D1026551

Exploring the
History &
Philosophy
of Christian
Education

Exploring the
History &
Philosophy
of Christian
Education

Principles for the 21st Century

Michael J. Anthony
Warren S. Benson

Ashland
Community & Technical College
Library

College Drive Car

Kregel
Academic & Professional

82523

Exploring the History and Philosophy of Christian Education: Principles for the 21st Century

© 2003 by Michael J. Anthony and Warren S. Benson

Published by Kregel Publications, a division of Kregel, Inc., P.O. Box 2607, Grand Rapids, MI 49501.

All rights reserved. No part of this book may be reproduced, stored in a retrieval system, or transmitted in any form or by any means—electronic, mechanical, photocopy, recording, or otherwise—without written permission of the publisher, except for brief quotations in printed reviews.

Unless otherwise indicated, Scripture quotations are from the New American Standard Bible. © The Lockman Foundation 1960, 1962, 1963, 1968, 1971, 1972, 1973, 1975, 1977, 1995. Used by permission.

Scripture quotations marked NIV are from the Holy Bible, New International Version®. NIV®. © 1973, 1978, 1984 by International Bible Society. Used by permission of Zondervan Publishing House. All rights reserved.

Scripture quotations marked KJV are from the King James Version of the Holy Bible.

ISBN 0-8254-2023-7

Printed in the United States of America

03 04 05 06 07 / 5 4 3 2 1

To
Warren S. Benson
(1930–2002)

This book is dedicated to one of the finest men I have known in the field of Christian education. He was a wonderful husband to Lenore, father to Bruce and Scott, grandfather to Annie, Emily, and Scotty Jr.

He will be particularly missed by his colleagues from the educational institutions where he held a faculty appointment. These include: Dallas Theological Seminary, Trinity Evangelical Divinity School, Southern Baptist Theological Seminary, and Talbot School of Theology.

In addition, his absence will be felt each year by his colleagues attending the annual meeting of the North American Professors of Christian Education. It was always a highlight of each conference to speak with Warren and attend his frequent seminars and workshops. He was one of my closest friends in the field of Christian education and I will forever look back with fondness to his personal mentoring and friendship.

CONTENTS

ACKNOWLEDGMENTS

IN A VENTURE OF THIS MAGNITUDE, it is obvious that many people contribute to the final outcome. Although two of us have our names on the cover, there are many people who made significant contributions to the project. I am very grateful for my wife, Michelle's, patience during this past year and a half as this manuscript has taken shape. She has a very successful and dynamic ministry as Pastor of Children and Student Ministries at Coast Hills Community Church, and her willingness to process this material with me to be sure it is relevant to real-life ministry was invaluable. In addition, my two children, Chantel and Brendon, have been very patient with me while I was upstairs studying and writing when they would have preferred to spend summer vacation at the beach.

My dean at the seminary, Dr. Dennis Dirks, was very generous in providing release time for me to pursue this project. I was the recipient of a sabbatical and had several semesters when I was able to receive a course reduction. Talbot School of Theology is a wonderful work climate for faculty members who have a passion to impact the world beyond the classroom. Dr. Dirks has made this possible, and for that I am most grateful.

Special thanks goes to Dr. David White, one of my former Ph.D. students, and, also, Joshua Simpson, my undergraduate research assistant, who provided me with the materials for the "What in the World" section of each chapter. Also at the top of my list is my friend and editor Jim Weaver at

Kregel Publications. Jim served as my editor for an earlier book, and I was so impressed with his professionalism and Christian character that I looked for another opportunity to join in partnership again. When you find someone you trust and respect in the Christian publishing field, you look for ways to continue the bond.

INTRODUCTION

THE SPANISH PHILOSOPHER SANTAYANA reportedly once quipped, "Those who do not know history are destined to repeat it." If this is true, then we must pay careful attention to those who have gone before us. Lessons must be learned and warnings must be heeded. History is replete with examples of those who have ignored valuable insights from the past and charged into the future ill equipped and unprepared. Those who serve in positions of ministry leadership are not immune from such mistakes.

BACK TO THE FUTURE

The purpose of this book is to provide the reader with more than just valuable insights regarding the past. Unlike the tack of some authors before us, our intention is not simply to string together biographies in a seamless list. Although such an approach might accomplish the task of reviewing history's facts, it does nothing to reveal the meaning of history and to glean valuable insights for how we live today. The emphasis of this history book is the future. We desire to review the past so that the ministry leader will be better equipped to serve in his/her future ministry location and that, having learned some valuable lessons from those who have gone before them, the readers will, in turn, be better prepared to meet the challenges that await them after graduation.

A Cry for Help

A couple of years ago, I finally reached my limit. I couldn't stand to hear one more student complain about having to take the course History and Philosophy of Christian Education. Countless students came to me, their student advisor, and complained about it. "That course," they would say, "puts me to sleep!" As one who valued the course, yet rarely taught it, I couldn't understand why a student wouldn't walk away from the course a changed person. The more I asked students who came through my office, the more I came to realize why it seemed like such a waste of their time. The material was taught in a lecture format with an emphasis on the names, dates, facts, and figures associated with history. When the philosophical material was taught, it left the students convinced that philosophy had little, if anything, to do with the daily practice of Christian educational ministries. In essence, they just didn't get the relationship between theory and practice.

The finest book in the field was *Christian Education: Its History and Philosophy,* written by two of my dear friends and colleagues, Kenneth Gangel and Warren Benson. The day Moody Press stopped printing their book was a dark day in our field. The most popular alternatives became James Reed and Ronnie Prevost's *A History of Christian Education* and George Knight's *Philosophy and Education.* Both books were excellent at their intended focus. However, philosophy is best understood in light of its historical context, and reading each book independent of the other results in the material seeming fragmented and disjointed. Both subjects must be processed simultaneously.

I spoke to Warren about the need for a new history and philosophy of Christian education text and shared my passion for relating theory to practice. I asked Warren if he would partner with me on this new venture, and he enthusiastically agreed. Warren had recently retired from Trinity Evangelical Divinity School and was then a senior professor of Christian education at Southern Seminary, where I teach each year as a visiting professor. Warren had more time on his hands now that he was "retired" and was willing to take on the demands of a new writing assignment. In addition, his son Scott had taken a pastoral position at Mariners Church in Irvine, just a few miles from my house, and whenever Warren came out to visit his grandchildren, we would often go out to lunch together.

THE NEED FOR A NEW PARADIGM

The proposed book would have to be different from any other previously published book on history and philosophy. We were both emphatic about making the subject relevant to ministry. We wanted pastors to understand how important theory was to the practice of ministry. We had each known too many ministry leaders who were forced to move from their ministries prematurely because they simply ran out of tricks and didn't understand how to make the necessary changes. They had enough material for a couple of years but then were forced to move on to another setting. If only they understood the "why" of ministry, then they would be able to change the "how" of ministry.

We determined that each chapter of the book would have three major emphases. First, because the material in each chapter occurred within a greater historical context, we decided to introduce each chapter with a section titled "What in the World?" The purpose of this section is to introduce the student to what else was happening in the world beyond the scope of the particular chapter. For example, although the theme of chapter 1 is Hebrew education, the Hebrews were not the only people in existence. China and India had thriving populations at the time. In addition, Europe, Great Britain, and many parts of Africa were known to be well populated and had highly developed cultures as well. Knowing this fact allows the reader to gain a greater degree of perspective regarding the material found in each chapter. Although chapters 8–10 cover the same period, we have nonetheless included the "What in the World?" feature for each chapter.

The second major emphasis of each chapter is the frequent use of text boxes to provide a summary of the material being discussed. Sometimes a simple chart can bring clarity to a topic. As they say, "A picture (in this case, a chart) is worth a thousand words." We hope that these text boxes will provide meaningful summaries and supplementary materials while saving the reader the work of reading more verbiage.

The last unique aspect of each chapter is the final section labeled "So What? Lessons from the Past for Twenty-first-century Christian Education." In these sections, we have specifically addressed the complaints of our students about the relevance of both history and philosophy as applied to Christian education ministries. These sections draw out three or four principles or lessons that can be derived from the particular period of history just discussed.

These lessons have specific relevancy to the way we do ministry today. In some cases, they inform us about priorities or perhaps highlight the essential elements of a particular historical era. In a few cases, they provide us with a warning so that we don't repeat the failures associated with that particular era. Sometimes we learn more by observing someone's mistakes rather than their successes.

We have tried not to overemphasize the great achievements found in each period without taking an honest and accurate look at its shortcomings as well. Indeed, not everyone lived happily ever after. Life didn't always have a happy ending for some people. Where appropriate, we point out the failures of the church and various leaders in an effort to prevent others from repeating their shortcomings.

Finally, our goal has been to present the philosophical dimensions of ministry within the historical setting of their development so the reader can see the evolution of a particular philosophical position. For example, humanism is discussed in three different chapters because it meant different things to different people in each of those eras. During the time of Aristotle, it had a different emphasis than it did when it resurfaced during the Renaissance and Reformation. Likewise, it took on a decidedly different meaning during the twentieth century at the hands of Dewey and his associates. It isn't enough to discuss humanism without also knowing under what historical context and definition it is being discussed. It meant different things to different people at different periods of history. To state that Jesus was a humanist educator might seem outright blasphemy unless one defines *humanism* according to Aristotle's conceptualization or perhaps even that espoused during the Renaissance. However, if one is using the definition and construct that became popular during the twentieth century, then clearly Jesus would have nothing to do with the latter form of humanism. Our point is that philosophy must be addressed within its historical context, or it becomes convoluted and entangled in misunderstanding and vague definitions. We sought to avoid this in our text.

The original plan was for me to write the first ten chapters and then send them to Warren for his editing and input. He was going to write the last few chapters and then send those to me for my review. Warren had edited my first four chapters when he was called home to be with his Savior. Before his homegoing, he had written major sections on colonial America and the eighteenth, nineteenth, and twentieth centuries. I state this so that the reader will know that if the book has shortcomings, I assume full responsibility for them. I am sure that if Warren had been around to complete the final editing, he would have caught a number of my errors and foolish observations. To say that his passing was a tremendous shock would be an understatement. His loss has been felt by many of us who called him friend and colleague. Warren's wife, Lenore, has been gracious in providing me with his materials, and I can only hope that this last of Warren's written work is worthy of his characteristically high professional standards.

What in the World?

➤ The first agricultural communities of Asia are developed in c. 4000 B.C.

➤ Egypt is comprised of two kingdoms: upper (south) and lower (the Delta).

➤ Britain establishes a large population by c. 4000 B.C.

➤ Egypt is united under King Menes c. 3000 B.C. with his capital in Memphis.

➤ A large population of people have developed in the central Andes Mountains c. 1500 B.C.

➤ The main population areas of Europe around 1000 B.C. are recorded as being what is known today between the Rhine and Danube Rivers.

➤ India and China have vast empires established by c. 600 B.C.

Chapter 1

HEBREW ORIGINS OF CHRISTIAN EDUCATION

CHRISTIAN EDUCATION IS INDEBTED TO THE Old Testament saints who provided us with an example of how to live in a covenant relationship with our Creator. God provided us with guidance and direction about how we could nurture our ongoing relationship with Him. God's desire has always been to see His children mature in their faith and pass that faith on to subsequent generations. To accomplish that aim, He chose patriarchal leaders such as Abraham, Isaac, and Jacob to model godly familial and national leadership. Soon after that, He gave us written instructions, known as the Torah, or Old Testament Law. Later, He commissioned priests, judges, and prophets with the task of instructing His people with the proper application of those laws to everyday life. Eventually, this task was given to synagogue leaders such as rabbis and scribes. After the Jews returned from exile, they established schools for the education of their children.

Tracing these early origins of Hebrew education provides a glimpse into God's original design for education. His Word gives clear guidance regarding His plans and purposes. Scripture tells us that God created the world and breathed life into mankind. Clearly, one of mankind's objectives was to populate the earth and instruct those who came along about how to enjoy a personal walk with their Creator.

What Do You Mean?

b.c.e.	Before the common era; a secular term denoting the period before the birth of Christ.
Gemara	A commentary on the Mishnah compiled about A.D. 500.
Jew	A descendant of the people who survived the destruction of Israel in 722 B.C.
Judaism	The term first used by Greek-speaking Jews in the intertestamental period to distinguish themselves from Hellenists.
Midrashim	Homiletical commentaries of the Hebrew Scriptures.
Mishnah	The oral law composed about A.D. 200.
Rabbi	Master, teacher.
Septuagint	The Greek translation of the Old Testament.
Shema	The first Hebrew words that a boy learns: "Hear, O Israel! The LORD is our God, the LORD is one!" (Deut. 6:4).
Talmud	Consists of the Mishnah and the Gemara, spanning a time from shortly after Ezra at about 400 B.C. to A.D. 500.
Tanakh	Hebrew acronym designating the three major sections of the Hebrew Bible: Torah, Prophets, and Writings.
Torah	In its narrowest sense, the first five books of Moses (i.e., the Pentateuch); in its broader sense, it comprises the written and oral law.
YHWH	God's proper name, Yahweh.

PATRIARCHS

In the early pages of human history, God was man's first instructor. Creation itself helped mankind learn of God's omnipotent power and creative spirit. He also put within man a conscience to understand right from wrong. We find on three occasions Elihu referred to God as a teacher (Job 33:16; 35:11; 36:22). "These early recipients of God's oral teaching included, among others, Adam, Eve, Enoch, Noah, Abraham, Isaac, Jacob, Job (assuming he lived in patriarchal times), and Moses."[1]

---

1. Roy B. Zuck, *The Evangelical Dictionary of Christian Education*, ed. Michael J. Anthony (Grand Rapids: Baker, 2001), s.v. "Education in the Pentateuch."

These patriarchs lived a nomadic existence. They owned large herds and flocks and traveled throughout the countryside seeking fertile land for their flocks to graze. Abraham began his journey from a region known as Ur of the Chaldees in Mesopotamia. This land between the Tigris and Euphrates Rivers was a fertile delta where a civilization had developed with rich cultural amenities. Recent archaeological excavations at Ur have discovered evidence of their culture by translating inscriptions from clay tablets. One such document, known as the Code of Hammurabi, speaks of matters regarding moral, social, civic, and economic development. Hammurabi lived about 1792–1750 B.C.

The Early Sumerian Civilization

Though one hundred years ago the Sumerian culture was relatively unknown to us, archaeological and linguistic studies have now established their primacy as a civilized people. It was initially thought that Egypt was the cradle of civilization, followed by Babylon and Assyria. However, such was not the case.

An authority on the Sumerian civilization writes, "From the point of view of the history of civilization, Sumer's supreme achievements were the development of the cuneiform system of writing and the formal system of education which was its direct outgrowth . . . it was from Sumer that writing and learning spread the world over."[2]

The Sumerians, a non-Semitic people, developed the first urban culture in the lower part of Mesopotamia, which the Bible calls Chaldea (2 Kings 25:5; Ezra 23:15). Sumer was located in the extreme south of the Euphrates Valley, and Akkad was just north of Sumer. Starting in the beginning of the third millennium B.C., Sumerian city-states such as Ur, Lagash, and Nippur already were old. They were independent of each other and almost constantly at war.

---

2. Samuel N. Kramer, *The Sumerians: Their History, Culture and Character* (Chicago: University of Chicago Press, 1963), 229; as cited in R. Freedman Butts, *The Education of the West* (New York: McGraw Hill, 1997), 36.

Genesis 12:1–3 records God's command for Abraham to leave the land of his ancestors so that he might establish a new nation that had God as its spiritual and national leader.

> Now the LORD said to Abram,
> "Go forth from your country,
> And from your relatives
> And from your father's house,
> To the land which I will show you;
> And I will make you a great nation,
> And I will bless you,
> And make your name great;
> And so you shall be a blessing;
> And I will bless those who bless you,
> And the one who curses you I will curse.
> And in you all of the families of the earth will be blessed."

This theocratic design was intended as a means of world evangelism. Note the phrase "And in you all of the families of the earth will be blessed." This does not reflect the early origins of prosperity theology but rather speaks of a spiritual blessing that would be available to other nations as they observed the special covenant that God had with Abraham's descendents. God's intention was for the other nations of the earth to learn about His character by observing how Israel related to Him. As Israel obeyed God's Word and received His blessings, other nations would come to Israel, asking how they, too, could establish a covenantal relationship with Jehovah.

> The covenant was not merely a social, but also an individual contract. It meant that every member of the Hebrew faith had a personal obligation to God. While this personal element was not so strong in early Hebrew life, it became the central message of the prophets who dwelled upon the subjective relationship between man and God.[3]

---

3. Fredrick Mayer, *A History of Educational Thought* (Columbus: Charles E. Merrill, 1966), 82.

The patriarchs were supposed to instruct their children about godly living. Genesis 18:19 reads, "For I have chosen him [Abraham], so that he may command his children and his household after him to keep the way of the LORD by doing righteousness and justice; so that the LORD may bring upon Abraham what He has spoken about him." As Abraham's children began living a distinctly righteous lifestyle among the other inhabitants of the land, his neighbors would inquire of his God and desire a special relationship with Him as well.

Pagan Deities

Baal	Name refers to "Lord"; controlled storms, rain, and fertility.
El	Seen as the king or father of all other gods and the creator of man.
Anat	Baal's sister, who had power over life, love, and conception.
Yam	Controls the sea, rivers, and sea monsters; viewed as an opponent of Baal.
Mot	Controlled death, drought, desert, and the underworld; the father of all creatures.
Ashtar	Associated with Venus and worshiped through human sacrifice.
Milkom	The Ammonite equivalent of Ashtar.
Astarte	Fertility goddess of lust and sexuality.
Dagon	The god of grain and the bestower of fertility.
Resheph	The god of peace and prosperity.
Moloch	Worshiped through child sacrifice.[4]

Abraham, and the other patriarchs who were to follow, never fully grasped their responsibility to instruct the nations about the uniqueness of their God. Jehovah was not like the gods of other nations. The God of Abraham, Isaac, and Jacob was a personal God who wanted to be engaged in the details of His creation. The pagan deities of Mesopotamia, Egypt, and Canaan, however, were gods to be feared for their destructive power and dominance.

---

4. Merrill F. Unger, *Unger's Bible Dictionary* (Chicago: Moody, 1972), 411-18.

Jehovah sought to bring out the best in man through a relationship based upon compassion and love. Retribution and justice were available for those who chose to disregard His instructions but such punishment was always the consequence of man's choices, never the intended purpose of God for His people.

THE LAW

According to His prophetic promise, God's people were led down to Egypt for a period of four hundred years (Gen. 15:13), after which time they were led out by Moses. Moses was instrumental in guiding the nation toward a new means of understanding Jehovah. God would now reveal Himself through the written text of laws and regulations. The Torah comprises the Pentateuch: Genesis, Exodus, Leviticus, Numbers, and Deuteronomy. In addition, the written Torah also includes two other parts: the Prophets (Joshua, Judges, Samuel, Kings, Isaiah, Jeremiah, Ezekiel, and the twelve Minor Prophets) and the Writings (Psalms, Proverbs, Job, Song of Songs, Lamentations, Ecclesiastes, Ruth, Esther, Daniel, Ezra, Nehemiah, and Chronicles).[5] These books were given for the purpose of instruction and guidance.

The Law required people to assemble several times each year for festivals, feasts, and religious ceremonies. One of these major events was the Passover Feast, which reviewed the historical events preceding their exodus from Egypt. The Feast of Tabernacles, with its week of tent camping, caused them to reflect on their forty-year journey through the wilderness. The Day of Atonement was an impressive event designed to remind them of God's holiness and justice. God designed these and other events such as the Feast of Trumpets, Feast of Pentecost, Year of Jubilee, and the weekly Sabbath to be moments of reflection to instruct His people and impress upon them the importance of righteous living. Discerning Hebrew citizens would ponder these events throughout the year.

The Law prescribed standards of conduct regarding most aspects of Hebrew life. It included regulations regarding the washing of clothes, food preparation, crime, marriage, divorce, inheritance, court proceedings, agricultural practices, medical procedures, human and animal sexuality, and a host of other areas. Little was left out of God's instructions about how

---

5. Jacob Neusner, ed., *World Religions in America* (Louisville: Westminster John Knox, 1994), 161.

people were to live. The Law provided humanity a certain degree of assurance that as long as they were living according to God's prescribed standards, they would not have to fear retribution or punishment. The Law served as a divine owner's manual on how to live.

Keeping the Sabbath Holy

Perhaps the most defining moment in the life of the Jew is the Sabbath. It is said, "As Israel has kept the Sabbath, so the Sabbath has kept Israel."[6] Sabbath begins for the Jew at Sundown Friday evening. It is celebrated with the family assembled around the table, fresh with a clean tablecloth and lit with candles. It is marked as a different evening of the week for it is holy unto the Lord. It is viewed as a time to break from the allure of materialism, the self-interest of one's professional ambition, the seduction of myriad forms of entertainment that prevent us from hearing the stillness of our soul's breath. It is a time to reflect upon the Lord and His mercies to us. We are together, we are at peace, and we are with God. It is a family event that has duties and functions for even the smallest of children present.

The two dominating reasons why no work is to be done on the Sabbath are found in Exodus 20:10 and Deuteronomy 5:15. According to the passage in Exodus, God spent six days creating the universe and then rested thereby making it a hallowed day. Mankind is told to do the same. The passage in Deuteronomy has a different emphasis. The Jewish people were commanded to remember that they were once enslaved in Egypt and God brought them deliverance from their suffering. They were released from the bondage of their work and are reminded to take this weekly opportunity to rest and reflect on God's salvation.[7]

---

6. *Gates of Prayer* (New York: Central Conference of American Rabbis, 1955), 191.
7. C. L. Wirtschafter, "Families in a Fractured World," *Proceedings of the Center for Jewish-Christian Learning* 11 (fall 1996): 34.

"The law," according to Galatians 3:24, "was our schoolmaster to bring us unto Christ, that we might be justified" (KJV). This verse helps us understand that one of the main reasons for the Law was for the people's instruction. The Law set the standard of moral absolutes. It revealed to man the nature of sin, the consequences of disobedient living, and the core of human depravity. It revealed God's expectations concerning man's conduct. It tells us of God's holiness and righteousness and His impartial standard of justice for all. He expects nothing less from us as well. The realization that we cannot live up to this standard of sinless living compels us to approach God requesting mercy and grace. Fortunately, both of these qualities are found in abundance through a personal relationship with Jesus Christ.

The Bible

The first five books of Moses are designated in Hebrew as "Torah," which means literally, *Teaching*. This term is sometimes seen in a more restrictive dimension in which only these five books are used, or it is sometimes seen in a broader sense by including two further categories described in Hebrew as *Nevi'im* and *Ketuvim*. The *Nevi'im*, or prophets, includes the historical and prophetic books, whereas the *Ketuvim* include a miscellaneous collection of poetry, sermons, songs, etc. The order that these books appear may have varied soon after they were formed into one collection, however, once established, this order has changed very little. It totals thirty-nine books in all.

Christians refer to this collection of books as the Old Testament, and they add to this their own supplement of writings known as the New Testament. For obvious reasons, this distinction does not exist to the Jew. This latter collection contains writings about the life of Christ (Gospels), the transitionary work of the Holy Spirit (Acts), and the writings of various apostles (Paul, Peter, John, and the unknown author of the book of Hebrews).

The Hebrew Bible has been translated into hundreds of languages and dialects. The first Greek translation came about during the centuries just before Christ. According to one story, Eleazar the high priest from Jerusalem, at the request of Emperor Ptolemy, who wanted to provide an enriched culture in Alexandria, sent seventy-two elders from Israel to make the translation. This version became known as the Septuagint, Latin for *seventy*. The Septuagint became the basis for numerous secondary translations by the early churches throughout Europe and the Far East.

The earliest Christian translation of the Bible is known as the Vulgate, Latin for *common*. This translation was made in the common language of the people and was completed in 404 A.D. by the church father Jerome. Further translations would follow by John Wycliffe (1383), William Tyndale (1525), King James Version (1611), and the Revised Standard Version (1952).[8]

THE FAMILY

Early educational efforts among these first Hebrews was not very well structured by modern standards, although that is not to say that they lacked intentionality. Life itself was the content of instruction. A child learned by living in community with others and at the feet of his/her parents. These early origins of home schooling formed the basis of passing down the Hebrew culture and religious practices from generation to generation.

> For He established a testimony in Jacob
> And appointed a law in Israel,
> Which He commanded our fathers
> That they should teach them to their children,
> That the generation to come might know,
> even the children yet to be born,
> That they may arise and tell them to their children,
> That they should put their confidence in God
> And not forget the works of God,
> But keep His commandments.
>
> —Psalm 78:5–7

Parents were required to be actively engaged in teaching their children the Mosaic Law. For this reason, the family was the primary means of schooling and instruction. A host of methods were available for parents to use. For

---

8. B. Z. Bokser, *Judaism and the Christian Predicament* (New York: Knopf, 1967), 45–48.

Ashland
Community & Technical College
Library

College Drive Campus

825 23

example, they could teach by example (Deut. 6:5-8; 31:12), oral communication (Deut. 6:6-7; 11:18-19), informal discussions that occurred during the day (Deut. 6:7; 11:19), while answering their children's questions (Exod. 12:26; 13:14; Deut. 6:20-21), through the use of visual aids and object lessons (Deut. 6:9; 11:20), and while observing or participating in religious festivals and ceremonies during the year (Deut. 16:16).[9]

The Shema was the starting point for most Hebrew family instruction. It is found in Deuteronomy 6:4-9, and they memorized it at an early age.

> Hear, O Israel! The LORD is our God, the LORD is one! You shall love the LORD your God with all your heart and with all your soul and with all your might. These words, which I am commanding you today, shall be on your heart. You shall teach them diligently to your sons and shall talk of them when you sit in your house and when you walk by the way and when you lie down and when you rise up. You shall bind them as a sign on your hand and they shall be as frontals on your forehead. You shall write them on the doorposts of your house and on your gates.

God certainly expected each parent to take an active role in the spiritual development of their children. Rabbis believed that the Hebrew home should be viewed, much like the tabernacle, as a private sanctuary for religious observances, including the worship of God (house of prayer), the instruction in the Torah (house of study), and meeting needs found in the community (house of assembly). In the same way that God's presence, or *Shechinah*, filled the temple, each Hebrew home was expected to light the Menorah (seven-branched lamp stand) as a reminder to everyone in their community that this family was dedicated to a greater purpose than simply providing shelter. Everyone would know that this was a family that took the teachings of Scripture seriously and that they were committed to following Jehovah.[10]

The community in which the Hebrew child was raised represented a rich heritage of curriculum development. The child lived in an environment that

---

9. Zuck, *Evangelical Dictionary of Christian Education*, s.v. "Education in the Pentateuch."
10. Marvin R. Wilson, *Our Father Abraham: Jewish Roots of the Christian Faith* (Grand Rapids: Eerdmans, 1989), 215.

was intentional in its educational focus. Monuments of stone were set up to memorialize important events in Hebrew history. Festivals and feasts that commemorated important historical events punctuated the year. Many of these events allowed children to participate and play active roles. Occasionally, the Levitical priests would assemble the entire community to proclaim the law and expound upon its meaning. Children were expected to participate in these events as well. The entire experience of a child's development was interwoven with instructional overtones.[11]

Hebrew girls were not sent to school for formal instruction but rather remained at home, where their mothers taught them how to manage the affairs of the home. Their instruction included sewing, caring for their younger siblings, and cooking and cleaning according to strict dietary laws. The woman's place in the Hebrew culture amounted to her being in the home, caring for the needs of her family. Because no civic or business roles were available for them, to provide girls an education beyond rudimentary homemaking skills made no sense.

Women could learn to some degree by observing the religious ceremonies at the temple or during special national festivals. However, even this was somewhat limited because they were forbidden to enter the innermost parts of the temple to share in the ceremonial offerings by assisting the priests. When it came time to observe the proceedings that took place in the temple, women stood off to the side out of the way. The women's court was set apart from the area that contained the brazen alter, the focal point of presenting one's offering.[12] Once the synagogue was established in postexilic Israel, women were able to receive some limited instruction there.

Boys were educated and trained by their fathers. In most cases, the son followed in his father's career and was apprenticed by him from a young age. The young man's education was primarily vocational in nature, although that is not to say that it was void of spiritual meaning. Indeed, much of what was included in the child's early educational experience was integrated into a religious theme or focus. Thus, Judaism affected all aspects of the child's development.

---

11. Severe E. Frost, *Historical and Philosophical Foundations of Western Education* (Columbus: Charles E. Merrill, 1966), 35.

12. Jacob Neusner, *Judaism in the Beginning of Christianity* (Philadelphia: Fortress, 1984), 31–32.

Priests, Judges, and Prophets

The home was certainly not the only means of education available to the Hebrews. The Levitical priests were commissioned with the task of providing instruction to the masses at significant religious events throughout the year. In addition, unlike the other tribes, they were not given a specific piece of land on which to settle (Num. 35:1-8). Instead, they were given cities throughout the country so their religious training and influence would be available to everyone throughout the land.

The educational tasks of the priests were seen as twofold. First, they were to provide religious instruction to those who were being apprenticed in the priestly vocation. They trained younger priests how to present the sacred offerings and how to maintain the various altars (brazen and incense) and the table of shewbread. Second, they were to instruct the people who came to the tabernacle (or later the temple) regarding the proper procedures for the presentation of their offerings. They were also involved in explaining the meaning behind the various festivals, religious observances, and special days in the Hebrew calendar. Their instruction was instrumental in helping people understand the character and nature of God Himself.[13]

They interpreted the Law to those who needed guidance and were relied upon for settling civil disputes and disagreements. For this reason, "the priests became the primary public educators of the nation until the exile. They were generally held in high regard by the people and were amply relied upon for instruction."[14]

Once the Hebrew nation settled in Canaan and migrated to their apportioned piece of land, they slowly began to assimilate the cultural and religious practices of the nations around them. Although they had been warned repeatedly about doing so, they soon lost their religious fervency and began to take on the idolatrous ways of the nations around them. The result was judgment from God in the form of border raids from hostile nations. As these nations invaded their land and took their valued possessions, the Hebrews cried out to God for help and deliverance. God responded by raising up one of their own to serve as a deliverer. The book of Judges in the Old

---

13. Charles B. Eavey, *History of Christian Education* (Chicago: Moody, 1964), 55.
14. James E. Reed and Ronnie Prevost, *A History of Christian Education* (Nashville: Broadman & Holman, 1993), 47.

Testament chronicles the lives of several men and a woman who served as judges to deliver God's people from calamity.

These judges spoke for God and rebuked the people for their failure to maintain a pure and unadulterated relationship with Jehovah. They spoke out forcefully against intermarrying with the nations around them. They worked hard to redirect the Hebrew nation back to their "first love" relationship with God. Through the methods of rebuke, correction, military intervention, and religious instruction, the judges were tireless in their efforts to turn the nation back to God. However, it was to no avail. The people chose to do what was right in their own eyes (Judg. 17:6) and ignored the instruction of the judges.

Although it is apparent that the people gave up and abandoned their distinctive relationship with Jehovah, God did not give up on them. As the last of the judges faded from the scene, a new breed of religious zealots entered with a passion to steer the nation back to God. These were the prophets. Some of their names are familiar to us from the stories we heard as children in Sunday school. A partial list of prominent prophets includes Jeremiah, Isaiah, Ezekiel, and Jonah. The stories of Samuel, Elijah, Elisha, and Nathan transfixed us the first time we heard of their exploits. These prophets were rugged individuals who were assigned the task of confronting Israel's national leaders with the consequences of their poor leadership decisions.

Many of these prophets seemed to be quite obscure and peculiar. They inhabited desert caves and led a solitary, nomadic existence. They often burst on the scene from obscurity with prophetic words destined to pierce the heart of their intended listener. Some of them were members of the king's court (e.g., Nathan, Elijah, Gad, and Iddo), whereas others were uncomfortable being around royal settings. Undoubtedly, each of them had the call of God on his life in a profound way for the specific purpose of turning a nation from their course toward certain destruction.

The message that these men brought was a call back to a purer faith. They protested social injustice, spiritual apostasy, idolatry, immorality, hedonism, overindulgence, class divisions, and the growing secularization of society as a whole.[15]

Probably no nation has ever produced a group of religious or moral teachers comparable to the prophets of ancient Israel. Through their spoken public

---

15. Daniel J. Silver, *A History of Judaism* (New York: Basic Books, 1974), 88.

addresses and writings, they became creators of national religious and social ideals, critics and inspirers of public policies, denouncers of social wrongs, preachers of individual and social righteousness, and the source and channel of an ever loftier conception of God and of the mission of Israel. In fulfilling each of these roles, they were acting as public teachers. In every national crisis, they were at hand to denounce, encourage, comfort, and always instruct. "They were the public conscience of Israel, the soul of its religion, the creators of its public opinion, its most conspicuous, its most revered, its most convincing teachers."[16]

As the number of prophets increased, a need arose for schools to instruct and train them in their duties. Schools for the "sons of the prophets" were begun. However, it is generally thought that these were not schools in the traditional sense but rather informal and temporal. They were probably begun by a popular prophet and comprised men who banded together to follow his teachings and share his mission. Eventually, larger communities of prophets were established that, in turn, attracted large numbers of students. The curriculum of these latter schools was based upon inducing prophetic utterance, instruction in the Law, prayers, meditation, and rituals of worship. The prophet Samuel is believed to have founded such a school at Ramah. Other schools were known to have existed in Bethel, Gilgal, Jericho, Carmel, Gibeon, and Samaria.[17]

THE MONARCHY

The Hebrew nation compelled the prophet Samuel—who held the unique position of prophet, priest, and seer—to select an individual to serve as their king. All of the other nations around them had their prominent national leader, so Israel desired one as well. In so doing, they rejected the theocratic reign of Jehovah Himself for a man-made institution destined to fail and disappoint them.

Samuel anointed a tall and reluctant man from the tribe of Judah to serve as Israel's first monarch. Saul's reign was relatively short (approximately 1050–1000 B.C.) and was eventually transitioned to a man who had his origins as a

---

16. Fletcher H. Seift, "Education in Ancient Israel from Earliest Times to 70 A.D.," quoted in Charles B. Eavey, *History of Christian Education* (Chicago: Moody, 1964), 59.

17. Frost, *Historical and Philosophical Foundations,* 36.

shepherd. King David also had a background in music and wrote eloquent songs. Many of David's songs were collected into a songbook that we know as the Old Testament book of Psalms. These orations were rich in instructional curriculum. They testified of God's power to create and control His universe. Unlike pagan deities, which were viewed as objectively removed from the affairs of mortal men, the Psalms reveal a God who relentlessly seeks fellowship with His creation and is engaged in the daily affairs of every man's life.

The songs written by King David provide his people with a chronicle of lessons that were learned by a sometimes imperfect monarch. By reading or singing these psalms, King David's people would have learned that there were consequences for personal sin and that no one, not even great kings, were immune from what Paul would state many years later: "For whatever a man sows, this he will also reap" (Gal. 6:7). These psalms reveal to the nation the character of God. God was seen as a deity Who was concerned with personal and national justice, as One Who served as an advocate of the homeless, a father to those who were themselves fatherless, and a benefactor of the weak. These psalms stood as more than a standard songbook for worship and praise; they also provided mankind with a glimpse into the very heart of the eternal God, the sovereign ruler of the universe. In many respects, these songs were a theology textbook for the world. The character of God is richly portrayed in the book of Psalms.

After King David died, his son Solomon reigned from 961–922 B.C. He, too, had a special relationship with God. First Kings 3 reveals a personal visit that God had with him early in his reign. The meeting occurred in a dream in which God asked Solomon what He could do for him as the new king. Solomon was intimidated by the task and pleaded with God for only one item: a soft and sensitive heart so that he could rule God's people with discernment. God granted him his wish, and as a result, we learn about the magnitude of God's patience, mercy, and grace. King Solomon was a writer himself and penned the books of Song of Solomon and Ecclesiastes. These books are instructive in their scope and content. They reveal the nature of an intimate love between a husband and wife as well as the folly of living a life based upon man's standard of ethics and morality.

The monarchy may be viewed with mixed opinions in terms of its overall effectiveness. However, these particular kings (and others who followed them) left us with a legacy of rich curricular content that became fodder for debate for thousands of years to come. The monarchy provides us with an understanding of God's nature and character as well as His involvement in human governments.

THE EXILE

In 931 B.C., the nation of Israel experienced a nonviolent civil war that resulted in its division. Ten tribes, under the leadership of King Jeroboam, reigned in the north with Samaria as their capital city. The remaining two tribes (Judah and Benjamin), under the leadership of King Rehoboam (922–915), remained in the south with Jerusalem as their capital city. In 732 B.C., the Assyrian king Tiglath Pileser III ravaged the tribes in the north. Ten years later, his successor, Sargon, destroyed Samaria and carried the inhabitants into exile in Assyria. In their place, the Assyrian leaders brought other people to inhabit the land. Only by God's immeasurable grace did the two remaining tribes in the south survive this transport. This period of grace, however, was to be short-lived.

By 586 B.C., Jerusalem surrendered to Nebuchadnezzar, who, in turn, transported the people in three separate movements back to Babylon. It was a bitter experience for them as they were far removed from the land that had been promised to their patriarchal ancestor Abraham. The finality of their exilic existence provided the wake-up call they needed to repent and turn back to God. God had chosen them from all of the other nations of the earth (Exod. 19:5), but they rejected Him. God had given His people a name and a land for an inhabitance (Josh. 1:3); yet, they turned away from God's blessings and preferred to rely upon their own resources. God gave them His laws to guide and lead them into righteous living (Josh. 1:7); yet, they chose to reject His teachings and instead worship the idols and false gods of the pagan nations around them. God was patient with them throughout the thousand years that they lived in their new land, but the time had come for God's patience to turn into wrath. God used an evil nation with a wicked world leader to execute His judgment upon His people.

Yet even in His anger, He did not leave them without hope. Although His punishment might have seemed harsh at the moment, He was still working for their benefit. The prophet Jeremiah was a spokesman to those who had been taken captive to Babylon and provided words of hope and encouragement. He wrote,

"Behold, days are coming," declares the LORD, "when I will make a new covenant with the house of Israel and with the house of Judah, not like the covenant which I made with their fathers in the day I took them by the hand to bring them out of the land Egypt, My covenant which they broke, although I was a husband to them," declares the LORD. "But this is the covenant which I will make with the house of Israel after those days," declares the LORD, "I will put My law within them and on their heart I will write it; and I will be their God, and they shall be My people. . . . [f]or I will forgive their iniquity, and their sin I will remember no more." (Jeremiah 31:31-34)

The exile shook the Hebrew nation to its core. It required a major re-thinking of theological perspectives. Where once they had felt like a chosen people set apart by God through the use of supernatural miracles, now they were struck by the insecurity of not knowing God's plans and purposes for them. Would God choose another nation to reveal His plan for worldwide salvation? Would God bring further calamity their way? Would the nation in exile ever be allowed to return, or would they pass into obscurity, never to be mentioned again in human history? These must have been their thoughts as they languished in their strange surroundings.

But God had not forgotten them. And no other nation would be chosen to replace them, at least not for the foreseeable future. God would use this exilic experience much like He had used the harsh conditions of the Egyptian bondage as a means of revealing His caring and loving heart. God would hear their cries for help, and He would see their tears of repentance, and in so doing, He would once again reveal His character and nature to them.

During the years of their confinement, the Hebrew people had plenty of opportunity to reflect on their heritage. Far removed from the distractions of maintaining safe borders, rebuilding their economy, or the common complaints of taxes and the conditions of their flocks, the Hebrews now had time to reflect on more important matters such as their relationship with God and each other.

Dating back to the period when the Hebrews would have been sent to Babylon are the short writings of the prophet Obadiah and the five brief chapters that comprise the book of Lamentations. In this latter book, the prophet records his grief and sorrow over the destructive siege of Jerusalem and the city's desperate condition. He reminds the people of God's steadfast love, that the resources of His mercy never expire, and to be patient during this time of suffering (3:22-26). He also informs them that a day of reckoning will come when God will visit the nation of Babylon in judgment for their sin (3:64-66). The book of Psalms contains a brief passage (137:1-6) directed at the Babylonian captives as well. These passages became words of hope for the captives.

At this time, the Hebrew people softened their heart and recognized their idolatrous sin. They saw with fresh vision the error of their ways and the apostasy that had so slowly crept into the fabric of their nation. They needed to do only one thing: they needed to claim the promise that had been given to King Solomon about 350 years earlier in 2 Chronicles 7:14:

> [If] My people who are called by My name humble themselves and pray and seek My face and turn from their wicked ways, then I will hear from heaven, will forgive their sin and will heal their land.

With hearts renewed from repentance, the Hebrews—now referred to in history as Jews—would make a concerted effort to instruct their people how to abide by God's laws and commands. To do so, they needed a new form of educational institution. They no longer had access to the temple, and the home was insufficient for their purposes. In this context, the Jews established the synagogue.

THE SYNAGOGUE SCHOOL

Developed around the sixth century B.C., the synagogue was set aside as a place of prayer, worship, fasting, and teaching of the Torah. It probably coexisted with the place where Jews met for prayer and other religious festivals. That place might have been the town's community building, a large house, a public patio, or another such setting. It is doubtful that separate buildings were designated as synagogues until the third century. The "synagogues" that were discovered in the fortresses at Masada and Herodium were assembly halls, which had other civic purposes beyond religious meetings. At first, the same prominent or learned men who led the civic or political affairs of the community were probably also in charge of the religious affairs of the synagogue because political and religious society were almost one. Perhaps this explains why Jesus was so seldom welcomed by the leaders of a village's synagogue. They viewed Him as an outsider and a threat to their well-established way of life.[18]

Because the synagogue system was already operating with success as a place of worship and adult instruction, Jewish leaders decided to use this facility as the basis for developing an educational system for children as well. Using the books of the Mosaic Law as a basis of the curriculum, they required boys to memorize large portions of the Law. Content also included mathematics and writing. Although attendance was voluntary at first, it became mandatory in A.D. 64, when Joshua ben Gamala, the high priest during the last days of the temple, ordered it. Every community that had ten Jewish families was required to maintain such a school for their children. Schooling generally began at the age of five.[19]

Aramaic became the spoken language of the population of Jews in exile. This presented a serious problem because the Torah was written and read in Hebrew. Children were growing up without a firsthand understanding of their mother tongue. Before long, the Torah would be an unused book by the next generation. It was critical to the survival of Israel that they teach their children to read, write, and speak Hebrew. The synagogue school became the obvious institution of choice for such activities. Young boys attended once they reached the age of manhood at thirteen. This milestone was marked by a celebration called bar mitzvah.

The term *bar* means "son," and *mitzvah* refers to "a command given by God." In essence, the young boy who undergoes the bar mitzvah ceremony becomes a "son of the commandments." Once he celebrates his bar mitzvah, he has four privileges available to him. First, he is counted with the men of the community to make up a *minyan*—a group of ten men needed to hold a public worship service. Second, the young man is now able to wear phylacteries—two small leather boxes containing slips of paper with Old Testament passages written on them. He wears these on his forehead and on his left arm during the morning prayers. Third, he is able to read the Torah in the synagogue service if called upon to do so. Fourth, he is eligible to become a member of the Jewish court that arbitrates disputes brought up within the community.[20]

---

18. Anthony J. Saldarini, *Pharisees, Scribes, and Sadducees in Palestinian Society: A Sociological Approach* (Wilmington, Del.: Michael Glazier, 1988), 52.

19. Michael J. Anthony, ed., *The Evangelical Dictionary of Christian Education* (Grand Rapids: Baker, 2001), s.v. "Synagogue Schools."

20. Jerry C. MacGregor, *The Evangelical Dictionary of Christian Education*, ed. Michael J. Anthony (Grand Rapids: Baker, 2001), s.v. "Bar Mitzvah."

Unfortunately, women were not viewed with the same level of acceptance as the young men; therefore, the women were not allowed to attend synagogue school and learn the Hebrew language. In recent years, more liberal Jewish sects have broadened the restrictions and held bat mitzvah ceremonies for young girls. Rabbi Hayin Haley Donin, speaking of the need to educate young Jewish women, pleads with contemporary Jewish parents to stop neglecting the education of their girls.

> If the Jewish people are to survive, the education of daughters may be even more important than that of sons. It is the woman who usually determines the spiritual character of the home. It is the mother who is most often called upon to answer her children's daily questions. It is the extent of the woman's faith, the strength of her values and beliefs, that plays the dominant role in shaping the spiritual character of the next generation.[21]

Although he might overstate his case a bit, he does make a good point about the equal access of Hebrew instruction that is needed in our contemporary setting. That such training was not available to young women beginning in the days of the Exile was indeed unfortunate.

After the Exile, the synagogue school developed into the leading educational institution of its day. The Torah emerged in written form in the Talmud, and it was taught by the rulers of the synagogue school. Students were required to memorize lengthy portions of it and be able to explain its meaning. For those who sought a deeper understanding of God and His revelation, schools of the prophets were formed.

RELIGIOUS LEADERS

With the destruction of the temple and their seventy-year exile in Babylon, the nation returned to their land in several migrations. In approximately 538 B.C., Ezra led back one group that consisted of a even few Levitical priests. God had commissioned the priest and scribe Ezra to rebuild the temple and to reinstall a place of Jewish assembly for national worship. A second group

---

21. Haymin H. Donin, *To Raise a Jewish Child: A Guide for Parents* (San Francisco: Basic Books, 1977), 113.

returned with Nehemiah, whose primary task was to rebuild the walls around the city of Jerusalem.

Although scribes existed before the Exile, they had grown in prominence during the exilic period. Those who were intellectually astute or verbally articulate attracted a gathering of faithful students. Thereafter, this prominent scribe would be seen as the religious leader of his school and was referred to as a *rabbi,* meaning "master." These rabbinical schools were a powerful force in postexilic Judaism for the duplication and interpretation of the Hebrew scrolls.

The scribes viewed their work as holy and unto the Lord. They never wavered in their concentrated effort to replicate God's Word precisely and accurately. They were forbidden to dip their reed pen in the ink just before or after writing the name for God for fear that they might accidentally smear or blot out God's name. Once they had copied a scroll, they counted the words of the old scroll to determine the middle word. They then compared that with their calculation on the new scroll to ensure that it was exactly the same. Likewise, they determined the middle letter of the old scroll and compared that with the middle letter of the new scroll. They randomly selected a word and counted how many times that word appeared in the old text and again compared that count with the one found in the new scroll. If the new scroll was found to be erroneous in any way, they burned the faulty scroll and began a new scroll. One can see why the scribe was soon revered for his knowledge of God's Word and his respect for it. To be viewed as the leader of such a school was a high honor indeed. It was hard to win a doctrinal dispute with a scribe unless you had been one yourself. Seldom did the common farmer or merchant dare to challenge the knowledge or interpretation of a scribe—especially a rabbi.

Once the people returned from Exile they returned with a renewed zeal to follow the teachings in the Talmud. They had learned their lesson, and now with a deeper understanding of God's laws, in part the result of the effectiveness of the scribes and rabbis, they were determined not to follow in the path of their ancestors. Watching over them to ensure that they did not return to the apostasy of their fathers were the prophets.

Ezekiel and Daniel prophesied during the Exile, whereas Haggai, Zechariah, and Malachi prophesied after the Exile. These men had a special, and in many cases spectacular, call of God on their lives. They were committed to maintaining a pure faith among God's chosen people. They maintained vigilance in their duties, and their commitment to national piety earned them respect among the common people. Again, in time, some of these men developed "schools of the prophets" to train and equip others to fill the ranks of this important religious position. Founded as a means of preparing men for prophetic service to God, these educational institutions were rigorous in both their curricular offerings and their instructional methodologies.

So What? Lessons from the Past for Twenty-first-century Christian Education

This period of human history chronicles God's dealings with mankind and His initial strategy for fellowship with His creation. We can learn much from this piece of recorded history. Several principles of ministry can be drawn from our observations as well. These stories not only record past events but also live on for our instruction. The observant student can draw several important implications for ministry practice today through careful analysis, of which the following are a few suggestions.

1. God desires to use people to accomplish His purposes on earth.

From the unique advantage of hindsight, we have come to learn much about the character of God in His dealings with the Hebrew nation. At first, God preferred to deal with just one person, a patriarch, with whom to share Himself. Whether that person was Adam, Noah, Abraham, Isaac, or Jacob, we see a God who desires fellowship and communion with His creation. He is worthy of praise and worship because of all that He has done in the initial act of creation.

Unfortunately, these early bearers of God's message to humanity were ineffective in their methods of presentation. God, however, will not be limited by man's inefficiencies. He places His mantle of anointing upon an entire nation with the express intention of using it as an object lesson of His great mercy and love. He did not choose Israel because of their great military strength and might but in spite of their limited population, geographical location, and political prowess. He chose the nation of Israel for reasons known only to God Himself. His plan was to communicate Himself to this people through special revelation (e.g., Jesus Christ, miracles, signs and wonders, etc.) and general revelation (e.g., His Word, priests, scribes, etc.).

What is helpful for us to realize today is that God is still in the business of using people. But not just anyone! God is looking for the man or woman whose heart is committed to doing God's will (2 Chron. 16:9). That means that he/she has humbly committed themselves to considering God's will to be more important than their own. The famous missionary to South America, Jim Elliot, said it so well when he stated, "Man has yet to see what God can do with a man (or woman) whose heart is completely committed to Him."

2. God's character is that of a nurturing parent/teacher.

Although the Old Testament saints were rarely faithful to God for long durations of time, their fluctuating relationship with Him again reveals God's character and nature as a patient and merciful Father. Eventually, even God's patience expires, and He must punish His children like an earthly father—once again revealing His character to those who have an ear to hear and a heart to understand.

Throughout this process, God seeks to instill His commands, instructions, and guidelines to His people. His primary means was through the home—a spiritually minded father and mother who cared enough about their children to rear them in the fear of the Lord. God prescribed annual events to reinforce this instruction through feasts, festivals, and temple sacrifices. Beyond the home, God used community-based institutions such as the synagogue to communicate His truth. Eventually, this latter method worked well, and synagogues became focused exclusively on the teaching and instruction of children and adults.

We can learn a great deal about God as a teacher through the early origins of Hebrew education. We discover a God who has His lesson aims clearly in focus. They are well reasoned and for the benefit of the learner. Although His learner might be somewhat slow and reluctant to learn the lesson, God continues to pursue His learner and is even willing to take into consideration the unique environmental conditions of the learning experience to determine which method will be most effective. God, the divine teacher, helps future Christian educators learn many valuable lessons about the teaching-learning process that will be beneficial for countless generations to come.

3. Ministry is about relationships.

In the twenty-first century, we get caught up in ministry programs. We develop curriculum, three-ring binders with handouts and overhead transparencies, and a full array of instructional support materials. But from time to time we must stop to realize that they are no substitute for getting into the lives of our students. Ministry is people, not programs. In your ministry careers, you will be tempted to get swept up in the busyness of making events and programs happen successfully, but remember one of the lessons from this era of human history: God desires a personal relationship with each of His children. Ministry programs can help facilitate that goal or they can get in the way of it. Seek to find ways to allow people to deepen their personal relationship with God through your ministry efforts, and don't lose sight of this important goal of ministry.

FOR FURTHER READING

Anthony, Michael J. "Synagogue Schools." In *The Evangelical Dictionary of Christian Education.* Edited by Michael J. Anthony. Grand Rapids: Baker, 2001.

Bokser, Ben Zion. *Judaism and the Christian Predicament.* New York: Knopf, 1967.

Crenshaw, James L. *Education in Ancient Israel: Across the Deadening Silence.* New York: Doubleday, 1998.

Donin, Haymin H. *To Raise a Jewish Child: A Guide for Parents.* San Francisco: Basic Books, 1977.

Eavey, Charles B. *History of Christian Education.* Chicago: Moody, 1964.

Forhrer, Georg. *History of Israelite Religion.* Translated by David E. Green. New York: Abingdon, 1972.

Frost, Severe F. *Historical and Philosophical Foundations of Western Education.* Columbus: Charles E. Merrill, 1966.

Graendorf, Werner C. *Introduction to Biblical Christian Education.* Chicago: Moody, 1981.

Kaufmann, Yehezkel. *The Religion of Israel.* Chicago: University of Chicago Press, 1960.

MacGregor, Jerry C. "Bar Mitzvah." In *The Evangelical Dictionary of Christian Education.* Edited by Michael J. Anthony. Grand Rapids: Baker, 2001.

Mayer, Fredrick. *A History of Educational Thought.* Columbus: Charles E. Merrill, 1966.

Neusner, Jacob. *Judaism in the Beginning of Christianity.* Philadelphia: Fortress, 1984.

——. *World Religions in America*. Louisville: Westminster John Knox, 1994.

Person, Peter P. *An Introduction to Christian Education*. Grand Rapids: Baker, 1958.

Proceedings of the Center for Jewish-Christian Learning, vol. 11. St. Paul: University of St. Thomas, p. 34, fall 1996.

Reed, James E., and Ronnie Prevost. *A History of Christian Education*. Nashville: Broadman & Holman, 1993.

Saldarini, Anthony. *Pharisees, Scribes, and Sadducees in Palestinian Society: A Sociological Approach*. Wilmington, Del.: Michael Glazier, 1988.

Seift, F. H. *Education in Ancient Israel from Earliest Times to 70 a.d.* Chicago: Open Court, 1919.

Seltzer, Robert M. *Jewish People, Jewish Thought*. New York: Macmillan, 1980.

Silver, Daniel J. *A History of Judaism*. New York: Basic Books, 1974.

Taylor, Marvin J. *An Introduction to Christian Education*. Nashville: Abingdon, 1966.

Wilson, Marvin R. *Our Father Abraham: Jewish Roots of the Christian Faith*. Grand Rapids: Eerdmans, 1989.

Zuck, Roy B. "Education in the Pentateuch." In *The Evangelical Dictionary of Christian Education*. Edited by Michael J. Anthony. Grand Rapids: Baker, 2001.

What in the World?

➤ The Trojan War; expansion of Mycenaean Greeks c. 1250 B.C.

➤ Jewish political power peaks with King Solomon c. 950 B.C.

➤ Siddhartha creates new religion later known as Buddhism in 528 B.C.

➤ The Greek Parthenon is built to honor the goddess Athena in 447–432 B.C.

➤ The great Greek philosopher, Socrates, is sentenced to death in 399 B.C. because his teaching challenged traditional ideas.

➤ The Hellenistic Age in Greece in 323–31 B.C.

➤ Alexander the Great dies in 323 B.C.

➤ The Great Wall of China is reinforced and lengthened as a defensive wall c. 221–206 B.C.

Chapter 2

GREEK EDUCATION AND PHILOSOPHICAL THOUGHT

NO CULTURE HAS HAD SO PROFOUND an impact upon the way we live today as that of the Greeks. The modern academic disciplines of education, art, science, medicine, and many other aspects of society can trace their roots to the Greeks. Our own educational system, aesthetic values as expressed within the fine arts, and of course, our quintessential philosophical presuppositions about life have Greek heritage. Freedom and democracy within a civilized society were the fruits of Greek thought. The Greeks by their very nature were inquisitive and encouraged the free exchange of opposing views. They feared only a closed mind. To the Greeks, the heart of a man who refused to entertain another point of view led to racism, bigotry, and intolerance.

Many famous ancient men came from the ranks of the Greeks. The great philosophers Socrates, Aristotle, and Plato were Greek, as were the renowned poets Homer, Aristophanes, and Sophocles. Whether they were in the arts, science, medicine, or law, many of history's greatest thinkers came from the ancient Greeks. It was a rich culture with limitless opportunities for discovery.

GREEK CULTURE

Because of its location along the coast of the Mediterranean Sea, ancient Greece enjoyed a cosmopolitan existence. Traders brought fine silks from

Mesopotamia, beaten copper and brass utensils from Egypt, spices from Morocco, silver from Spain, and olive oil and leather from Italy. Greece lacked few essentials for daily living and even seemed to have a plentiful supply of luxuries in the marketplace. Along with their wares, merchants also provided an abundance of stories about customs and local traditions. Cultural patterns from distant lands were accepted and assimilated into their own.

Greek civilization sought to assimilate the best from these foreign lands and held open arms toward people of differing or even opposing views. The Greeks were insatiable in their quest for artistic expression. In the fields of art, literature, poetry, drama, rhetoric, athletics, and music, the Greeks enjoyed boundless expression.

Throughout most of Greece was an attitude of tolerance for others. Such open-mindedness allowed people of differing faiths to find freedom of expression without fear of reprisal. Many Greek towns had a middle class—something that was absent from many cultures that we have seen up to that time. Slaves did most of the menial tasks, and because they were treated with relative respect, few threats to their existence as a nation came from within their borders. However, such was not always the case from outside their regions.

Perhaps the aspect of Greek culture that gained the most notoriety was their love for athletic competition. These sporting contests were more than demonstrations of physical power; they also showcased the mental, emotional, and spiritual conditioning of Greek youth. They were times to demonstrate to the world how well balanced the Greek culture was.

The Olympic games originated in ancient Greece and were dedicated to the god Zeus. Preparation for the games lasted nearly a year, during which time the military returned from distant conquests to ready themselves for competition. The events themselves were conducted every four years at Olympia in western Greece. Sporting events such as the pentathlon, marathon, swimming, wrestling, and boxing were the preferred contests. All freemen were encouraged to attend, and men came from miles around to participate as representatives of their village or hamlet. Because the participants wore few, if any, clothes, women were strictly forbidden to observe. Neighboring countries sent diplomatic delegations as well. After the events were over and the victors had been identified, a huge banquet was held in their honor at which the olive branch crown was placed upon their head.

In addition to the Olympic games, the Pythian games were celebrated at the city of Delphi every four years. These events differed from the Olympic games because they also included musical competitions. The focal point of these games was singing a hymn to the god Apollo, in whose honor the games were held. Other events included painting, dramatic productions, poetical renditions, and playing the flute and lyre. The Nemean games were conducted every two years and also were dedicated to Zeus. Most of these events were athletic in nature, but some limited music competition occurred. Finally, the Panathenaic games were celebrated in Athens at the beginning of every fourth year with laughter and merriment. Because these games celebrated the union of the tribes that inhabited the region of Attica around Athens, great pomp and ceremony were characteristic of the occasion. The entire city shut down to observe the events. Among the contests were boating, torch races, horse races, chariot races, dancing in full armor, leaping in and out of moving chariots, throwing the javelin, and musical competition such as playing the flute and the lyre and singing. The main event was when the entire population of Athens marched into the streets in parade formation wearing gold robes to commemorate the goddess of the Parthenon.[1]

Beyond the cultural boundaries of sporting events, the Greeks enjoyed music, drama, poetry, and art. Archaeological discoveries reveal a rich culture of fine arts. Mosaics, paintings, and sculptures evidenced their feelings about life. Even everyday flower vases and water jugs were viewed as canvases for painting and recording historic events. Much of what we know about ancient Greek culture comes from these remnants of their society.

The Greeks enjoyed a temperate climate that could accommodate a diverse array of outdoor pursuits. In addition, they had many lakes, mountains, and ocean retreats for those people who were inclined to enjoy them. Clothing was light and loose fitting. Both the rich and the poor wore relatively the same style of tunic, thereby minimizing distinctions among the classes. Homes were decorated modestly. Most homes were one story with few windows.

GREEK RELIGION

Discussions of Greek culture and Greek religious expression are seemingly inseparable. Walter Otto described in his 1926 lecture series titled *The*

---

1. Fredrick Eby and Charles F. Arrowood, *The History and Philosophy of Education: Ancient and Medieval* (Englewood Cliffs, N.J.: Prentice-Hall, 1940), 169–70.

Ancient Greek Idea of God the relationship that existed between the two. He stated, "Wherever religion and culture are still found in their native strength, they are fundamentally one, and more or less to be identified one with another. In such a case religion is not valued additional to cultural goods but the most profound revelation of the peculiar content and essence of a culture."[2] In other words, to know and understand one is to know and understand the other.

Whereas the Hebrews believed that only one God existed and that He could be known personally, the Greeks had no such limitations. Their religious beliefs and practices were based upon polytheism. Although they had many gods from which to choose, they viewed a select group of twelve as the dominate leaders. To abbreviate oaths made to these deities, worshipers simply announced, "I swear on the Twelve," thereby ensuring that no god was left out. After all, who wanted to take a chance on offending one of the supreme deities and thereby incurring his wrath? The names of these twelve gods were inscribed upon the east frieze of the Parthenon: Zeus, Hera, Poseidon, Demeter, Apollo, Artemis, Ares, Aphrodite, Hermes, Athena, Hephaestus, and Hestia.

A Who's Who of Greek Gods

Zeus	Father of the gods and supreme deity
Apollo	God of agriculture and weather or prophecy, healing, and music; patron of the Olympian games and intellect
Poseidon	Temperamental sea god with influence over earthquakes and floods
Ares	God of war and military conquests
Athena	Patron goddess of protection for Athens and her soldiers
Hera	Preeminent goddess of marriage and childbirth
Demeter	Goddess of fruits and corn; controlled the crops and ultimate harvests
Aphrodite	Goddess of love, beauty, passion, and fertility

---

2. Walter F. Otto, *Die Gestalt und das Sein*; as cited in C. Kerenyi, *The Religion of Greeks and Romans* (New York: Dutton, 1962), 13.

Hestia	Goddess of the hearth and home
Hephaestus	Controlled fire and was the special protector of smiths
Artemis	Fertility goddess with additional control over forests and hills
Hermes	Patron of the wayfaring; he also escorted the dead to hell

According to Greek religion, the gods controlled everything. There was a god who determined the growth of the corn, the direction and flow of rivers, the movement of the sun and stars, childbirth, fire, rain, and just about everything else that was seen as important to human existence. It all started, so states the myth, when the ancient god Kronos no longer reigned in the universe. His three sons cast lots to determine who would have control over the various regions of influence. Zeus got heaven, Poseidon the sea, and Hades the underworld.

Greek mythology records the activities of and the interaction between these gods and humanity. Stories that depicted their existence were passed down from generation to generation. These fables, or myths, provided the background information necessary to understand the influence of a particular god and by what means he/she preferred to be worshiped. "A myth then is firstly, man's attempt to explain the world and the things he sees in it, and to make intelligible to himself the natural phenomena which condition his way of life in that world."[3]

Some poets depicted the affairs of these gods and their interaction with mankind through poems, stories, and plays. One of the most famous Greek poets who illustrated the life of the gods and their interaction with humanity was Homer. His two great epics *Iliad* and *Odyssey* are to this day among the finest examples of Greek lore. *Iliad* describes the war between Troy and Archaen (Greeks), which took place after Paris, the Trojan prince, abducted Helen.

Odyssey is the account of Odysseus, the king of Ithaca, who makes an arduous journey home from the battlefield. These stories, and others like them, represented some of the curriculum that the Greeks used to pass down their culture, values, and traditions to children in subsequent generations.

Because no single inspired source of information about these gods existed, each author added his perspective through stories. Some authors built upon the observations of their predecessors, whereas others contradicted

---

3. Richard Pattrick, *All Color Book of Greek Mythology* (London: Octopus, 1972), 4.

previous writers. No basis existed by which to judge the validity of one man's opinion on such matters. Some gods were referred to in the singular tense (e.g., Pan, the god of herdsmen, who was characterized as having a human body to the loins and goat legs, ears, horns, etc.) yet they appear in other writings in the plural (e.g., Panes). Worshiping a god about whom you were not sure was a significant challenge.

> The plain man, then, in ancient Greece lived in a world full of all manner of supernatural powers, great and small, friendly and unfriendly, and naturally tried to get and maintain right relations with them. This was done partly, by avoiding unlucky actions and days as much as possible. . . . If men will do justly both by fellow-countrymen and strangers, the gods will reward them with prosperity; their fields will yield bounteous harvests, the oaks will bear plenty of acorns and wild bees make their hives in them, the flocks and herds will increase, the women will bear healthy children. But for those who practiced the wanton disregard for the rights of others there are none of these blessings, but rather plague, famine, sterility, and disaster in war, or shipwreck at sea.[4]

People worshiped Greek gods more out of fear for how the gods could hurt them than out of a genuine desire to express their appreciation and affection for the gods. They presented offerings more to avoid future punishment than to express heartfelt thanksgiving. They seldom viewed gods as personal and approachable, so they worshiped them out of ignorance and isolation.

GREEK EDUCATION

When one speaks of the educational system of ancient Greece, one must clarify what geographical parameters are placed on the discussion. As was described earlier, the physical geography of Greece allowed it to maintain many variations in its cultural distinctives. Nowhere was this fact more apparent than in its educational system because no single standard regarding curriculum, discipline, grading practices, employment credentials, etc., was applied

---

4. Herbert J. Rose, *Religion in Greece and Rome* (New York: Harper & Brothers, 1959), 28-29.

across the country. Each district exercised a great deal of freedom in all of the preceding elements of an educational system; therefore, discussions about Greek education must be limited to the locale. For purposes of our discussion, we will limit ourselves to two of the most predominant cities to illustrate the significant differences that existed among Greek citizens.

Sparta

This prominent Greek city was situated about 650 to 700 feet above sea level between two tributary rivers. The city itself was small by today's standards, measuring only about two miles from north to south and a mile from east to west. Made up mostly of agrarian peasants, the city, perhaps in part the result of its closeness to the sea, was a much-desired piece of real estate. Hence, the city always seemed to be at war with some neighboring village or was preparing to defend itself from attack. Two of the most famous wars include the Third Messenian War (c. 465-460) and the Peloponnesian War (c. 431-404). Sparta's end in history seems to have come at the hands of the Goths under Alaric in A.D. 396[5]

The majority of the people who inhabited the city lived a meager and relatively poor existence; hence, the popular phrase, "He lived a Spartan's life." Society in Sparta placed a heavy emphasis upon the needs of the state. The people lived for the state and were exploited by those who were in control of civil government. The needs of government superceded personal aspirations. For this reason, children were viewed as a means to an end, and that end was political and military dominance. Records found from this era describe the majority of its citizenry as "living in a perpetual armed camp."[6] Children were indoctrinated at an early age to believe that no higher virtue existed than to defend one's city against all opposing forces.

> The great social problem of all later Greek educators was to determine how individualism might be repressed and the character of every citizen might be developed on one communal model. The Spartan state, with its rigid authoritarianism, appeared to be the

5. N. G. L. Hammond and H. H. Scullard, eds., *The Oxford Classical Dictionary* (Oxford: Clarendon, 1970), 1006-7.
6. Werner Jaeger, *Paideia: The Ideals of Greek Culture* (New York: Oxford University Press, 1939), 2:83.

solution of this problem in actual practice; and as such it occupied Plato's mind throughout his life.[7]

In Sparta, the child did not belong to the parents but rather to the state. If the child were born with a defect of any kind, the city elders had the authority to rid themselves of an unwanted burden. If the child survived this first examination, he/she was allowed to remain at home under the watchful care of the parents for approximately seven years, at which time the boys entered a dormitory where they lived among their peers.

Boys were divided into companies according to their ages. Once established, these companies were merged into larger organizations called troops. The leader of the company and the troop was a superintendent chosen from among his peers. His duty was to ensure cooperation and unified discipline within the ranks. He was allowed a great deal of latitude in terms of corporal punishment, and some of these youth were ruthless in maintaining their position. The overall training of the boys themselves was delegated to trainers who were under the control of a Board of Inspection. Every Spartan citizen could invoke a measure of discipline to raise the "children of the state" in a most effectual manner. Obedience to their elders was one of the highest ideals taught to these boys. This character quality became a distinguishing element between Spartans and the boys from other cities.[8]

Spartan education was marked by fanatical discipline. The intent of their education was to harden the body and develop the greatest degree of bodily skill. At the age of twelve, the boys were given only the items essential for survival. For example, their clothing, even in the cold of winter, consisted of only a robe. Likewise, their food was meager. They were given only enough to sustain existence, never enough to produce slothful overindulgence. Their bed was made of straw gleaned from the field. At fifteen, they were allowed a bed of reeds or bulrushes. They were conditioned to tolerate endurance and physical pain. Intellectual development was void and seen as wasteful. A few of the boys might have been able to learn to read, but such activity was frowned upon and came only at great personal expense through the hiring of personal tutors known as pedagogues. These boys learned neither literature, art, nor science.

---

7. Ibid.
8. Hugo Blumner, *The Home Life of the Ancient Greeks* (New York: Cooper Square Publishers, 1960), 99–100.

What little mathematics they learned was for the purpose of pragmatic living. Some basic musical instruction, such as learning to play a kithara or flute, occurred mixed with singing choruses approved by the state.[9]

Spartan education was directed toward producing soldiers who could fight with unwavering discipline. One unique aspect of their training is seen in the "art" of robbery and theft. Spartan boys were taught to steal from one another as a tool for developing stealth as a scout. They needed such skill while conducting surveillance. If the child was caught in the act of stealing, he was beaten severely—not for stealing but for getting caught. Isocrates once declared that skill in stealing was an essential step in the road toward holding a political office in the city of Sparta.[10]

Girls were educated in Sparta, but their education consisted primarily of curricula that had benefit to the state as well. They were taught how to be mothers of future warriors, always nurturing and sacrificing for their sons. Gymnastics was a dominant course of instruction, and it included dancing, singing, and music.[11] To bear strong children, the girls were instructed in wrestling, gymnastics, swimming, and running.

> The result of all this outdoor training was great physical perfection: Lampito, the Spartan woman in Aristophanes' *Lysistrata,* is greatly admired by the women from other cities for her beauty, her complexion, and her bodily condition: "she looks as though she could throttle a bull." She ascribes it to her gymnastics and vigorous dancing.[12]

It was said that the greatest honor of a Spartan mother was to see her son return from the battlefield carried on his shield, having given his life for the protection of his country.

Athens

Athens was located approximately four miles inland and built about the Acropolis, a hill some 512 feet high and 1000 feet long. Owing to the

---

9. Ibid., 101.
10. Kenneth J. Freeman, *School of Hellas* (New York: Teachers College Press, 1969), 23-24.
11. Hammond and Scullard, *Oxford Classical Dictionary,* 370.
12. Freeman, *School of Hellas,* 30.

prominence of this peak, the city was accessible from only one side, thus giving it an unexcelled means of defense. A high wall connected the city with its closest harbor, which was known as Piraeus. The town was fed by aristocratic leaders who owned and farmed Attica, the nearby peninsula. Eventually, the aristocratic elite secured slaves to cultivate their land while they built fashionable homes inside the security of the city walls. In its glory days, Athens boasted a population of 125,000 freemen and almost as many slaves. Because most Athenians were too poor to own even one slave, those who were rich obviously had a great many.[13]

With extra time on their hands, the aristocratic landowners gave themselves over to the quest of art, architecture, philosophy, science, politics, music, and drama. To enhance these pursuits, they built theatres, stadiums, museums, gymnasiums, and outdoor amphitheaters. The Athenians were a cultured population. They dedicated themselves wholeheartedly to the pursuit of knowledge in a diverse array of fields.

In the city of Athens, the educational system stood in sharp contrast to the form of instruction that was indicative of Sparta. Whereas the Spartan system valued physical prowess displayed by supreme military might, the Athenian system was dedicated to the development of the mind. No public schools existed in Athens. Wealthy people hired private tutors for their children. They also hired pedagogues, older Greek slaves who had lost their ability to do physical labor in the field, to serve as chaperones. They carried the child's school supplies, ensured they made it to school safely and on time, and generally oversaw the child's moral and ethical development within society. Today, we might refer to such individuals as older mentors.

Athenian children remained home with no formal instruction until the age of six, at which time their formal education began. Basically four types of schools were available: elementary school for boys aged six to thirteen; secondary school for boys aged fourteen to eighteen; school for higher education, where a young man could learn advanced studies in medicine, law, music, or science; and military academy for students who desired such training.

Most children attended at least a few years of basic instruction so they could learn to read and write. Included in this elementary instruction was also music and art. The Athenians valued a balanced, well-rounded education. Physical education was important but not at the expense of other interests. The training of young children, known in the Greek culture as *paideia*,

---

13. Eby and Arrowood, *History and Philosophy of Education*, 219-22.

was a respected profession. "Paideia did not involve doing things for the child, but rather the guiding of his spontaneous activity into artistic and graceful forms. It signified in a general way the natural and harmonious development of physical and mental powers, to bring about an all-around perfecting of human nature."[14] Such a well-rounded liberal education holds the origins of humanism, an educational philosophy that we will address in greater detail in the Reformation period.

To the Athenian Greeks, no distinction between body and soul, or mind or muscle, existed. Little differentiation was made between the content that affected the mind and that which affected the heart. Values, meaning, and clear understanding were just as important as facts. A concerted effort was made to integrate academic pursuits with democratic responsibilities. Content was not taught purely to prepare a child for examination and further graded advancement. To the Greeks, an educated individual was one who could assume responsible living and hold a contributing role in greater society. As such, they were not limited to or fixated on the myopic view of the mere acquisition of knowledge. To get good grades but be unable to think rationally about the meaning and purpose of life was unheard of within the system. Education was individual, not done in groups the way we do it today, so time could be taken with each child to ensure that the child grasped the full meaning of the material being taught.

Music instruction was an important element of Greek education because through music the emotions were engaged. Children learned to play a musical instrument and to value the sounds of music. They sang hymns and songs, many of which held religious or moral instructional value. The great Greek philosopher Plato once said of musical instruction,

> Musical training is a more potent instrument than any other, because rhythm and harmony find their way into the inward places of the soul, on which they mightily fasten, imparting grace, and making the soul of him who is rightly educated graceful, or of him who is ill-educated ungraceful; and also because he who has received this true education of the inner being will most shrewdly perceive omissions or faults in art and nature, and with a true taste, while he praises and

---

14. Ibid., 234. Mortimer Adler used the term "paideia" to describe his urban instruction program for North America's city curriculum. See his *Paideia Proposal: An Educational Manifesto* (New York: Macmillan), 1982.

rejoices over and receives into his soul the good, and becomes noble and good, he will justly blame and hate the bad, now in the days of his youth, even before he is able to know the reason why; and when reason comes he will recognize and salute the friend with whom his education has made him long familiar.[15]

At fourteen, the child completed his studies and returned home to learn a trade. He might have been apprenticed by his father or a relative. Those who were wealthy enough not to have to work progressed to secondary schools, where the children of nobility studied under learned men called Sophists. Sophists were itinerate teachers who were hired for a specific period of time to teach intensive subjects beyond those studied in elementary school. They taught mathematics, astronomy, geometry, advanced literature, and music theory. Because the Sophists were paid by the parents, they were hired to teach whatever subjects the parents deemed important for their sons.[16] Those who were able to convince wealthy parents of their wisdom commanded large sums for their instruction and became quite wealthy.

> The Sophists represented a radical change in education in at least three ways: (1) They helped popularize intellectual inquiry to the detriment of physical activity; (2) they placed great value on oratory, which for the Greeks meant the arts of persuasion, generally; and (3) they extended formal education well into young manhood.[17]

Although popular, these traveling professors were not without their critics. Plato labeled them "disputatious, controversial, pugnacious, combative, acquisitive, a dissembler, a dealer in appearances, and a word juggler."[18] They gained a reputation for being more concerned about the inflated tuition they charged than with impartial truth and intellectual integrity.

An alternative form of secondary education was established by teachers who preferred not to travel selling their intellectual prowess like produce in the marketplace. Instead, they developed residential schools to which stu-

---

15. Plato *Republic* 401-2.
16. Freeman, *School of Hellas,* 157-65.
17. James J. Jarrett, *The Educational Theories of the Sophists* (New York: Teachers College Press, 1969), 18.
18. Ibid., 20.

dents came for four years of study (fourteen to eighteen years of age) to focus their learning on prescribed subjects. The curriculum for these schools was divided into two broad categories: trivium—which consisted of grammar, rhetoric, and dialectic; and quadrivium—which consisted of geometry, arithmetic, astronomy, and music. These combined categories are often referred to in the field of education as the seven liberal arts.

Plato established one such school known as the Academy, where he specialized in the subjects of mathematics and literature. Aristotle developed the Lyceum, where he instructed his students in biological sciences. Epicurus founded the Epicurean School in Athens, where he emphasized the study of ethics and moral philosophy. He was also a prolific writer, completing thirty-seven books during his life.[19] The fourth residential school of higher education was the Stoic school founded by Zeno, a rich merchant from the island of Cyprus.

The Academy

Plato established a residential school on the outskirts of Athens around 385 B.C. Here he taught students for the service of the state for a period of forty years. Ample evidence exists that many of his students became influential members of Athenian politics. Although he instructed his students in this subject, his curriculum also consisted of astronomy, mathematics, science, and philosophy. The latter subject brought him highest acclaim. Plato was instrumental in providing this higher form of learning free of charge to citizens of the state. This early form of state-funded education would form the basis for what North America would later develop in its public school system.

GREEK PHILOSOPHICAL THOUGHT

Philosophy can be defined as the love and pursuit of wisdom. Greek philosophy was a serious endeavor to understand the universe and man's

---

19. Eby and Arrowood, *History and Philosophy of Education*, 390.

relationship to it. The chief aim was to discover the right way to live and to bring others to a similar conclusion.[20]

If you were to survey the philosophical giants of ancient Greece in the same way that you would observe a distant mountain range, three "peaks" would rise prominently above the rest. These philosophical pinnacles would seem to dwarf the rest by both their magnitude and their grandeur. On the mountain range of Greek philosophical thought, Socrates, Plato, and Aristotle would be the names of these prominent mountain peaks. Socrates is seen as the founder of moralism, Plato as the founder of idealism, and Aristotle as the founder of realism. A brief exploration of each individual and their respective philosophical presuppositions will provide the reader with an overview of essential educational philosophies.

Socrates and Moralism

Socrates (469-399 B.C.) was the child of a wealthy sculptor or stonecutter. He served for a time in the army and demonstrated heroism and courage at battles in Potidea, Amphhipolis, and Delium. Educated in Athens and blessed with a sharp mind, he soon rose to the position of president in the city's assembly.

Although contradictory accounts are given of his physical stature, most authors agree that he was not a particularly attractive man. In fact, he is described as a portly man who wore worn-out clothing and walked barefoot throughout Athens. However, what he lacked in physical appearance he more than made up in mental aptitude. He sought to define important terms such as *justice, piety,* and *courage.* He rarely answered a student's question but guided the student toward self-discovery by asking a series of questions that placed him in a state of mental disequilibrium (see "The Socratic Instructional Method"). He argued and contended with his students to the point where they found themselves hopelessly lost and confused by contradictory statements.

Socrates came on the scene at a time when mankind was inundated with prejudice and arrogance. Society had become categorized and finely differentiated by socioeconomic class, status, rules, standards, protocols, and taboos. These social restraints were communicated through cultural norms,

---

20. J. Burnet, "Philosophy," in *The Legacy of Greece,* ed. R. W. Livingstone (Oxford: Clarendon, 1951), 58.

standards, laws, rules, regulations, and restrictions. Until Socrates' time, no one dared challenge the presuppositions of these limitations. Socrates investigated the rationale for such living by using systematic observation, critical reflection, and detailed analysis. This methodology would later be called the scientific method. His investigations into the moral reasoning of mankind and his ethical decision making set him apart as a moral philosopher.[21] "Socrates declared the soul to be the source of the highest values in human life."[22]

Although he himself never wrote anything, he has been the subject of myriad volumes. Much of what is said about his philosophy of life is recorded by Plato, who had been his disciple. For Socrates, the question of whether virtue could be taught was of paramount importance. Virtue, defined then as civic responsibility, was the nonnegotiable quality of a citizen of the state. Socrates sought to determine whether such national pride and patriotism was taught to children at a young age or was an innate quality? Thus began the age-old question of nature versus nurture. Socrates was committed to the sound training of youth (preferably through state-sponsored public schools) with the goal of producing contributing members of society. Virtue was demonstrated in one's defense of the state, in the respect granted to a community elder, or in raising one's children to obey the laws of the land.

Two specific areas of Socrates's thought are of particular interest here: universal definitions of terms and dialectical argument. The first concept refers to a term's being defined such that its meaning remains the same regardless of cultural or contextual differences. The second concept refers to his method of arguing with his students to confuse them and challenge their reasoning process.[23]

Socrates was committed to a world governed by a moral order and a definite reason for existence. To Socrates, only the moral individual could possess true knowledge. He would have agreed with Jesus that knowledge sets one free. Plato's *Apologi* quotes Socrates as saying, "The unexamined life is not worth living." In this statement, he challenges his audience to consider life's true meaning and purpose. Socrates found personal meaning

---

21. Eby and Arrowood, *History and Philosophy of Education,* 328.
22. Jaeger, *Paideia: The Ideals of Greek Culture,* 2:45.
23. James E. Reed, and Ronnie Prevost, *A History of Christian Education* (Nashville: Broadman & Holman, 1993), 30.

and fulfillment in the field of teaching. Having abandoned the vocation of his father, he chose the career path of a teacher. After thirty years of national prominence, he was put on trial for introducing strange gods to the community and for leading the youth of the city astray. His indictment reads, "Socrates is guilty because he does not acknowledge the gods which the State acknowledges, but introduces new divinities; he is guilty because he corrupts youth." During this trial, he was given the opportunity of either renouncing his teaching career or being condemned to death. He said that he would cheerfully choose death rather than give up his "divinely appointed" vocation. Therefore, Socrates became the world's first educational martyr. Thirty days after his trial he was sentenced to death by drinking a potion laced with hemlock.[24]

Socrates was well known for his unique method of instruction. He began his day walking throughout the school yard asking questions of his students. These were not simple questions that required a short verbal response. Rather, they were specifically crafted such as to force the student to think critically before responding. Socrates' questions required that the student integrate previously learned materials with new insights being taught in the curriculum. Socrates had a way of penetrating the heart of the learner and required contemplative introspection before providing an answer. His was a unique approach because it required a different response. Socrates was not satisfied with simply obtaining a factual answer. He wanted responses that required higher levels of reasoning. Using Bloom's taxonomy as an example, Socrates worded his questions such as to require students to analyze and synthesize before formulating a response. Plato and Aristotle, who modeled their schools and philosophical training after Socrates, replicated this approach in their instructional methodology as well.

Socratic Method of Instruction

While any teaching method based upon questioning could be considered Socratic, modern applications of this ancient mode of teaching are the various forms of the small group discussion. Discussions range in format from completely undirected buzz groups or rap sessions to the seminar that has a

---

24. Eby and Arrowood, *History and Philosophy of Education*, 322.

specific topic and purpose. Discussions involve asking open-ended questions, questions that require more than a simple yes or no answer, from asking for an opinion or basic information to deeper questions of meaning and application. The latter can make seminars particularly powerful when dealing with issues and ideas.[25]

In the Socratic discourses three stages can generally be distinguished: first, the stage called Plato "opinion," in which the individual is unable to give valid reasons for his knowledge or supposed knowledge; second, the destructive or analytical stage, in which the individual is brought to realize that he does not know what he assumed he knew, and that leads to a contradiction and a mental condition of doubt or perplexity; third, a synthetic stage for the results of which Plato would reserve the term "knowledge." When this last stage is attained, the individual's experience is critically reconstructed and he can justify his beliefs by giving reasons for them.[26]

Plato and Idealism

Plato (427–347 B.C.) is viewed as the first systematic philosopher. His real name was Aristocles. The name *Plato* means "the broad one," which might have referred to the rather liberal views that he held. He came from a distinguished aristocratic family in Athens and lived to the age of eighty. Much of what we know about Plato's thoughts come from his writings, which exist in dialogue form. In almost every dialogue, the major figure is Plato's teacher, Socrates, who personally mentored Plato, so we should not be surprised to discover that Plato does not wander far from his master's philosophical underpinnings. He established a residential school in Athens called the Academy in 387 B.C. The great philosopher Aristotle became one of his students.

Plato's publications consist of twenty-five dialogues and *Apology*. They also include an additional thirteen letters, although their authenticity is debatable. Plato's philosophical presuppositions can be found in his three major writings: *The Republic, The Laws,* and *Protagoras*. In these dialogues, we

---

25. Douglas Falls, *The Evangelical Dictionary of Christian Education*, ed. Michael J. Anthony (Grand Rapids: Baker, 2001), s.v. "Socratic Method."

26. Leonard and Gertrude, in *The Doctrines of the Great Educators*, by Robert R. Rusk (New York: St. Martin's, 1957), 5.

discover his views about the nature of man, the purpose of government, and a systematic view of public education.

Before embarking on a discussion of Plato's philosophy of idealism, it is imperative that we understand his view of man because it is within this worldview that his perspectives have meaning. A summary of his notions regarding the nature of man includes the following propositions.

1. Man is composed of two basic substances, matter and spirit (a body and a soul).
2. The superior substance is spiritual and immortal.
3. Evil tendencies in man are usually associated with matter.
4. Although there is a universal and immutable human nature, important differences are found in men; these differences are rooted in the different levels of intelligence.
5. Social classes are determined by levels of intelligence; the intellectual elite are charged with the function of governing the masses.
6. Man possesses a free will and is wholly responsible for his behavior.
7. Reason alone gives true knowledge, and sense knowledge is wholly unreliable.[27]

Continuing the investigation of virtue begun by his master Socrates, Plato believed there to be four supreme virtues, each forming a natural bridge between mankind and society: temperance, courage, wisdom, and justice.[28] The first two virtues, according to Plato, were "formed in the soul in the course of time by habit and exercise." Development of the latter two virtues required a more intentional process. Thus, an educational philosophy that included a rationale for public education was the natural consequence of his reasoning.

Following is a brief overview of idealism from Plato's allegory "The Cave," presented from *The Republic*. Imagine if you will, that you and a few of your friends have been chained together in a dark cave. You are seated on a ledge facing the wall and you are unable to see anything except the wall in front of you. Behind you is a large fire that is giving off a good deal of light. You are separated from the fire by enough room to allow objects to pass between you, but because you have your eyes fixed on the wall of the cave in front of

---

27. Plato *Republic* 6:510f.
28. Reed and Prevost, *History of Christian Education*, 31.

you, you are unable to see the actual objects themselves, only the shadow of the object on the wall of the cave. Now, let's take this one step further and imagine that the people who are chained together have been there for their entire lives, never having known life outside the cave. Their only concept of the world around them is based on the shadows of the objects they have seen on the cave's wall. They have no concept of three-dimensional life and have never seen color.

Over the years of their existence, shadows of objects such as animals, eating and drinking utensils, and even people have been projected on the wall. These shadows represent their world of reality. The shadowy image of a dog represents all they have come to know concerning the idea of "dogness."

Now let's suppose that someone comes and releases them from their chains and they are free to move about within the boundaries of the cave. They now discover that their idea of "dogness" was inadequate because they see a dog as a three-dimensional object. They have a fuller and more robust idea of "dogness" now that they have been allowed to move about the cave.

Now, let's take this one step further. In the final episode of Plato's story, the people are allowed to exit the cave into a world full of creative expression. They hear music, see color, and smell objects that they never dreamed were possible. Once more, several dogs pass alongside them, and the people realize that dogs come in descriptive variances (e.g., size, weight, colors, and hair length). They have now expanded their idea of "dogness" to include the full scope of reality.

According to the father of idealism, human beings are restricted to the confines of their earthly cave, limited in what they have come to know as real based upon only the five senses (i.e., sight, sound, smell, taste, and touch). But, according to Plato, these objects that we have come to experience are mere images of reality. Just the way our knowledge was limited to the shadows on the wall of the world's cave, we know the objects around us (e.g., man, woman, chair, or tree) only in a greatly limited and imperfect dimension. As when one tries to look up into the sun, the light blinds our ability to see the planetary objects.

Plato's problem, therefore, resolves itself to this: how can we get at the essences of beauty, truth, justice, stability, number, etc., that give meaning to our claims to knowledge? If we could get at these essences, we should be able to show students how to discover them for themselves and to justify the statements that they make in support of this discovery. Therefore, Plato considers that the ability to justify our claims to knowledge is the essence of education.[29]

In his major discourse, *The Republic,* Plato develops his concept of the ultimate state. Although it is not a defense of totalitarianism, it does advocate the benefit of state control over important agencies, chief among them being the education of society's children. He writes,

> Civil authorities will begin by sending out into the country all the inhabitants of the city who are more than ten years old, and will take possession of their children, who will be affected by the habits of their parents; these they will train in their own habits and laws, I mean in the laws which we have given them: and in this way the state and constitution of which we are speaking will soonest and easily attain happiness, and the nation which has such a constitution will gain most.[30]

To say that Plato believed that the end justified the means is no understatement. He believed that taking control of a child's education was in the best interest of the state and therefore strongly encouraged it. *The Republic* portrayed a state that was devoid of individualism. As an idealist, Plato believed that only through common education controlled by the state could be created a society that had *esprit de corps* that could withstand internal and external threats. He had witnessed the results of parental control over education in Sparta and was determined not to let Athens descend to such a level of social destruction.

Another significant contribution of Plato's educational philosophy relates to his belief that women should be equal recipients of education along with men. This was no minor detour from traditional Greek educational instruction. He believed that the educational neglect of one half of the population of Athens undermined the future success of the state. He insisted on women being admitted to the same educational institutions as men if they had the financial means to attend. In *Laws* he writes, "I affirm that the practice which at present prevails in our districts is a most irrational one—namely, that men and women should not all follow the same pursuits with one accord

---

29. Allen Brent, *Philosophical Foundations for the Curriculum* (Boston: George Allen & Unwin, 1978).
30. Plato *Republic.*

Platonic System of Public Education

Age	School	Curricular emphasis
0–3	Infancy	Physical growth and development, sensory life, no fear, child reacts to pleasure or pain.
4–6	Nursery	Play, fairy tales, nursery rhymes, myths, seek to eliminate the self-will of the child.
6–13	Elementary school	Play, poetry, reading, writing, singing, dancing, religion, social etiquette, numbers, geometry.
13–16	Instrumental music	Play the kithara, sing religious hymns, memorize poetry, arithmetic.
16–20	Gymnastics and military	Formal gymnastics and military training. No intellectual training done at this stage.
20–30	Sciences	Coordination of reason and habits; integration of the physical sciences.
30–35	Dialectic	Philosophy, psychology, sociology, law, government, and education.
35–50	Service to state	
50–death	Philosophers	Higher philosophy.[31]

31. Eby and Arrowood, *History and Philosophy of Education*, 389–90.

and with all their might." His conclusion is that "the female sex must share with the male to the greatest extent possible, both in education and in all else."

An Evangelical Critique of Idealism

Although a number of elements of idealism have value and are worthy of note, several aspects of idealism as a philosophy of education are untenable to evangelicals. A critique of idealism from an evangelical perspective include the following observations.

1. The metaphysic of idealism denies the general revelation of nature. The Scriptures affirm the revelatory worth of the physical creation (Ps. 19:1ff.; Rom. 1:16–20). As previously noted, while realism places value on the study of nature as a means of discovering truth, idealism rejects this notion and hence devalues God's general revelation.
2. Idealism is concerned with preservation of the *status quo*. While for some this would be an acceptable stance for Christian education, any stance that *only* preserves the church's culture rather than *professing* the faith *to* the culture in which the church exists is not only inadequate but compromises the mission and educational emphasis of the church.
3. While idealism does affirm the existence of a Supreme Being/Mind, the god of idealism is not equivalent in attributes to the God of Scripture.
4. Idealism advocates the detachment of faith and reason. While evangelicals acknowledge the difference between faith and reason, they likewise maintain a symbiotic connection between the two.[32]

Plato's idealism did not end with his views on public education. His also speaks of important topics such as the role of government in forming laws, the free expression of ideas regardless of political party affiliation or socio-economic status (a dialogue that the aristocracy did not appreciate), the

---

32. James R. Estep, *The Evangelical Dictionary of Christian Education*, ed. Michael J. Anthony (Grand Rapids: Baker, 2001), s.v. "Idealism."

proper division of labor within society, the international code of conduct during war, and a host of other important issues. To say that he was ahead of his time is no exaggeration. A political and philosophical trailblazer, he was not always appreciated for the positions he held, but because he held a superior intellect and rhetorical ability, he seldom lost debates.

Aristotle and Realism

Aristotle (384–322 B.C.) was the third of Greece's great philosophers. He supported many of Plato's major premises such as the mind-body dualism (with the mind being superior), the immaterial and indestructible nature of the soul, the universality of human nature (i.e., that it is the same everywhere and at all times), and the same distrust of democracy, preferring instead a monarchical system.[33] That is not to say, however, that he always agreed with his mentor. On a number of occasions, Aristotle disagreed quite vehemently with Plato.

Aristotle came from a wealthy family in Athens. His father and many of his relatives were trained physicians. No doubt, he had cultural and educational opportunities that far surpassed those of his peers. Although he was intrigued by the study of science, he enrolled in Plato's Academy at the age of seventeen and remained under his tutelage for twenty years. Plato referred to him as the "Reader," which no doubt referenced his love of research and study. When Plato died in 347 B.C., Aristotle left Athens and traveled throughout Asia Minor. He was enlisted to become the private tutor for Alexander the Great from the age of thirteen to sixteen. At the age of forty-nine, Aristotle returned to Athens and founded a school of higher education, the Lyceum, where he remained until his death at sixty-two.

No one should be surprised that Aristotle's philosophy was highly analytical and systematic. His love for the scientific method, which he no doubt learned from his father as a child, influenced his detailed categorization of philosophic thought. His analysis of life bordered on the extreme. Whereas Plato sought to reflect on the meaning of life, Aristotle dissected it much like a medical examiner would conduct an autopsy. The answers to life's mysteries were found and recorded but held little that resembled life once the exploration was complete.

---

33. Adrian M. Dupius, *Philosophy of Education in Historical Perspective* (Chicago: Rand McNally, 1966), 50.

Plato's motives for directing his investigation had a practical outcome because he sought to preserve and strengthen the beloved city of his birth. For Aristotle, however, the end result of his inquiry did not have to have practical application. Inquiry served its own purpose without having to possess utility. He was not a reformer of politics, education, or society as a whole; he advocated the acquisition of knowledge for its own sake.[34]

The following points may be helpful to summarize Aristotle's views.

1. He reiterated the dualistic nature of man and attributed to reason or intellect the highest rank among human abilities.
2. Although he believed that the knowing process begins with sensation of the external world, true knowledge is found only in universal ideas.
3. Intellectual virtues are superior to moral virtues.
4. In educational theory, he recommended no major revisions in Plato's conservation.[35]

Aristotle's philosophical position, particularly as it relates to the educational system, is far less structured and coherent than either Socrates or Plato. It is difficult to understand his writings and even more difficult to categorize his views in terms of scope and sequence of curriculum. From what we have been able to determine from multiple sources, the following academic levels with their corresponding curriculum seems apparent:

0–7	Remained at home	Socialization as a child of the state
8–13	Elementary school	Reading, writing, counting
14–18	Secondary school	History, drama, poetry, science, public speaking, and physical education
19+	Military training	

If one finds difficult the differentiation between the various forms of realism, he or she is certainly not alone. Those who call themselves realists (e.g., classical realists, neorealists, and critical realists) rarely agree on a common set of terms and principles. It might even be due to the manner in which the term *real* is used that contributes to this confusion. Regardless of

---

34. Eby and Arrowood, *History and Philosophy of Education*, 395.
35. Dupuis, *Philosophy of Education in Historical Perspective*, 52.

the reasons, the following four meanings are attributed to the concept of realism.[36]

1. Realism is the belief that matter (i.e., the physical world) is independent of cognition; consequently, human experience and knowledge are of an independent, external world, and this world is in no way affected by our awareness of it.

2. Realism is the belief that the universe cannot be reduced to forms, ideas, or minds; consequently, something (i.e., matter) would continue to exist even if all men, minds, ideas, or consciousness did not exist. On this view, the tides would rise and fall as long as the moon orbits, even if every single human were destroyed in an atomic war.

3. Realism is the belief that ideas (i.e., the ideal world) are independent of material objects; consequently, while experience may be with sensible objects, knowledge is of the ideas giving form to these objects. On this view, circles and justice, triangles and beauty, would exist even if there were no mathematics, social organization, or art.

4. Realism is the belief that universals exist, and that they exist independently of the particulars that manifest the existence of these universals. On this view, "red" or "redness" has an existence separate and independent from red flags, red sweaters, red lipstick, red blood, etc.; thus, if no particular with the property we call "red" existed, "redness" would nevertheless exist. (The theories contrary to this kind of realism are called nominalism, where universals are said to be names, and conceptualism, where they are said to be ideas.)

Numerous philosophical differences exist between Plato's idealism and Aristotle's realism. Chief among those differences was the concept of reality. To Plato, an object was real and possessed form only if it existed in the mind of someone, including the mind of a transcendent being, or if personal knowledge of it existed. To the realist, matter was independent of mind; therefore, an object was real apart from one's mind. Aristotle held that the basic constituents of every object were form and matter. An object could

---

36. Hobert W. Burns and Charles J. Brauner, *Philosophy of Education* (New York: Ronald Press, 1962), 94.

exist without form (as in the case of gravity, God, a conscience, etc.), but it is impossible for matter to exist without form.[37]

> In the debate between the philosophies of idealism, realism and nominalism, the issue centered about the essence of reality. Plato was known as the "idealist," positing that all individual objects were expressions of a reality, or "form" which gave meaning and essence to those objects. Aristotle, the "realist," on the other hand, suggested that one could know nothing except that which first came through the senses. For Aristotle reality consisted of the objects themselves. Universals were not "reality" itself, only an extension of the true reality residing in the objects.[38]

Truth verified realty through the senses. As a student used his senses to explore his world, the sensory receptors—taste, sight, touch, smell, and/or hearing—confirmed its existence. To the idealist, reality occurred once the object entered the mind. To the realist, its existence was substantiated through one of the senses.

GREEK INFLUENCES ON MODERN EDUCATION

The lasting influences of classical Greek education still remain long after its inception. A comparison of contemporary educational philosophy and practice reveals a number of antecedents. First, the basis of what we have come to know as the liberal arts has its roots in classical Greek education. Developing a comprehensive scope and sequence of curriculum guarantees that students will receive both a well-rounded education and the necessary academic prerequisites as they progress from grade to grade.

Second, the age-old debate of a liberal (broad-based) arts education versus a more pragmatic vocational focus in higher education remains to this day on most college campuses. Such debate has its roots in classical Greek thought. The argument was not settled in 400 B.C. by either Plato or Aristotle, nor is it likely to be solved anytime soon.

---

37. George R. Knight, *Philosophy and Education: An Introduction in Christian Perspective* (Berrien Springs, Mich.: Andrews University Press, 1998), 46.
38. Robert C. De Vries, *The Evangelical Dictionary of Christian Education*, ed. Michael J. Anthony (Grand Rapids: Baker, 2001), s.v. "Realism."

Third, classical Greek educational thought insisted on the education of the masses. Public school education for all has its roots firmly in Greek education. Plato advocated the importance of educating all members of society. He realized that an informed and educated society would form the strongest foundation for lasting democratic existence.

Fourth, the manner in which the Greeks identified and differentiated the curriculum according to the learner's developmental stages has influenced education today. During the age of the Greeks, serious thought was given toward what a child could learn at age seven and what would have to wait until a later stage of development when the child could understand abstract concepts.

Fifth, the manner in which many of our scientific classifications came about was influenced by the Greeks. Aristotle spent a number of years mentoring the young leader Alexander. Once Alexander came to power and began his military conquest of the known world, Aristotle requested that Alexander bring back specimens of the local flora and fauna for him to analyze and study. Alexander the Great achieved phenomenal success and was able to return with samples beyond Aristotle's highest expectations. Aristotle began to study these specimens and organize them into groupings. The Latin names and classifications that he ascribed to these samples remain many years later.

So What? Lessons from the Past for Twenty-first-century Christian Education

The Greeks might have lived more than twenty-five hundred years ago, but the influence of their culture remains with us today. The benefit of their experience remains for us in the church as well. We can learn much from their example if we have ears to hear and hearts that are open. Following are a few important insights.

1. Christian education must be more than rote memory.

If Christian education is going to have a lasting benefit in the lives of those in our church and parachurch ministries, we must find ways to affect more than the lowest level of their cognitive domain. Having knowledge is important but knowledge for knowledge's sake alone is never enough. Jesus condemned no one as much as He did the scribes and Pharisees. Why?

Because they should have known better. No one knew the sacred Scriptures as well as the scribes because it was their task to duplicate the scrolls painstakingly by hand. The Pharisees studied the law and knew it better than most people did. Most of them were from the middle class, so they not only had the knowledge of how to make a difference in the world for God but also had the means to do so. In spite of this overwhelming knowledge, however, they sat back and criticized others for what they should have been doing themselves.

Bible memory games, activities, and programs are important in the lives of young children, but they should never be seen as the end. They are simply the means to the end of balanced spiritual formation. Young children should be questioned about the meaning of the verses they are memorizing. Where understanding is weak, it should be reinforced. Stickers in a book or patches on a vest do not constitute spiritual maturity. Meaningful understanding and practical application must precede memorization or we are guilty of creating modern day Pharisees. This goal can be achieved, in part, through well-crafted questions that challenge the students' thinking. Forcing them to think through the ramifications of the Bible content must be an integral part of our instruction. But it can't stop there. The Greeks understood the need for critical thinking and challenged the mind to investigate new ways of thinking about traditional ways of living.

Ministry to children and youth absolutely must include an element of service by which the passages of Scripture that have been learned are put into practice. Children should be guided in the proper application of Scripture. Teachers should have firsthand knowledge of the child's family life to help them apply passages to the way they live at home. Will it take more work? Yes! Will it require additional training of workers to help them take their teaching to additional levels of application? By all means! But what are the consequences of inaction? We will have raised a generation of children and youth who are bored in our churches because, as they put it, "We've heard it all before." The problem is not that they have heard it before but that they have never been guided to move beyond knowledge to application. The Greeks ensured that children applied what they learned as they learned it.

2. The curriculum of Christian education must be fully integrated.

The children living in Sparta were concerned only with learning that which was applicable to only their limited perspective of military superiority. The

Athenian children learned multiple subjects at the same time. In essence, the curriculum was multidisciplinary and fully integrated with real life (e.g., music, gymnastics, and sporting ethics were all taught at the same time). In the church, this point means that teachers and sponsors must understand what the children or youth are studying at school and look for ways to provide a biblical basis for their instruction. Public schools are based on a secular metaphysic that leaves God out of the equation. The church must not be timid. We are in a battle for the minds of our children and youth, and we must provide them with the resources they need to withstand the pressures of contemporary secular humanism.

Children, and particularly youth, must be taught a biblically based apologetics curriculum that will enable them to stand firm on the day of testing so they can provide a reasoned defense for the hope that is within them. Teaching young people the same old Sunday school stories that they learned in preschool and Vacation Bible School is not enough. What is needed is a firm foundation of solid theological instruction. Many of the strange philosophies that are circulating in society today can be addressed with a thorough knowledge of what the Scriptures teach regarding the nature of God, the deity of Christ, the inerrancy of the Scriptures, the purpose of the church, and other essential doctrines of the Bible.

Curriculum that is presented in our churches and parachurch ministries must be multidimensional in that they address and critique the postmodern philosophies that have permeated our public school systems. Teaching in our church must not shy away from confronting the dangers of drug use, chemical dependency, the gay/lesbian agenda, safe sex (as opposed to abstinence), responsible dating/courting, and preparing to live in a pluralistic world filled with relativism. Our students need resources to defend against evolution being taught in school. The Scripture must be taught as authoritative and plausible answers must be provided to those who are being challenged by modern cults.

3. Scope and sequence of Bible-related curriculum must consider basic tenants of human development.

To introduce concepts that are spoken of in abstract terms will only frustrate the child who has not yet learned to reason to that degree. Some forms of advanced philosophical discussions did not take place in the life of the Greeks until middle adulthood. Symbolic and abstract concepts such as the nature and ministry of the Holy Spirit, details of eschatology, and elements of soteriology will be of limited benefit to individuals who have not yet learned to reason with abstract terminology.

We have not taken the time to compare and contrast the differences between Hebrew education and classical Greek education. Suffice it to say that there are many differences and some similarities. While Hebrew parents were busy raising their children in the fear of the Lord, Greek parents were turning the responsibility of education over to the government. Plato and Aristotle advocated a firm "hands-on" approach to the education of society's children. Educational institutions had become a differentiated system based on the child's age and capabilities, with selective scope and sequence of curriculum, and highly paid instructors.

For Further Reading

Blumner, Hugo. *The Home Life of the Ancient Greeks.* New York: Cooper Square Publishers, 1966.

Bowyer, Carlton H. *Philosophical Perspectives for Education.* Glenview, Ill.: Scott, Foresman & Company, 1970.

Burns, Hobert W., and Charles J. Brauner. *Philosophy of Education.* New York: Ronald Press, 1962.

Cahn, Steven M. *The Philosophical Foundations of Education.* New York: Harper & Row, 1970.

Calder, William M. *Schools of Hellas.* New York: Teachers College Press, 1969.

Castle, E. E. *Ancient Education and Today.* New York: Penguin Books, 1961.

Chambers, John H. *The Achievement of Education.* San Francisco: Harper & Row, 1983.

Eavey, Charles B. *History of Christian Education.* Chicago: Moody, 1964.

Eby, Frederick, and Charles F. Arrowood. *The History and Philosophy of Education: Ancient and Medieval.* Englewood Cliffs, N.J.: Prentice-Hall, 1940.

Gangel, Kenneth O., and Warren S. Benson. *Christian Education: Its History and Philosophy.* Chicago: Moody, 1983.

Guthrie, William K. C. *The Greeks and Their Gods.* Boston: Beacon, 1956.

Hammond, N. G. L., and H. H. Scullard. *The Oxford Classical Dictionary.* 2d ed. Oxford: Clarendon, 1970.

Jaeger, Werner. *Paideia: The Ideals of Greek Culture.* 3 vols. New York: Oxford University Press, 1939-45.

Jarrett, James L. *The Educational Theories of the Sophists.* New York: Teachers College Press, 1969.

Kerenyi, C. *The Religion of the Greeks and Romans.* New York: E. P. Dutton, 1962.

Knight, George R. *Philosophy and Education: An Introduction in Christian Perspective.* Berrien Springs, Mich.: Andrews University Press, 1980.

Livingstone, R. W. *The Legacy of Greece.* Oxford: Clarendon, 1951.

Noll, James W., and Sam P. Kelly. *Foundations of Education in America.* New York: Harper & Row, 1970.

Patrick, Richard. *The Color Book of Greek Mythology.* London: Octopus, 1972.

Reed, James E., and Ronnie Prevost. *A History of Christian Education.* Nashville: Broadman & Holman, 1993.

Rusk, Robert R. *The Doctrines of the Great Educators.* 2d ed. New York: Macmillian, 1957.

Schmitz, L. *Classical Mythology: The Myths of Ancient Greece and Ancient Italy.* Chicago: Ares, 1902.

What in the World?

➤ Mayan civilization is dominant in Central America in 300 B.C.–A.D. 900.

➤ The Han Dynasty rules in China in 206 B.C.–A.D. 220.

➤ Greece is conquered by the Romans in 31 B.C.

➤ Augustus becomes the first Roman emperor in 27 B.C.

➤ The birth of Jesus Christ in 4 B.C.

➤ The crucifixion of Christ c. A.D. 29.

➤ Fire burns two-thirds of Rome in A.D. 64.

➤ Titus destroys Jerusalem in A.D. 70.

Chapter 3

ROMAN EDUCATION AND PHILOSOPHICAL THOUGHT

TRADITION TELLS US THAT ROME WAS founded in 753 B.C. on Palatine Hill, one of the seven hills surrounding that particular geographic location, and although the historical origins of the Italian people might be somewhat obscure, it is generally understood that Roman influence in the centuries just before the birth of Christ was dominant and well established. Unlike the harsh lifestyle of the Spartans or the aristocratic Athenians, the Romans were a relatively quiet people who preferred the simplistic agrarian lifestyle of farming. Their emphasis was not so much on intellectual elitism or the physical prowess of a military warrior as on character development and personal integrity. Energy was spent in the pursuit of honesty, courage, dignity, and filial duty.[1]

Many contemporary texts on the antecedents of Christian education omit a discussion of Roman education as if to imply that little came out of this era that contributed to the origins of Christian education. However, when one considers the fact that God chose to send His Son into the world at a time when the Roman system dominated the world in terms of its laws, commerce, education, and social structure, one concludes that the Roman approach to

---

1. Dan K. Ball, *The Evangelical Dictionary of Christian Education,* ed. Michael J. Anthony (Grand Rapids: Baker, 2001), s.v. "Roman Education."

government and religious orientation had a great deal of importance to God. In essence, the Roman form of education, society, and governance laid the foundation for the birth of Christianity. The impact of Rome upon the entire world was profound for more than a thousand years. Although the Romans were different from the ancient Greeks, we should highly regard and value them for their contributions to the origins of Christian education.

ROMAN CULTURE

The Romans were never seen as a particularly homogeneous people group. An Indo-European population provided the early origins of the Italian tribes. A second racial stock, the Etruscans, had entered Italy probably around 800 B.C. The Etruscans, presumably originating in Asia Minor, were viewed as a more advanced civilization than those who inhabited the land before them. In the seventh and sixth centuries, Greek settlements began to develop along the southern borders of Italy and Sicily. Jews, Egyptians, and Gauls from what is modern France, settled within their borders, providing them with a rich and varied cultural perspective.[2]

Rome's influence soon grew far beyond the confines of its Italian peninsula. Expansion brought it into contact with varied cultural traditions from far and wide, and with this awareness of new ways of living, change inevitably occurred throughout the land. The independent agrarian lifestyle that had held its grip on the people for so long gave way to a national state comprised of large landholdings owned by wealthy aristocrats. The manufacturing and distribution of items such as tools, machinery, and furniture flourished. In addition to the influences and effects of commerce on the nation, the Roman army, with a host of international conquests, brought back to their homeland the riches and cultural practices of their despoiled adversaries.[3] This wealth challenged tradition and eventually led to a new, more cosmopolitan approach to life. For this reason, Horace, the great Roman poet, maintained that it was *Greece that conquered Rome*–culturally.[4]

---

2. Frederick Eby and Charles F. Arrowood, *The History and Philosophy of Education: Ancient and Medieval* (Englewood Cliffs, N.J.: Prentice-Hall, 1940), 520.

3. Adrian M. Dupuis, *Philosophy of Education in Historical Perspective* (Chicago: Rand McNally, 1966), 53.

4. Horace *Epistle* 1.156, as quoted in Dupuis, *Philosophy of Education in Historical Perspective*, 53.

Although Roman society as a whole was predominantly agrarian, that is not to say that they were devoid of social classes. Definite class distinctions were apparent throughout its history. For example, there were the aristocrats with their emphasis upon land ownership and the enjoyment of artistic expression, the plebeians occupied what would now be referred to as a middle class, and finally, slaves provided the foundation of its social stratification.

The Greeks provided the most profound impact upon Roman ways. However, in all fairness, we must say that "Rome was more by far than a transmitter of Greek culture. She was a creator of culture. Her genius was practical, not contemplative. She was a builder of material marvels, not philosophical systems. She was realistic and pragmatic, not idealistic. In her way she gave to future generations much that made them what they were and are."[5]

One of the most predominant cultural contributions of Roman life was its political system. No other culture in the world had developed as elaborate a means of governmental control and oversight of vast populations as the Romans.

> When she boasted of an empire reaching the Tigris and Euphrates rivers in Asia to the Firth of Forth in Great Britain, from the pillars of Hercules to beyond the Black Sea, and from the Rhine and the Danube deep into the Sahara Desert, she could also boast of a governmental structure that staggers the imagination and a legal pattern that was just and humane.[6]

The Roman system of providing citizenship to its people was remarkable. It provided its citizens with national pride, guaranteed protection wherever they traveled, and gave them a valuable tool for negotiating with neighboring countries. The apostle Paul benefited from his Roman citizenship by avoiding a beating at the hands of the Roman centurion (Acts 22:24-29) and when he demanded his right of legal appeal before Caesar (Acts 25:11).

The Romans were a pragmatic people by nature. What was valued was what could be used to enhance their crop production or defend their state. They were not obsessed with the condition of their physical bodies. As long as they were healthy and could plant and harvest their crops, they were

---

5. S. E. Frost, *Historical and Philosophical Foundations of Western Thought* (Columbus: Charles E. Merrill, 1966), 79.

6. Ibid.

content. Likewise, neither were they overly concerned about the arts. Although they enjoyed music and art forms, they did not consume themselves with the pursuit of such ambitions. The average Roman citizen had only utilitarian concerns. Politics was of no consequence as long as he was free to live his life without inordinate interference. He was, for all intents and purposes, devoid of philosophical curiosity.[7] What mattered more than anything else was an emphasis upon the family, particularly as it related to the education of their children.

ROMAN EDUCATION

The history of Roman education can be divided into five broad categories, starting with the establishment of the city of Rome in 753 B.C. through the closing of the pagan schools by Justinian in A.D. 529. A brief discussion of each period's characteristics follows.

Home Instruction Period (753–272 B.C.)

Roman education was first and foremost dominated by the family, and in the Roman family the father held the undisputed role of supreme authority. The family was the unit of the Roman constitution, the custodian of ancestral tradition, and the focal point of religious and educational activities. By Roman design, the father had absolute control over his wife, children, property, and slaves. He determined the fate of all within his household. At the birth of his child, he could choose to keep the baby or expose it in the wilderness if it seemed unfit or was not the gender he preferred. He could sell his children into slavery, and subject only to the customary obligation of holding a family council, he could condemn his son to death if he so desired. Whatever was owned by his son was, by law, also under the control of his father for even a marriage contract did not prevent the father from usurping control over his extended household. He was seen as the teacher, lawgiver, and priest of the family.[8] He took each role seriously.

The subsequent respect (or fear) of the father's dominant role did not end in the home. Within the greater community as a whole, the elder was treated

---

7. E. B. Castle, *Ancient Education and Today* (Bungay, U.K.: Richard Clay & Co., 1961), 108.
8. Ibid., 109.

with the respect and honor that he had grown accustomed to expect. This fact may best be illustrated by drawing upon several scattered quotations and literary fragments that provide a picture of how senior citizens were treated in Roman society.

> For instance, it was accepted as a natural token of respect to rise and offer one's seat at the arrival of an older person, generally, to yield place to him. Younger men regarded it as a privilege to escort elders to the Senate House, where they would wait at the doors and then accompany them home. At festival gatherings, preliminary inquiry was made as to who the guests were likely to be, in order that the younger might not take their places before their seniors; and there was reluctance to leave before the elders had arisen. If a party of three should be walking along the street, the oldest man would be given the middle place in the group, if it were two only, the younger man would take the outer, more exposed position. Children noticed these things, and put them into practice themselves. But the important point was that the elders merited these attentions not only in view of their position or experience, but by reason of their own conduct; serious in outlook, dignified in manner, and sensitive to any breach in decorum, they were conscious of the importance of their personal example. They benefited from a wider extension of parental respect, in that older citizens were regarded as the common parents of the community.[9]

The parents were the first educators of their children. It was a pragmatic form of instruction that presumed that the son would follow in the footsteps of his father's trade and that the young girl would become a homemaker, much like her mother. The young girl learned to spin and weave because the mother was responsible for clothing her family. Because education was based on these expectations, little in the way of formal instruction was offered to the child in this early period of Roman education. From birth until the age of seven, the child remained at home under the care of the mother. At the age of seven, he was transitioned to the father, who began the process of educating him to become a citizen of Rome.

---

9. Stanley F. Bonner, *Education in Ancient Rome: From the Elder Cato to the Younger Pliny* (Berkeley: University of California Press, 1977), 6–7.

The character of the young man was the focus of the father's instruction. Tremendous emphasis was placed upon the character development of the child at an early age, even before the more formal disciplines of reading, writing, and mathematics were introduced. After all, what value would there be if the child learned these subjects but was unable to use them honorably? "To the Roman father education was not a matter of instruction from books or of cultivating aesthetic appreciation in his children, but rather a means of inculcating an indelible reverence for a few definite moral qualities, and of imparting such practical skills as were essential to good farming and brave fighting."[10]

Chief among the ideals taught by the Romans was *virtus,* which was defined as the ability to stand tall among one's peers as proud and unwavering, conscious of his virility, second to no one else in loyalty and strength of character. The second ideal was *pietas,* the realization that the Roman child lived in a world of unseen but powerful spirits. These spirits of his ancestors watched over him and demanded his allegiance and respect. Likewise, the gods were worthy of his unwavering devotion. Social mores hewn out of countless centuries of civic and spiritual living were not to be ignored but held in high honor and esteem. A Roman child that was worthy of his citizenship learned the value of both of these critical elements of his early childhood education.[11]

At the age of sixteen, the child participated in a rite of passage that transitioned him from boyhood to manhood. During this ritual, the individual took off his childish clothes, the *toga praetext,* and was presented with the *toga virilis,* clothing of a full-grown man. At this point in the young man's life, an older relative or close friend of the family took on the responsibility of educating him. Those who were merchants or wealthy members of the middle class were able to provide their young men with an education that consisted of reading, writing, history, gymnastics, and the proper use of weapons.[12]

An important event occurred during this period that had a significant impact on the education of Roman citizens. In 509 B.C., the Etruscan kingdom came to an end as the result of a revolt by the nobles and the patristic

---

10. Castle, *Ancient Education and Today,* 113.

11. Frost, *Historical and Philosophical Foundations,* 80.

12. James E. Reed and Ronnie Prevost, *A History of Christian Education* (Nashville: Broadman & Holman, 1993), 36.

families living in Rome. The Etruscans had given the Romans their alphabet, cultic worship, an enlarged vocabulary, and the beginnings of what would later be known as mechanical and structural engineering. After the departure of the Etruscans, a power struggle ensued between the ruling party—known as the patricians—and the commoners—known as the plebs. The latter group eventually won the rights of recognition and as a result published a code of laws called the *Laws of the Twelve Tables*. These laws formed the intellectual basis of Roman life and were memorized by both patrician and plebeian boys from early childhood.[13] The ensuing class struggle resulted in the restructuring of the Roman government in 287 B.C.[14]

Transformation Period (272-132 B.C.)

With the military conquests of Rome expanding into other regions, the Roman form of education took on a decidedly different perspective. A decisive event occurred in 272 B.C. when Rome conquered the city of Tarentum. Many of the Hellenized captives were brought to Rome as slaves to serve in a variety of capacities. One such capacity was the role of hired tutor. As Rome began to assimilate the cultural distinctives of other countries, education began to take on a broader perspective.

Some of the educated slaves that had been brought to Rome from conquered regions, referred to as *litteratores,* served a purpose similar to that of the Greek *paidadogues*. They provided more detailed instruction beyond that given by the boy's father. This practice eventually transitioned into the Roman elementary school for children six to twelve years old. At twelve, the boy progressed to secondary school, the curriculum of which consisted of history, geography, mythology, literature, and the study of the Greek and Latin languages.

One of the more notable *litteratores* of this period was a Greek captive named Livius Andronicus who, in 250 B.C., translated Homer's *Odyssey* into Latin. School during this period was usually held on a veranda. The teacher sat at a desk or wooden platform while the children sat on wooden benches. When the students wrote their lessons, they used wax tablets, a wooden stylus for writing, and some large scrolls. Discipline was harsh, and boys who

---

13. Eby and Arrowood, *History and Philosophy of Education,* 521.
14. Reed and Prevost, *History of Christian Education,* 37.

misbehaved were the recipients of severe corporal punishment.[15] It is thought that this form of discipline was needed because the Roman boy would have had little respect for his slave or freedman teacher. As such, the *litteratores* would have been forced to maintain classroom management through the harshest of terms.

Imperial Period (132 B.C.-A.D. 100)

During these days, the Roman Empire expanded on all sides. During the second century B.C., Rome annexed Spain, Carthage, Illyria, and Greece. During the following century, she subjugated northern Africa, Egypt, Asia Minor, and Gaul to the Elbe and the Danube. Rome had become the mistress of the entire Mediterranean world.[16] Of all of the cultures that were assimilated, that of the Greeks was cherished most. Greek culture, which was considered to be several hundred years advanced beyond the Romans, was evidenced everywhere. Greek literature, art, and music were all but worshiped as being in form and structure superior to anything the Romans possessed. In essence, although Rome possessed the land of Greece, Roman military might never conquered the Greek mind.

By the beginning of the first century B.C., the Latin *Odyssey* had become the primary textbook in educational curriculum. This led to a desire for further studies in Greek literature. As a result, additional Greek materials were studied and became a staple in their entire school system. In the grammar schools, the course of instruction became purely literary and humanistic and was conducted in both Greek and Latin. Homer, Hesiod, and Menander were the favorite authors studied. Only later, after the full bloom of the Augustinian literature, did the Latin poets, especially Virgil and Horace, become of almost equal importance in the curricula. The instructional methodologies during this time included the teaching of language, grammar, meter, style, and subject matter. Literature was read aloud in class to refine their oratorical skills.[17]

---

15. Luella Cole, *A History of Education: Socrates to Montessori* (New York: Holt, Rinehart & Winston, 1962), 61-64.
16. Elwood P. Cubberly, *The History of Education* (Boston: Houghton Mifflin, 1948), 60.
17. W. Warde Fowler, *Social Life at Rome: In the Age of Cicero* (Norwood, Mass.: Norwood Press, 1909), 188.

One dominant figure during this period was Marcus Tullius Cicero (106–43 B.C.). His father was an influential city leader and could afford the finest education for his son. A studious young man, Cicero memorized the *Twelve Tables* and also the Latin translation of *Odyssey* at an early age. He also studied Greek and Latin literature, drama, and rhetoric. After having received the *toga virilis*, he studied law under Quintus Mucius Scaevola, one of Rome's leading legal experts. In addition, he developed a fascination for religion and philosophy. Armed with a keen mind and a well-rounded education, he set out to write a treatise about the grammar and rhetorical schools of Rome titled *De oratore* ("On the Education of an Orator").[18] Viewed as the greatest Roman orator of his day, he espoused an education based on pragmatic ideals. He thought that an educated man must also be one who made a contribution to his community. The educated adult must be honest, public minded, devoted to public service, and pure in mind and heart. His actions and behaviors must be in keeping with the best interests of his country. Steeped in tradition that values his ancestors, the educated adult would look for ways to pass on this heritage to future generations.[19]

The Epicurean Philosophy of Lucretius

One of the most prominent Roman philosophers of the day was a poet named Titus Lucretius Carus. Although the exact dates of his birth and death cannot be confirmed, the majority of evidence indicates that he lived 94 to 55 B.C. Very little is actually known about Lucretius's life. To assume that he was a member of the aristocratic upper class and enjoyed a well-educated upbringing would be natural. The only fact with which we have confidence is that he was a close friend—or possibly a dependent—of an aristocrat named C. Memmius, the patron of Catullus and Cinna, to whom he dedicated an extensive poem titled *De rerum natura*. He was also rumored to have been friends with the Roman leaders Atticus, Cicero, Cassius, and Brutus.

In his six-book poem, Lucretius expounded his thoughts about the physical

---

18. Reed and Prevost, *History of Christian Education*, 39.
19. Frost, *Historical and Philosophical Foundations*, 85.

theory of Epicurus, which included abolishing superstitious fears about the interference of gods in the affairs of mankind, the punishment of the soul after death, and a defense for the atomic view of the universe. He extrapolated the latter perspective from the writings of Leucippus and Democritus, who wrote in the middle half of the fifth century b.c.

Lucretius's Epicureanism espoused the naturalistic view that God had atomic structure identical to that of other materials in existence and, as such, was of no significant influence in the universe. Although Epicureans did not deny the existence of God, they denied His universal power to influence the affairs of mankind. Man was released to seek his own pleasure without the constraints placed upon him by any moral absolutes. Epicureans believed in the moral theory that pleasure was the end in life. Man lives a life of free will controlled by only the constraints and restrictions that he chooses to place upon himself. To Lucretius, the soul was mortal and died with the body; therefore, any fear of punishment after life was nullified because everything about life existed only in the present. As a philosopher, he accomplished a great deal by expounding atomism in poetic verse and often with a depth of understanding, passion, and feeling that even his critics praised. The teachings of contemporary moral philosophy have many of their roots in this early Greek and Roman philosophy of life.[20]

The Latin grammar school came into its own during this period. The teaching of medicine and law, the latter in regular schools, was established at Rome. Also during this period the greatest Roman treatises on architecture and oratory were produced. Schools were mostly private, financed by the parents of those who sent their children to them. However, during this period the publicly financed school system began.[21] In 38 b.c., Asinius Pollio established the first public library in Rome.[22] Obviously, during this time Jesus Christ was born, and the Christian church was established.

---

20. N. G. L. Hammond and H. H. Scullard, *The Oxford Classical Dictionary* (Oxford: Clarendon, 1969), 622–23.
21. Eby and Arrowood, *History and Philosophy of Education*, 516.
22. Bonner, *Education in Ancient Rome*, 97.

The Schools of Rhetoric

Up until this point in Roman educational history, the schools had served a practical and useful purpose. Beyond the elementary and secondary levels of instruction grew a form of higher education that we might refer to today as college. These schools were designed to prepare students in rhetoric and oratory, which in turn trained them for the great professions of law and public administration in Rome. These schools were the direct descendents of the Greek rhetorical schools of the Sophists. In these schools, the teachers were known as *rhetors,* because of their emphasis upon public speaking and debate. A young man who aspired to enter into the legal or political professions found attending these schools a requirement. They were attended for two to three years by boys over the age of sixteen. Due to their cost only the children of wealthy aristocrats could afford the tuition. Beyond the obvious instruction in oration, the schools also provided instruction in mathematics, literature, linguistics, science, and philosophy. The famous "seven liberal arts" of the Middle Ages (grammar, rhetoric, dialectic, music, arithmetic, geometry and astronomy) all seem to have been included in the Schools of Rhetoric.[23]

A second figure of note during this period was Marcus Fabius Quintilian (A.D. 35-c. 90s). Born at Calagurris in Spain but reared in Rome from his youth, he was provided with a thorough education in Roman elementary, secondary, and rhetorical schools. He was trained in oratory by Palaemon and viewed Cicero as the man he most admired. In A.D. 88, he retired from teaching to devote himself to writing a book titled the *Institutes of Oratory,* a manual that described the training of young orators. To Quintilian, the orator was a most important personage in Roman life. An orator's responsibilities included giving eulogies of famous men, delivering motivational speeches to armies about to enter battle, discussing public matters, pleading legal cases before the judicial system, and performing other duties that required verbal eloquence. Beyond the emphasis upon training an orator, Quintilian's *Institutes* also discussed the educational system of Rome in general. He

---

23. Cubberley, *History of Education,* 69-70.

believed that a child was better motivated by positive rewards than by harsh punishment. He was also a strong advocate of group learning as opposed to hiring private tutors. He looked down upon teachers who charged for their services but was not opposed to those who accepted payment as a gift rather than as a requirement for services rendered. To Quintilian, a thorough education included studies in history, literature, language, astronomy, philosophy, geometry, music, rhetoric, logic, law, and professional ethics.[24] A robust education indeed!

Period of Continuance (A.D. 100–275)

Roman literature came into its own at this period. No longer was the emphasis upon Greek thought because the Roman scholars had now established their own literature base. Roman literature and schooling continued to play a large part in the structure of the nation.

The leading figure during this period was Mestrius Plutarch (A.D. 46–120). Having grown up in Chaerones, not far from Athens, he traveled throughout Greece, Egypt, and Italy lecturing on the topic of law. He often cited his father, Autobulus, and his grandfather, Lamprias, in his many writings. During his lifetime, he wrote several hundred works that cover a broad range of topics. He often used the dialogue form in his writings as though the reader were sitting across a dinner table conversing with this great Roman educator. Interestingly, the last thirty years of his life he served as a priest at Delphi. Plutarch's contributions have been long lived. His works were popular during medieval times. Indeed, Shakespeare, Dryden, and Rousseau are among Plutarch's debtors.[25]

Period of Decline (A.D. 275–529)

During this period, the Roman government began to issue edicts that mandated and controlled the educational system across the empire. The resulting state monopoly over education and the corresponding lack of free speech had a profound effect upon education as a whole. Roman higher education came to an end in A.D. 529 when Emperor Justinian closed the

---

24. Frost, *Historical and Philosophical Foundations*, 90.
25. Hammond and Scullard, *Oxford Classical Dictionary*, 849.

schools of philosophy and law in Athens and all schools of higher education in Rome. The only schools that were spared were the schools of law.[26]

This was an era of declining economics throughout the Roman Empire. Maintaining control over regions that were spread out so far from the seat of government was difficult requiring large sums of money to equip, train, and support the vast armies of Rome. The upper class grew disproportionately in economic influence. The middle class, if we would call it that, became extinct. Those who were poor and who had come to Rome to seek a better way of life for themselves and their families were sorely disappointed. One Roman leader, Tiberious Gracchus, commented of the living conditions of the average Roman citizen living in Rome that "the wild animals that range over Italy have a hole, but the men who fight and die for Italy . . . have not a clod of earth to call their own."[27] Roman educators faired no better as they were not allowed to charge tuition and had to rely upon gifts brought to them by their students several times a year. Consequently, many of them had to seek additional employment opportunities and spread their interests between instructing their students and surviving.

Although Rome was creative and deliberate in its legal system, it lacked a great deal of innovation when it came to its educational system. Although it was based upon the Greek model of education in terms of curriculum and structure, it lacked a great deal of public support. Whereas Greek education was concerned with lofty ideals and expanding intellectual horizons, the Romans were known more for their pragmatism. Ultimately, Roman education became boring and predictable. It failed to meet the challenges that an increasingly pluralistic society brought to them.[28]

Although the reasons for the decline of Rome have been debated over the centuries, that the issues contributing to its decline are many and varied stands to reason. Some people point to the lowering of public standards of moral conduct, whereas other people conclude that it was caused by an overemphasis on politics and law. Some people espouse a view that as the educational system goes, so goes the nation. As the Romans began to lose their exuberance and focus in their educational curriculum, academic

26. Ball, *Evangelical Dictionary of Christian Education*, s.v. "Roman Education."
27. Frederick Mayer, *A History of Educational Thought* (Columbus: Charles E. Merrill, 1966), 121.
28. Ibid.

disciplines, professional standards of teaching, and economics associated with schooling, they also experienced a concomitant decline in the product of their schooling. No longer were they graduating students who desired to see the greater good of society as a basis for determining their professional aspirations. Society had become increasingly self-indulgent as altruism gave way to personal and national hedonism. Schools were closed, teachers were required to apply for national credentials, and textbooks lacked creativity. In the context of rigid legalism, governmental constraints, and lack of creative expression, the Middle Ages were born.

Educational Structure in Summary

The manner in which the Romans conducted their educational system differs across the various time periods that we have described. Overall, four levels of schooling grew out of the Romans' perspective on education: home, elementary, grammar, and rhetorical. Education began in the home with training from the mother (before age seven) and the father (after age seven); the elementary school, in which the subject matter consisted primarily of reading and writing taught by the *ludi magister,* or the *litterator;* the grammar school, which emphasized the seven liberal arts taught by the *grammaticus,* or the *litteratus;* and the schools of rhetoric, in which young men were prepared for careers as professional orators, or advocates. The latter schools were taught by *rhetors,* men skilled in the art of public presentations and articulate debate.[29] In addition to the preceding levels of schooling, the Romans were also influential in giving us our modern language.

Of all of the Roman contributions to modern civilization, perhaps the one that most completely permeates our modern life is their alphabet. This alphabet has become the common property of almost all of the civilized world. The English language, which is spoken throughout a large part of the civilized world and by one-third of its inhabitants, has also received so many additions from Romanic sources that today we scarcely utter a sentence without using some word once used by the citizens of ancient Rome.[30]

---

29. Eby and Arrowood, *History and Philosophy of Education,* 536.
30. Cubberley, *History of Education,* 77.

Roman Levels of Education

Level	Age	School	Instructional Curriculum
Home	0–6	Home	Basic Instruction in the duties related to the home. Girls: Homemaking, cooking, cleaning, making clothes, etc. Boys: Character and moral development, respect of elders, etc.
Elementary	7–11	Elementary schools	Taught by the *ludi magister,* or *litterator;* the content consisted primarily of reading, writing, and arithmetic.
Grammar	12–15	Latin grammar schools	Taught by the *grammaticus,* or the *litteratus;* the content consisted of the seven liberal arts: grammar, rhetoric, dialectic, music, arithmetic, geometry, and astronomy.
Collegiate	16–18	Collegiate	Known as the Schools of Rhetoric; the content consisted of grammar, rhetoric, and dialectic.
University	25–40	University	The University of Rome taught courses in law, medicine, philosophy, architecture, mathematics, and rhetoric.

To point out the differences that existed between the Greek and Roman systems of education might be helpful. The differences are many, and the following chart summarizes some of the most apparent ones. For purposes of this comparison, the Greek educational system that was evident in Athens will be used.[31]

Greek Education	Roman Education
Imaginative	Unimaginative
Creative	Concrete
Subjective	Practical
Artistic	Constructive
Idealistic	Realistic
Minimal administrative capabilities	Extensive administrative capabilities
Few practical tendencies	Minimal intellectual pursuits
Made contributions to the fields of art, philosophy, and literature	Made contributions to the fields of law, architecture, and civil government
Lifestyle of aesthetic enjoyment and an appreciation for natural beauty	Little value for aesthetic enjoyment in life because their values were more utilitarian
Worshiped the beautiful and good	
Sought to enjoy life rationally and nobly	Worshiped force and effectiveness
	Lived by rule and authority
Preferred immediate gratification	Were willing to wait for happiness
Taught beauty, virtue, poetry, and art	Taught law, duty, respect, civility

A cursory comparison illustrates the differences between the two cultures as evidenced in their education systems. In essence, the Greeks gave the world an appreciation for the fine arts, aesthetics, philosophy, literature, and music. The Romans were far more pragmatic and provided the world with a model of civil government, a system of laws, legal codes, commerce, and engineering. Together, they form a rich heritage upon which modern civilization would to be developed.

---

31. Adapted from ibid., 74–75.

So What? Lessons from the Past for Twenty-first-century Christian Education

The part that Rome played in the development of Western culture and thereby in determining the educational ideals across Europe and America is monumental. For hundreds of years, Rome held a firm grip over the cultures of Europe, Asia, and Africa. Her domination over so much of the world united language, government, laws, commerce, and cultural understanding. In addition, Rome contributed to the fusion of art, forms of thought, and ways of feeling for more than one thousand years. In this capacity, she was the great transmitter of culture.[32]

1. Be a student of the culture.

Rome was the contextual and cultural birthplace of Christianity. By creating a dominant language, alphabet, system of laws and government, and a highly developed means of commerce (and therefore communication), the stage was set for mankind to receive the greatest message that humanity would ever know. God had foreordained before the foundations of the world were laid that His Son would be born into such a world condition. This development contributed to the effectual spread of Christianity throughout the known world and allowed the Great Commission to be effected with greater speed and power.

Effective ministers who influence their communities for Christ are students of contemporary culture. As twenty-first-century ministry leaders, we must be aware of how culture affects ministry. Reaching the lost for Christ does not happen in a vacuum but rather in a cultural context. In the midst of ministry preparation, don't neglect to read the newspaper, study current events magazines, and examine forms of entertainment that reveal culture. Remember, culture forms the context for ministry.

2. The moral and character development of the child starts in the home.

For the Romans, the home was the primary means of instilling values in the child. Both the mother and the father partnered to train their children such as to reflect the cultural, religious, moral, and ethical values of the parents. A task of such magnitude could not be trusted to anyone outside the home. Much like that of the Hebrews, whom we considered in an earlier

---

32. Ibid., 517.

chapter, the home life of the Romans held supreme over anything that was developed in society at large, in either a school system or civil government. Plutarch, the great Roman rhetorician, after praising Cato the Censor for the manner in which he lived as a husband, father, and supervisor of his estate, commented as follows on how seriously he took his responsibilities as a teacher for his son:

> . . . Cato took upon him the office of a schoolmaster to his son, though he had a slave named Chilo, who was a good grammarian, and taught several other children. But he tells us that he did not choose that his son should be reprimanded by a slave, or pulled by the ears, if he happened to be slow in learning; or that he should be indebted to so mean a person for his education. He was, therefore, himself, his preceptor in grammar, in law, and in the necessary exercises. For he taught him not only to throw a dart, to fight hand to hand, and to ride, but to box, to endure heat and cold, and to swim the most rapid rivers. He further acquaints us, that he wrote histories for him with his own hand, in large characters, that, without stirring from his father's house, he might gain a knowledge of the great actions of the ancient Romans and of the custom of his country. He was careful not to utter an indecent word before his son, as he would have been in the presence of the vestal virgins.[33]

The Romans understood the importance of raising their children and were intentional about their instruction. Twenty-first-century parents and ministry leaders should do no less. We must guard what comes into their world to ensure that it is wholesome and constructive for their personal, academic, social, and spiritual development.

3. We must integrate curriculum with real-life training.

The Romans were convinced that the study and pursuit of a subject should not be an end in itself. The final aim in education was a well-rounded individual who could take the tenets of several disciplines (e.g., law, ethics, and philosophy) and weave them together to form a cohesive and fully integrated mind. Therefore, the study of medicine or law was not devoid of a knowledge of ethics. The Romans believed that a noble and virtuous

---

33. Eby and Arrowood, *History and Philosophy of Education*, 530.

physician or attorney could not practice his profession outside the boundaries of ethical conduct. In addition, stringent physical conditioning was part of educational curriculum at all levels of instruction. To the Romans, disciplining the mind was of little value if one did not have a corresponding degree of physical discipline as well. The various subjects that were taught in the elementary, grammar, and rhetorical schools were fully integrated and taught as a composite.

In the same way, modern Christian educators should seek to find ways to bring together the various subjects that are affecting their students today (e.g., science, sociology, history, and religion). Instruction in many public schools treats curriculum design as if the student were progressing down a cafeteria line selecting items a la carte. They leave the integration of these topics for a later date, presumably college or beyond. The problem with this approach is twofold: first, it implies that the student can afford the luxury of waiting until this integration takes place (which is a high-risk assumption); second, it presumes that someone will come along and assist the student in this integrative process later in life. However, no one is held accountable if it doesn't happen. As Christian educators, we do not have the option of handing over something as important as the integration of faith to an unknown teacher without accountability. God holds the Christian teacher accountable, and we are not allowed the freedom of passing off that responsibility to someone who may or may not come along in the future (James 3:1).

4. Twenty-first-century ministry leaders need balanced programs.

A final insight for contemporary Christian educators is the degree to which the Romans considered even the physical conditioning of a student. The Roman student's training included all forms of conditioning because their teachers understood the value of living a balanced life. Education included mental conditioning, but it didn't stop there; it also included physical, social, and emotional aspects as well.

Luke 2:52 tells us that "Jesus grew in wisdom [mental] and stature [physical], and in favor with God [spiritual] and men [social]" (NIV). Obviously, Jesus was able to maintain a balanced perspective in all facets of His life. No single element grew disproportionately in relation to the other elements. We, particularly those of us who are working with children and young adults, must approach education in the local church in the same way. We should develop programs that include elements of each of these four categories to ensure balanced and wholistic disciples.

For Further Reading

Ball, Dan K. "Roman Education." In *The Evangelical Dictionary of Christian Education*. Edited by Michael J. Anthony. Grand Rapids: Baker, 2001.

Barclay, William. *Educational Ideals in the Ancient World*. Grand Rapids: Baker, 1959.

Bonner, Stanley F. *Education in Ancient Rome: From the Elder Cato to the Younger Pliny*. Berkeley: University of California Press, 1977.

Carcopino, Jerome. *Daily Life in Rome*. Westford, Conn.: Yale University Press, 1940.

Castle, E. E. *Ancient Education and Today*. New York: Penguin Books, 1961.

Cole, Luella. *The History of Education: Socrates to Montessori*. New York: Holt, Rhinehart & Winston, 1962.

Cubberley, Ellwod P. *The History of Education*. New York: Houghton Mifflin, 1948.

Dupuis, Adrian M. *Philosophy of Education in Historical Perspective*. Chicago: Rand McNally, 1966.

Eby, Frederick, and Charles F. Arrowood. *The History and Philosophy of Education: Ancient and Medieval*. Englewood Cliffs, N.J.: Prentice-Hall, 1940.

Fowler, W. Warde. *Social Life at Rome*. New York: Macmillan, 1910.

Frost, S. E., Jr. *Historical and Philosophical Foundations of Western Education*. Columbus: Charles E. Merrill, 1966.

Gangel, Kenneth O., and Warren S. Benson. *Christian Education: Its History and Philosophy*. Chicago: Moody, 1983.

Hammond, N. G. L., and H. H. Scullard. *The Oxford Classical Dictionary*. 2d ed. Oxford: Clarendon, 1970.

Kerenyi, C. *The Religion of the Greeks and Romans*. New York: E. P. Dutton, 1962.

Mayer, Frederick. *A History of Educational Thought*. 2d ed. Columbus: Charles E. Merrill, 1966.

Pellison, Maurice. *Roman Life in Pliny's Time*. New York: Chautaugua, 1897.

Reed, James E., and Ronnie Prevost. *A History of Christian Education*. Nashville: Broadman & Holman, 1993.

Rose, H. J. *Religion in Greece and Rome*. New York: Harper & Brothers, 1959.

What in the World?

➤ The city of Teotihuacan dominates the valley of Mexico in A.D. 100–650.

➤ Death of Marcus Aurelius and onset of Roman decline in A.D. 180.

➤ Constantine gives Christians the freedom to worship in A.D. 313.

➤ Gupta marks the classical age of India in A.D. 320–500.

➤ Nicaean Council: milestone in solidifying Christianity in A.D. 325.

➤ Adrianople: Visigoths victorious over Roman legions, which marks the beginning of German breakthrough in A.D. 378.

➤ The last Roman emperor loses power in A.D. 476.

Chapter 4

CHRISTIAN EDUCATION
IN THE EARLY CHURCH

"BUT WHEN THE FULLNESS OF THE time came, God sent forth His Son" Jesus into the world (Gal. 4:4). Although this passage speaks of the opportune time for Mary to deliver her new son Jesus into the world, it also has another dimension because God seemingly had prepared more than Mary for the coming of the Savior into the world. God had also been preparing the world itself for the coming of His Son.

THE CONTEXT OF EARLY CHRISTIAN EDUCATION

Upon the conquest of Macedonia in 146 B.C., Greece became a province of the Roman political state, but in many respects Rome had been captured by Greek culture and intellect. Scarcely did any great Roman leader between Cato and Augustus Caesar ascend to the throne who was not heavily influenced by Greek teachers through the important role they played in preparing him for leadership in Roman affairs. Crassus, Pompey, Mark Antony, Cicero, Julius Caesar, and Octavius (who later became known as Augustus Caesar) all continued in the educational centers of the East the Hellenistic Latin studies that they had begun in Rome. Of these men, none held greater influence in Roman life than Cicero. He held that a Greek literary and philosophical education was useful and necessary in the basic educational curriculum of every Roman citizen if he were to become a contributing member of society.[1] Thus, many Roman citizens who were learned could understand both classical Greek and Latin. The acquisition of the Greek language was by no means a small factor. "With the Greek language a whole world of concepts, categories of thought, inherited metaphors, and subtle connotations of meaning enters Christian thought."[2] Those who lived during the time of Christ and His immediate followers were well versed in Greek philosophic thought, yet they preferred the more pragmatic emphasis of Roman education. Theirs was a fine blending of both educational systems.

What contributed to the collapse of the mighty Roman Empire has been the focus of debate for countless centuries. Of what we are sure, the aristocracy voted themselves out of the tax system and granted to many new citizens a reduced levy as well. Consequently, the finances required to maintain the vast empire fell to the commoners and the working class who did not hold Roman citizenship. Accommodation and compromise were essential for lasting harmony, and the Romans recognized this fact by initiating twofold categories of laws, the *ius civile,* which applied to Roman citizens, and the *ius gentium,* which applied to all other people.[3] Eventually, the financial hardships required of the masses to fund Rome's military conquests and building campaigns went beyond that which they could bear. Simultaneous with these internal pressures were the border disputes with the Celts and the Germanic tribes in the west and the warring countries from the east. The empire had become too vast to manage, and eventually it lost control. In 476, Germanic tribes handed Romulus Augustus a rousing military defeat, and most historians view this defeat as the end of the empire.

The contribution of the great Roman Empire to the beginnings of Christianity cannot be overstated. The Son of God was born into a world that valued learning. The Hebrews had contributed an emphasis upon monotheism and family-life education; the Greeks had provided an emphasis upon philosophic thought united under a common language; and the Romans gave the world a strong civil government with secure borders, commerce, communication, and stable means of transportation. Together, these national

---

1. Edward H. Reisner, *Historical Foundations of Modern Education* (New York: Macmillan, 1928), 113-20.
2. Werner Jaeger, *Early Christianity and Greek Paideia* (Cambridge: Belknap Press of Harvard University, 1961), 6.
3. E. H. Gwynne-Thomas, *A Concise History of Education to 1900 a.d.* (Kansas City: University of Missouri, 1981), 31.

and cultural contributions laid the foundation for early Christian church education.

When considering the educational changes that occurred between the Roman Empire and the Christian church, one must follow two distinct lines of development. The imperial schools provided their students with one type of training and the Christian schools provided another type. As the centuries progressed, the number and influence of the pagan schools diminished while those established by the church slowly grew to dominate European education. The latter schools will be the focus of this chapter's investigation.[4]

JESUS AS THE MASTER TEACHER

Jesus had humble human origins. Born into a small town far removed from the political leadership of Rome and the mighty learning centers of Athens and Corinth, Jesus came into the world as the son of a commoner. God could have chosen the lineage of a Greek aristocrat or a Roman politician of His day. Instead, much to the dismay of both aristocrats and politicians, Jesus' entry into the world was witnessed by simple shepherds. He spent most of his life surrounded by those who had little power or influence. He chose to associate with the weak, the disenfranchised, and the lowly of society. He never studied in any of the great universities of His day and was trained in neither Greek rhetoric nor Roman military planning. Yet, He has become the leading force in politics, religion, science, economics, and philosophy since His days on earth. Jesus rarely called Himself a teacher, yet that role seems to be the one that others most often ascribed to Him. He was indeed the great Master Teacher.

The Gospels provide a glimpse into the early years of Jesus, but they focus more on His adult life and teachings. Because Jesus was not born into an economically affluent or socially prominent family, He most likely would not have had the luxury of higher education. His instruction, like that of other people of His socioeconomic background, would have comprised basic synagogue school after His *bar mitzvah* at the age of thirteen. In addition to this formal instruction, He would have been exposed to Jewish cultural and religious influences while observing the religious festivals and by participating in the temple sacrifices while He was visiting Jerusalem. During His young

---

4. Luella Cole, *A History of Education: Socrates to Montessori* (New York: Holt, Rinehart & Winston, 1962), 72.

adult years, He would also have become an apprentice in the trade of His earthly father Joseph until the age of thirty, at which time He obviously chose a different career path and became a teacher of some national renown.

Jesus was a skillful educator. Although He was not a formal teacher per se, such as the Greek philosophers or the Roman orators who were paid for their services, He was dedicated and committed to the task of instructing His learners in the knowledge of spiritual truth. He was viewed differently than the rabbis of His day because He was perceived as one who taught with authority (Matt. 7:29). Although He was unlearned in the science of educational instruction, He nevertheless possessed a vast repertoire of instructional methodologies. For example, He often spoke in parables (see Matt. 25:1–30; Mark 4:2–20; Luke 10:25–37), which created a degree of intellectual disequilibrium in his learners. He also used parables because they required higher levels of critical thinking (i.e., more than the simple acquisition of facts) from His disciples and those who came to challenge Him. Parables revealed biblical truths and values through the medium of stories. These stories remained fixed in the mind of the listener and were more easily recalled.

Jesus also taught through proclamation. This form of instruction engaged both the mind and the heart of the learner. Jesus' statements of "You have heard it said . . . but I say to you" (see Matt. 5:21–22, 27–28, 33–34) challenged the learner to encounter and assimilate new forms of meaning and purpose into otherwise old forms of knowledge. We see frequent opportunities of Jesus to lecture to the masses through His sermons on the mountain (Matt. 5–7), on the plain (Luke 15), and in synagogues (Matt. 4:23; Luke 4). Because Jesus' followers were not highly educated, He often adjusted his instructional methodologies such as to relate His message to their worldview.

Jesus taught through simple object lessons. Jesus revealed some of His most profound symbols by this method (Matt. 13). For example, Jesus used water to communicate the nature and purpose of biblical worship to a Samaritan woman at a roadside well (John 4). He used old wineskins to speak of Old Testament curriculum and the need for new paradigms of thinking (Matt. 9:17). He used children as an object lesson to point people to the true nature of kingdom living (Matt. 19:13–15), a lost coin to reveal God's quest for the misplaced soul (Mark 12:13–17), and a ripened field to portray the spiritual harvest that is available to those who serve as ministers of the gospel (John 4:35). Perhaps the most profound object lesson was the one that He gave to His disciples during their last meal together. Taking the loaf of bread and the cup of wine, He revealed a new spiritual meaning by stating, "This is My body . . . this is My blood of the covenant" (Mark 14:22, 24). The use of object lessons helped the listeners bring new spiritual meaning and insights to otherwise common elements of their world.

Jesus taught using various methods of speech as well. He used similes in which two different objects are brought together to reveal explicit comparisons. For example, "The kingdom of heaven is like a mustard seed, which a man took and sowed in his field; and this is smaller than all other seeds, but when it is full grown, it is larger than the garden plants" (Matt. 13:31). He also used metaphors in which an implicit comparison is made between two objects. For example, "I am the vine, you are the branches" (John 15:5), and "I am the good shepherd" (John 10:11).

Jesus also used poetry in His teaching. The ancient Greeks used this approach frequently as it became a standard element of their curriculum. Speaking of this method as employed by Jesus, Prevost and Reed write, "Jewish poetry in Jesus' day was not based on rhyme but on rhythm and parallelism. The educational effectiveness of ancient poetry lies in its repetitive nature and repetition of the rhythmic beat or of parallel thoughts."[5] Examples of such parallelism used by Jesus include, "Do not judge, and you will not be judged; and do not condemn, and you will not be condemned" (Luke 6:37).

Another figure of speech that Jesus used in His teaching is hyperbole. Hyperbole is a controversial method because of the methods of hermeneutics employed to interpret the passage and make relevant application of the instruction. The difficulty lies in trying to sort through the difference between what is said and what is meant. How literally does Jesus expect us to take Him? An example of this method is found in His admonition to pluck out your eye or cut off your hand if it causes you to sin (Matt. 5:29–30). Perhaps a more controversial example would be the extent to which a Christian is suppose to avoid physical confrontation when Jesus commands us, "Do not resist an evil person; but whoever slaps you on your right cheek, turn the other to him also" (Matt. 5:39). A literal interpretation of the latter example would certainly preclude one from service in either the military or any law enforcement agencies. Although Jesus often overstated certain commands, a good deal of cross-referencing is needed to bring a balanced perspective to bear on His message.

---

5. James E. Reed and Ronnie Prevost, *A History of Christian Education* (Nashville: Broadman & Holman, 1993), 66.

Jesus was a master of varied methods as well. At times, He taught in a small village hamlet, whereas at other times He purposefully approached the synagogue that was filled to capacity. At times, He pulled away from the crowds to reveal His teachings to a smaller audience, whereas at other times He taught at the doorstep of the temple while the city was swollen with the multitudes. At times, He addressed the religious leaders with a fiery message filled with passion and conviction; at other times, He spoke with the gentleness and grace of a father to his young child. He revealed an expertise that was anything but expected from such a formally unlearned man. In some ways, this paradox was what attracted to His teaching those who knew the difference between the sophists and the commoners. The Pharisees and other religious leaders of His day knew that Jesus was something beyond ordinary. Many people feared Him and were threatened by His success. They knew that something about His ways was supernatural; indeed, His ability to perform miracles added a great deal of authenticity to His message. Regardless of how the world might have understood His message, however, there was no mistaking His unique ability to communicate biblical truth such as to captivate and convict the multitude.

CHRISTIAN EDUCATION IN THE APOSTOLIC AGE

It did not take long for the impassioned followers of Christ to get about the task of communicating the gospel to the lost and needy world around them. The apostles began to spread the good news of the gospel message to those with whom they made contact during the daily occurrences of life. After healing a lame man who was sitting at the entrance of the temple, Peter and John boldly preached a message that resulted in the salvation of five thousand men. The next day, the religious rulers, elders, and scribes assembled in the temple courtyard to challenge these two apostles. Even the high priest Caiaphas and several others of high-priestly descent had gathered for the occasion. It wasn't often that the high priest entered into public debate to defend Judaism, so undoubtedly the crowd was enormous. It was an unfortunate day indeed for Caiaphas because he was about to be publicly humiliated by an unlearned fisherman and the Holy Spirit of God. So impressive was Peter's eloquence that at the debate the multitude began asking themselves how such an unlearned man could speak with such persuasive power and conviction: "they were amazed, and began to recognize them as having been with Jesus" (Acts 4:13).

Recognizing that the unlearned disciples of Jesus had begun speaking and teaching with a boldness to which the rabbis and the sophists of their day were unaccustomed, the Jewish authorities sought quickly to extinguish the influence of these seemingly academically untrained commoners. While they were meeting to discuss how to rid themselves of such intellectually ignorant men, the acclaimed Jewish scholar Gamaliel warned the Jewish council of elders that had assembled to be cautious. He stated,

> Men of Israel, take care what you propose to do with these men. For some time ago Theudas rose up, claiming to be somebody, and a group of about four hundred men joined up with him. But he was killed, and all who followed him were dispersed and came to nothing. After this man, Judas of Galilee rose up in the days of the census and drew away some people after him; he too perished, and all those who followed him were scattered. So in the present case, I say to you, stay away from these men and let them alone, for if this plan or action is of men, it will be overthrown; but if it is of God, you will not to able to overthrow them; or else you may even be found fighting against God. (Acts 5:35–39)

What is significant about this passage is that the council of the elders flogged Peter and John for what they were teaching, and the response of the disciples was that "they went on their way from the presence of the Council, rejoicing that they had been considered worthy to suffer shame for His name" (v. 41). Such was the effectiveness of being under the tutelage of the Master Teacher for three years of in-depth studies.

In spite of the resulting persecution, the apostles continued to teach and preach the Scriptures to those who would listen. Acts 5 concludes with this summary statement: "And every day, in the temple and from house to house, they kept right on teaching and preaching Jesus as the Christ" (v. 42). The obvious result is that the Jerusalem church continued to grow numerically and spiritually.

Those of Jewish descent were learning for the first time the true meaning of the Old Testament prophecies concerning the coming Messiah. Those who knew the scriptural predictions were comparing current events with biblical references. Many of them were becoming convinced that Jesus was the Messiah and that His death on the Cross and His subsequent resurrection provided mankind with the hope for which they had been waiting so many years. Having accepted the message of the apostles' teachings and become partakers of the new covenant, these new Jewish converts began meeting together in small fellowships to study the Scriptures in more detail and provide needed encouragement to one another.

The structure and forms of worship in the Jerusalem church would have looked very Jewish at first. They continued to meet at the temple (Acts 3:1; 5:20), met for worship on the Sabbath (1:12), observed daily prayers (3:1), kept the Jewish dietary laws (10:14), read from the Old Testament Scriptures (2:17-21, 25-28; 6:4), and maintained the practice of circumcision. To the outside observer, Christianity would have looked like a mild revision of Judaism. But for a few differences, such as assembling for worship on the first day of the week instead of the Sabbath, meeting in homes for small group fellowship, and structuring the church according to one's giftedness (as opposed to being born into the priestly tribe), the church would have looked much like a Jewish community of believers. In a short time, however, this situation would all change.

The religious leaders in Jerusalem did not take lightly to seeing their Jewish faith compromised by such apostasy. The only reasonable response was to put an end to such cultic practices. Persecution began to spread through the region (Acts 8:2). Those who had come to faith in Christ had to weigh their decision in light of the possibility of facing economic, social, and perhaps even physical consequences. Jewish merchants who had converted to Christianity found that they were unable to buy and sell their products in the marketplace. Members of their own family and community shunned these new believers. Some of them were put on trial and mocked in front of their peers. When that failed to stem the tide, physical retaliation became a reasonable option. Many Jewish converts to Christ were put in prison, and some of them were put to death. The result was surprising to those who had planned these events. Rather than eliminating Christianity, such harsh means only resulted in a purification of the faith and a resolve not to bow to such pressure. Enduring under the hardships of persecution gave these new believers a sense of satisfaction that somehow they had been found worthy to share in the suffering and identification with Christ. Jesus had told them before departing not to give up on the city of Jerusalem but to remain there and establish a foothold for the new faith (Acts 1:4, 8). The apostles remained firm to their commission and taught the Scriptures to these new converts daily. Converts who were not of Jewish descent simply decided to return to their homelands, where the pressure would be inconsequential.

The book of Acts records that many tradesmen and merchants from distant lands were present in Jerusalem during the Passover celebration when Christ was put to death. Many of these individuals remained in Jerusalem an additional fifty days so they could continue their business of selling and trading (Acts 2:6-11, 41). They also witnessed the events of Pentecost and were amazed at what they had seen and heard with their own eyes and ears. Armed with the conviction that they had just witnessed the dramatic hand of God, many of these individuals also became believers. With Passover and Pentecost over, they returned home to resupply their goods and share with their family and friends what they had just experienced. No doubt, many of them were now living radically transformed lives, and the evidence that something profound had taken place was hard to deny. The result was that small fellowships of this new religion began to develop outside the confines of Israel's borders.

The Jewish religious leaders were concerned about these new pockets of resistance and commissioned a zealous young man with impeccable credentials to see what could be done to rid the land of these cultic followers. The Jerusalem council of elders sent Saul with the express purpose of exterminating Christians wherever he could find them. Along the way, on his way to persecute Christians in the city of Damascus, Syria, he had an unexpected encounter with the resurrected Christ Himself (Acts 9). The resulting conversion of Saul was miraculous given the extent of his success as a religious bounty hunter. His reputation preceded him, so it is not surprising to discover that the apostles at the Jerusalem church were somewhat skeptical of him once he returned (v. 26).

Simultaneous with these events, new churches were being founded in villages, towns, and cities all along the Mediterranean coast. One such city was Antioch to the north. No one knows for sure who brought the gospel message to this bustling city, but we do know that it was not one of the apostles (Acts 8:1). Perhaps one of the merchants discussed earlier brought the good news to them (11:19-22). At any rate, the church in Antioch took root and began to flourish, and it soon garnered the attention of the apostles in Jerusalem. Because it had not been founded by one of the apostles, and neither had any of the apostles been present to teach them the Scriptures, they agreed that an envoy from the Jerusalem church should be sent to examine the legitimacy of what was happening (v. 23). They decided to send Barnabas, who in turn invited Saul (now renamed Paul) to join him. At Antioch, Barnabas discipled Paul for about a year while providing him with the direction he needed to serve as a church leader (vv. 25-26).

From this point, with the notable exception of Acts 15, the prominence of the apostles' ministry diminished while the service of Paul increased substantially. Paul embarked on three missionary journeys with the intent of taking the gospel message to Jews and Gentiles throughout the European region. No other man is as deserving of our adulation and respect as Paul for his many sacrifices and service to our Lord. He established new churches; mentored and trained church leaders; provided necessary discipline like a father to his children; chronicled his teaching and instruction, which have remained for our benefit; and eventually laid down his life for the cause of world evangelism and discipleship.

The Teaching Ministry of the Apostle Paul

In his letter to the Christians at Philippi, Paul identified a comprehensive curriculum for his teaching: "whatever is true, whatever is honorable, whatever is right, whatever is pure, whatever is lovely, whatever is of good report, if there is any excellence and if anything worthy of praise, let your mind dwell on these things. The things you have learned and received and heard and seen in me, practice these things, and the God of peace will be in you" (Phil. 4:8–9). All that philosophers have sought over the ages in order to gain wisdom became the teaching agenda for Paul and for Christians in their thought and practice. All that Christians gain from their pursuit for truth and wisdom was to be passed on to others who in turn could teach (2 Tim. 2:2). Paul was clear about the source of this truth for it is in Christ Himself that "are hidden all the treasures of wisdom and knowledge" (Col. 2:3), and the task before Christians is "taking every thought captive to the obedience of Christ" (2 Cor. 10:5).[6]

---

6. Robert W. Pazmino, *The Evangelical Dictionary of Christian Education*, ed. Michael J. Anthony (Grand Rapids: Baker, 2001), s.v. "Teachings of Paul."

Tradition tells us that the other apostles spread throughout the other countries of the known world, conducting similar church planting enterprises. As they journeyed, they wrote letters that remain to this day as books in our New Testament. Tradition tells us that they also developed a church manual for the training of new believers. This sixteen-chapter book, called the *Didache*, instructs the new convert in matters pertaining to properly living the Christian life (chaps. 1-6); teachings regarding baptism, communion, and fasting (chaps. 7-10); distinguishing between false teachers and godly prophets; qualifications for church leaders (chaps. 11-15); and living a godly lifestyle in light of the imminent return of Jesus Christ (chap. 16).

In partnership with the Holy Spirit, the apostles established the foundation for the church that remains throughout the world to this day. Although they were relatively unlearned men by the world's standards, they were faithful servants to a living God. They established churches and schools where the teachings of Christ would prevail.

CATECHUMENAL INSTRUCTION

The apostles' teachings continued to establish and strengthen the church body. As new believers were added to the church, some systematic form of instruction was necessary to ensure authenticity of faith and consistency in practice. People with the gift of teaching and shepherding took the lead in providing this training.

Catechism Curriculum

With such new forms of catechism, a broad—even contradictory—range of opinions swept across the church's pedagogical philosophies: on the one hand, Tertullian (c. 160–215) contrasted sacred and secular knowledge with his famous rhetorical inquiry that pitted "Jerusalem" against "Athens." On the other hand, some latter church leaders valued a broad-based, general education, by advocating that the most comprehensive education provided a great advantage to Christians; these leaders included: Basil the Great (c. 329–79), Gregory of Nyssa (330–89) and Augustine of Hippo (354–430).

> Correspondingly, Augustine is generally credited with the now popular motto: "All truth is God's truth."
>
> A standardized curriculum soon emerged from these early centuries, a core of resources that would make their mark on the Reformation era of cathechetical instruction. Specifically, an analysis of most early church education revealed the consistent pattern of the Lord's Prayer and the Apostle's Creed. By the thirteenth century, the Ten Commandments were added, to this uniformed list, even though spokespersons like Augustine had lobbied for the Decalogue's inclusion almost one thousand years before.[7]

The words *catechism* and *catechumen* are derived from the Greek word that is translated "instruct." They occur in the New Testament seven times (Luke 1:4; Acts 18:25; 21:21, 24; Rom. 2:18; 1 Cor. 14:19; Gal. 6:6). These passages reveal the systematic nature of the instruction that was provided as preparation for accepting the new convert into fellowship. The period of preparation lasted two to three years and was comprised of three distinct levels. Those in the first level were called *hearers* because they were allowed to listen to the reading of the Scriptures and to sermons in the church service. They also received instruction in the basic tenets of the faith. Those at the second level were referred to as *kneelers* because they remained for corporate prayer after the hearers were dismissed from class. They received more detailed instruction in matters pertaining to living the Christian life. Finally, the *chosen* were people who received intensive training in doctrines and church liturgy and were prepared to receive baptism.[8]

The Catechumenate

The modern discipline of Christian education has its roots in the early church's practice of baptism. At the birth of the church, adult converts were baptized with little formal instruction as seen in Acts 2:38–41; 8:12–13, 35–39; 9:17–

---

7. Ronald T. Habermas, *The Evangelical Dictionary of Christian Education*, ed. Michael J. Anthony (Grand Rapids: Baker, 2001), s.v. "Catechism."

8. Charles B. Eavey, *History of Christian Education* (Chicago: Moody, 1964), 84.

19; 10:44–48; and 16:14–15. But as the number of converts began to increase, seven reasons made it necessary to subject these individuals to a probationary course of instruction and discipline preparatory to baptism and admission into the church. First, non-Jewish people who were being converted out of paganism who needed to be instructed in the Hebrew Scriptures. Second, it was necessary to determine the reasons why people who were joining the church. Third, a biblical lifestyle was a process and not a product, and so, time and opportunity to change a convert's personal lifestyle was needed. Fourth, care had to be taken for those who professed conversion to Christianity because of the possibility that the stress of persecution might cause them to recant their faith. Fifth, few converts could read. Writing materials were difficult to obtain, which made oral instruction imperative. Sixth, the oral method of question and answer aided in the memorization of the content because of the opportunity for repetition and the personal relationship between the one who asked the questions and the one who answered the questions. Seventh, the Christian community became concerned about the doctrinal purity and survival of the content that was being transmitted to the new converts.[9]

This form of Christian education reached its peak of popularity around A.D. 325-450. It declined in effectiveness once it became expected of children to be baptized and when pagans, lacking genuine motivation for joining the faith, were commanded by law to attend church. The early church fathers Origen (A.D. 185-255) and Cyril of Jerusalem (A.D. 310-86) warned catechumens not to take lightly the teachings of Christ.[10]

CATECHETICAL AND CATHEDRAL SCHOOLS

Many of the new converts to Christianity came from the lower class. It took time for the gospel to spread across the Mediterranean to Athens and Rome, which were considered the seats of higher learning. The Jews had given little attention to studying classical Greek philosophers and poets. Neither

---

9. J. E. Harvey Martin, *The Evangelical Dictionary of Christian Education*, ed. Michael J. Anthony (Grand Rapids: Baker, 2001), s.v. "Catechumenate."
10. Werner C. Graendorf, ed., *Introduction to Biblical Christian Education* (Chicago: Moody, 1981), 40.

did they hold the Roman system of education in high esteem because the Jews had been the recipient of the Romans' harsh control. Jews were hesitant to send their children to formal schools where their children would receive instruction in the secular Greek or Roman curriculum.

Eventually, a learned generation of believers recognized the value of educating their children. Heretical philosophies of Greek and Roman origin began to creep into the church and required an educated and rational response. Scholarly preparation in the literature and the philosophical teachings of ancient Greece and Rome put one at par in a rhetorical debate. Soon, believers began attending schools where they could be taught sound biblical doctrine integrated with the seven liberal arts. The result was a powerful defense of the faith among the learned class.

The educational institutions that prepared these learned Christian leaders were known as catechetical schools. Chief among these schools was one located in Alexandria, Egypt. The city was established by Alexander the Great three hundred years before Christ. There scholars translated the Old Testament into Greek. This translation was known as the Septuagint. Tradition says that Mark planted the church in Alexandria and no doubt began the basic catechetical school there to help strengthen the new converts. In 179, Pantaenus, a converted Stoic philosopher, became the director of the school. By 185, it was a recognized catechetical institution. He expanded the curriculum to include an integration of biblical doctrines with discussions in classical philosophy. Clement, viewed as the first Christian scholar, succeeded Pantaenus, and with him came an ever more expanded curriculum that included instruction in Greek literature, science, dialectic, physics, geometry, astronomy, logic, and history.[11] Later, Clement fled from Alexandria, and his young student Origen became the new director. Viewed as one of the finest Christian institutions of higher learning in its day, it earned a reputation as a premier place of Christian scholarship. The conservative church, however, viewed it with some skepticism because no topic was forbidden and heresies were often given ample discussion among formative minds.

The educators in Alexandria were anxious to develop a theology that used Greek philosophy and yet would give a systematic explanation of Christianity. Because the faculty had been trained in the Scriptures and Greek philoso-

---

11. Frederick Eby and Charles F. Arrowood, *The History and Philosophy of Education: Ancient and Medieval* (Englewood Cliffs, N.J.: Prentice-Hall, 1940), 611.

phy, they were confident that they could integrate the two subjects. In time, however, under Origen, it was anything but positive; instead of emphasizing the historical-grammatical interpretation of the Scriptures, they preferred a more confusing mix of philosophical allegory. This latter approach was based upon the assumption that Scripture has several meanings. Using the analogy of a man's body, soul, and spirit, they argued that the Scriptures possessed a literal and historical interpretation that corresponded to the physical body; a hidden moral meaning that corresponded to the soul; and a much deeper, underlying spiritual meaning that only the most spiritually astute Christian leader could comprehend. This approach grew from a desire to link Judaism and Greek philosophy by finding a hidden meaning in the language of the Old Testament that could be associated with Greek philosophy. Rather than trying to determine the meaning of the passage as it related to the particular people to whom it was written in its historical context and perhaps an application for present believers, the Alexandrian scholars were fixated on trying to find hidden and coded meanings. Eventually, absurd and aberrant theological teachings spread throughout the church.[12] The result was a destructive sense that Scripture had lost its ability to impact people's lives. It had become simply another textbook added to the curriculum of study.

Although Alexandria was seen as the most prominent of the catechetical schools, others also developed in Jerusalem, Antioch, Edessa, Nisibis, and Constantinople. Origen also founded one in Caesarea after he departed Alexandria to avoid persecution. These schools supplied the early church with some of its greatest minds and able apologists.[13]

As Christianity spread, it was incumbent upon the leadership to appoint able men who could administrate the affairs of several churches within a particular geographical region. These leaders, known as bishops, soon became a powerful force in the development of the church. The political power they wielded over their churches was extensive, and few people could challenge their authority. The finest church among those that they supervised was usually the one over which the bishop presided. The church building was known as a cathedral, and the asssociated school was referred to as an episcopal, or cathedral, school. They were highly structured and administered with detailed supervision. Unfortunately, in time, the bishop became

---

12. Earle E. Cairns, *Christianity Through the Centuries: A History of the Christian Church*, 3d ed. (Grand Rapids: Zondervan, 1996), 108.

13. Eavey, *History of Christian Education*, 88.

preoccupied with maintaining political and economic control over his region and often lost his spiritual vibrancy. These cathedral schools slowly drifted away from their original purpose of training an educated clergy and created instead a new sense of superiority among those who attended.[14]

Early Christian Educators: Church Fathers, Apologists, and Polemics

During the second and third centuries, the church continued to suffer persecution at the hands of the Jews. However, in addition to the Jewish opposition, they also faced confrontation from Roman authorities. Roman politicians were bent on the wholesale destruction of the Christian faith. During this time, the church needed encouragement from its leaders. In addition, church leaders needed to provide an apology (defense) of their faith. Also, in those days sharp heresies arose that threatened to divide the church. The church needed leaders who could refute the false teachings that had entered the church. Each of these unique needs required a distinct type of scholar or orator to face the challenge. The church fathers wrote letters to and on behalf of Christians to encourage their endurance under persecution. Apologists provided a detailed defense of their faith before governmental leaders in an effort to provide a rational defense for the Christian faith. Finally, a third type of Christian educator known as a polemic wrote in an effort to maintain purity within the church and to dispel the false doctrines of misguided teachers. We will summarize the work of several Christian educators from each of these three categories.

Justin Martyr (A.D. 100–165)

Justin Martyr was born into a pagan family near the biblical town of Shechem. At an early age, he explored the various philosophical presuppositions of Plato, Aristotle, and Pythagoras. He started a school in Ephesus to expound on Stoicism and Platonism, although neither of them met the deep needs of his soul. One day, while walking along the coast, an old man shared with him the gospel message of salvation in Christ. He became a Christian and sought to find ways to integrate Greek philosophies with the tenets of

---

14. Ibid., 89.

Christianity. He established a new Christian school for this purpose in Rome.[15] Perhaps the most famous of the second-century apologists, he wrote several books to provide a defense of the faith.

Around 150, he wrote his *First Apology* to Emperor Antonius Pius to examine the accusations against the Christians living in Rome (chaps. 1–3) and to challenge him to free them if they were found innocent of the charges. He provided a convincing defense that Christians were neither atheists, idolaters, nor a threat to the state (chaps. 4–13). A substantial portion of his address presents the moral and spiritual teachings of Christianity (chaps. 14–60). He sought to prove that Christ's superior teachings as demonstrated by His lifestyle and character had been declared prophetically in the Old Testament and that Rome had nothing to fear from those who further the teachings of ethical living and respect of authority (chaps. 61–67). Once having determined that Christians were not a threat to the state, they should be released and allowed to live life free from the coercive constraints of the empire. His *Second Apology* is similar in tone to his *First Apology*. He also wrote an extensive apology to the Jews titled *Dialogues with Trypho* in which he sought to demonstrate to the Jews that Christ was the Messiah who had been foretold in the Old Testament Scriptures.[16] He was beheaded in 166.

Clement of Alexandria (150–215)

Probably born in Athens, Clement received a superior education in the classic disciplines of Greek learning. He followed his mentor Panteus as director of the catechetical school in Alexandria. As was mentioned earlier in this chapter, this school attempted to integrate Greek philosophy, primarily the ethical base of Plato, with Christian theology. Clement was a winsome apologist for Christianity although he thought that Greek culture was as sacred to God as Hebrew culture and that Hellenistic philosophy and ethics could live harmoniously with Christian theology and practice. He left Alexandria in 202.[17]

---

15. Cairns, *Christianity Through the Centuries,* 104.
16. Ibid.
17. Eby and Arrowood, *History and Philosophy of Education,* 612.

Tertullian (A.D. 150–230)

An apologist from the Western church, Tertullian wrote in defense of the Christians who were being persecuted back in Rome. Trained as an attorney, he spoke with legal eloquence and often used legal arguments to put forth his claims. In his book titled *On Schoolmasters and Their Difficulties,* Tertullian revealed his lack of patience for those who sought to integrate Greek philosophy with Christianity. From his perspective, it was a vain pursuit, and he believed that efforts would be better spent trying to find ways better to live the Christian life within society. His other book, titled *Apologeticus,* provided a defense for those whom the Roman authorities were persecuting.

Origen (A.D. 185–254)

Clement's successor at the school in Alexandria, Origen, was one of the most complex thinkers of the Greek church fathers. Both of his parents were Christians. His father was a teacher of rhetoric, and Origen assisted his father by serving as an instructor at the young age of sixteen. His father died the next year, and Origen was appointed chief catechist of the Christian school. Just one year later, he was appointed director, a position that he held for the next thirty years.[18] A voluminous writer, he devoted himself so wholeheartedly to the reconciliation of pagan and Christian writings that some people thought him to be a heretic. In his efforts to unify the two views, he was not opposed to setting aside the teachings of Christianity if he thought that they were incompatible with logic and reason.[19]

Obviously suffering from a conflicted mind, he applied the teachings of Matthew 19:12 literally and underwent castration. He preferred the ascetic lifestyle and frequently visited the desert with his books for extended study. One of the most prolific church fathers, Origen wrote extensively on matters related to exegesis, textual criticism, and systematic theology. He espoused the allegorical approach to biblical interpretation characteristic of his Alexandrian school; therefore, his views were often suspect. "Origen quoted Scripture extensively yet embarked on speculations for which only minimal support was available. He produced the *Hexapla,* the finest piece of biblical scholarship in

---

18. Ibid.
19. Eavey, *History of Christian Education,* 92.

the early church. His major work in theology, *First Principles,* introduced basic Christian doctrines in a systematic manner."[20] One of the most noted and acclaimed apologists and theologians among the early church fathers, Origen is highly respected for his keen mind and Christian scholarship.

Cyril of Jerusalem (A.D. 330-379)

As bishop of the church in Jerusalem, Cyril understood the significance of his position. Realizing that his church had been the birthplace of Christianity, he desired to maintain a pure faith among his followers. His twenty-four catechetical lectures instructs catechumens in the basic doctrines of the Christian faith. They are seen as the foundational tenets of the early church creeds.

Basil the Great (A.D. 331-396)

Born into a wealthy family, he was educated in Constantinople and Athens. After his conversion to Christianity, he became a teacher. At a young age, he developed a friendship with the pagan Sophist Libanius. He often referred students to Libanius's school, and the two men remained good friends for many years. He retired from the field of education and sought a monastic lifestyle. In 370, he became the bishop of Caesarea. Writing to Libanius at an old age, he testified of his love for the Scriptures and their superiority over Greek literature: "I am now spending my time with Moses and Elias, and saints like them, who tell me their stories in a barbarous tongue. . . . If ever I learned anything from you, I have forgotten it."[21] He developed Greek monasticism and sought to live an ascetic lifestyle of self-denial and simplicity. More will be said about monasticism in the next chapter on Christian education in the Middle Ages.

Jerome (A.D. 340-399)

At a young age, Jerome was brought to study in Rome where he fell in love with the works of Cicero, Horace, Virgil, and others. He later studied

---

20. Kenneth O. Gangel and Warren S. Benson, *Christian Education: Its History and Philosophy* (Chicago: Moody, 1983), 88.

21. *A Select Library of Nicene and Post-Nicene Fathers of the Christian Church* (New York: Christian Literature, 1895), 8:322.

at the famous catechetical school in Antioch, where he mastered the Greek language.

While exploring the life of an ascetic in the Chalcis desert, he learned Hebrew with great effort. His academic training was eclectic to be sure, but it brought him little peace of mind because he could not reconcile classical literature with the Scriptures.[22] "What communion does light have with darkness?" He could not fathom what connection could exist between Horace and the apostle Paul, between the teachings of Homer and Peter. The two could not be harmonized without significantly compromising the latter. He related a dream that he had had when he was quite sick with a fever:

> Suddenly I was caught up in the spirit and dragged before the judge's judgment seat; and here the light was so dazzling and the brightness shining from those who stood by so radiant that I flung myself upon the ground and did not dare to look up. I was asked to state my condition and replied that I was a Christian. But he who presided said, 'Thou liest; Thou art a Ciceronian, not a Christian. For where thy treasure is, there will thy heart be also.' Straightway I became dumb.[23]

From that point, Jerome forsook his previous passion of classical literature and sought to maintain a disciplined study of the Scriptures. He was not always successful in his resolve, however, because his love for Greek and Latin classics was well engrained.[24]

Because of Jerome's expertise in the original languages of the Bible, Pope Damasus compelled him to revise the old Latin texts of the Gospel accounts of Christ in 383. Of all of the classical Latin authors of the early church, Jerome is most known for his translation of the Bible, the Latin Vulgate.

John Chrysotom (A.D. 345–407)

John received his education in the finest public schools of Antioch under the supervision of Libanius, a noted professor of rhetoric. His mother led him

---

22. N. G. L. Hammond and H. H. Scullard, *The Oxford Classical Dictionary* (Oxford: Clarendon, 1970), 563.

23. F. A. Wright, trans., *Select Letters of Saint Jerome* (Cambridge, Mass.: Loeb Classical Library, 1933), 127.

24. Eby and Arrowood, *History and Philosophy of Education*, 596.

to the Lord; consequently, he abandoned his pursuit of secular studies to become the director of a catechetical school. He was one of the first Christian educators to look seriously at the education of children. In his work *Concerning the Education of Children,* he spoke of the need to blend a child's love for storytelling with the scope and sequence of the early childhood education curriculum. He clearly understood the limitations of a child's concrete-based reasoning ability and sought to take complex Old Testament stories and put them into concepts and vocabulary that a child could understand.[25]

As an acclaimed church father, his school in Antioch rivaled the school in Alexandria. The Antioch school became a seminary dedicated to the training and instruction of the clergy. Unlike the school in Alexandria, Chrysotom did not hold to the more liberal approach of taking an allegorical interpretation of Scripture and preferred the more conservative historical-grammatical approach to Scriptural interpretation.[26]

Augustine (A.D. 354-430)

Born in Thagaste, North Africa, in 354, Augustine was educated in Latin grammar and rhetoric. The son of a Christian mother, Monica, he preferred the works of the great Latin authors over those written by the Greeks. He taught rhetoric at Carthage, Rome, and Milan. At the age of nineteen, he read Cicero's *Hortensius* and became captivated by the study of philosophy. He subsequently converted to Manichaeism, a gnostic sect that promised great wisdom to its followers, and in 386 to a Christianized neo-Platonism patronized by St. Ambrose, bishop of Milan.[27] "He went through a period of deep trauma and came to faith in Christ in a dramatic encounter in which Romans 13:13-14 provided solace as he wrestled with his immoral past. This took place in August, A.D. 386, and the following Easter he was baptized. On arriving back in Africa, he spent three years in solitude and study."[28] He later became bishop of Hippo, a city in Africa not far from his birthplace.

One of the leading Western church fathers, Augustine was viewed as the most learned, noble, and acclaimed leaders of the early church. He wrote several highly acclaimed books. *Confessions* is a book that is autobiographical

---

25. Eavey, *History of Christian Education,* 92.
26. Eby and Arrowood, *History and Philosophy of Education,* 614.
27. Hammond and Scullard, *Oxford Classical Dictionary,* 148.
28. Gangel and Benson, *Christian Education,* 100.

in nature and speaks of the profound grace of God and its benefit to the new believer. In his work *The City of God*, Augustine developed the distinct differences between the earthly kingdom and our future heavenly kingdom.

Augustine has much to offer the twenty-first-century Christian educator. His discussions regarding the grace of God represent a message that is desperately needed today as well. His instructions to teachers to provide comfort to their students and to treat them with respect is admirable. Regarding the significant contributions made by this early church father, Davies writes,

> Augustine's philosophical and educational writings make significant contributions to Christian education. For the western church, he was able to successfully fuse Neoplatonic philosophy with Pauline Christianity. He believed that the universe is an ordered structure in which the degrees of being are at the same time degrees of value. This universal order requires the subordination of what is lower on the scale of being to what is higher—body is subject to spirit, and spirit to God. Philosophically he maintained wherever one may find truth, in the final analysis it has come from God. The individual thinker does not make truth, he finds it; he is able to do so because Christ, the revealing Word of God, is the *magister interior,* the "inward teacher," who enables him to see the truth as she listens to it. As an educational thinker, Augustine transcended his generation. He combined deep respect for the cultivation of reason with a passionate concern for heart feelings stirred by God. A human being's ability to reason was what set him apart from other animals. But sensitivity to "the light within" was necessary for true wisdom.[29]

Many of these early church fathers, apologists, and polemics were what we would call today authentic Christian leaders. They struggled with the same issues that we face. A number of these leaders faced battles between the desires of the flesh and the desire to serve Christ with wholesale abandon. One should demonstrate caution, however, in placing these men on so high a pedestal that we fail to see the manifestation of God's grace in their daily lives. Although they were significant Christian educators of the first few

---

29. James A. Davies, *The Evangelical Dictionary of Christian Education,* ed. Michael J. Anthony (Grand Rapids: Baker, 2001), s.v. "Augustine."

centuries of the Christian church, they also understood what it meant to live in a fallen world. Yet, in spite of these human limitations, these early church leaders dedicated themselves to providing the church with resources, either through their own leadership or through written letters and books, that were needed to take the young church to her next level of spiritual maturity.

To understand the circumstances under which these church leaders lived and ministered, it is important to remember the condition of learning as a whole during these four centuries of Greek and Roman education. It was profoundly Hellenistic and pagan. It was an education that emphasized human existence over the supernatural and was in many respects in direct opposition to the biblical truths espoused by many of the leaders whom we have surveyed in this chapter. Pagan literature was filled with references to polytheism, and for Christians who desired to provide a rational defense of the Christian faith, it was imperative that they subject themselves to the ungodly instruction of many Greek and Latin professors. Only as these and other church leaders grappled with the professed enlightenment of Greek and Latin literature were they able to point others to a better way in Christianity.

These church fathers were responsible for shepherding churches through turbulent times. Upon their shoulders rested the future of the Christian faith. They attempted to make the message of the gospel consistent with the Greek and Latin philosophical teachings of their day. Although their motives might have been admirable at the time, the consequences of their actions have had a lasting effect on the church. In spite of efforts to eradicate the church of such humanistic philosophies through edicts such as that issued by the Council of Carthage in 401, it is abundantly clear to us (through the advantage of hindsight) that men have continued ever since this attempt to humanize the gospel message.[30]

PHILOSOPHICAL HERESIES IN THE EARLY CHURCH

During the first few centuries after the birth of the church, society as a whole grew more secular and pagan. In an effort to accommodate the many cultures that were captured during the Roman military campaigns, it became apparent that a high level of give-and-take would be needed for peaceful

---

30. Eavey, *History of Christian Education,* 96–98.

coexistence. As a result, polytheism was characteristic of most religious beliefs, and moral relativism permeated the legal and ethical systems across the empire. Philosophers traveled the land espousing new ways of reasoning. Church leaders grew to despise these "men of learning." That their teachings contradicted the Scriptures was quickly apparent. Tertullian wrote of the special satisfaction he would receive on the day he saw these vain philosophers thrown into the fires of hell. He writes,

> How vast the spectacle that day, how wide! What sight shall wake my wonder, what my laughter, my joy, my exaltation as I see . . . those sages the philosophers blushing before their disciples as they blaze together, the disciples whom they taught that God was concerned with nothing, that men have no souls at all, or what souls they have shall never return to their former bodies! And then the poets, trembling before the judgment seat, not of Rhadamanthus, not of Minos, but of Christ whom they never looked to see![31]

With no morals and ethical absolutes with which to govern civil affairs and personal decision making, the Roman Empire became a breeding ground for heretical philosophies such as Gnosticism, Docetism, Manichaeism, Neo-Platonism, Marcionism, and Arianism. Each of these damaging philosophies had an impact on the church.

Gnosticism

Chief among the aberrant teachings that came into the church at this time was a philosophy known as Gnosticism. By now, the majority of the new believers being added to the church were coming from backgrounds of Greek and Roman culture. They brought with them their perspectives about life and sought to find ways of integrating Greek philosophy into Christianity.

Gnosticism had its roots in a platonic dualism that held that physical matter was evil and the realm of the spirit was superior. Anything associated with the creation of matter, such as the biblical creation account, simply added support to their belief that Jehovah depicted in the Old Testament was a secondary,

---

31. Tertullian *De Spectaculis* 30; quoted in William Barclay, *Educational Ideals in the Ancient World* (Grand Rapids, Baker, 1959), 202–3.

perhaps inferior, manifestation of a lesser created being, or demiurge. He certainly could not be God Himself. The gnostics developed a system by which God as a spirit could be disassociated from material substance.

This philosophical reasoning had profound implications for discussing the deity of Christ; how could a pure god inhabit a physical body when to do so would be to participate in evil? To the gnostic, the idea that God would clothe Himself in human form as described in the Gospel accounts was absurd. The apostle Paul countered this teaching in his address to the church in Philippi: "Jesus, . . . who, although He existed in the very form of God, did not regard equality with God a thing to be grasped, but emptied Himself, taking the form of a bondservant, and being made in the likeness of men" (Phil. 2:5–7).

> The Gnostics, like the Greeks of the first two chapters of 1 Corinthians, sought by human wisdom to understand the ways of God with man and to avoid what seemed to them to be the stigma of the cross. If the Gnostics had succeeded, Christianity would have simply become another philosophical religion of the ancient world.[32]

In addition to the letter addressed to the church in Philippi, Paul also confronted gnostic heresy in his writings to the church in Corinth and especially Colossae. Colossians 2:8–15, 20–23; 3:1–11 take a firm stand against the influences of Gnosticism in the church. The apostle John in his first epistle also seems to address this issue directly (see 1 John 1:1–3).

Docetism

Docetism was a variation of Gnosticism in that it held that Christ, being a purer form of god, could not associate with evil physical matter such as a human body. Therefore, Jesus must simply have been a phantom image of a man and not a real human being at all. They believed that Christ came into the body of Jesus for the brief time between His baptism and when He appeared on the Cross. Once on the Cross, Jesus was left to His own demise. According to Gnosticism and Docetism, God would neither create a material world, live in it, nor allow Himself to become subject to its constraints.

---

32. Cairns, *Christianity Through the Centuries*, 96.

Manichaeism

Manichaeism was similar to Gnosticism in that it held to a dualistic view of man. It was founded by Mani, also known as Manichaeus (216–77) of Mesopotamia. He developed his peculiar philosophical framework around the middle of the third century. Convinced through a series of dreams that he was the Paraclete promised by Jesus, his concept of salvation was depicted in a struggle between the forces of light and the forces of darkness. A precosmic invasion of the realm of light by the forces of darkness resulted in the present intermingling of good and evil on earth. In essence, divine matter was imprisoned in our physical bodies and the latter needed to be held under subjection.[33]

Salvation was achieved by releasing the light from the constraints of its physical boundaries. As a result, the body was subjected to harsh isolation and given as few liberties as possible, resulting in an ascetic lifestyle of abstinence from any form of human pleasure. Food and water were provided only out of necessity for survival, but other forms of pleasure gained through participation in the fine arts, physical activity, or sexuality were absolutely forbidden. Those who held to these strict standards rose in ranks to the priestly sect. Those who were still in process were called hearers and provided the monetary means to enable the priests to continue their spiritual ascent. Augustine sought to refute this philosophical teaching in his book *Against Manichaeans.*

So What? Lessons from the Past for Twenty-first-century Christian Education

A great many principles from this epic period of human history influence the way ministry is conducted today. The example of Christ's life, His followers, and the spread of Christianity during the initial centuries of the early church provide us with a rich heritage to guide and shape Christian living.

1. What Would Jesus Do (WWJD)?

The life of Christ is our ultimate example of Christian education. The Gospel accounts of the life of Christ provide our example of what God expects

---

33. Hammond and Scullard, *Oxford Classical Dictionary,* 643.

of His creation. We are to live according to the instructions set out for us in the Old and New Testaments. One does not need a seminary degree to understand the fundamental teachings of Christ. Taken at face value, they are easy to understand yet decidedly difficult to apply. Our fallen nature is set in direct opposition to the things of the Spirit. Strict discipline is needed to live the Christian life although not to the extremes set by the ascetics.

2. Live in partnership with the Holy Spirit.

The Holy Spirit was sent, in part, to empower the church toward godly living. The Spirit of God has been placed inside each believer as evidence of God's guarantee of our redemption. The Spirit brings with Him a gift, which, when used correctly, allows us to strengthen and build up the body of Christ (Rom. 12:3–8; 1 Cor. 12; Eph. 4:11–16). Together, we can form a working partnership that will continue the work started by the Lord Jesus Christ when He lived among us.

The New Testament records countless principles to govern the manner in which we lead, serve, train, evangelize, and minister in the world today. We are called to be about the task of making disciples (Matt. 28:19–20). This is a twofold process of first bringing them to faith in Christ through evangelism and then building them up in the faith through edification. Twenty-first-century Christian educators must use every technological advantage available to us to bring the timeless message of hope to a lost and needy world. The Holy Spirit will give us the wisdom and the energy to carry out these important tasks.

3. Keep the contributions of philosophy in perspective.

Yes, there is value in being able to use logic and sound reasoning in the formation of our worldview, but we must also conclude with the apostle Paul that the "wisdom of man is foolishness to God." It's important to keep a balanced perspective regarding the value of philosophy. Many of the early church fathers and apologists had training in Greek and Latin philosophy and, armed with that knowledge, were able to provide an effective defense of the faith before emperors and regional rulers. Knowledge of philosophy gave them an additional weapon in the defense of the faith.

Many of the Christian apologists were themselves skilled and trained in all Greek knowledge and lore before they became Christians. Even Tatian, who speaks with the greatest of violence and virulence about pagan culture, was himself trained in it. Aristides was an

Athenian philosopher before he became a Christian. Melito was also a most cultured philosopher.[34]

To say that the study of secular philosophy is evil and spiritually corrupting would be a gross overstatement. Knowing the metaphysical and epistemological presuppositions of those who would stand in opposition to our faith is of tremendous value. However, one must realize the intoxicating effect that these philosophies have had on men throughout the ages. Philosophies help us understand the fascinating world that God gave to His created beings. Our minds allow us to know and understand the vast universe of His created order. However, we need to keep our priorities in line and view Scripture as absolute truth. Knowledge of the inerrant Word of God becomes the lens through which we develop our worldview and philosophical beliefs. Taken in that order and with that priority, the study of secular philosophy can teach Christians a great deal. We can become critical learners and use our minds as a powerful force to overthrow the evil influences of this present age.

A number of Christian universities and seminaries in North America have recognized the need for an integrated approach to understanding philosophy and have developed contemporary Christian apologetics programs with a solid biblical and theological core of instruction. Having established that foundation, they provide training in the use of philosophy as a tool that can be used to defend the faith. Graduates of these programs are entering fields of law, media, medicine, education, and politics to give a defense for the hope that is within them.

Christianity was born with the coming of Christ. His life provided an example of how we ought to live and treat one another. His death and resurrection give us the hope and security of eternal life. The subsequent provision of the Holy Spirit enables us to continue with His mission of reaching the world with the message of hope and eternal life. The written Word of God found in the New Testament books gives us all that we need to provide a rich heritage for our children's faith. By the time the apostles died, they had trained other men to take on the responsibility of fulfilling the Great Commission. That task is now handed to us, and we must be found faithful in continuing the job of evangelizing and strengthening the church for the generations to come.

34. Barclay, *Educational Ideals in the Ancient World*, 209.

FOR FURTHER READING

Castle, E. E. *Ancient Education and Today.* New York: Penguin Books, 1961.

Cole, Luella. *The History of Education: Socrates to Montessori.* New York: Holt, Rhinehart & Winston, 1962.

Eby, Frederick, and Charles F. Arrowood. *The History and Philosophy of Education: Ancient and Medieval.* Englewood Cliffs, N.J.: Prentice-Hall, 1940.

Gwynne-Thomas, E. H. *A Concise History of Education to 1900 a.d.* Kansas City: University of Missouri, 1981.

Hadas, Moses. *Imperial Rome.* New York: Time, 1965.

Jaeger, Werner. *Early Christianity and Greek Paideia.* Cambridge: Belknap Press of Harvard University, 1961.

Laurie, Simon S. *Historical Survey of Pre-Christian Education.* New York: Longmans, Green & Company, 1900.

Reisner, Edward H. *Historical Foundations of Modern Education.* New York: Macmillan, 1928.

Ashland
Community & Technical College
Library

College Drive

82523

What in the World?

➤ Muhammad, a prophet of Islam, is born in Mecca in c. 570.

➤ Charlemagne is crowned emperor of the Romans on Christmas Day in 800.

➤ Vladimair, prince of Russia, is converted to Christianity in 988.

➤ The schism of the Eastern Orthodox Church and the Roman Catholic Church occurs in 1054.

➤ The first crusade is preached by Pope Urban II in 1095.

➤ The University of Cambridge is founded in England in 1209.

➤ The Magna Carta is signed in England in 1215.

➤ Genghis Khan, the Mongol conqueror, dies in 1227.

➤ Thomas Aquinas dies in 1274.

Chapter 5

CHRISTIAN EDUCATION IN THE MIDDLE AGES

(500-1300)

THE MIDDLE AGES WERE A CHALLENGING and difficult time for most of the people living in Europe and the Middle East. After the demise of the Roman government came an era of general turmoil and strife. Regional territories became the target of countless battles as neighboring countries sought to expand their power base and become the dominant force of the world. People were torn between living in the glory days of the classical past and their desire to carve out a more robust future for themselves and their families. Contrary to what many people would have us believe, life was anything but sweet and romantic during this time.

Part of the challenge for us as we look back in hindsight is to establish precisely when the Middle Ages began. The end of the Roman Empire and the beginning of the Middle Ages did not take place at the conclusion of a strategic battle or the birth of a new king. Establishing a date for the beginning of the Middle Ages has been the focus of countless historians over the years. None of them has been successful in identifying a particular event that marked the beginning of the Middle Ages, although that fact has not stopped their trying.

Of the dates that have been suggested as the start of the Middle Ages, some people have drawn their line at the deposition of the Roman emperor

Romulus Augustus in 476. Other scholars cite 395, when Theodosius I died, and with him ended the last reunification of the Roman Empire. The historian Earle Cairns provided one of the most detailed discussions regarding this topic. He wrote,

> Some begin medieval church history in 313 with the grant of freedom of religion. Others begin at the Council of Nicaea in 325. Others prefer 378 because the battle of Adrianople resulted in the migration of the Visigoths into an empire. Still others think that the ancient period of church history ended with the fall of the last Roman emperor in 476. The year 590 is chosen for this work because Gregory I ushered in a new era of power for the church in the west in that year.
>
> The end of the Middle Ages of the history of the church is also debatable. It has been variously set at 1095, the beginning of the era of the Crusades; at 1453, the fall of Constantinople; and at 1648, the peace of Westphalia. The writer (Cairns) has chosen 1517 because the activities of Luther in that year ushered in an entirely different era, in which the emphasis was not so much on the church as an institution as it was on the church constituted as a body of individual believers by a personal faith in the redemptive work of Christ.[1]

Perhaps the reason why it is so difficult to establish precise beginning and ending dates for the Middle Ages is that human history is not as clean and well ordered as some historians would have us believe. The reasons why the term *ages* is used (and always in the plural) is that it seems to be the most accurate way of describing what actually happened during this period of time. One era, specifically classical Greek and Roman, was drawing to a close just as another period was beginning to unfold. However, a significant overlap exists between the various elements that are involved. Political, economic, artistic, philosophical, and religious themes each had their various seasons of strength and weakness. As one element came to fruition and dominance, another might have been waning. Hence, the beginning and the end of the Middle Ages might depend more on the focus of one's exploration than on anything else.

---

1. Earle E. Cairns, *Christianity Through the Centuries: A History of the Christian Church*, 3d ed. (Grand Rapids: Zondervan, 1996), 159.

For example, if one historian prefers to focus his or her efforts on political themes, then his or her start (and end) date will be different than those of another historian who prefers to emphasize religious themes. Obviously, the people involved in the political arena will be different than those in the philosophical arena, so it stands to reason that dates will be different among historians. Suffice it to say for our purposes that we are discussing events that occurred between the fifth and the sixteenth centuries. This broad period can be further divided into the early Middle Ages (fifth to eleventh centuries) and the late Middle Ages (twelfth to sixteenth centuries).

Perhaps more important to our introduction in this chapter is not so much *when* the Middle Ages began as *why* and *how* they began. The real value in studying the Middle Ages is not in establishing a starting or ending date but is found in exploring the differences between what came before and what came after this season of time. The discerning reader will ask, "What was God doing that so affected the world that it ushered in a completely new way of thinking and a new way of relating to the world around us?" "In the gradual submergence of the ancient and the emergence of the medieval civilization there is a remarkable contrast and interplay between old and new institutions and values."[2]

Many people have looked back on this era and referred to it as a dark season of human existence. Some historians refer to this period as the Dark Ages but such a label is not an accurate description of what occurred during those years. The term *dark* is ascribed to this period because it was, in part, a time in which few new discoveries were made in contrast to either the era just completed or the one that was to come. Following after the great classic authors and philosophers of Greece and Rome is a tough act to follow. The Reformation period, which would come later, was replete with gifted thinkers, scientists, and artists. In comparison, the period of time between these epic eras seems to lack a certain luster and resilience. However, this is not to say that no significant contributions came to humankind during these particular years. Indeed, the church came from a period of intense persecution and in the Middle Ages blossomed in a phenomenal season of rapid growth and expansion. Things were anything but dark for the church. Our purpose in this chapter will be to highlight a few of the pertinent discoveries and

---

2. William C. Bark, *Origins of the Medieval World* (Garden City, N.J.: Doubleday, 1960), 5.

demonstrate their contributions to Christian education and the kingdom as a whole.

The Decline of the Roman Empire

The Roman Empire came to be divided into three geographical portions: the Southern portion, populated primarily by Muslims, in North Africa; the Eastern Asiatic portion, known as the Byzantine Empire, remained until 1453; and the Western portion existed in the European papal areas. Each portion had its own ebbs and flows in terms of power and dominance. One can say with some certainty that the Western region began its decline with the defeat of Romulus Augustus, the last Western emperor, in 476, as a result of attacks by German warlords and their organized bands of warriors. The other two portions remained longer.

What contributed to the demise of the vast Roman Empire as a whole has been the subject of conjecture over the years. Although no single event brought down the empire, a combination of events likely took its toll. First, apparently the degree to which it had extended its borders could not be sustained over time because of the expense of its political, military, and civil bureaucracies. Conquering weaker nations proved much easier than maintaining them. As we said in the preceding chapter, many of the empire's elite citizenry opted out of paying taxes, and it fell to the peasants to provide the necessary finances. By the fourth century, little, if any, middle class survived, and because the upper class did not provide any financial base, the lower class was taxed beyond their ability to pay, and the empire went into financial insolvency.

Second, some people have espoused that the Roman Empire fell because of the phenomenal growth of the church. As the church gained in power and influence, the pagan influences of Greek and Roman culture were undermined. A number of historians blame Christianity for the decline of the empire because the church provided a moral and ethical standard by which Roman civilization could be judged. Greek and Roman art, poetry, philosophy, and literature became the target of the church's purification, resulting in the loss of such cultural essentials.

A third hypothesis for the decline of the empire lies in the inability of Rome to defend its extensive borders. At some point, the borders expanded beyond Rome's ability to sustain them, and neighboring countries that had withstood the onslaughts of the Roman army found Rome's weakness; Rome's overextended reach could no longer be sustained, and bordering countries seized their opportunity to march on a share of the empire closest to their land. As we said, probably no one factor brought down so great an empire. However, the combination of these and perhaps other factors certainly had their cumulative effect.

One unfortunate outcome of Rome's demise was the disintegration of education and scholarship. Most public and many private educational institutions came to an abrupt halt in terms of expansion and growth. Many schools lost their support once Rome was brought to an end. Teachers who had come to depend on their financial support from Rome lost their jobs and were forced to look for other means of employment. Libraries were unable to sustain themselves and had to close. Art museums, gymnasiums, and other forms of cultural influence paid a heavy toll as a result of the empire's decline. Schools that were associated with a church or group of churches survived. In fact, some schools began to flourish during this period. Soon, the Roman Catholic Church began to realize that educational institutions could have a profound influence on their own stability and long-term growth. More will be said of this later in the chapter.

THE RISE OF FEUDALISM

As the three portions of the empire collapsed, various entities took control of what remained. The Muslims held firm control over the countries around the Mediterranean, especially North Africa. They were relentless in their desire to seize additional land from the eastern and western leaders. The eastern portion had its own distractions, wresting control from the Catholic Church to form the Greek Orthodox Church. With the successful German warlords moving into the western portion, the empire was fragmented beyond repair. "The decline of city life and trade after the fall of the Roman Empire forced people back to the land to make a living. Feudalism had precedents both in Roman and German customs concerning the holding of land and service. These and other chaotic conditions of the ninth century encouraged the rise of the feudalistic way of life in western Europe. It put public power into private hands."[3]

---

3. Cairns, *Christianity Through the Centuries*, 184.

Feudalism divided society into distinct classes of people. At the top of the social structure was the king and his *nobility*. Second, were the *protectors*, who comprised the feudal knights with the privilege of land ownership in exchange for their services. Third were the *producers*, the serfs of the manors, who had to work the land to survive. Last were the *prayers*, or the priestly class of clergy, who held spiritual authority over all within their reach. Each individual knew his rightful place in society and followed a strict allegiance to his master while at the same time governing those under his control. An exceptionally high level of authority existed in this social hierarchy.[4]

What Do You Mean?

Abbot	Clergyman who supervised land on behalf of the church.
Feudal lords	Those who owned several manors.
Fief	That which generated income for the lord (e.g., mill or toll bridge).
King	At the top of the social pyramid; the only one who could own land.
Knight	Those who fought to protect their vassal or lord.
Magna Carta	Feudal contract between King John and his vassals.
Manor	An area of land that could support an armed knight.
Monk	Clergyman who lived in a monastery according to strict rules.
Serf	Those who had to work the land and serve the lord.
Serfdom	Being destined to serve a lord for as long as you lived.
Vassal	Those who resided at the top of the social pyramid.

Opinions differ concerning what life was like under feudalism. Modern media would have us believe that it was filled with chivalry and jousting competitions. Some people have sought to rewrite history for their own purposes. William Bark, a twentieth-century medieval historian, writes, "Some of the romantics . . . tended to view the Middle Ages only through pleasantly tinted glasses. They too found what they looked for, the picturesque pag-

---

4. Ibid., 186.

eant, knights in shining armor on coal-black steeds, ladies of high station on milk-white palfreys, castles, tournaments, maidens in distress, jolly priests and monks, quaint peasants, and a cruel Saracen or two."[5] Those who take a serious and more historically accurate look at the period known as feudalism, however, paint a much more stark picture of life. It was, for all intents and purposes, a relatively bleak and desperate time unless you were fortunate enough to know the right person who would appoint you to become the lord of a manor or the priest over a church.

Although the system of feudalism began with clearly defined boundaries between landowners and their areas of jurisdiction, before long, infighting and greed raised their ugly heads. Soon vassals wanted more power and authority, which was achieved only by controlling larger portions of land. Knights were sent in marauding parties to undermine and kill those in neighboring fiefs. In time, the feudal system was undermined by political and economic infighting.

Education in the Age of Chivalry

Children of nobility needed an education if they were going to be prepared for the future. Those children needed to learn the various methods of government, land management, military techniques of battle, etc. In all, four basic stages of education existed during the Middle Ages.

During the first six years of the boy's life (women were not educated in this period of history), he remained at home and learned what he could from his parents. Second, at the age of seven, the young lad was referred to as a *page,* and he served in the manor house of his lord, in the castle of the great lord, or in the court of the king. The royal lady supervised the early education of the child by teaching him such subjects as religion, music, poetry, manners and social etiquette, rules of honor, basic reading and writing skills, Latin, and the vernacular. The gentleman of the house taught him basic skills of personal defense such as boxing, wrestling, gymnastics, and some forms of early military training.

The third stage began at the age of fourteen, when the young man was

---

5. Bark, *Origins of the Medieval World,* 8.

called a *squire*. His jobs included setting the table for his lord, doing general work around the house, grooming the horses and performing other responsibilities of animal husbandry, cleaning his lord's shield and sword, and accompanying his lord at the various tournaments or in battle. He also prepared himself for fighting in battle one day by learning to fence, hunt, swim, and joust. He also learned falconry. In addition to such physical activities, he developed his mind through the study of advanced music, and by singing and playing chess.

Finally, at age twenty-one and when he had advanced through the previous stages of educational training, he could attain to the noble title of *knight*. The initiation into knighthood took place at a church, castle, or palace, where he placed his sword on the altar for a night while he devoted himself to prayer and fasting. He vowed his allegiance to the church, his lord the king, his superiors, his fair lady, and honor and gallantry itself. He was touched on each shoulder with his sword and declared to be a knight. He then received the symbols of his knighthood, accepting a gold chain, sword belt, sword, and spurs.[6]

In the thirteenth century, knights wore suits of armor made of chain mail (a mesh of small ringlets) to prevent injury from arrows, lances, and small arms. In the fourteenth century, chain mail was replaced with plate armor suits that were constructed such as to protect the knight from weapons such as the crossbow or the mallet. These suits were made of large pieces of hammered steel. This plate armor offered excellent protection, but it was very difficult to wear and eventually grew expensive to produce (some suits of armor cost as much as a small farm). Eventually, full dress armor became impractical to use in battle.[7]

One of the reasons we discuss feudalism is because it had such a detrimental influence on the church. "During the Feudal Age, Christianity under-

6. Tony Lane, *Harper's Concise Book of Christian Faith* (Cambridge, Mass.: Harper, 1984), 81-82; and also Hugh Wamble, *History of Christian Thought CH0212* (Nashville: Seminary Education Extension Department of Southern Baptist Seminaries, 1969), 163; as cited in James E. Reed and Ronnie Prevost, *A History of Christian Education* (Nashville: Broadman & Holman, 1993), 125.

7. "World of Wonder: Exploring the Realms of History, Science, Nature, and Technology: Knights of the Middle Ages," *The Press Enterprise: Orange County Register,* 20 September 2002, sec. B, p. 8.

went so many significant developments from its early medieval character that it seemed in some respects to be almost a new religion."[8] Large pieces of land were held by the church in western Europe. Much of this land was given to the church by pious or penitent men who were seeking atonement for their sins. Because only the church could offer such benefits, they soon found ways to extract larger and larger portions of land from the populace. The challenge was in finding worthy individuals who could manage these resources such as to provide a healthy return on the investment for the church. The church could not help but be heavily influenced by the feudal system of land management. Abbots and bishops became the beneficiaries of large land grants from the church. As feudal lords, they were vulnerable to marauding knights, so they, too, employed vassal knights who could protect the land on behalf of the church.

This feudalization of the church's land had two damaging effects. First, those who were placed in charge of the land as abbots and bishops were not always spiritually guided men. Sometimes they were ruthless scoundrels with little concern for anything other than their own financial gain and power. Second, the ecclesiastical vassal faced the problem of divided interests between the spiritual affairs of the church and the secular affairs of the land. Should his allegiance be to the temporal lord, to whom he owed significant sums of money in taxes and fees, or should his allegiance be to the pope, who ultimately determined his authority and controlled his destiny? Such divided interests made for anything but a healthful spiritual climate for himself or those under his spiritual shepherding.[9]

THE CHURCH DIVIDED

By the beginning of the fourth century, Christianity had become the dominant religion of the land. The Emperor Galerius's edict of tolerance in 311 was an admission that Christianity had become too large a religion to be ignored or persecuted out of existence. By a series of further decrees between 380 and 392, Christianity was viewed as the only lawfully recognized faith of the Roman Empire. But Christianity had hardly emerged as victorious over its rivals than dissatisfaction from within threatened to bring it

---

8. Edward Burns, *Western Civilizations: Their History and Their Culture* (New York: Norton, 1949), 282.

9. Cairns, *Christianity Through the Centuries*, 187.

down.[10] Arguments over theological interpretation and philosophical distinctives soon undermined her expansion. The church in the West disagreed with the church in the East over important issues such as the deity of Christ; the role of the Holy Spirit in the Trinity; the importance of Mary, Jesus' earthly mother, the authority of those in the priesthood; the proper use of the sacraments; and other critical doctrinal issues.

Early in the fourth century, Emperor Constantine the Great came to power in Rome after having succeeded Emperor Diocletian. He became a Christian himself and took a bold move by declaring in the Edict of Milan (A.D. 313) that Christians were free to worship without persecution. This declaration of religious tolerance also provided for Christians who had been the recipient of Rome's harsh persecution to receive just and fair compensation for their losses. As a result of his taking such a bold move, his popularity was enormous. Around 330, he decided to abandon Rome and settle in a remote location in what is now known as Istanbul, Turkey. The effect was to divide the political kingdom between the East and the West, but it would also have a lasting impact by dividing the church's sphere of influence.

Eventually, the church split, and the Roman Catholic Church maintained its ecclesiastical headquarters under the leadership of the pope in the city of Rome. The Greek Orthodox Church stood firm under the leadership of the patriarch of the church in the city of Constantinople. The Western church and the Eastern church were constantly at odds over differences in theology and praxis. For more than eleven hundred years, Byzantium, as it was also known, stood as the capital of the Eastern Roman Empire and the Greek Orthodox Church until the Ottoman Turks conquered the city in 1453.

THE CONDITION OF THE CLERGY

During the second and third centuries, the church experienced significant growth. This in turn required a more formalized clergy to establish what was orthodox and acceptable doctrine and what was aberrant belief. During this period, some ecclesiastical structure and order was needed to manage the affairs of church districts.

> As the number of congregations multiplied, and as the official religion of Rome, distinctions of rank among the bishops themselves

---

10. Burns, *Western Civilizations,* 200.

began to appear. Those who had their headquarters in the larger cities came to be called metropolitans, with authority over the clergy of an entire province. In the fourth century the still higher dignity of the patriarch was created to designate those bishops who ruled over the oldest and largest of Christian communities—such as Rome, Constantinople, Antioch, and Alexandria with their surrounding districts. Thus the Christian clergy by A.D. 40 had come to embrace a definite hierarchy of patriarchs, metropolitans, bishops, and priests.[11]

The church emphasis began a slow transformation from being about a personal faith held by someone who desired an intimate relationship with his or her creator God to a corporate faith that was marred by multiple layers of structural hierarchy. In time, the clergy grew distant from God. Immersed in concern for political and economic control over land and the people who lived there, the clergy began to make appointments to church leadership on the basis of expediency rather than spiritual qualifications. The need for increased economic support made the church adopt nonbiblical means of fund-raising. This led to charges of corruption and fraud.

> Charges centered on the "sale of grace," whereby the church and the Papacy received a large income in return for such unauthorized practices as the appointment to church offices made in return for a fee (simony), expense accounts of papal inspectors levied upon local churches (procurations), permission sold in advance to do things ordinarily prohibited by the church (dispensations), exorbitant legal fees, and, above all, the sale of indulgences.[12]

Over the period of the Middle Ages, the church was experiencing a paradoxical metamorphosis. On one hand, the church was flourishing with unprecedented growth and expansion. Multiple layers of ecclesiastical management provided the church with the ability to plan strategically its expansion to countries through the world. The Great Commission seemed to be within reach, and the church was keen to take advantage of every

---

11. Ibid., 203.
12. R. Freeman Butts, *A Cultural History of Education* (New York: McGraw Hill, 1947), 204.

opportunity to present the gospel to unreached peoples. However, on the other hand, the means by which the church often employed its evangelistic efforts did not justify the ends. Granting absolution from sin with no call to repentance but merely for financial gain might have proved effective for fund-raising purposes, but from a biblical or theological point of view it was a complete disaster. To make matters worse, some church missionaries who traveled to foreign countries coerced pagans to convert to Christianity through threat of bodily harm. It was felt that the end (converting pagan souls to the kingdom of Christ) was worth whatever means (physical coercion and control) was necessary. After all, it was thought, the new converts would thank them one day in heaven for helping them see the error of their earthly ways.

ASCETICISM AND THE MONASTIC SCHOOLS

A disillusionment of sorts regarding the role of the clergy and their level of spiritual formation brought an increased desire on the part of some church leaders to distance themselves from many of the excessive practices of the illiterate clergy and demonstrate a sincere faith, unstained by the world (James 1:27). Following the example of Jesus to retreat into the desert wilderness for prolonged periods of solitude and fasting, these men dedicated themselves to celibacy (again because of the example set by Jesus) and lived a life of poverty and physical denial. This form of asceticism continued to grow in popularity among religious devotees and eventually led the way for a movement known as monasticism. The earliest ascetics were hermits who chose to live in isolation far removed in the Eastern desert. Others who were not so committed to that degree of isolation yet still valued a more reclusive lifestyle gathered and formed associations, known as monasteries. Many of these monasteries developed schools for training and educating the priests.

One of the first of these desert fathers was St. Basil, to whom we referred in the previous chapter. Although it is widely held that Anthony the Egyptian (251–356) was the founder of Eastern monasticism, the leader of Western monasticism was Benedict of Nursia (c. 480–550). St. Benedict established a rigid set of standards that a devotee must follow. Trying to steer away from some of the excesses of those who tortured themselves in an attempt to gain God's favor, the Benedictine order obligated its followers to strict poverty, obedience, hard physical labor, and long hours of practicing spiritual disciplines.

The monastic life appealed to some people for the wrong reasons. Instead of a love for God and a desire to serve Him, some men were attracted to it because it seemed to be a life of ease and relative comfort. Lounging in a library in a remote forest castle while praying and reflecting on the meaning of life seemed like a great way to live. The truth, however, was that the life of most monks who resided in a monastery was anything but easy. It was often associated with harsh manual labor, long hours of Bible reading, vesper services, and community service. St. Benedict, a sixth-century monastic leader, drew up a set of guidelines by which a monastery was to be governed. It became the rule for governance of monastic societies throughout the Middle Ages. They are recorded in this chapter for your review.

Monastic Guidelines for Service

The qualities necessary for an abbot. The abbot who is worthy to rule over a monastery ought always to bear in mind by what name he is called and to justify by his life his title of superior. . . . The abbot should know that the shepherd will have to bear the blame if the Master finds anything wrong with the flock. . . . The freeman is not to be preferred to the one who comes into the monastery out of servitude, unless there be some other good reason. . . . For whether slave or free, we are all one in Christ [Gal. 3:28] and bear the same yoke of servitude to the one Lord, for there is no respect of persons with God [Rom. 2:11]. . . . Therefore, the abbot should have the same love toward all and should subject all to the same discipline according to their respective merits. . . .

Above all, the abbot should not be too zealous in the acquisition of earthly, transitory, mortal gods, forgetting and neglecting the care of the souls committed to his charge, but he should always remember that he has undertaken the government of souls of whose welfare he must render account. . . .

Taking counsel with the brethren. Whenever important matters come up in the monastery, the abbot should call together the whole congregation [that is, all the monks], and tell them what is under consideration. After hearing the advice of the brothers, he should reflect upon it and then do what seems best to him. . . .

Humility. Brethren, the Holy Scripture saith: "And whosoever shall exalt himself shall be abased; and he that shall humble himself shall be exalted" [Matt. 23:12]. . . .

Now the first step of humility is this, to escape destruction by keeping ever before one's eyes the fear of the Lord, to remember always the commands of the Lord. . . .

The second step of humility is this, that a man should not delight in doing his own will and desires, but should imitate the Lord. . . .

The third step of humility is this, that a man be subject to his superior in all obedience for the love of God, imitating the Lord. . . .

The fourth step of humility is this, that a man endure all the hard and unpleasant things and even undeserved injuries that come in the course of his service, without wearying or withdrawing his neck from the yoke. . . .

The sixth step of humility is this, that the monk should be contented with any lowly or hard condition in which he may be placed, and should always look upon himself as an unworthy laborer, not fitted to do what is intrusted to him. . . .

The seventh step of humility is this, that he should not only say, but should really believe in his heart that he is the lowest and most worthless of all men. . . .

The eleventh step of humility is this, that the monk, when he speaks, should do so slowly and without laughter, softly and gravely, using few words and reasonable, and that perfect love of God which casteth out all fear [1 John 4:18]. . . .

Divine worship at night [vigils]. During the winter, that is, from the first of November to Easter, the monks should rise at the eighth hour of the night; a reasonable arrangement, since by that time the monks will have rested a little more than half the night and will have digested their food. . . .

How the monks should sleep. The monks shall sleep separately in individual beds, and the abbot shall assign them their beds according to their conduct. If possible all the monks shall sleep in the same dormitory, but if their number is too large to admit of this, they are to be divided into tens or twenties and placed under the control of some of the older monks. . . .

Monks should not have personal property. The sin of owning private property should be entirely eradicated from the monastery. No one shall presume to give or receive anything except by the order of the abbot; no one shall possess anything of his own, books, paper, pens, or anything else. . . .

The weekly service in the kitchen. The brothers shall serve in their turn in the kitchen, no one being excused, except for illness or because occupied in work of greater importance.

The weekly reader. There should always be reading during the common meal, but it shall not be left to chance, so that anyone may take up the book and read. On Sunday one of the brothers shall be appointed to read during the following week. . . .

The amount of food. Two cooked dishes, served either at the sixth or the ninth hour, should be sufficient for the daily sustenance. We allow two because of differences in taste, so that those who do not eat one may satisfy their hunger with the other, but two shall suffice for all the brothers, unless it is possible to obtain fruit or fresh vegetables, which may be served as a third. . . .

The amount of drink. A half-measure of wine a day is enough for anyone, making due allowance, of course, for the needs of the sick. . . .

The daily labor of the monks. Idleness is the great enemy of the soul, therefore the monks should always be occupied, either in manual labor or in holy reading. The hours for these occupations should be arranged according to the seasons. . . .

The ordination of the abbot. The election of the abbot shall be decided by the whole congregation or by that part of it, however small, which is of "the wiser and better counsel." . . . But if the whole congregation should agree to choose one simply because they know that he will wink at their vices, and the character of this abbot is discovered by the bishop of the diocese or by the abbots and Christian men of the neighborhood, they shall refuse their consent to the choice and shall interfere to set a better ruler over the house of God.[13]

Such a life might seem strange to us as we look back at these religious leaders who chose to live in relative isolation from the world, but perhaps it would be helpful to try to understand just what motivated them to accept voluntarily such harsh living conditions. Edward Burns states the reasons for its popularity as being fivefold.

1. The desire of many pious Christians to protest against increasing worldliness of the church. The farther they might go to the opposite

---

13. W. T. Jones, *A History of Western Philosophy: The Medieval Mind,* 2d ed. (New York: Harcourt Brace Jovanovich, 1969), 146–47.

extreme of the luxurious lives of some of the clergy, for example, the more effective that protest would become.

2. The choice of morbid self-torture as a substitute for martyrdom. With the abandonment of persecution by the Romans, all chances of winning a crown of glory in heaven by undergoing death for the faith were eliminated. But the desire to give evidence of one's religious ardor by self-abasement and suffering was still present and demanded an outlet.

3. The desire of some Christians who were sincerely devoted to the faith to set an example of exalted piety and unselfishness as an inspiration to their weaker brethren. Even though most men should fail to attain the ideal, the general level of morality and piety would be raised.

4. The influence of the Oriental religions, especially Gnosticism and Manicheism, with their exaggerated spiritualism, contempt for this world, and degradation of the body.

5. The influence of pessimistic and defeatist philosophies, such as Cynicism and Neo-Platonism. The former taught contempt for society and exalted the life of the recluse as an ideal. The Neo-Platonists affirmed that matter was evil and preached what amounted to the denial of life through mystical absorption into the divine.[14]

At first, the curriculum of education in a monastery was designed to train and equip young men for the priesthood. Eventually, it was broadened to include nonvocationally oriented instruction. The focus of education was religious instruction in the Word of God and in prayer, fasting, and meditation. The men gathered together several times a day for vesper services in which they would read Scriptures, sing chants, and listen to the exposition of the Word from the monastery's spiritual director. The language of instruction was Latin, and in this way they showed their allegiance to the Western church and the pope. Beyond this was instruction in the seven liberal arts (i.e., grammar, rhetoric, dialectic, arithmetic, geometry, music, and astronomy), chief among them being the study of grammar. The finest monastery schools included those of Tours in France, Fulda in Germany, Jarrow in Northern England, Monte Cassino in Italy, Iona in Scotland, and Clonmacnois in England. The monastic schools dominated the educational system of Europe from the sixth to the eleventh centuries.[15]

---

14. Butts, *Cultural History of Education,* 204.
15. Kenneth O. Gangel and Warren S. Benson, *Christian Education: Its History and Philosophy* (Chicago: Moody, 1983), 108.

THE CRUSADES

The portion of the former Roman Empire in North Africa that was dominated by Muslims began to expand. They began an eastern expansion and in the seventh century they conquered Syria and Palestine. This created a significant threat to believers in the Western church because the papacy encouraged those who sought penance for their sins to go on a religious pilgrimage to the Holy City, Jerusalem. By going there, they would receive a spiritual blessing and assurances of a shortened stay in purgatory. Those who made this pilgrimage began facing increased mistreatment and even persecution by the Muslims. When Jerusalem fell to the Seljuk Turks in 1071, the Byzantine church appealed to the Western church leadership for help. With the Muslims in control of Christianity's holy sites, trade and communication with the West was stifled. This put an economic strain on the Western church, and soon the church was forced to act. Something had to be done to remove the Muslims from controlling Palestine. What was needed was an army to force them out. However, such an army would cost a small fortune, and the church could not afford to finance such an expedition. Instead, the church would recruit volunteers to go and fight by promising them spiritual blessings and eternal rewards. Volunteers came by the thousands for an opportunity to serve God thus.

Muhammad and the Birth of Islam

The prophet Muhammad was born in Mecca around A.D. 570. We know very little about his early life, but we do know that in midlife (A.D. 610) he experienced a series of revelations from the angel Gabriel. Soon afterward, he began preaching publicly. The people of Mecca were pagans and they did not like Muhammad's harsh criticisms of their practices; in 622, he and his family emigrated to Medina. This move is called the *hijra* (or *Hegira*) and marks year 1 of the Islamic calendar.

Muhammad was much more successful at Medina. It was here that he began preaching that his followers were commanded by God to convert or else conquer the neighboring tribes. Expansion followed rapidly, and in 630 they had conquered Mecca. Muhammad himself died in 632.

> He was recognized by his followers to be what he claimed to be: the final and true prophet, following in a direct tradition from Abraham, Moses, and Jesus. We have nothing from Muhammad's hand. The sacred book of Islam, the Koran *(Quran)*, was written down in final form in 651 and 652, by his followers who knew him directly and intimately.[16]

In 1095, Pope Urban II launched the first of what would be eight separate crusades to free the holy lands from Muslim domination. In this first assault, the army was comprised mostly of peasants from France, Hungry, Germany, and the Balkans. Not being trained in military methods, they were no match for the well-equipped defenders. When trained reinforcements arrived from France, Belgium, and Italy in 1097, they eventually achieved success and captured Jerusalem in 1099. However, its freedom would be short-lived because not long afterward the Muslims regrouped and retook the land. This process of losing and retaking the land would continue for several hundred years. During those years, wave after wave of reinforcements came by land and sea in an attempt to free the Holy City and its priceless sites. Hundreds of thousands of lives were lost as Christians and Muslims fought each other for control of this sacred land.

Perhaps the most noteworthy of the Crusades was one motivated by a sermon preached by a twelve-year-old boy named Stephen of Cloyes. This French shepherd was responsible for inciting more than thirty thousand French children, many of them younger than himself, to join in the quest to free the Holy Land. They marched through France on their way to the Mediterranean to board ships heading east. Because travel was often perilous and hard, many of them died from hunger and disease. For those who did manage to survive the journey, they were sold into slavery by merchants once the ships landed in Algiers. Although thirty thousand departed France on this crusade, only one child returned home in 1230 to report what had happened along the way. What a waste of an entire generation of French children!

---

16. E. L. Skip Knox, "The Crusades," Boise State University, 1998, (sknox@bsumail. idbsu.edu), 2.

The Children's Crusade

The "Crusade" was preached in France by a peasant boy named Stephen from a village near Vendome. In Germany, a boy named Nicholas from Cologne started the movement. The sorry business was summarized by a chronicler in these terms:

In this year occurred an outstanding thing and one much to be marveled at, for it is unheard of throughout the ages. About the time of Easter and Pentecost, without anyone having preached or called for it and prompted by I know not what spirit, many thousands of boys, ranging in age from six years to full maturity, left the plows or carts which they were driving, the flocks which they were pasturing, and anything else which they were doing. This they did despite the wishes of their parents, relatives, and friends who sought to make them draw back. Suddenly one ran after another to take the cross. Thus, by groups of twenty, or fifty, or a hundred, they put up banners and began to journey to Jerusalem. They were asked by many people on whose advice or at whose urging they had set out upon this path. They were asked especially since only a few years ago many kings, a great many dukes, and innumerable people in powerful companies had gone there and had returned with the business unfinished. The present groups, moreover, were still of tender years and were neither strong enough nor powerful enough to do anything. Everyone, therefore, accounted them foolish and imprudent for trying to do this. They briefly replied that they were equal to the Divine will in this matter and that, whatever God might wish to do with them, they would accept it willingly and with humble spirit. They thus made some little progress on their journey. Some were turned back at Metz, others at Piacenza, and others even at Rome. Still others got to Marseilles, but whether they crossed to the Holy Land or what their end was is uncertain. One thing is sure: that of the many thousands who rose up, only very few returned.[17]

17. James Brundage, trans., *Chronica Regiae Coloniensis Continuatio prima*, s.a.1213, MGH SS XXIV 17-18, *The Crusades: A Documentary History* (Milwaukee: Marquette University Press, 1962), 213; as cited in The Internet Medieval Sourcebook, ed. Paul Halsall, Fordham University Center for Medieval Studies. Web site URL: http://www.fordham.edu/halsall/sbook.html.

One of the detrimental effects of the Crusades was an increasing distrust between the church in the West (Rome) and the church in the East (Constantinople). Vast resources were poured into these eight campaigns by both churches, and it drained each of necessary funds. In addition, the location of the Eastern church to the borders of the Muslim fighters made it a likely target of their incursions. As a result, the capital Constantinople fell in 1453.

The Crusades in Review—Important Dates

Crusade	Date	Event
1	1095–1101	Pope Urban II encourages the First Crusade. It fails initially, but an organized army of knights takes Jerusalem in 1099.
2	1147–49	The Second Crusade is initiated.
3	1189–92	The Third Crusade forms and fails.
4	1202–04	The Fourth Crusade begins and successfully takes Jerusalem.
5	1217–21	The Fifth Crusade is undertaken.
6	1228–29	The Sixth Crusade is undertaken.
7	1248–54	The Seventh Crusade is led by King Louis IX.
8	1270	The Eighth Crusade ends. Knights resume life at home, which includes tournaments and court life.
	1346–51	The Black Death kills one-fourth of the population of Europe.
	1453	The Ottoman Turks take Constantinople, cutting off trade routes to the Far East.

It is hard to look back at this time and see many positive benefits that came from the Crusades. One of the most significant positive effects was an increase in trade between the regions around Palestine and Western Europe. "They created a constant demand for transportation of men and supplies, built up themselves a great carrying trade, improved the art of navigation, opened new markets, taught the use of new commodities, created new needs, made known new routes and new peoples with whom to trade, stimulated exploration, and in a hundred ways which cannot be mentioned introduced a new commercial age whose character and results must be examined in detail hereafter."[18]

SCHOLASTICISM AND THE DEVELOPMENT OF UNIVERSITIES

During the late Middle Ages, an attitude developed even among church leaders for the need to study theology. Theology was considered to be the lens through which education would be viewed. The problem was that so few clergymen were trained in the study of theology. Realizing that the survival of the church depended on an educated clergy, the cathedral and monastic schools that developed during the early Middle Ages grew into more rigorous academic institutions. Curriculum was broadened, and intellectually trained faculty were secured. "The function and balance of the Roman Catholic system had been worked out. Bishops, abbots, and the Pope himself were promoting and fostering scholarship and schools. Under that fostering care two of the most important developments in the intellectual history of the western world were soon to take place: the intellectual revival of the twelfth century and the founding of European universities."[19]

It was as though the intellectual mind of Europe had reawakened from a deep slumber. A renewed interest in Greek and Latin studies came to the forefront of education. "At a time when a European scholar could assemble a library of not more than 50 books, educated Arabs had 500 or more; one library was known to have contained 600,000 books."[20] The contributions of

---

18. George B. Adams, *Civilization During the Middle Ages* (New York: Scribner's, 1922), 269.
19. Frederick Eby and Charles F. Arrowood, *The History and Philosophy of Education: Ancient and Medieval* (Englewood Cliffs, N.J.: Prentice-Hall, 1940), 713.
20. K. Schmidt, *Geschichte der Pädagogik*, P. Schettler, 4 vols. (1873–76), 2:111–3; as cited in Luella Cole, *A History of Education: Socrates to Montessori* (New York: Holt, Rinehart & Winston, 1962), 151.

Arab scholarship and culture blended well with the cosmopolitan makeup of many European cities, especially in Spain, to where many of the Arabs had emigrated. The increased trade and commerce that came about after the Crusades contributed a great deal to the free flow of intellectual reasoning as well. This renaissance of thinking began to permeate European minds.

Scholasticism was as much about helping the believer become a more critically thinking individual as it was about simply teaching the curriculum of the seven liberal arts. The end result of scholasticism was a mature believer who employed the mind to come to a reasonable and rational faith. It was a blending of theology and philosophy such as to make a reasonable faith.

> Educationally, the purpose of Scholasticism was to develop the ability to organize beliefs into a logical system and the power to set forth and defend such systems against all arguments brought in opposition to them. Along with this, there was avoidance of developing an attitude critical of the basic principles established by recognized authority. Thus, scholastic education aimed at systematization of knowledge, thereby giving it, incidentally, scientific form. However, to Scholasticism, knowledge was almost entirely theological and philosophical in nature, so its prized form was deductive, not inductive, logic. A third phase of the educational purpose of Scholasticism was to give the individual mastery of this knowledge systemized into a logical whole in the form of propositions and syllogisms.[21]

One of the most brilliant and remarkable leaders of this renewed renaissance was Peter Abelard (1079-1142) from the University of Notre Dame in Paris and also the collegiate church of St. Geneviève. "Many of his opinions were declared heretical by the ecclesiastical authorities. This fact, combined with his boldness in theological controversy, the title of one of his books, *Yes and No,* and a phrase of his 'By doubting we are led to enquire; by enquiry we perceive the truth,' long gave color to the theory that he was a spokesman of science and the father of liberal studies."[22]

The technique of scholasticism involved the ability to argue with another individual, usually in a public forum. Often, one master challenged another

---

21. Charles B. Eavey, *History of Christian Education* (Chicago: Moody, 1964), 109.
22. Ibid., 746.

to a debate, and they argued between themselves with one verbal exchange after another until one of them seemed to have a more sound reasoning than the other. Abelard had gained at a young age a reputation as the undisputed prince of dialectic skill. This ability to use logic and reason was a powerful weapon in the church toward the end of the Middle Ages.

> Logic was, however, a sword that cut in two directions. It gave the pious Christian a means of proving his faith—not in the modern sense of empirical proof but in the same sense as proving a proposition in geometry—but it gave the heretic a means for attacking the church much more effectively than ever before because the weapon was better. The desire to train scholars to defend the faith with reason and to refute doubt was one basic cause for the development of higher education especially at the University of Paris.[23]

However, just as his ability to debate forcefully a fellow scholar had been one of Abelard's most powerful weapons, it also became the lightening rod for opposition against him. Abelard's ability to humiliate his adversaries publicly brought him great disdain among the scholarly elite of Paris. His popularity as an instructor motivated students from all over the city and neighboring countryside to seek out his instruction. This enraged his fellow teachers because they lost the income that their departing students had formerly brought them. These colleagues formed a strong alliance and eventually forced him out of the public arena of instruction. He withdrew from teaching at the University of Paris and became a monk, lived in a monastery, and sought a quieter existence. His life was marred by turmoil, disappointment, and hardship. It was an unfortunate ending for so brilliant an educator.[24]

Another exceptional educator during this period of scholasticism was Thomas Aquinas (1225-74). Viewed as the greatest theologian and philosopher of the Middle Ages, he was born in Roccasecca in southern Italy. He began his studies at the age of fourteen, enrolling in the University of Naples, where he studied the seven liberal arts. He completed this training at the age of eighteen. A year later, he declared his intention of joining the Dominican order, which was famous for its emphasis on Catholic theology and

---

23. Luella Cole, *A History of Education: Socrates to Montessori* (New York: Holt, Rinehart & Winston, 1962), 159.
24. Ibid., 151-76.

scholarship. His family, however, refused to allow him to do this because joining the Dominican order would have prevented his assuming control over the family's estate upon the death of his parents. His mother and brothers arranged to kidnap him and held him in the family's castle at Roccasecca for one year. Realizing the futility of holding him against his will and being unable to change his mind, however, they granted him his freedom and he soon joined the Dominican order.

He was sent to the monastery of the Holy Cross in Cologne, Germany, where he studied theology under the tutelage of Albert Magnus, the only academic scholar ever to be awarded the title "the Great." Magnus and Aquinas had the distinct advantage of being able to study Aristotle from recently translated manuscripts that had been in the possession of Arab scholars. Together, they sought to reconcile the philosophical tenets of Aristotle with theology. Aquinas believed that all truth was God's truth, and if it seemed unreasonable to integrate biblical teaching with philosophy, then the fault must lie in man's ability to understand clearly what God intended in His Word. Faith was always to be viewed as superior to reason.

Aquinas began his teaching career at the age of twenty-seven at the pre-eminent theological institution of Europe, the University of Paris. As an instructor, he lectured on the subject of dogmatic theology, a course that highlighted the basic doctrines of Scripture. Using the prevailing instructional methodology of the day, Aquinas began the class by espousing a particular theological truth and then argued rationally to a conclusion based upon that truth. He then proceeded to review the lesson by presenting all of the reasons for and against a particular perspective. His teaching was heavily lecture driven, and students were required to take copious notes throughout the presentation.[25]

History books have described Thomas Aquinas as being either a theologian or a philosopher, depending on the particular perspective of the historian. In reality, he was both. Well trained in both academic disciplines, he had a remarkable ability to integrate the two subjects with skillful craft. In one of his books, *De Magistro*, he developed a theory of education that is worthy of citing here because it clearly demonstrates the manner in which he was able to see the blending of these two important fields.

---

25. Gerald L. Gutek, *Historical and Philosophical Foundations of Education: A Biographical Introduction* (Upper Saddle River, N.J.: Merrill Prentice-Hall, 2001), 61.

Thomas Aquinas in the Classroom

One of his principles was that students learned not only by instruction but by the discovery of knowledge through their own senses and powers of reasoning. Teacher and student are like doctor and patient. A teacher can no more instill his own knowledge in his student than a doctor can transmit his own good health to his ailing patient. The teacher's role is to aid the student in the acquisition of knowledge. Thomas trusted the power of human intellect and considered its development a way to glorify its Creator.

Teachers must not only know their material but be able to communicate it in simple terms, building a bridge between what the student already knows and what he needs to learn. Curriculum should begin with what is material before advancing to what is abstract. Start with what can be plainly seen.

Thomas maintained that teachers should be involved in the lives of their students as well as their own scholarly pursuits. Despite Thomas's urging to lead a life that was both active and scholarly, scholasticism tended to overemphasize intellectualism. Critics declared that debate and discussion had little to do with everyday life. By separating informal schooling that contributed to character formation from more formal training, Thomas managed to drive a wedge between the two.[26]

1. Education, like life itself, is purposeful; it is a means to an end. Human beings' ultimate destiny is the beatific vision of God, and education should contribute to realizing that goal.
2. Reality exhibits two dimensions, one spiritual and one physical. Education relates to both dimensions of human nature: the soul and the body. It should prepare the human being for what needs to be done on Earth and what will contribute to the salvation of the soul.
3. Reality—both supernatural and natural—is hierarchically structured as is society, both secular and religious. Because not all things are equal, education, especially areas of study receiving the greatest priority.[27]

---

26. Robert J. Choun, *The Evangelical Dictionary of Christian Education*, ed. Michael J. Anthony (Grand Rapids: Baker, 2001), s.v. "Thomas Aquinas."
27. Ibid.

Neo-Thomism, as his educational philosophy is called today, has been highly instrumental in shaping the way in which we teach in Christian educational institutions today. Rather than seeing biblical instruction as completely separate and distant from the way we live, Aquinas would have us find ways to bring theology (biblical teaching) together with the practice of daily living. This blending of theory and practice was a valuable contribution of Aquinas.

In addition to this educational emphasis of Aquinas, he was helpful in articulating the interrelationship between faith and reason. His approach to the integration of faith (theology) and reason (philosophy) has been highly instrumental in combating the forces of anti-intellectualism prevalent in many evangelical colleges and seminaries today.

> To summarize Thomas' position on this point, it may be said that he made a double distinction. First, he distinguished between philosophy and theology: Philosophy is what can be proved by the natural light of reason; theology is whatever rests on faith. Second, he distinguished between revealed and natural theology: The latter is the part of the former that is susceptible of proof. Thus, philosophy and theology overlap. Some of the truths that rest on faith (and so belong in the field of theology) are demonstrable (and so belong in the field of philosophy). Natural theology is the name Thomas gave to the set of propositions that constitute the field of knowledge on which faith and reason overlap.[28]

The preuniversity education that a young man received varied according to his family's circumstances and the particular location of his training. Some elementary and secondary schools had better resources to offer their students than did others. Some students were educated by private tutors; others learned at grammar schools that were established and maintained by the town, guild, or local church. Some students were trained by a literate church priest. This preliminary education consisted of studies in grammar and basic arithmetic. Above all else, the young man needed to have a firm grasp of the Latin language before he hoped to enter university studies because Latin was the language of instruction. He entered university at the age of fourteen and matriculated four years later. In those days, a student didn't just enroll in

---

28. Jones, *History of Western Philosophy*, 212.

university and show up for class. He placed himself under the authority and tutelage of a particular master. That master would serve an expanded role beyond mere instruction because he would also serve as a kind of academic parent, providing discipline, advisement, counsel, and mentoring to the young men under his supervision.[29]

The structure of the medieval university would look remarkably similar to that of students today. For example, the colleges were first set aside as residence halls where students came to board while they learned. The faculty determined matters of curriculum and set general academic standards for the conferral of degrees. The rector (college president) selected the faculty and exercised a high degree of oversight to guarantee quality control. Beyond the basic level of the bachelor's degree, many universities also housed colleges that allowed a student to advance in a particular vocational subject such as law, medicine, or science. The bachelor's degree was designed to be achieved in four years, and graduate (master's and doctoral) degrees were achieved only after the completion of additional years of instruction. The culmination of the latter degrees occurred after a public demonstration and oral defense of the student's learning.

Some things will never change regarding life away from home at the university. The following translation of a student's letter to his parents helps us realize that students from all generations need financial assistance from their parents.

> Well-beloved father, I have not a penny, nor can I get any save through you, for all things at the University are dear: nor can I study in my Code or my Digest, for they are all tattered. Moreover, I owe ten crowns to the Provost, and can find no man to lend them to me; I send you word of greetings and money.[30]

---

29. Richard Dales, *The Intellectual Life of Western Europe in the Middle Ages* (Washington, D.C.: University Press, 1980), 218.
30. G. G. Coulton, *Life in the Middle Ages* (Cambridge: Harvard University Press, 1929), 3:113; as cited in Crane Brinton, John B. Christopher, and Robert L. Wolff, *Prehistory to 1715*, vol. 1 of *A History of Civilization* (Englewood Cliffs, N.J.: Prentice-Hall, 1967), 306.

So What? Lessons from the Past for Twenty-first-century Christian Education

The Middle Ages was a time of transition. The glory years of classical Greek and Roman education had drawn to a close. It is difficult to imagine how soon the profound elements of so great a culture could be lost on the one to follow, but such was the case. The immediate needs of survival and a general lack of concern for culture led to the beginning of the Middle Ages. Civil governments were too busy trying to maintain their own existence to afford their people much concern. The church was no different in many respects. Arguments over authority, jurisdiction, and power also stifled the church's ability to help its people. The church divided along geographic and philosophic boundaries and eventually fragmented into warring factions. Battles ensued that cost the lives of countless thousands of souls. Looking back, we must ask, "What lessons can we learn from the period of the Middle Ages that will help us be more effective ministers of our Lord in the twenty-first century?" Following are principles drawn from this period to guide contemporary ministry practice.

1. Stay focused.

The church became too distracted in its own quest for survival to care about the current spiritual needs of its members. The political concerns of the civil government and the quest for power and authority in the church were one and the same. In fact, in some cases, the leadership of one was simultaneously the leader of the other, creating an obvious conflict of interests. Little, if any, separation of church and state existed. Where this happened, disaster followed. If we have learned anything from this chapter of human history, it is that interests and concerns of the civil government are not the same as those of the church. Civil government is entrusted with protecting and providing for the physical resources of its citizens, whereas the church is entrusted with protecting and providing for the spiritual resources of its members. When a conflict of interest occurs between the two, the people generally lose. The separation of church and state was a principle that grew out of this era, and it has become a valuable contribution to our times.

2. How you raise money is just as important as how you spend it.

Raising funds for worthy causes does not justify unethical or unbiblical means. No government has enough money to do all that its citizens want. Likewise, every church finds itself unable to do all that it would like because of the limitation of available funds. God might own the cattle on a thousand hills, but that doesn't mean that He gives us everything we want. The need to raise funds for ministry ventures is obvious; however, the means by which those funds are raised is just as important as what those funds are being raised to do.

The Crusades stand as testimony that the church abused its trust by the people. The average person did not possess sufficient education to determine whether what the church was saying was accurate. When the clergy guaranteed men eternal salvation without risk of punishment if they died in battle on a crusade, it was guilty of fraud and misrepresentation of truth. Nowhere do the Scriptures make such a promise. Yet, countless thousands of innocent people laid down their lives for what their priests had taught them. The political influence that the church won by these crusades was not worth the price that was paid.

In the same way today, the church must speak clearly and honestly to its membership. At times, the leadership of the church must separate itself from personal gain and advancement and consider the needs of its members to be of more value than itself. Church leaders today are not needlessly sending young men off to war, but many churches are guilty of trying to manipulate the will and desire of its people on the basis of ecclesiastical prestige rather than on the basis of God's will. Statements made from the pulpit such as "We can never reach the lost in our community if you don't give sacrificially to the new building campaign" might sound pious and well intentioned. However, when church leaders make such pleas to build their own religious fiefdoms rather than the kingdom of Christ, they are guilty of the same spiritual negligence.

3. The mind is a terrible thing to waste.

Once again, we are reminded of the importance of using our minds to reason our faith. The Christian does not need to fear a critical mind. God gave us our minds to use as a means of understanding Him. His ways are not our ways, and they require a good deal of reflection to understand. Like Aquinas, we should believe in the power of the human intellect and realize that as we develop its capabilities, we glorify God in the process.

Middle school and senior high ministries (the ages when young people begin to reason and think through their faith) would do well to find ways to challenge their students to engage their minds and intellects. The study of apologetics and a renewed interest in public speaking skills would be helpful additions in the curriculum of twenty-first-century youth education. We must equip our young people with the tools that will give them an edge in their ability to defend their faith at school and elsewhere in the world.

4. The head and the heart belong together.

We desperately need Aquinas's approach of blending theory and practice today. Time spent in mindless and brain-numbing instruction that has no lifestyle application could be better spent in praxis activities designed to engage our faith and our hearts. The study of theology has many valuable contributions to make; however, it should not be viewed as an end in and of itself. Theology that has no application to life is void of meaning and purpose.

Jesus sought to connect the heart of His student with the message that He was teaching. Knowledge of doctrine alone is insufficient to fulfill the Great Commission. What is needed is a careful and deliberate blending of ways that we can apply biblical doctrines to the way we live. As James stated, "Even so faith, if it has no works, is dead" (2:17).

FOR FURTHER READING

Adams, George B. *Civilization During the Middle Ages.* New York: Scribner's, 1922.

Bark, William C. *Origins of the Medieval World.* New York: Doubleday, 1958.

Brinton, Crane, John B. Christopher, and Robert Wolff. *Prehistory to 1715.* Vol. 1 of *A History of Civilization.* Englewood Cliffs, N.J.: Prentice-Hall, 1967.

Burns, Edward McNall. *Western Civilizations.* New York: Norton, 1949.

Butts, R. Freeman. *A Cultural History of Education: Reassessing Our Educational Traditions.* New York: McGraw Hill, 1947.

Cairns, Earle E. *Christianity Through the Centuries: A History of the Christian Church.* 3d ed. Grand Rapids: Zondervan, 1996.

Choun, J. Robert. "Thomas Aquinas." In *The Evangelical Dictionary of Christian Education.* Edited by Michael J. Anthony. Grand Rapids: Baker, 2001.

Dales, Richard C. *The Intellectual Life of Western Europe in the Middle Ages*. Washington, D.C.: University Press of America, 1980.

Eavey, Charles B. *History of Christian Education*. Chicago: Moody, 1964.

Eby, Frederick, and Charles F. Arrowood. *The History and Philosophy of Education: Ancient and Medieval*. Englewood Cliffs, N.J.: Prentice-Hall, 1940.

Gutek, Gerald L. *Historical and Philosophical Foundations of Education: A Biographical Introduction*. Upper Saddle River, N.J.: Merrill Prentice-Hall, 2001.

Hoyt, Robert S., ed. *Life and Thought in the Middle Ages*. Minneapolis: University of Minnesota Press, 1967.

Johnson-Miller, Beverly. "Medieval Education." In *The Evangelical Dictionary of Christian Education*. Edited by Michael J. Anthony. Grand Rapids: Baker, 2001.

Jones, W. T. *The Medieval Mind*. New York: Harcourt Brace Jovanovich, 1969.

Le Goff, Jacques, trans. *Time, Work, and Culture in the Middle Ages*. Chicago: University of Chicago Press, 1977.

MacKinney, Loren C. *The Medieval World*. New York: Rinehart, 1956.

Painter, Sidney. *A History of the Middle Ages: 240–1500*. New York: Knopf, 1956.

Rand, Edward K. *Founders of the Middle Ages*. New York: Dover, 1928.

Reed, James E., and Ronnie Prevost. *A History of Christian Education*. Nashville: Broadman & Holman, 1993.

Setton, Kenneth M., and Henry R. Winkler, eds. *Great Problems in European Civilization*. Englewood Cliffs, N.J.: Prentice-Hall, 1957.

Taylor, Henry O. *The Medieval Mind: A History of the Development of Thought and Emotion in the Middle Ages*. 2 vols. Cambridge: Harvard University Press, 1959.

Walsh, James J. *High Points of Medieval Culture*. New York: Library Press, 1969.

What in the World?

➤ The Aztec Empire dominates Mexico, 1325–1519.

➤ John Wycliffe oversees English Bible translation in 1380.

➤ The first great work of English literature is *The Canterbury Tales,* written by Geoffrey Chaucer in 1390.

➤ Jan Hus, Czech forerunner of Protestanism, is burned at the stake in 1415.

➤ Joan of Arc is burned at the stake in Rouen in 1431.

➤ Leonardo Da Vinci, leading Italian Renaissance painter, is born in 1452.

➤ France is victorious in the Hundred Years' War in 1453.

➤ The Gutenberg Bible is printed in Mainz, Germany in 1455.

➤ The Inca Empire is in power in 1440–1537.

➤ Christopher Columbus "discovers" America in 1492.

➤ French invasion of Italy in 1494 marks the beginning of "modern" power politics.

Chapter 6

CHRISTIAN EDUCATION
IN THE RENAISSANCE
(1350–1500)

As the Middle Ages began to draw to a close, a number of learned scholars and philosophers began to stir up the hearts and minds of their students. The university was becoming a safe haven where the free exchange of ideas could take place without the threat of reprisal. For obvious reasons, the church felt threatened by this new academic freedom and was not always resolved to allow the resident scholars to express their minds as freely as they would have liked. In time, however, civil governments wrestled control of these prominent cathedral schools away from the church, and they became sanctuaries of freedom for the pursuit of new ideas and philosophical inquiry.

This resurgence of life was like a breath of fresh air to those who had been held under the repressive control of the church. Soon, new philosophers, artists, scientists, and literary scholars would spread their wings and explore this forgotten horizon of inquiry. Unfortunately, not all of them were greeted with welcome arms.

Unlike the Middle Ages, which we discussed in the preceding chapter, the period known as the Renaissance is easier to delineate. It generally extends from the fourteenth century to the sixteenth century. This period is characterized by a shift from the stifling control of the church over the affairs of mankind to a general sense of freedom for man to control his own destiny.

THE CULTURAL CONTEXT OF THE RENAISSANCE

The term *renaissance* means literally "rebirth." It was the rebirth of the ancient Greek and Roman classical cultures in the modern age. Art, literature, and architecture would revisit the wondrous days of their former glory. The fields of science, philosophy, and education would also discover new horizons of inquiry. Each area had experienced a virtual stagnation during the Middle Ages and was anxious to begin with fresh new opportunities. "In these intervening centuries, the thirteenth to the fifteenth inclusive, there existed a place in social organization for an intellectual life, exerting profound influence, permitting much freedom, having definite character, possessing peculiar merits, and developing an appropriate educational system."[1]

Renaissance Literature

In an effort to explain both his own unique personage and the historical and cultural contexts of his writings, Dante Alighieri (1263-1321) provided in *The Banquet (Il Convito)* an exposé of the ideas, the intellectual life, and the overall meaning of educational life throughout the period known as the Middle Ages. It was a type of literary bridge between the Middle Ages and the Renaissance. It was not intended to provide so much a chronology of activity as one author's penetrating interpretation of the spiritual dimension of life. It is unique in that it established a credible defense for the use of the vernacular in his works, an approach that was seldom practiced in his day.[2]

The work of this period that received the most acclaim throughout the years, however, was Dante's *Divine Comedy,* in which he takes the reader on a pilgrimage through the afterlife. Among the figures in the story are classical personalities such as Homer, Plato, Socrates, and Caesar. He admits into purgatory a number of these classical personalities and a few distinguished pagans and reveals his central belief that the supreme purpose of man is to live in this finite world, where all natural phenomena have their

---

1. Paul Monroe, *A Textbook in the History of Education* (London: Macmillan, 1915), 327.
2. Ibid., 341-42.

meaning in a quest for peace and justice on earth and salvation in the life thereafter. Interestingly, he placed a number of prominent popes in hell.[3]

> In a literal sense the *Commedia* is a presentation of the rewards and punishments, the destiny of man in the hereafter; allegorically, it is a presentation of the virtues and vices of the human soul as illustrated in concrete examples and in the details of the plan; morally, it has as its social, political, and ethical purposes, the making of worthier citizens, better neighbors, nobler men; mystically, it typifies the struggle of the human soul to become free, its growth through sin to holiness, its progress from the finite to the divine.[4]

To state his commitment to making a contribution to the lives of the commoner, Dante wrote his work in the vernacular of Tuscany rather than in the more respectable Latin. Ever the quintessential Renaissance poet, Dante will forever be remembered as the man who lived with one foot firmly planted in the Middle Ages and the other in the Renaissance.

A second Renaissance poet who personified the essence of the period was Francesco Petrarca, or simply Petrarch (1304-74). Commonly known as the father of Italian Renaissance literature, he, like Dante, wrote in the Tuscan dialect. Although he wrote a number of works that were well received, his best known work is *Sonnets*, which he wrote to his beloved Laura in the chivalrous style of love poetry associated with troubadours. Unfortunately, his life's true love died during the Black Death when it swept across Europe.

Petrarch exemplified the humanistic thought that sought to form a literary bridge between the classical authors of the Graeco-Roman age and the works of Augustine and other more contemporary Christian authors of his day. He is dearly loved among those who look back at Renaissance literature and acclaim him as "the first modern man."

A third and final Renaissance poet worth mentioning is a famous Florentine named Giovanni Boccaccio (1313-75). Although he never rose in prominence to the master Dante or his mentor Petrarch, he still managed to make a name for himself through his use of Italian prose. In *Decameron*,

---

3. Edward McNall Burns, *Western Civilizations: Their History and Their Culture* (New York: Norton, 1949), 309.

4. Monroe, *Textbook in the History of Education*, 342.

he reveals the worldly side of Renaissance life during this transitional time in history.

Renaissance Art

The Renaissance period brought a fresh new approach to the fine arts. Before the thirteenth century, Byzantine conventions dominated most art forms. Even before serious dialogue about bringing back art forms from classical antiquity occurred, Giotto (1266-1336) introduced a new natural-ism into painting. For example, when most artists painted a picture of the Madonna, she was always surrounded by angels and a host of other saints, perhaps even Greek nymphs to emphasize her role as the mother of God and to establish a strong religious theme in the painting. However, when Giotto painted a picture that included a Madonna, he portrayed her as a lady of feeling and true virtue. She was revealed as an individual with great depth of spiritual passion. He sought to portray Christ as being real and approach-able, full of love and compassion. His pictures were anything but stiff and stylized icons that were characteristic of the Byzantine era.[5] Giotto's work marked the turning point of a fresh new awakening of the soul. It invited the heart of the painter into the piece itself to reveal the inner beauty of the person being depicted on the canvas or the chapel wall.

Because we look through the hindsight of many years, it might be difficult for us to imagine that the great Renaissance painters were actually consid-ered lower middle-class laborers. But as men who worked with their hands, they were not held in particularly high esteem by society. Once an artist was invited to paint a piece by a wealthy merchant or nobleman, his art became officially commissioned. As such, the artist was employed for as long as it took to complete the work. These patrons of the arts held great sway over the artists' livelihoods but were essential to the artist's survival.

Renaissance artists and sculptors such as Leonardo da Vinci (1452-1519), Leon Battista Alberti (1404-72), Sandro Botticelli (1444-1510), Raphael Sanzio (1483-1520), and Michelangelo Buonarroti (1475-1564) came to their trade at a time of significant transition. The church often commissioned these particular artists, and others like them, to paint or sculpt pieces of art that

---

5. Lewis W. Spitz, *The Renaissance and Reformation Movements* (Chicago: Rand McNally, 1971), 193.

would reveal the Christian faith through a new lens, now marked by deep feelings and passion.

Leonardo da Vinci was the son of a Florentine lawyer named Piero and was from the city of Vinci, a small hillside village outside Florence. After receiving his apprenticeship under Verrocchio, he left for Milan, where the patrons of that city commissioned his work. There he painted *The Virgin of the Rocks* and *The Last Supper,* the latter being a fresco in the refrectory of the convent of Santa Maria delle Grazie. *The Last Supper* characterizes the Renaissance period with its classic symmetrical pattern (e.g., four groups of three disciples). Leonardo left Milan and went to live in Rome, where Pope Leo X commissioned his work. In his final years, he served in the court of King Francis I in France, bringing with him three paintings: *John the Baptist; Anne, Mary, and the Christ Child;* and, presumably, the *Mona Lisa.*[6]

No discussion of Renaissance art would be complete without a brief reference to one of the greatest artists of this period, the venerable Michelangelo. His accomplishments in painting, sculpture, architecture, drawing, and lyric poetry have long exemplified the fine arts of this period.

Like many of the other Renaissance artists of his day, Michelangelo used allegory in his art as a means of expressing himself beyond the brush. Two of his pieces reveal not only his unqualified expertise as an artist but also his penchant for allegorical expression. He did not originally want to be commissioned to paint the ceiling of the Sistine chapel; however, after repeated appeals by Pope Julius II, Michelangelo relented. The panels depict a neoplatonic theory of the ascent of man and his conquest over the forces of darkness. Likewise, in the painting *The Last Judgment* on the front wall of the Sistine chapel, Michelangelo—who often sought refuge from his troubled spirit by escaping into the writings of his favorite author, Dante—chose to express through allegory the struggle of man in the battle between good and evil, in relationship with a God of mercy and wrath, and in the afterlife. These themes were evident in Dante's writings and in the prominent neoplatonic philosophy of his day.

Michelangelo was also a gifted sketch artist. He knew that a relationship existed between the eye and the mind. His detailed drawings reveal a keen sense of awareness that more was being depicted in the tablet than the mere physical representation of the object itself. "The mind and the eye are not

---

6. Ibid., 216.

antithetical, for intelligent vision is informed vision. In a way, we *think* because we see and see *because* we think. It is thus no exaggeration to say that Renaissance painters taught men so to look at the world about them that a detailed knowledge of the structure and function of the things natural became possible."[7] Renaissance artists expressed their philosophy and theology through their art forms, whether it be painting or sculpting; the artists moved beyond the darkness of traditional Gothic art forms into a new light of meaningful and passionate expression.

Renaissance Architecture

In architecture, the Gothic style that had developed during the twelfth century formed the basis for all development in Northern Europe. Almost all of the Gothic cathedrals and other building enterprises reflected the tastes of the great nobles who had come to dominate the politics of the age. They were traditional in nature with characteristically large stained-glass windows. Gothic architecture was dark and foreboding. Renaissance architecture, however, was based on precise calculations and mathematical principles of linear perspective. These principles allowed architects to revolutionize the structural composition of Europe's cathedrals. Such was certainly the case with the design of both the dome on the Florence cathedral by Filippo Brunelleschi (1377-1446) and the dome of St. Peter's cathedral in Rome by Michelangelo Buonarroti (1475-1564).[8]

Expressing the allegorical and neoplatonic philosophy of the architects themselves, cathedrals were built that put man in a different focal point. Now, man entering the cathedral was drawn to the heart of the building as though by an unseen force. The architect's desire for man to be drawn into a restorative relationship with his Creator in the final victory in the battle of good versus evil was expressed as the penitent's sense came alive as he was caught up in the grandeur of God's majesty and approachability. Renaissance architecture made a statement about God's desire for relationship with mankind.

---

7. Joseph Anthony Mazzeo, *Renaissance and Revolution: The Remaking of European Thought* (New York: Pantheon Books, 1965), 177-78.

8. Charles G. Nauert, *The Age of Renaissance and Reformation* (New York: University Press of America, 1981), 100-101.

Renaissance Science

The Renaissance marked a turning point in the field of scientific inquiry. During the Middle Ages traditional methods of instruction in the universities consisted in doing little more than reading the manuscript while the professor made incidental comments. The traditional central doctrine in philosophic speculation was the relation of particular objects to general types, or the study of universals. Great quarrels broke out in lecture halls across Europe in an attempt to settle the argument. As a result, two streams of philosophic reasoning emerged. Nominalism held that only the particular object was real, whereas realism insisted that only the type was real. The result of this debate was a barrenness in university studies.[9]

An English Franciscan friar and Oxford professor named Roger Bacon (1214-94) shook the hallowed presuppositions about the world and man's relationship to it. He was not satisfied with the system of inquiry established by St. Thomas Aquinas. He thought that the Thomist views regarding universal authority and absolutes could no longer go unchallenged. Instead, he provoked those who had developed an unhealthy reliance upon Aristotle for authority in scientific matters.[10] He believed that truths must be discovered and that the means by which they could be known was through what has come to be known as the scientific method. This process allowed one to develop a hypothesis about the natural world and then seek to verify that hypothesis through controlled experimentation. What could not be explored or open for scientific inquiry was suspect.

Bacon's most significant writing was *Opus maius,* in which he pointed out the need for studying nature and science within the curriculum. As a devout believer, he believed that science should enhance the study of theology, which he viewed as the queen of the sciences. His writings on optics remained authoritative for many years, and his discoveries related to magnifying lenses might have led him to create the first microscope. He was not only the best geographer of his day but also one of the first scientists to perceive the inadequacies of the Julian calendar and to advocate the need to correct its deficiencies.[11]

---

9. Henry S. Lucas, *The Renaissance and the Reformation* (New York: Harper & Brothers, 1934), 133.

10. R. Freeman Butts, *A Cultural History of Education: Reassessing Our Educational Traditions* (New York: McGraw Hill, 1947), 156-57.

11. Burns, *Western Civilizations,* 303.

Classical humanists contributed little to the new discoveries of science because they preferred in their methodology to examine the classical authors rather than to explore the possibility that old paradigms might be perceived incorrectly. This was not the case for a new breed of Renaissance thinkers who were in stark contrast to the educational humanists. Renaissance contributions to the field of science include the new paradigmatic views of Nicolaus Copernicus (1473-1543), who had decided that Ptolemy was wrong about the earth's being at the center of the universe. This provided the groundwork for Galileo (1564-1642) to espouse his heliocentric theory of the universe. In the same way, Andreas Vesalius (1514-64) laid the foundation for the modern science of anatomy, Ambroise Pare (1517-90) became known as the father of modern surgery, Bernard Palissy (1510-99) provided new insights into the natural sciences from his post in Paris, and Rodolphus Agricola (1443-85) promoted the scientific study of mining. New ways of thinking and exploring the natural world were coming of age. Change was not radical at this point, but it was the beginning of a movement that would sweep across Europe and influence science for centuries to come.[12]

Renaissance Education

The traditional influence on education during the Renaissance was educational humanism. Because so much should be said about this topic, a separate section will be devoted to its discussion later in the chapter. However, educational humanism was not the only driving force in the field of education during this period. In addition to educational humanism was the influence upon character building. The central purpose of education was more than merely to instill information into the mind of the learner; something more lasting was necessary. An emphasis on behavioral change might bring about different actions, but because it did not touch the heart of the learner, no guarantee of sustainable change was possible; a redirection toward heart change was necessary.

The Renaissance educator emphasized the value of moral considerations and sought to replicate the virtuous acts of the great Greeks and Romans who had come before them. He also paid careful attention to religious train-

---

12. Butts, *Cultural History of Education,* 214.

ing because it reinforced the tenets of moral instruction. Last, because the educational system was geared toward those of noble heritage who could afford formal instruction and who were destined for military or political leadership, educational theory and praxis emphasized the importance of physical training and even military exercises.[13]

Renaissance Philosophy

Little was added to the landscape of philosophy during the period of the Renaissance because of the overpowering efforts of the humanists, who were more concerned with literature and style than with philosophy itself. In the field of logic, attacks were made on Aristotelianism, but these were brought more by the naturalists and scientists than by the philosophers themselves. About the only organized effort by humanists to probe the depths of philosophic thought during this period was brought about by the establishment of the Platonic Academy in Italy during the fourteenth century. There they sought to revel in the contemplative life, relying on allegory to explain religion and trying to integrate philosophy, religion, and science into one cohesive unit.[14]

PHILOSOPHICAL ANTECEDENTS OF THE RENAISSANCE

During this period, the philosophical threads of mysticism began to spread across the land. Roman Catholic dogma had fostered a harsh form of legalism that valued a strict adherence to church laws and doctrinal teachings. Over time, the motivation of understanding why these rules and teachings were important began to diminish; in its place came an emphasis more upon the practice of overt behaviors (attending church, paying one's absolutions, cooperating with the priest's social and political agenda, etc.) rather on the condition of a believer's heart toward God. Turning the hearts of a believing society back toward God would not be easy because even many of the clergy were against such a move; they feared the loss of their prestige, power, and influence.

Mysticism was an effort on the part of some ministry leaders to sensitize

---

13. Nauert, *Age of Renaissance and Reformation*, 102.
14. Butts, *Cultural History of Education*, 213.

their hearts toward the Spirit's moving in their lives. "The mystical movement, the classical form of Roman Catholic piety, developed as a reaction against formal and mechanical sacerdotal ritual and dry Scholasticism in the church of the day. It reflected the perennial tendency toward the subjective aspect of Christianity, which always occurs when too much emphasis is laid on outward acts in Christian worship."[15]

Mysticism was concerned with trying to engage the heart of the worshiper as well as his mind. The emphasis, however, was clearly more on the former than on the latter. This, in turn, led to a danger of placing more emphasis upon the subjective nature of one's faith than on the truths of Scripture. Hermeneutical interpretation was subject to the whims of feeling rather than being based on the more solid foundation of historical-grammatical interpretation. It did, however, begin to stir the hearts of people toward considering God in a different, more caring light. The veil was lifted, and it revealed a more sensitive and compassionate God who was deeply concerned about the issues of helpless man. God became more than a judge to be feared and a deity always in need of our financial resources; the mystical movement revealed a God of grace and mercy.

Whereas scholasticism emphasized the reasoning side of man at the expense of man's feelings and subjective nature, mysticism sought to return to a more balanced state of being. One of the most prominent leaders of mysticism was a woman named Catherine of Siena, who claimed that God often spoke to her. She sought to turn the heart of Pope Gregory XI to a closer walk with Christ. She denounced sin wherever she encountered it and tried desperately to turn the heart of her Catholic clergy associates back toward a genuine faith in Christ.

In Germany, the mystical movement centered in the Dominican order. Under the leadership of Meister Eckhart (1260-1327), mysticism in Germany developed a firm philosophical foundation. Eckhart differentiated between the Godhead, which, to him, represented God as the philosophical unity behind the universe, and God, who was the Creator and the caretaker of the universe itself. His ultimate aim in preaching was to return man's soul to union with his Creator. He is reputed to have said, "God must become I, and I God." His beliefs bordered on a neoplatonistic form of pantheism, and for this reason the pope held him in contempt. A papal bull was issued

---

15. Earle E. Cairns, *Christianity Through the Centuries: A History of the Christian Church*, 3d ed. (Grand Rapids: Zondervan, 1996), 244.

against him after his death. His followers, known as the Friends of God, sought to keep the spirit of his teachings alive and in so doing emphasized the importance of an individual's personal relationship with Christ as opposed to mere adherence to external ceremonies and traditions.[16]

THE BRETHREN OF THE COMMON LIFE

Continuing this emphasis upon personal intimacy with God was a movement in the Netherlands known as *Devotio Moderna*, or the Brethren of the Common Life. Influenced by John of Ruysbroeck (1293–1381), the father of practical mysticism, this movement emphasized applied Christian service yet was able to steer clear of the negative aspects of pantheism. A friend of John of Ruysbroeck was able to blend the positive elements of mysticism with solid biblical instruction. It was the best of both worlds with a perfect combination of a reasoning mind guided by the teachings of the New Testament and the stirring of the heart impassioned by the leading of the Holy Spirit. With this combination of heart and mind, the movement spread across the Netherlands, Europe, and eventually to North America itself.

Geert Groote

As a brilliant young man, Groote (1340–84) was well educated, ambitious, and sought fame and fortune. But during a life-threatening bout with the Black Plague, Groote had a profound and life-changing experience with God and saw the emptiness of his life goals. He saturated himself in the Scriptures and gave his life to spreading the gospel. He preached on the streets and on the hillsides. Soon he had a number of followers who helped in his ministry: later, these followers of Groote were called "The Brethren of the Common Life" or the "Devotio Moderna."

Some of Groote's disciples were schoolteachers: one of these was Johannes Cele. Groote took Cele with him on a walking trip and began sharing with Cele a vision for reform of the schools that Groote said was given to him by God. The elements of this vision included lofty aims and revolutionary

---

16. Ibid., 243.

> teaching methods. Cele began to put these into practice in his school in Zwolle, Netherlands. Other Brethren teachers did this as well.
>
> Meanwhile, Groote's success in preaching and evangelization caused some consternation among local clergy. Eventually Groote received a communication from the pope forbidding him to preach. This was a serious blow to the movement, because these early reformers felt the pope was God's spokesman on earth. Shortly after that, their leader, Geert Groote died.[17]

The Brethren took no vows and placed no emphasis upon rules and regulations. They recognized that such an emphasis could lead to a modern pharisaical adherence to Christianity. Instead, the Brethren organized into homes in which believers lived in community with all represented levels of society—nobles, priests, scholars, peasants, artisans, students, etc. Together, members of this common life worked hard and shared their resources with the poor and needy. They lived a rather primitive and simple existence with an emphasis upon living the Christian life as the New Testament taught it. One book that has survived, the *Imitation of Christ,* attributed to Thomas à Kempis, reveals the heart of the movement. It held firmly to the dogmas of the Catholic Church but also encouraged believers to move beyond ritual practice to genuine spiritual sensitivity to the work of God in an individual's life.[18]

The Brethren of the Common Life never intended their community to become a reformation movement per se. They sought to influence the church and society as a whole through their unique curriculum and instructional methodologies. Their curriculum emphasized Bible study in the vernacular so people could form their own understanding of a passage's meanings and applications. "The burden of their teaching (and preaching) was more purity, more charity, more tolerance, more enlightenment, and more respect for human faculties. Their concern for the common man was behind their use of the vernacular—even to the point of translating the Bible into Dutch, a move that was attacked by the Roman Catholic church."[19]

---

17. Ibid., 95.
18. Charles B. Eavey, *History of Christian Education* (Chicago: Moody, 1964), 130.
19. Julia Henkel, "Gerte Groote," in *A History of Religious Educators,* ed. Elmer Towns (Grand Rapids: Baker, 1975), 72; as cited in Kenneth O. Gangel and Warren S. Benson, *Christian Education: Its History and Philosophy* (Chicago: Moody, 1983), 132.

The Brethren of the Common Life were unique in their educational practice because rather than managing their classes with strict punishment for those who were not able to learn their lessons properly, they provided generous praise and rewards for those who were able to master the necessary material. They taught the trivium and the quadrivium but also included studies in Greek, Hebrew, and Latin. They initiated a different means of dividing the class. The grade plan taught students in smaller groups according to the students' levels of progress. These and other innovations were responsible for radical educational reforms in schools across Europe. A number of significant leaders came up through the ranks of schools sponsored by the Brethren of the Common Life, including Martin Luther (1483-1546), Martin Bucer (1491-1551), John Calvin (1509-64), and Ulrich Zwingli (1484-1531).[20]

HUMANISM AND THE RENAISSANCE

Chief among the ideologies of the Renaissance was the concept that man should be in control of his destiny rather than the church or the state. In reality, this was not such a new concept but was taken from Aristotle and other Greek philosophers of his day. Renaissance humanism had its origins in the writings of Aristotle and Plato. Chief among its beliefs was the idea that the educational curriculum should be comprised of certain core subjects, including the seven liberal arts (i.e., grammar, rhetoric, dialectic, arithmetic, geometry, music, and astronomy), the classic Greek authors (Aristotle, Plato, Homer, etc.), Roman authors (Cicero, Ovid, Virgil, Horace, etc.), the early church fathers (e.g., Basil, Chrysostom, and Augustine, etc.), and the Bible. This body of literature comprised the essence of what has come to be known as the humanities. The one who had disciplined himself in their academic studies and was able to grasp the full scope of this literature was referred to as a *humanitus*, or humanist.

Many of these subjects were taught in their original languages; therefore, the humanist was one who had learned both classical Greek and Latin as well as his own vernacular. In 1459, an Italian Greek scholar named Guarino Guarini (1374-1460) espoused that the Greek language be an essential

---

20. Julia Henkle-Hobbs, *The Evangelical Dictionary of Christian Education*, ed. Michael J. Anthony (Grand Rapids: Baker, 2001), s.v. "Brethren of the Common Life."

component of an educated man. He declared, "I have said that the ability to write Latin verse is one of the most essential marks of an educated person. I wish now to indicate a second which is of at least equal importance, namely, familiarity with the language and literature of Greece. The time has come when we must speak with no uncertain voice upon this vital requirement of scholarship."[21] Therefore, a humanist was one who had a well rounded education in all of the various fields of study that pertained to making a fruitful contribution to one's world.

The first humanist educator, and by far the most successful schoolmaster of the Renaissance, was Vittorino Rambaldoni, also known as Vittorino da Feltre (1378–1446). He entered the university at Padua at the age of eighteen and upon graduation accepted their invitation to remain as their Latin professor; he taught there for more than twenty years. He left to establish a school in Venice, but that venture was short-lived, and he returned to the University of Padua.

In 1423, he received an invitation from the Marquis of Mantua to establish a private school for his children. "The master here gave the Greek idea of a liberal education its first embodiment, and taught to the youth for the first time the literature, history, and civilization of the Romans instead of the mere form of their language."[22] His popularity grew, and soon children of other nobility desired to attend. In time, he allowed these children to join his instruction and his school soon filled the entire palace. His desire was for the educational setting to be such an enjoyable experience that his school was named "The Pleasant House." He integrated sports with the seven liberal arts although literature was the dominant field of study. This new direction represented his desire to move beyond mere rote memorization of the curriculum to include a moral component as well. His school also included a unique system of self-governance for the boys, a dependence upon the natural desires and interests of the students, and a component whereby the boys worked during part of the day.[23]

Perhaps no individual so personified Renaissance humanism as much as

---

21. W. H. Woodward, *Vittorino da Feltre and Other Humanist Educators* (Cambridge, U.K.: Cambridge University Press, 1905), 166; as cited in Fredrick Eby and Charles Flinn Arrowood, *The History and Philosophy of Education: Ancient and Medieval* (Englewood Cliffs, N.J.: Prentice-Hall, 1940), 908.
22. Monroe, *Textbook in the History of Education*, 376.
23. Ibid., 377.

the Dutch scholar Desiderius Erasmus (1466-1536). Born in Rotterdam, in the Netherlands, he is alleged to have been the illegitimate son of Geradus Gerardi, a priest, and Margaret Rogerius, who was under Gerardi's employ as his housekeeper. In an effort to conceal his illegitimacy, he avoided using his last name. In 1497, he added the name Desiderius and later adopted the name of the city of his birth.[24]

Erasmus's early training was in the school of the Brethren of the Common Life at the famous church school at Deventer. There he was influenced by the dynamic teaching of Hegius and Agricola. Upon the death of his parents, his guardians placed him in an Augustinian monastery. There he mastered Greek and Latin and became proficient in reading the classical works in their original languages. He had a rich background in a broad range of subjects, including the liberal arts, biblical studies, and contemporary literature. He was, for all intents and purpose, the ultimate Renaissance man. He became an itinerate teacher of private students as he traveled throughout Europe. He was a prolific author, and few scholars saw their work disseminated during their lifetime as much as did Erasmus.[25]

Referred to as the "prince of humanists," this leading educator of his day held a disdain for the intrusion of the state into the affairs of mankind. In the most famous of his pointed discourses, *The Colloquies,* he details the abusive nature of the Catholic Church, the state government, monastic life (which he had rejected), and the university system. He was a forerunner of the great German reformer, Martin Luther.

> While a professor at Cambridge, Erasmus continued research and writing into areas in which he specialized: the teaching of classical languages and biblical scholarship. In 1512, he published *de Copia,* a compendium of Latin words, phrases, and idioms designed to aid students in enlarging their vocabularies. Four years later, he completed his Greek version of the New Testament.[26]

---

24. Albert Hyma, *The Youth of Erasmus* (New York: Russell & Russell, 1968), 51-53, 55-56, 59; as cited in Gerald Gutek, *Historical and Philosophical Foundations of Education: A Biographical Introduction* (Upper Saddle River, N.J.: Merrill Prentice-Hall, 2001), 75.
25. Monroe, *Textbook in the History of Education,* 380.
26. Gutek, *Historical and Philosophical Foundations of Education,* 77.

"Erasmus emphasized studying the nature of children, the importance of games in education, praise and rewards instead of discipline, helping students, and providing more education for women. Moreover, he was one of the first people to champion systematic teacher training."[27] Erasmus lived in Basel, Switzerland, and Freiburg im Bresigau. He died in 1536. His unfaltering career in defense of scholarship, exemplary standards of literary taste, and a life of reason won him the acclaim of scholars worldwide. He has been referred to as the most civilized man of his age.[28]

Unfortunately, much of what we have come to know as humanism in the twenty-first century has become synonymous with atheism and naturalism. It would be many years later, however, before the naturalistic philosophy of Darwin and others would have a determining influence on humanistic education. Indeed, twenty-first-century Christian educators could agree, in terms of scope and practice, with much about humanism as it originally came to us during the Renaissance. Although running the risk of being misunderstood or taken out of context, given the essential teachings of Renaissance humanism, one could easily declare that Jesus Christ was a humanistic teacher as well. To illustrate this assertion, perhaps a summary of humanism as applied to an educational context would be beneficial. The summary that follows[29] is a composite of the more narrowly defined Renaissance humanism and input from those who have built upon its foundation since its inception. As applied to education, humanism encompasses a variety of assumptions about the teacher, the learner, the curriculum, and the context of learning.

This man-centered approach to education that came to prominence in Italy influenced educational theory and practice all across Europe. In other countries, humanist educators made significant changes in the educational structure of their schools. Curriculum was restructured to provide students with instruction in the classical writings of Greek and Latin scholars, detailed study of the Scriptures, the writings of the church fathers, and a comprehensive examination of the liberal arts. These curricula became the standard for educational centers all across Europe. This humanistic approach to learning

---

27. Lin Johnson, *The Evangelical Dictionary of Christian Education*, ed. Michael J. Anthony (Grand Rapids: Baker, 2001), s.v. "Desiderius Erasmus."
28. Burns, *Western Civilizations*, 345.
29. For a more exhaustive description and discussion, see my article in *The Evangelical Dictionary of Christian Education*, ed. Michael J. Anthony (Grand Rapids: Baker, 2001), s.v. "Christian Humanism."

Principles of Educational Humanism

1. Central to the humanistic movement in education is a desire to create a learning environment that is free from fear, punishment, harsh discipline, and manipulative instructional methods. This is done in order to move away from the adversarial role of teachers in the traditional approach. The humanist's desire is to create an atmosphere that facilitates a free flow of discussion.[30]

2. Teachers should create a learning environment where they are free to develop interpersonal relationships with their students. These relationships should be marked by trust, sincerity, and empathetic concern for their students. They should prize their students and hold them in high regard.[31]

3. Factors that influence the affective domain should also be considered essential to the development of the educational curriculum.[32] Recent research indicates that children who are taught in an atmosphere where affective factors are integrated into the curriculum will develop a more positive self-concept compared to those situations where it is excluded from the learning environment.[33]

4. A healthy learning environment is one that is marked by mutual respect and appreciation for what the teacher and student bring to the encounter. This relationship should be marked by healthy dialogue and interaction of ideas. The teacher is not viewed as an educational autocrat. Learning takes place through a dynamic process of verbal interaction between teacher and student.

5. Teachers should consider using a variety of instructional methodologies that enable the student to develop an appreciation for the worldview of other members of the classroom. Such techniques could include

---

30. George R. Knight, *Philosophy and Education* (Berrien Springs, Mich.: Andrews University Press, 1980), 105.

31. R. F. Biehler and J. Snowman, *Psychology Applied to Teaching* (Boston: Houghton Mifflin, 1986), 399.

32. Ibid.

33. D. L. Bayer, "The Effects of Two Methods of Affective Education on Self-Concept in Seventh-Grade Students," *The School Counselor* (November 1986): 130–31.

> the use of drama, role plays, case studies, initiative tests, and simulation games.[34]
>
> 6. Teachers should consider using various instructional methodologies that will help students become more aware of their own attitudes and values. Instruction that focuses only on the cognitive development of the learner limits its ability to have a lasting impact on the student's life. Instruction of this nature is limited in scope and usefulness.

was at the heart of a new awakening among people throughout the continent. Education was more than mere adherence to a harsh and seemingly ruthless set of disciplinary standards of conduct. Teachers took the time to explore the meaning of their instruction to ensure that their students were capable of explaining the concepts rather than merely repeating them on an exam.

Johann Reuchlin (1455-1522), a German who studied in Italy, returned to his homeland, where he devoted himself to the study of the Old Testament and published the first Hebrew grammar in northern Europe. In France, Jacques LeFever d' Etaples (1455-1536) was a dedicated believer and New Testament scholar. In Great Britain, John Colet (1467-1519) served as the dean of St. Paul's Cathedral, where he was instrumental in the administration of one of England's finest schools of higher education.[35] His friend and colleague Thomas More (1478-1535) published in 1516 a groundbreaking manuscript titled *Utopia,* in which he details an ideal society on an imaginary island. He portrays civilization as tolerating different opinions and abolishing war and monasticism forever. Sir Francis Bacon (1561-1626), also from Great Britain, made a monumental contribution to humanist thought through his glorification of the inductive method of inquiry.[36] Many of these humanistic educators had a deep respect for Christian education, and their desire was to further the cause of Christ by making educational contributions to the church.

---

34. Ibid., 400.
35. Kenneth O. Gangel and Warren S. Benson, *Christian Education: Its History and Philosophy* (Chicago: Moody, 1983), 130.
36. Burns, *Western Civilizations,* 352.

FORERUNNERS OF THE REFORMATION

One of the most profound influences that preceded the Reformation was the spiritual awakening led by John Wycliffe (c. 1330-84) in England. Much like Groote and his followers in the Brethren of the Common Life, Wycliffe did not start out to reform the Catholic Church. His intention was to bring a renewed awareness of the need for the clergy to sustain a vibrant and dynamic personal spiritual life. Disillusioned by the excesses of the priests, he sought to reform the church from within. Once he realized that the church authority did not recognize their need for reform, he broke ranks and began to denounce what he saw as the unbiblical abuse of ecclesiastical power and control. In 1378, he took a stand against the church and preached the primary authority of the Scriptures for everything pertaining to spiritual formation. He recognized the pope as the leader of the Catholic Church but could find no biblical basis for his prominence in the universal church. He rejected wholeheartedly the Catholic Church's claim that it was the sole reflection of Christ's rule on the earth. To add further contempt for the role of the Catholic Church, he translated the Bible into English so that the commoner could see for himself that the clergy had misrepresented the teachings of Christ to the masses.

By 1380, Wycliffe reached the conclusion that the pope is the Antichrist, since his deeds opposed those of Christ. In his later writings, he advocated the abolition of the papacy. The conclusion, regarded as most heretical by his contemporaries, was Wycliffe's denial of the doctrine of transubstantiation. He also condemned monasticism and taught that all authority, ecclesiastical and secular, is derived from God and is forfeited by one who lives in mortal sin. So great was his influence in the direction of revolt that he has been called "The Morning Star of the Reformation."[37]

John Wycliffe was a professor of theology and philosophy at Oxford University. From this prestigious position of authority, Wycliffe was unrelenting in his desire to see the Catholic Church become more relevant and meaningful to the masses. His appeals would fall on deaf ears in Rome, so he called for

---

37. Eavey, *History of Christian Education*, 132.

England to establish a new state church, one that would view the Scriptures as the sole basis of church authority and in which the priests would demonstrate through their own lifestyles the teachings of Christ. This early attempt to reform the church, although inadequate to effect change in his lifetime, represented a foreshadow of what was to come. A summary of his most important positions on religious reform includes the following.

1. Because each person is a direct vassal of God and holds his possessions by grace, he should enjoy them only on condition that he render service and loyalty to God.
2. The terms by which we enjoy these possessions are set forth in the Bible; therefore, everyone should have access to the Scriptures to know these terms.
3. The duty of the clergy is to be pious, to live modest lives, and to give up worldly concerns. If the clergy fail in these respects, it is the duty of the state to reform the church.[38]

After Wycliffe's quiet death in 1384, his disciples, known as Lollards, continued to spread throughout England his message of necessary reform. The Catholic Church did not take kindly to such talk and unleashed a wave of persecution against the Lollards. As a movement without a persuasive leader, however, it did not last long into the sixteenth century.

Simultaneous with the preaching of Wycliffe in England, another reformer named Jan Hus (1373–1415) living in Bohemia was also trying to instigate change in the Catholic Church. Like Wycliffe in England, this Czech religious vanguard condemned the amount of power and control that the pope had over believers. Hus searched the Scriptures and could find no evidence of such authority. Instead, he believed that the Scriptures were the only true source of authority that should govern the affairs of individual believers and the church (corporate believers). As a result of his views about papal authority and the church, he was arrested, tried, and condemned as a heretic at the Council of Constance. He was burned at the stake on July 6, 1415. Although the church had killed him, they could not stop his teachings from influencing those who followed in his steps. The Hussites, as they were known, fervently defended their doctrinal distinctives. This position forced the pope to launch a crusade into the Czech homeland in an effort to force their

---

38. Butts, *Cultural History of Education*, 204.

obedience. The move backfired, however, and only strengthened the resolve of the Czech nation to stand against the coercive influence of the church.

John Wycliffe and Jan Hus were viewed as heretics for their efforts to bring about church reform in England and Bohemia, respectively. In Florence, Italy, Girolamo Savonarola (1452–98) focused his efforts on both state and church reform. He became a Dominican monk in 1475 and was committed to furthering the cause of Christ regardless of personal sacrifice or discomfort. When his passion for personal holiness put him at odds with the lifestyle of the pope, it signaled the beginning of his end. His preaching against the evil lifestyle of the pope did not endear him to the entrenched church leadership, and it resulted in his execution in 1498.[39]

Calls for church reform were being voiced from multiple venues. Reforming councils were formed to try to bring stability and clarity to the situation. These councils were comprised of national representatives of the church, and their focus of attention was reform. This need became even clearer when, in 1378, Urban VI and Clement VII each claimed to be the rightful successor of the apostle Peter. Because this situation required the various countries across Europe to decide whom they would follow and acknowledge as their ecclesiastical authority, the Great Schism of the church occurred as each country chose sides in the argument of papal succession. To try to bring about a peaceful resolution, the Council of Pisa met in the spring of 1409. It deposed Benedict XIII (who was in control of Avignon) and Gregory XII (who was in control of Rome) and chose rather to elect Alexander V as the rightful pope. But the other two popes would not abdicate so the church now had to deal with three popes, each of whom was claiming to have power and authority as God's chosen messenger for the church. A final Council of Constance was called to end the Great Schism, end heresy, and bring about internal and external reform. As a result, Gregory XII resigned and after a great deal of negotiation, both Benedict XIII and John XXIII were deposed by 1415. The council went on to condemn the teachings of John Wycliffe and order the execution of John Huss.[40] Over the years, such councils would continue to meet and discuss the ongoing problems associated with reform, heresy entering the church, and the residual effects of the Great Schism.

---

39. Cairns, *Christianity Through the Centuries*, 247.
40. Ibid., 249–50.

THE INQUISITION

Long divided by cultural and religious differencies, Spain needed to find a way to bring together the various factions that had divided it for generations. The two central sources of power were Ferdinand, king of Aragon (1452-1516) and Isabella, queen of Castile (1451-1504). Each ruled a significant piece of territory but sought a way to bring together their two parts into a national whole. Neither was strong enough to secure domination over the other, so they decided to form a partnership sealed in marriage. As husband and wife, they would bring their forces together and forge a union that would be a dominant force in Europe. Having joined their efforts, they began ridding their nation of influences that sought to divide them, chief among which were the Muslim and Jewish landowners and merchants. The creative solution to their problem was getting each of these religious minorities to renounce their faith and convert to Catholicism.

Because the church would also benefit from this consolidation of power (and commerce), the Spanish Inquisition was unleashed among those members of the Spanish populace who opposed the new king and queen. Unlike the French Inquisition, which occurred at the hands of Louis VIII during the thirteenth century to rid his country of the Albigensian heresies, the Spanish Inquisition was an effort on the part of King Ferdinand and Queen Isabella to consolidate their political and geographical power across Spain. It had little to do with preserving orthodox theology or maintaining a more vibrant personal faith. Simply stated, the church was used as a front to exploit and dominate people of differing religious persuasions. In 1492, King Ferdinand and Queen Isabella seized the last fragment of Muslim-occupied Spain while Columbus was launching a new Spanish conquest on the shores of North America.[41]

The Renaissance was one of history's most significant transitional periods. Moving from the somewhat dark and depressive atmosphere that characterized the Middle Ages, the Renaissance was a time of rebirth. At the heart of the Renaissance were renewed patterns of thinking about life, death, the struggle between good and evil, and God Himself. Great men took advantage of an increased freedom and allowed themselves to dream big

---

41. Crane Brinton, John B. Christopher, and Robert L. Wolff, *A History of Civilization* (Englewood Cliffs, N.J.: Prentice-Hall, 1967), 398-99.

dreams about the natural world and man's relationship to his Creator. Some of this new thinking influenced various art forms, especially painting and sculpture. It was also seen in the architecture of the "modern" cathedrals. It permeated the minds of those who wrote some of the greatest literature of the day. "The Renaissance was, among other things, a revival of secular learning, another instance of man's endless search for true knowledge. In many ways this revival was a radical departure from medieval views of the world, of life, and of culture—views developed under domination of the church."[42] No longer bound by archaic and untrustworthy ways of thinking, man had unshackled himself from the narrowly defined parameters of the church and had begun to taste freedom of thought and mobility. The world would never be the same; there would be no turning back.

So What? Lessons from the Past for Twenty-first-century Christian Education

1. God always sends a forerunner to start the change process.

It is interesting to discover throughout human history how God works in the lives of His creation. God is never predictable; if any one character quality of God is obvious in the Scriptures, it is that He is creative. Nevertheless, we do see a number of times in human history when God acts in somewhat predicable ways. For example, in the Old Testament, God was forever sending His prophets to facilitate change. Countless times, the efforts of the prophets were met with resistance. Usually, the prophet himself lost his life trying to instigate the new paradigms that God intended. In each case, the blood of the prophet seems to have fertilized the soil of reformation. In the New Testament, we again see God's desire to change His approach in dealing with mankind. Instead of a corporate priesthood that was once the link between God and man, each believer became a priest with direct access to his heavenly Creator.

Beyond the historical framework of the Scriptures, we have many examples of God at work behind the scenes of human history to bring about change. Clearly we saw it in the Middle Ages, when God was at work preserving His

---

42. Gutek, *Historical and Philosophical Foundations of Education,* 133.

church in spite of its moral and doctrinal decay. The Renaissance was a time when we see God at work again in mystical and majestic ways. Forerunners of the mighty Reformation, including John Wycliffe and Jan Hus, tried with all of their hearts to bring reform to the church from within. Although their efforts failed, we see clearly God's knocking on humanity's door seeking to get man's attention.

God used these and other such men to challenge our thinking and to put our minds and hearts in a state of disequilibrium. The church was in desperate need of a wake-up call of grand proportions from God Himself. Only through the advantage of hindsight can we see just how hard and through how many means God has tried to get man's attention but to no avail. If change cannot come through the still, small voice of inner transformation, it will come in the form of a mighty storm. Either way, God's desires *will* be accomplished.

God continues to send His messengers to bring change to the church. We will see it happening again in a few chapters when we discuss the Great Awakening. More recently, we saw it in the Jesus Movement of the 1960s. Let's be careful not to miss the next time He moves in our midst. If we are careless and too busy, we will miss out on His intended blessings.

The forerunners of the Reformation were resolved to defend the supremacy of the Scriptures over any man-made authority. They sought to get the Bible into the hands of the common man and wanted to help him discover for himself the timeless truths of the Word. Finally, they challenged people to think beyond the confines of man's religiosity and sought to engage man's heart in a fresh, vibrant relationship with God. These have been and continue to be the hallmarks of twenty-first-century Christian education as well. We have had godly examples of those who have gone before us. Now it is our turn to continue the cause of Christ.

2. We see in the Renaissance a patient and tolerant God.

How many times have we read that the church's leadership had grown hard-hearted and callous toward the things of God? Concerned more about their own interests, those who were called to be stewards of God's resources squandered them on their own desires. Material assets were wasted, human resources were corrupted, and the politics of power swept through the church for centuries. No longer was the church concerned with fulfilling the Great Commission. It had lost its mission altogether. To preserve the charade of their own spiritual morass, church leaders forbade commoners to read the

Scriptures. Those who dared to translate and distribute the Word of God in the vernacular were either excommunicated or killed in the most brutal of fashions. The church was merely going through the motions of spirituality.

Yet, even in this period we see God reaching out to His own. He cares enough to send His prophets. Their mission was to return the hearts of mankind back to God. The message of the Renaissance was that the human spirit of discovery and inquiry could be free to explore God's natural creation. God is not threatened by our questions. He wills us to reason and to use our minds as a means of understanding His character. God was gracious in preserving Israel although they had to experience forty years of wilderness wandering. He was again gracious by calling His elect to serve in the distant land of Babylon while He purified the hearts of His children. And, once again, God moved in the minds and hearts of His elect to raise a consciousness of renewed thinking. God demonstrated His unending grace and mercy during the Renaissance by reminding the church that change was on the way. This change would bring lasting reformation to His church and a new way of relating to Himself. It would not be painless. Indeed, it would require radical means and methods. But the end result would be worth the journey because it would end in a closer and more intimate walk with God Himself. The benefits of the Reformation would be worth the pain that was experienced in the Middle Ages and the Renaissance.

3. Times, they are a changing.

Sometimes you just have to take a risk and dare to think about how things ought to be done and not just how they are. Change is an important part of God's dealings with mankind. In the church today are those who would dare to make us stop and think about what we are doing. It isn't always comfortable to be challenged. We get set in our ways and grow accustomed to tradition. What was once new and on the cutting edge when we were young will one day grow old and be challenged by the generation that follows. Over time, new methods become old methods and fail to reach a new generation with the timeless message of hope and eternal salvation. Risk takers start new organizations because they are no longer welcome in existing ones. A good lesson for us all to learn through the Renaissance is that change is good, and we should not be threatened by it.

FOR FURTHER READING

Anthony, Michael J. "Christian Humanism." In *The Evangelical Dictionary of Christian Education.* Edited by Michael J. Anthony. Grand Rapids: Baker, 2001.

Barlow, D. L. *Educational Psychology: The Teaching-Learning Process.* Chicago: Moody, 1985.

Bayer, D. L. "The Effects of Two Methods of Affective Education on Self-Concept in Seventh-Grade Students." *The School Counselor* (November 1986).

Bernard, H. W., and W. C. Huchins. *Humanism in the Classroom: An Eclectic Approach to Teaching and Learning.* Boston: Allyn & Bacon, 1974.

Biehler, Robert F., and J. Snowman. *Psychology Applied to Teaching.* Boston: Houghton Mifflin, 1986.

Brinton, Crane, John B. Christopher, and Robert L. Wolff. *A History of Civilization.* Englewood Cliffs. N.J.: Prentice-Hall, 1967.

Burns, Edward. *Western Civilizations: Their History and Their Culture.* New York: W. W. Norton, 1949.

Butts, R. Freeman. *A Cultural History of Education: Reassessing Our Educational Traditions.* New York: McGraw Hill, 1947.

Cairns, Earle E. *Christianity Through the Centuries: A History of the Christian Church,* 3d ed. Grand Rapids: Zondervan 1996.

Clark, D. H., L. Asya, and A. L. Kadet. *Humanistic Teaching.* Columbus: Charles E. Merrill, 1971.

Eavey, Charles B. *History of Christian Education.* Chicago: Moody, 1964.

Eby, Fredrick, and Charles Flinn Arrowood. *The History and Philosophy of Education: Ancient and Medieval,* Englewood Cliffs, N.J.: Prentice-Hall, 1940.

Gangel, Kenneth O., and Warren S. Benson. *Christian Education: Its History and Philosophy.* Chicago: Moody, 1983.

Gilmore, Myron P. *The World of Humanism: 1453–1517.* New York: Harper & Brothers, 1952.

Green, Vivian H. H. *Renaissance and Reformation.* London: Edward Arnold, 1959.

Gutek, Gerald L. *Historical and Philosophical Foundations of Education: A Biographical Introduction.* Upper Saddle River, N.J.: Merrill Prentice-Hall, 2001.

Henkel, Julia. "Gerte Groote." In *A History of Religious Educators.* Edited by Elmer Towns. Grand Rapids: Baker, 1975.

Henkle-Hobbs, Julia. "Brethren of the Common Life." In *The Evangelical Dictionary of Christian Education.* Edited by Michael J. Anthony. Grand Rapids: Baker, 2001.

Hulme, Edward M. *The Renaissance, The Protestant Reformation and the Catholic Reformation.* New York: Century, 1915.

Hyma, Albert. *The Youth of Erasmus.* New York: Russell & Russell, 1968.

Johnson, Lin. "Desiderius Erasmus." In *The Evangelical Dictionary of Christian Education.* Edited by Michael J. Anthony. Grand Rapids: Baker, 2001.

King, W. P. *Humanism: Another Battle Line.* Nashville: Cokesbury, 1931.

Knight, George R. *Philosophy and Education.* Berrien Springs, Mich.: Andrews University Press, 1980.

Kurtz, P. *The Humanistic Alternative.* Buffalo: Pemberton, 1973.

Lamont, C. *The Philosophy of Humanism.* New York: Fredrick, 1982.

Lucas, Henry S. *The Renaissance and the Reformation.* New York: Harper & Brothers, 1934.

Mazzeo, Joseph Anthony. *Renaissance and Revolution: The Remaking of European Thought.* New York: Pantheon Books, 1965.

Monroe, Paul. *A Textbook in the History of Education.* London: Macmillan, 1915.

Nauert, Charles G. *The Age of Renaissance and Reformation.* New York: University Press of America, 1981.

Reisner, Edward H. *Historical Foundations of Modern Education.* New York: Macmillan, 1928.

Spitz, Lewis W. *The Renaissance and Reformation Movements.* Chicago: Rand McNally, 1971.

Weinberg, C. *Humanistic Foundations of Education.* Englewood Cliffs, N.J.: Prentice-Hall, 1965.

Weinstein, G., and M. D. Fantini. *Toward Humanistic Education.* New York: Praeger, 1970.

Weller, R. *Humanistic Education: Visions and Realities.* Berkeley: McCutchan, 1977.

Woodward, W. H. *Vittorino da Feltre and Other Humanist Educators.* Cambridge: Harvard University Press, 1905.

What in the World?

➤ Luther posts his Ninety-five Theses in 1517.

➤ Luther is excommunicated from the church in 1521.

➤ King Henry VIII approves the Act of Supremacy in 1534, which makes the Church of England independent from the pope.

➤ Council of Trent opens in 1545.

➤ The English defeat the Spanish Armada in 1588.

➤ English playwright William Shakespeare pens *Romeo and Juliet* in approximately 1595.

Chapter 7

CHRISTIAN EDUCATION IN THE REFORMATION
(1500–1600)

THE RENAISSANCE WAS A PERIOD OF reawakening in the hearts and spirits of European thinkers. It marked the end of a dark period of human history and the beginning of a new dawn. Its work, however, was only begun during that period. The real resurgence of reform activity would take place during the next few centuries. What was begun during the Renaissance came to full fruition during the Reformation.

The work of the mystics, reformers, reforming councils, and humanists was an earnest attempt from different angles to bring about internal reform that would make religion more personal, the Scriptures the source of authority, and the Roman church more democratic in its organization. The defeat of these movements or their absorption by the Roman church ended all attempts at internal reform. At the same time external forces were creating opposition to the papal authority. These forces strengthened the movement that was eventually to break forth as the Protestant Reformation and to bring to an end the dominance of the papacy.[1]

---

1. Earle E. Cairns, *Christianity Through the Centuries: A History of the Christian Church,* 3d ed. (Grand Rapids: Zondervan, 1996), 252.

The period known as the Reformation began with Martin Luther's nailing his Ninety-five Theses to the door of the church at Wittenburg, Saxony, on October 31, 1517. Most historians end this period approximately 150 years later in 1650. The period has a clear, definitive beginning, but its ending is open to interpretation and personal opinion, although most historians date it with the end of the Thirty Years' War in 1648. One thing is known for sure: change was the primary characteristic of the world at that time. Looking back, everything seems to have been subject to change and transition. Much of what we knew about the world was going through radical rethinking.

In the field of science, new discoveries were being made about the origins of the universe. Because of new discoveries from transoceanic voyages, geopolitical boundaries were being redrawn as fast as the map and chart makers could keep up. New international trading partners had a profound effect on commerce, transportation, and national economics. Commerce and trade were occurring on a much larger scale than anyone had thought possible just a few hundred years earlier. Social class structure was being reworked to accommodate the emergence of a new middle class. Universities were free to challenge existing paradigms of thinking and were causing quite a stir with their new theories. No academic discipline was immune from new ideas. Math, science, physics, architecture, literature, and the fine arts were all going through radical transformation. Those were exciting days for the world.

How one labels the Reformation may depend on one's personal theological perspective. For example, the Catholic historian might view the Reformation as a Protestant revolt against the universal church. The Protestant historian, however, will view it as a break from a corrupt institution by those who desired to return to a more accurate New Testament approach to worship and service. The secular historian might choose to ignore the religious nature of this period of human history altogether and view it as a season of purely political, economic, intellectual, and social revolution.[2] Each view has an element of truth to it because the reformation that occurred in human history at that time must be attributed to more than just a theological difference of opinion. One cannot ignore the geopolitical changes that occurred simultaneously with the economic, moral, intellectual, social, and philosophical changes that seemed to collide at the apex of the sixteenth century.

---

2. Ibid., 268–75.

THE DECLINE OF THE PAPACY

The church, however, did not welcome all of these changes. The church had a growing number of parishioners who had become disenfranchised as a result of the coercive methods of the past. The papacy had grown entrenched in tradition and averse to change of any kind. Overall, the church faced the pressures of change: internally and externally. A brief overview of each source of pressure is beneficial for review.

Internal Contributing Factors

The church faced opposition from a number of sides, chief among which was within its own leadership. Near the end of the thirteenth century, a growing number of priests, monks, and friars were becoming increasingly frustrated by the lack of spiritual vitality they saw in church leaders (e.g., bishops, cardinals, and the pope). Two internal factors that contributed to the Reformation will be discussed (although many more could be included): a church renewal movement known as mysticism and the general state of decline in the church's leadership.

1. Mysticism's attempt at church renewal.

Mysticism, which had put down its roots in the Middle Ages (see chap. 6), flourished as a call to church renewal during the fourteenth century. Mysticism sought to reawaken the heart and passions of the people toward God. It strove to engage the heart and soul of the believer to worship and follow God beyond the duty of obedience, fear, and cultural expectations. Four leaders of this internal reform movement were priests named Johannes Eckhart (1260-1327), John of Ruysbroeck (1293-1381), Johann Tauler (1300-1361), and Henry Suso (1295-1366). Although these priests lived before the start of the Reformation, their influence on mysticism was so great that they are viewed as some of the leading internal forces of change from within the church.

Mysticism is difficult to define because of its highly subjective and personal nature. It has to do with the intuitive and emotional appeal of spiritual reality and is based on the assumption that they may know the ultimate nature of reality by means of apprehension, insight, and intuition. A mystic believer experiences union with God through ecstatic contemplation, utterance, trance, vision, or personal absorption.[3] Mysticism brought religion into

---

3. Lewis W. Spitz, *The Renaissance and Reformation Movements* (Chicago: Rand McNally, 1971), 38.

the realm of personal experience. The concept of personal faith was viewed as almost an oxymoron because no two terms could be farther apart in reality at this period of church history. These mystic priests tried to make the Catholic faith a more satisfying encounter with God through personal sensitivity and experience. They failed, however, to create momentum sufficient to facilitate any long-term change.

2. The state of decline in the church's leadership.

The second internal contributing factor for reforming the Catholic Church rested with the general state of decline among the clergy themselves. As was mentioned in earlier chapters, the church had acquired large land holdings, political influence and power, a blind obedience among the illiterate masses, and clergymen who were selected on the basis of political appointment rather than on their spiritual leadership. Many of the clergy had risen to their respective offices as a result of manipulation, nepotism, coercion, and/or bribery. Many of them had taken advantage of their social prestige and had grown accustomed to the rights and privileges of office.

Because marriage was forbidden among the clergy, some of the priests took concubines or had illicit sexual affairs with women in their congregations. Because few seminaries were dedicated to the preparation and training of the clergy and because many bishops would ordain almost anyone who requested (or paid for) it, a large contingent of underemployed and uneducated priests rose from the ranks of the lower class. Because they had never attended school, they could not read and were never formally trained for their responsibilities as priests. Therefore, they were totally unfit to raise their parishioners above the level of popular ignorance and superstition. Moreover, the clergy themselves were known for their ignorance, barbarism, rudeness, drunkenness, personal coarseness, and lack of spiritual understanding. The religious orders of monks, friars, and nuns were often held by individuals who did not even belong to their appropriate orders but did nothing other than collect the revenue assigned to the position.[4]

The papacy was no better off. For example, Pope Innocent VIII (1484–92) was known as being more concerned about maintaining his own power and control through the extensive use of nepotism than in the spiritual concerns of his high office.

Then came Pope Alexander VI (1492–1503), a depraved scoundrel who

---

4. Charles G. Nauert, *The Age of Renaissance and Reformation* (New York: University Press of America, 1981), 56-57.

bribed his way to the papal throne, used his spiritual authority to free his daughter Lucrezia Borgia to contract new marriages useful to papal politics, and allowed his brutal son Cesare Borgia to undertake the violent creation of a hereditary Borgia within the papal territories. The sexual incontinence of the pope himself was not, as in the case of Innocent VIII, a matter of his youthful past, and the families of his mistresses also were rewarded with church offices. For example, Alessandro Farnese, the brother of one of these women, became a cardinal at twenty-five solely because of his sister's relationship with the pope.[5]

The lack of genuine interest and concern for the spiritual condition of the populace eventually gave rise to a general state of cynicism and disgust for the leadership of the Catholic Church. Whether they were simple priests, monks, or friars or had risen to the high office of bishop, cardinal, or even pope, most of those who were in positions of spiritual leadership within the church were viewed with suspicion and contempt. The recognition of the need and demand for reform from within the church itself was largely ignored. These internal factors contributed to a significant decline in the effectiveness of the church.

External Contributing Factors

A number of external forces were also driving the church to reform its practices. Many such forces could be cited here with supporting evidence; however, two forces of significant note will be highlighted: first, the power struggle that existed between various European monarchs and the papacy; second, several inventions that created rapid social changes that caught the church off guard and unprepared.

1. Power struggles occurred between European monarchs and the papacy.
Rather than being content to administer spiritual leadership and influence among the peoples of Europe, the church insisted on also having final authority over the administrative judgments of national monarchs. As such, the papacy believed that it was its right and duty to hold final authority over all matters pertaining to international decision making. At this point, monarchs from all over Europe established their battle lines against what they perceived to be increasingly intrusive meddling from Rome.

---

5. Ibid., 54.

The population of Europe in 1500 was sixty-five to eighty million people and comprised possibly sixty or more kings, princes, archbishops, and other rulers with various structures of power and authority. New social forces such as capitalism and the bourgeois class that rose up with it, the new technology associated with the printing press, mining, commerce, transportation, and other enterprises were having a profound impact on previously established forms of governance.[6] Alliances that once existed between most European governments and the Catholic Church were being strained. The influences of a broad continental economy were complicating matters as never before. All of these factors resulted in a loss of revenue for the church and a desire on the part of the papacy to rein in rogue monarchs for their lack of compliance and cooperation.

So blatant was the power struggle between national monarchs and papal authority that some popes confronted the challenge with resolute force. Pope Boniface VIII (1294–1303) set forth the claim of ultimate papal authority over universal earthly kingdoms. His famous bull *Unam sanctam* (1302) stated bluntly that all legitimate authority came to the king only through the auspices of the supreme pontiff. He concluded that obedience to the pope was a necessary requirement for salvation. He claimed that a pope had the authority to depose a defiant monarch, to absolve the monarch's subjects of all oaths of loyalty, and even to stir up rebellion against him/her if the pope thought that such action was warranted and in the best interests of the church.[7]

> The rise of strong national monarchies made it certain that the State would do what it could to lessen the amount of papal interference in its internal affairs, to reduce papal control over church appointments, the break the Church's monopoly of education and to cut off the payment of money which was draining the country of its gold according to contemporary economic opinion. In particular the Papacy's intelligent exploitation of every possible source of revenue—annates, tithes, sales of dispensations and offices, indulgences, absolutions— aroused the jealous wrath of the national monarch.[8]

---

6. Spitz, *Renaissance and Reformation Movements,* 309.

7. Nauert, *Age of Renaissance and Reformation,* 59.

8. V. H. H. Green, *Renaissance and Reformation* (London: Edward Arnold, 1959), 117.

The claim of supreme authority over all earthly governments had gone too far. The battle lines were drawn, and the church lacked both the ability and the resources to do much more than watch as its grip on European governments declined with each new decade.

2. Several inventions contributed to rapid social change.

A second external factor that contributed to the need for a reform of the Catholic Church was the rapid social change that took place as a result of several important inventions. First was the invention of gunpowder, which has been attributed to Roger Bacon at the end of the thirteenth century. The feudal system of lords and land barons ended abruptly once knights' armor was discovered to be no match for the onslaught of a gun or a cannon. Castles could no longer be protected by knights equipped with only spears and swords. As a result, new forces came to power while traditional powers were eliminated. The wealthy aristocratic class of landowners could no longer prevent the establishment of a merchant middle class who heretofore had been prevented from using their entrepreneurial skills to create new industries and opportunities.

The Gunpowder Plot

King James VI had come to the throne in Scotland as a result of the abdication of his mother, Mary Queen of Scots. He came to the British throne as James I and began a campaign to persecute the Catholic population. A Catholic loyalist by the name of Robert Catesby felt compelled to take drastic action to preserve the British Isles for Catholic control. He enlisted the help of his cousin Thomas Wintour and formed a plot to blow up the House of Lords at the opening day ceremonies of Parliament on November 5, 1605. It was their hope that with the death of King James I, his son the Prince of Wales, and most of the members of Parliament they would send England into a state of turmoil. The end result would be that the Catholic Church would perhaps have an opportunity to recover control of the country.

Catesby enlisted the help of a Yorkshire mercenary by the name of Guy Fawkes to provide professional expertise in the use of explosives. Fawkes had distinguished himself while serving in the Spanish army. Catesby also enlisted the help of a group relatives, friends, and colleagues to enter the conspiracy and help finance his plans.

They rented a house near the Palace of Westminster, and the group began to dig a tunnel out under the Houses of Parliament. However, progress was slow for these gentlemen were not used to such hard labor. With opening day fast approaching and progress on the tunnel moving too slow, one of the conspirators was able to use his connections at the Royal Court to rent a cellar right under the House of Lords. Guy Fawkes posed as a servant by the name of "John Johnson" and filled the basement with thirty-six barrels of gunpowder hidden beneath coal and some wooden sticks.

The plot unraveled when one of the conspirators warned a relative, Lord Monteagle, who was a member of the House of Lords, not to attend the opening day ceremony. He was sitting down to dinner in his Hoxton home when a letter arrived for him that read:

My lord, out of the love I bear to some of your friends, I have a care for your preservation. Therefore I would advise you, as you tender your life, to devise some excuse to shift of your attendance of this Parliament, for God and man hath concurred to punish the wickedness of this time. And think not slightly of this advertisement but retire yourself into your country, where you may expect the event in safety, for though there be no appearance of any stir, yet I say they shall receive a terrible blow, the Parliament, and yet they shall not see who hurts them. This counsel is not to be condemned, because it may do you good and can do you know harm, for the danger is past as soon as you have burnt the latter: and I hope God will give you the grace to make good use of it, to whose holy protection I commend you.

The subsequent investigation led to the discovery of the gunpowder and those involved in the plot were apprehended, put on trial, found guilty, and hanged for treason. To this day, England celebrates the intentions of these men on November 5 of each year. On Guy Fawkes Day children light large bonfires and the entire community comes out to watch the pile burn.[9]

The second significant invention was the printing press by a German goldsmith named Johann Gensfleisch. He later changed his last name to

---

9. David Nash Ford, *The Gunpowder Plot*, http://www.britannia.com/history/kaboom.html.

Johann Gutenberg. Little is known about him because his name is not cited in any of his works. His goldsmith background enabled him to explore the varied uses of molten metal, one of which was the creation of individual metal letters that could be used to form movable type. Once these letters were inked and paper was pressed upon them, the pages could be removed and allowed to dry. The resulting page left an exact replica of the original, thus shortening considerably the amount of time it took for a scribe to copy a manuscript.

The Gutenberg Bible

Before Gutenberg's innovation, most books were produced by and for the church using the process of wood engraving. This required the craftsman to cut away the background, leaving the area to be printed raised. This process applied to both text and illustrations and was extremely time-consuming. When a page was complete, often comprising a number of blocks joined together, it would be inked and a sheet of paper was then pressed over it for an imprint. The susceptibility of wood to the elements gave such blocks a limited life span.

But metal type changed all this, and in 1455 what is known as the 42 Line Bible (also known as the Gutenberg Bible) was published in Mainz. It is considered to have been the first substantial publication and took Gutenberg fully two years to complete. In the same year his financier, Johann Fust, foreclosed on their agreements, and Gutenberg lost his press and other equipment, although he is believed to have reequipped himself soon afterwards.

Like him, others in the industry needed sympathetic financiers. They found greatest demand for their work from the church, and many early publications were of a religious nature, often in Latin, and took the form of pamphlets, booklets, and complete volumes. It was not until 1476 that the first printing press was established in England.[10]

---

10. N.a., http://www.dotprint.com/fgen/history1.htm. For additional sources regarding the contribution of Johan Gutenburg, see also Richard W. Clement, ORB Online Encyclopedia, Books and Universities, Medieval and Renaissance

The third invention of note was related to the second. Although to state that paper was invented during the Reformation would be incorrect, a number of major changes in its manufacture occurred that made it available to both those of the printing trade and the populace as a whole. This availability contributed to the rapid spread of correspondence and communication among the people on the European continent. Change and progress (e.g., freedom from tyranny) that was being enjoyed in one part of the Holy Roman Empire was communicated to other parts as a motivational force for further reforms. Now what one country had won was possible for others as well. A modern equivalent would be the development of the Internet, which made it possible to spread truth and counter biased propaganda across national boundaries via the World Wide Web.

THE ERA OF CHURCH REFORM

Martin Luther (1483-1546) was born on November 10, 1483, in the little town of Eisleben. His father was a peasant who had migrated with his family from their ancestral homeland to the region of Germany where opportunities existed for new mining investments. Martin learned the value of hard work and persistence while watching his parents endure hard labor. His parents' austerity and severe methods of corporal discipline instilled in him a depth of character. His mother allegedly whipped him to the point of drawing blood when she discovered that he had stolen a nut from the kitchen pantry. His early childhood days at school were also marked by harsh treatment. At one point, his teacher whipped him fifteen times in one morning. The teacher stated, "We must whip children, but we must at the same time

---

Book Production—Printed Books http://orb.rhodes.edu/encyclop/culture/books/medbook2.html; and also see Albert Hyma, *The Brethren of the Common Life* (Grand Rapids: Eerdmans, 1950); and Regnerus R. Post, *The Modern Devotion: Confrontation with Reformation and Humanism* (Leiden: E. J. Brill, 1968). On Gutenberg and the first half-century of printing, see Luigi Balsamo, "The Origins of Printing in Italy and England," *Journal of the Printing Historical Society* 11 (1975-1976): 48-63; C. H. Bloy, *A History of Printing Ink, Balls and Rollers 1440-1850* (London: Wynkyn de Worde Society, 1967). There is a vast literature on the "Gutenberg question," much of it flawed or outdated; for a good review of Gutenberg, see George D. Painter, "Gutenberg and the B36 Group: A Reconsideration," in *Studies in Fifteenth-Century Printing* (London: Pindar, 1984), 1-31.

love them." In spite of this brusque learning environment, Luther's teachers managed to instill in him the catechism, the Ten Commandments, the Apostle's Creed, the Lord's Prayer, and several hymns.[11]

Luther enrolled in a school administered by the Brethren of the Common Life in Magdeburg. There he heard for the first time from his early mentor Andrew Proles, provincial of the Augustinian order, that change and reform were warranted in the church.[12] His father wanted Luther to study law, but in 1505, while caught in a severe thunderstorm, Luther vowed to Saint Anne that if God would spare his life he would enter a convent and become a monk. Two weeks later, at the age of twenty-one, he entered the gates of the monastery of the Augustinian hermits at Erfurt. Two years later, he was ordained and celebrated his first mass.

Luther was resolved to give himself wholeheartedly to his religious studies. He had a deep yearning for a personal relationship with God that motivated him to excel in his religious instruction. However, this yearning was never satisfied by the rigors of academics or ascetic isolation. His "man-made" righteousness never seemed to satisfy the deep longing of his soul for the spiritual peace that only God could provide.

Luther taught theology at the new university that had been established in Erfurt. Soon afterward, he was sent to Rome on church business, and there he saw firsthand the abuses of the church upon the commoners. In Rome, he observed for himself the corruption of the clergy, their lack of spiritual disciplines, and their aggressive means of seeking financial gain through the sale of indulgences. He was astounded by their flippancy and returned to Wittenberg in 1511 resolved to see necessary reforms initiated. He had earlier written *Disputations Against Scholastic Theology* to address these abuses, but it had received little, if any, attention. Frustrated by the lack of response to his repeated calls for convening a council to address these questionable practices, he prepared his arguments in the form of ninety-five statements that he nailed to the door of the court church as an invitation to debate.

---

11. J. H. Merle D'Aubigne, *The Life and Times of Martin Luther* (Chicago: Moody, 1978), 14–15.
12. Ibid., 15.

Indulgences for Sale!

The theory of indulgences concerned the remission of the punishment of sins. Only God can forgive sin, but the repentant sinner also has to undergo punishment on earth in the form of penance and after death in purgatory, where sinners repentant on earth atone for their sins and are prepared for heaven. Indulgences could not assure the forgiveness of sins, according to the theory advanced by medieval schoolmen, but they could remit penance and part or all of the punishment in purgatory. The church claimed authority to grant such remission by drawing on the Treasury of Merit, a storehouse of surplus good works accumulated by the holy activities of Christ, the Virgin, and the saints. Only the priest could secure for a layman a draft, as it were, on this heavenly treasury.

The doctrine of indulgences was thus a complex matter, too complex for the ordinary layman to grasp completely. To the man in the street in sympathy with the Reformers, it must have looked as though a sinner could obtain not only remission of punishment but also forgiveness of sins if only he secured enough indulgences.[13]

It was not Luther's intention to divide the church. His love for and devotion to the church were unquestioned. What he sought was a venue where tradition could be challenged on the basis of scriptural teaching. So much tradition had crept into the church over the past fifteen hundred years that it was past time to review some of them and determine whether a biblical basis existed for their continuance. Chief among his issues was the practice of selling indulgences whereby the buyers hoped to secure God's forgiveness. However, that was not his only complaint. He was also beginning to question the whole notion of the priesthood and its supreme authority to forgive sin when the Scriptures did not teach such a position. Indeed, the more Luther studied the Scriptures, the more convinced he was that the church had drifted slowly away from its theological moorings and was in need of a course correction.

---

13. Crane Brinton, John B. Christopher, and Robert L. Wolff, *A History of Civilization* (Englewood Cliffs, N.J.: Prentice-Hall, 1967), 462.

Luther's main issues and the basis of his subsequent reform were threefold:

1. *Justification by faith.* Salvation could be acquired only by someone who had made a genuine confession of sin and was sincerely penitent. Salvation was a gift of grace that came through faith from God alone (Rom. 1:17). It could not be achieved through the purchase of an indulgence. Furthermore, those who were guilty of selling such indulgences were themselves guilty of spiritual negligence, and God would punish them severely for their fraudulent practices.
2. *The supremacy of Scripture.* The Scriptures can be interpreted by those in whom the Holy Spirit has taken up residence. The Bible was provided for all believers, not just those in the ecclesiastical hierarchy. No longer should believers be reliant upon the interpretation provided by the pope or his councils because history had already proven that such means were rife with fraud, contradiction, and inaccuracy. Luther translated the Bible into German so that everyone in his homeland could become acquainted firsthand with their loving Creator.
3. *The priesthood of all believers.* All individuals who have made a genuine commitment to follow Christ are themselves priests and have the rightful privilege of entering God's throne of grace without the mediating efforts of the clergy. This position threatened the entire structure of the Catholic Church, which Luther was now content to criticize. In his book *The Babylonian Captivity of the Church,* he compared true believers to Israel and referred to the pope as the Antichrist, who had taken believers captive by falsely interpreting the Scriptures concerning the sacraments. Luther believed that the only true church sacraments were baptism and the Lord's Supper.

It goes without saying that Luther's theological presuppositions were not well received by papal authorities. Soon after he published his views, the pope issued a papal bull declaring Luther a heretic. Fortunately for Luther, political transitions in France and Germany were taking center stage and competed for the pope's attention. This, in turn, bought Luther additional time to organize his doctrinal positions and put them in writing for future generations. Luther also enjoyed the protection of Fredrick the Wise, Elector of Saxony.

Luther continued his vigilant calls for church reform. In January 1521, Luther was excommunicated from the church, and in May 1521, the Diet of Worms also placed him under further restrictions. During his appearance before the Diet he defended his theological positions. When he was ordered to recant his views, he reportedly said to those assembled, "Here I stand. I cannot do otherwise. God help me. Amen!" The Diet also condemned those who followed Luther and anyone who so much as read his publications. Being associated with Luther in any way was dangerous. Shortly before his death in 1546, he wrote *Against the Papacy at Rome, Established by the Devil*, which was his final word on the illegitimacy of the papacy.

Luther's Ninety-five Theses

Much has been said over the years regarding Luther's Ninety-five Theses. Because they set off a virtual firestorm in the Catholic Church and across Europe, to produce them here for your review is worth the effort.

1. When our Lord and Master Jesus Christ said, "Repent" (Matt. 4:17), he willed the entire life of believers to be one of repentance.
2. This word cannot be understood as referring to the sacrament of penance, that is, confession and satisfaction, as administered by the clergy.
3. Yet it does not mean solely inner repentance; such inner repentance is worthless unless it produces various outward mortification of the flesh.
4. The penalty of sin remains as long as the hatred of self (that is, true inner repentance), namely until our entrance into the kingdom of heaven.
5. The pope neither desires nor is able to remit any penalties except those imposed by his own authority or that of the canons.
6. The pope cannot remit any guilt, except by declaring and showing that it has been remitted by God; or, to be sure, by remitting guilt in cases reserved to his judgment. If his right to grant remission in these cases were disregarded, the guilt would certainly remain unforgiven.
7. God remits guilt to no one unless at the same time he humbles him in all things and makes him submissive to the vicar, the priest.

8. The penitential canons are imposed only on the living, and, according to the canons themselves, nothing should be imposed on the dying.

9. Therefore the Holy Spirit through the pope is kind to us insofar as the pope in his decrees always makes exception of the article of death and of necessity.

10. Those priests act ignorantly and wickedly who, in the case of the dying, reserve canonical penalties for purgatory.

11. Those tares of changing the canonical penalty to the penalty of purgatory were evidently sown while the bishops slept (Matt. 13:25).

12. In former times canonical penalties were imposed, not after, but before absolution, as tests of true contrition.

13. The dying are freed by death from all penalties, are already dead as far as the canon laws are concerned, and have a right to be released from them.

14. Imperfect piety or love on the part of the dying person necessarily brings with it great fear; and the smaller the love, the greater the fear.

15. This fear or horror is sufficient in itself, to say nothing of other things, to constitute the penalty of purgatory, since it is very near to the horror of despair.

16. Hell, purgatory, and heaven seem to differ the same as despair, fear, and assurance of salvation.

17. It seems as though for the souls in purgatory fear should necessarily decrease and love increase.

18. Furthermore, it does not seem proved, either by reason or by Scripture, that souls in purgatory are outside the state of merit, that is, unable to grow in love.

19. Nor does it seem proved that souls in purgatory, at least not all of them, are certain and assured of their own salvation, even if we ourselves may be entirely certain of it.

20. Therefore the pope, when he uses the words "plenary remission of all penalties," does not actually mean "all penalties," but only those imposed by himself.

21. Thus those indulgence preachers are in error who say that a man is absolved from every penalty and saved by papal indulgences.

22. As a matter of fact, the pope remits to souls in purgatory no penalty which, according to canon law, they should have paid in this life.

23. If remission of all penalties whatsoever could be granted to anyone at all, certainly it would be granted only to the most perfect, that is, to very few.

24. For this reason most people are necessarily deceived by that indiscriminate and high-sounding promise of release from penalty.

25. That power which the pope has in general over purgatory corresponds to the power which any bishop or curate has in a particular way in his own diocese and parish.

26. The pope does very well when he grants remission to souls in purgatory, not by the power of the keys, which he does not have, but by way of intercession for them.

27. They preach only human doctrines who say that as soon as the money clinks into the money chest, the soul flies out of purgatory.

28. It is certain that when money clinks in the money chest, greed and avarice can be increased; but when the church intercedes, the result is in the hands of God alone.

29. Who knows whether all souls in purgatory wish to be redeemed, since we have exceptions in St. Severinus and St. Paschal, as related in a legend.

30. No one is sure of the integrity of his own contrition, much less of having received plenary remission.

31. The man who actually buys indulgences is as rare as he who is really penitent; indeed, he is exceedingly rare.

32. Those who believe that they can be certain of their salvation because they have indulgence letters will be eternally damned, together with their teachers.

33. Men must especially be on guard against those who say that the pope's pardons are that inestimable gift of God by which man is reconciled to him.

34. For the graces of indulgences are concerned only with the penalties of sacramental satisfaction established by man.

35. They who teach that contrition is not necessary on the part of those who intend to buy souls out of purgatory or to buy confessional privileges preach unChristian doctrine.

36. Any truly repentant Christian has a right to full remission of penalty and guilt, even without indulgence letters.

37. Any true Christian, whether living or dead, participates in all the

blessings of Christ and the church; and this is granted him by God, even without indulgence letters.

38. Nevertheless, papal remission and blessing are by no means to be disregarded, for they are, as I have said (Thesis 6), the proclamation of the divine remission.

39. It is very difficult, even for the most learned theologians, at one and the same time to commend to the people the bounty of indulgences and the need of true contrition.

40. A Christian who is truly contrite seeks and loves to pay penalties for his sins; the bounty of indulgences, however, relaxes penalties and causes men to hate them—at least it furnishes occasion for hating them.

41. Papal indulgences must be preached with caution, lest people erroneously think that they are preferable to other good works of love.

42. Christians are to be taught that the pope does not intend that the buying of indulgences should in any way be compared with works of mercy.

43. Christians are to be taught that he who gives to the poor or lends to the needy does a better deed than he who buys indulgences.

44. Because love grows by works of love, man thereby becomes better. Man does not, however, become better by means of indulgences but is merely freed from penalties.

45. Christians are to be taught that he who sees a needy man and passes him by, yet gives his money for indulgences, does not buy papal indulgences but God's wrath.

46. Christians are to be taught that, unless they have more than they need, they must reserve enough for their family needs and by no means squander it on indulgences.

47. Christians are to be taught that the buying of indulgences is a matter of free choice, not commanded.

48. Christians are to be taught that the pope, in granting indulgences, needs and thus desires their devout prayer more than their money.

49. Christians are to be taught that papal indulgences are useful only if they do not put their trust in them, but very harmful if they lose their fear of God because of them.

50. Christians are to be taught that if the pope knew the exactions of the indulgence preachers, he would rather that the basilica of St. Peter were burned to ashes than built up with the skin, flesh, and bones of his sheep.

51. Christians are to be taught that the pope would and should wish to give of his own money, even though he had to sell the basilica of St. Peter, to many of those from whom certain hawkers of indulgences cajole money.

52. It is vain to trust in salvation by indulgence letters, even though the indulgence commissary, or even the pope, were to offer his soul as security.

53. They are the enemies of Christ and the pope who forbid altogether the preaching of the Word of God in some churches in order that indulgences may be preached in others.

54. Injury is done to the Word of God when, in the same sermon, an equal or larger amount of time is devoted to indulgences than to the Word.

55. It is certainly the pope's sentiment that if indulgences, which are a very insignificant thing, are celebrated with one bell, one procession, and one ceremony, then the gospel, which is the very greatest thing, should be preached with a hundred bells, a hundred processions, a hundred ceremonies.

56. The true treasures of the church, out of which the pope distributes indulgences, are not sufficiently discussed or known among the people of Christ.

57. That indulgences are not temporal treasures is certainly clear, for many indulgence sellers do not distribute them freely but only gather them.

58. Nor are they the merits of Christ and the saints, for, even without the pope, the latter always work grace for the inner man, and the cross, death, and hell for the outer man.

59. St. Lawrence said that the poor of the church were the treasures of the church, but he spoke according to the usage of the word in his own time.

60. Without want of consideration we say that the keys of the church, given by the merits of Christ, are that treasure.

61. For it is clear that the pope's power is of itself sufficient for the remission of penalties and cases reserved by himself.

62. The true treasure of the church is the most holy gospel of the glory and grace of God.

63. But this treasure is naturally most odious, for it makes the first to be last (Matt. 20:16).

64. On the other hand, the treasure of indulgences is naturally most acceptable, for it makes the last to be first.

65. Therefore the treasures of the gospel are nets with which one formerly fished for men of wealth.

66. The treasures of indulgences are nets with which one now fishes for the wealth of men.

67. The indulgences which the demagogues acclaim as the greatest graces are actually understood to be such only insofar as they promote gain.

68. They are nevertheless in truth the most insignificant graces when compared with the grace of God and the piety of the cross.

69. Bishops and curates are bound to admit the commissaries of papal indulgences with all reverence.

70. But they are much more bound to strain their eyes and ears lest these men preach their own dreams instead of what the pope has commissioned.

71. Let him who speaks against the truth concerning papal indulgences be anathema and accursed.

72. But let him who guards against the lust and license of the indulgence preachers be blessed.

73. Just as the pope justly thunders against those who by any means whatever contrive harm to the sale of indulgences.

74. Much more does he intend to thunder against those who use indulgences as a pretext to contrive harm to holy love and truth.

75. To consider papal indulgences so great that they could absolve a man even if he had done the impossible and had violated the mother of God is madness.

76. We say on the contrary that papal indulgences cannot remove the very least of venial sins as far as guilt is concerned.

77. To say that even St. Peter if he were now pope, could not grant greater graces is blasphemy against St. Peter and the pope.

78. We say on the contrary that even the present pope, or any pope whatsoever, has greater graces at his disposal, that is, the gospel, spiritual powers, gifts of healing, etc., as it is written, 1 Corinthians 12[:28].

79. To say that the cross emblazoned with the papal coat of arms, and set up by the indulgence preachers is equal in worth to the cross of Christ is blasphemy.

80. The bishops, curates, and theologians who permit such talk to be spread among the people will have to answer for this.

81. This unbridled preaching of indulgences makes it difficult even for learned men to rescue the reverence which is due the pope from slander or from the shrewd questions of the laity.

82. Such as: "Why does not the pope empty purgatory for the sake of holy love and the dire need of the souls that are there if he redeems an infinite number of souls for the sake of miserable money with which to build a church?" The former reason would be most just; the latter is most trivial.

83. Again, "Why are funeral and anniversary masses for the dead continued and why does he not return or permit the withdrawal of the endowments founded for them, since it is wrong to pray for the redeemed?"

84. Again, "What is this new piety of God and the pope that for a consideration of money they permit a man who is impious and their enemy to buy out of purgatory the pious soul of a friend of God and do not rather, because of the need of that pious and beloved soul, free it for pure love's sake?"

85. Again, "Why are the penitential canons, long since abrogated and dead in actual fact and through disuse, now satisfied by the granting of indulgences as though they were still alive and in force?"

86. Again, "Why does not the pope, whose wealth is today greater than the wealth of the richest Crassus, build this one basilica of St. Peter with his own money rather than with the money of poor believers?"

87. Again, "What does the pope remit or grant to those who by perfect contrition already have a right to full remission and blessings?"

88. Again, "What greater blessing could come to the church than if the pope were to bestow these remissions and blessings on every believer a hundred times a day, as he now does but once?"

89. "Since the pope seeks the salvation of souls rather than money by his indulgences, why does he suspend the indulgences and pardons previously granted when they have equal efficacy?"

90. To repress these very sharp arguments of the laity by force alone, and not to resolve them by giving reasons, is to expose the church and the pope to the ridicule of their enemies and to make Christians unhappy.

91. If, therefore, indulgences were preached according to the spirit and intention of the pope, all these doubts would be readily resolved. Indeed, they would not exist.

92. Away, then, with all those prophets who say to the people of Christ, "Peace, peace," and there is no peace (Jer. 6:14)!
93. Blessed be all those prophets who say to the people of Christ, "Cross, cross," and there is no cross!
94. Christians should be exhorted to be diligent in following Christ, their Head, through penalties, death and hell.
95. And thus be confident of entering into heaven through many tribulations rather than through the false security of peace (Acts 14:22).

Luther's contributions to Christian education are many. He understood the value of disciplined study and sought to integrate it in the public schools of his day. He recognized the value of reading the Scriptures personally, and his German translation of the Bible enabled the masses to become enlightened in the Scriptures without an obvious bias or conflict of interest from the church. He supported the home and encouraged parents to become involved in the development of their children. However, when it came to private tutorials or home-based schooling, Luther thought that the public school was the better option. Church-based schools were an abysmal failure at their task of educating children. Greek and Hebrew were required languages to be learned in Lutheran schools because they enabled one to read the Scriptures in the original languages. This, more than any other factor, was that to which Luther ascribed his Reformation freedoms.

Luther wrote numerous hymns and spiritual songs. The most famous of his compositions is "A Mighty Fortress Is Our God." Based on Psalm 46, it became the battle hymn of the Reformation for decades to come. Although he never took time to systematize his educational philosophy, he expressed a great deal of concern regarding Christian education. Two of his works, *The Letter to Mayors and Aldermen of all the Cities of Germany in Behalf of Christian Schools* (1524) and *Sermon on the Duty of Sending Children to School* (1530), are viewed as Protestant manifestos on education.[14]

Philip Melanchthon (1497-1560) was one of Luther's closest friends and colleagues. A strong argument could be made for the view that the Reformation would not have had as great an impact on Christian education had it not been for the efforts of Melanchthon because he brought many of Luther's

---

14. James E. Reed and Ronnie Prevost, *A History of Christian Education* (Nashville: Broadman & Holman, 1993), 193.

educational reforms to the classroom. As a strong humanist and lover of classical languages, Melanchthon sought to maintain much of the momentum that had been started in the Reformation period.

Melanchthon was something of a child prodigy. At the young age of twelve, he enrolled at the University of Heidelberg, and by fourteen he had earned the Bachelor of Arts degree. Not being allowed to sit for the examination because of his youth, he transferred to the University of Tubingen, where he became a Master, that is, a university instructor, a feat nearly unheard of at the time. At the age of twenty-one, he became the Greek professor at Wittenberg and eventually a close colleague of Luther.[15]

At the Wittenberg university on August 29, 1518, he delivered his inaugural address, titled "The Reform of University Studies,"and called for an integration of humanistic educational principles and curriculum within the contemporary setting, reforms for which Luther himself had previously called.[16] Luther and Melanchthon shared a deep bond as a result of their compatible theological and philosophical positions. Indeed, they had differences of opinion to work out, but the bonds of friendship and camaraderie would carry them through many a turbulent struggle with the Holy See.

> The two great men were at once drawn to each other. Luther's clear understanding, deep feeling, pious spirit, heroic courage, overwhelmed Melanchthon with wonder, so that he reverenced him as a father. Melanchthon's great learning, fine culture and tender heart, acted as a charm upon Luther. Each found the complement of his own nature in the other. God had joined the two with marvellous adaptation. . . . Together they achieved what neither could have done without the other. Hence they are entitled to share equal honours for the work of the Reformation.[17]

As a humanist educator, Melanchthon was devoted to the importance of the classics and sought to incorporate them into the public educational system of Germany. As a professor at Wittenberg, he was also required to hold

---

15. Kurt Aland, *Reformers* (Minneapolis: Augsburg, 1979), 61.
16. Ibid., 63.
17. James W. Richard, *Philip Melanchthon: The Protestant Precepter of Germany* (New York: Lenox Hill, 1974), 41–42.

to the strongest of commitments regarding the authority of the Scriptures. With both priorities, Melanchthon was able to become one of the strongest forces for educational reform. As a dedicated Christian humanist, Melanchthon served for generations to come as a model concerning the ability to build a rigorous scholarship on genuine biblical foundations. His commitment to Christian scholarship is the flagship of modern Christian universities.

During the sixteenth century, European countries were experiencing a renewed spirit of nationalism. Ruled by monarchs who personified their national reputation, these nations set about adding structure to their idealism and dreamed of futures beyond what they had thought possible a century earlier. Their ties with the Roman Church threatened to weaken their growth and development, causing many people in authority to question their historical allegiance to the Holy See. Primary loyalty belonged to their state as people began to define themselves as English, French, Spanish, Swiss, etc.[18] This nationalism led to evangelistic efforts that were more nationally focused. Chief among those who directed their evangelical efforts at their homelands was John Calvin (1509-64).

The Reformation came to the French-speaking city of Geneva, Switzerland, in 1536 through the efforts of Guillaume Farel (1489-1565), but the work of John Calvin had the most lasting influence. Calvin turned the city into the center of evangelical thought and mission. He was an outstanding scholar and, except for a few brief years, spent his entire life ministering in Geneva. The influence and significant impact that Calvin had on the population has been traced to three primary factors: (1) his prolific output of commentaries and Bible study resources; (2) his *Institutes of Christian Religion,* which he published in 1536; and (3) his establishment of the Geneva Academy, a school dedicated to assisting refugees, many of whom caught his mission and traveled the world to spread the evangelical message of the gospel. Calvinism, as his teachings were called at the time, spread across Europe and became the dominant form of Protestantism in many of the countries where it was introduced. In France, Calvinists were called Huguenots. Although they suffered persecution at the hands of Catholic inquisitors, the Edict of Nantes (1598) granted them a degree of religious freedom and toleration. The Edict, however, was revoked in 1686

---

18. Gerald L. Gutek, *Historical and Philosophical Foundations of Education: A Biographical Introduction* (Upper Saddle River, N.J.: Merrill Prentice-Hall, 2001), 85.

forcing them to consider other alternatives for spreading the gospel abroad.[19] In Switzerland, the Calvinist church was the Reformed Church; in the Netherlands, it was known as the Dutch Reformed Church; and in Scotland, it was called the Presbyterian Church. Once the Calvinists arrived in the New England colonies, they were referred to as Separatists and Puritans, and those followers of John Calvin had a profound impact on the shaping of American values during the colonial era.[20]

> As a Protestant reformer, Calvin believed not only that it was necessary to purge the corruptions of Catholicism from Christian practice, but also that young members of the new church had to be instilled with correct doctrine. Like other reformers, such as Luther, Calvin turned to the catechistic method to impress the correct version of Christianity on the minds of the young. He condensed the religious principles of the *Institutues* and the confession into an abbreviated version in a catechism that could be studied by children in school.[21]

Calvinism is perhaps best known for its doctrinal distinctive of predestination. This view holds that God has already destined some people for eternal reward and other people for eternal punishment. God makes the choice even before the person is born. The individual has little to do with the decision because it all depends on God. What is less known about Calvin, however, is his influence on the school system and the national government. Calvin held to strict standards for teachers at his academy. He held them accountable for the student's learning and believed that strict corporal punishment was acceptable to ensure motivation for learning. He believed that the state had an obligation to share in the expenses associated with educating its children. He was instrumental in aligning the laws of the city with the teachings of Scripture. This emphasis, however, led to a series of abusive practices, and from that example we have learned the value of the separation of state and church. The following example should illustrate the dangers of church and state being too closely associated.

---

19. John Hannah, *The Kregel Pictorial Guide to Church History* (Grand Rapids: Kregel, 2000), 12.
20. Gutek, *Historical and Philosophical Foundations of Education,* 93.
21. Ibid., 91. See also John Calvin, *Institutes of the Christian Religion,* trans. Henry Beveridge (Grand Rapids: Eerdmans, 1993), 340-57.

He (Calvin) united the Church and State to such an extent that moral offenses were punishable by the State. During the first twenty-four years of his rule, fifty-eight people were executed, fourteen witches were burned to death, hundreds were exiled and hundreds were punished annually for moral offenses. All places of popular pleasure were closed. Dress regulations were severe. Prisoners were tortured to exact confessions of moral offenses.[22]

Lay Reform Movements

This was a turbulent time to live in Europe if you were not a Catholic. The inquisitors were on a mission to preserve the faith and purify the church. Even the simplest of observers could see that the church had lost its zeal and was using manipulation and coercion to maintain its popularity. Small embers of resistance began to glow until the fires of reform caught on across the continent. Once people had a chance to read the Scriptures in their own language and come to their own conclusions regarding the discrepancies between what the Scriptures taught and what the church was practicing, a groundswell of religious revolt was inevitable. From a Catholic point of view, a strong response was needed. This response came as councils and creeds forced people to state their unequivocal allegiance to the pope and the church. Those who did not swear such allegiance were dealt with severely. Persecution was harsh and was intended to make a strong statement about the resolve of the church to guard its own. Once groups of reformers were identified, they were to be eliminated much like a cancer has to be destroyed to preserve the health of the entire body. These groups of reformers included Waldensians, Hussites, Lollards, Albigensians, Anabaptists, Puritans, and Mennonites. A brief synopsis of each group will acquaint the reader with these important historic movements.

The Waldensians

Peter Waldo espoused a life of poverty, simplicity, and humility, and his followers were known as Waldensians. In keeping with the beliefs of their

---

22. Leo Daley, *History of Education* (New York: Monarch, 1966), 67; as quoted in James E. Reed and Ronnie Prevost, *A History of Christian Education* (Nashville: Broadman & Holman, 1993), 199.

leader, who in 1170 took a vow of poverty, they lived a simple existence and sought a genuine relationship with God. In 1184, Waldo was excommunicated, and his followers were persecuted for hundreds of years. At times, the persecution of the Waldensians became acute. Take, for example, the following account of one of many such episodes.

When Cardinal Tournon told the king that the Waldensians were in revolt and opposing his sovereign government, he revoked his refusal to deal harshly with them. The cardinal had no pity in his breast; he hurried away, and after fixing a seal upon the document himself and fabricating a false military order, launched a brutal soldiery upon the innocent villages. One reason for this dastardly act was the ambition of the Baron d'Oppede to possess the fertile lands that the Waldensians during six generations of toil had transformed into a blooming garden. The result was that Merindol, Cabrieres, and twenty-two other villages were denuded of their population by the most revolting barbarism (1545). The official conscience knew that it was one of the worst crimes in all history, and Francis I, king of France, commanded his heir, Henry II, to bring the guilty ones to justice, but all except one were exculpated.[23]

It was a difficult time in history to seek a simple life free of political or religious intrusion. Both the monarchy and the church had their eyes and hearts set on capturing the world through financial and military means. Tension existed between the two forces to see which entity could wield the most power in its dominance of the populace.

The Hussites

Beyond finding a solution to the Great Schism, the Council of Constance was established to counter the effects of heresy and false doctrines. One of the leaders whom the council condemned to death was Jan Hus. A reformer from Bohemia, he preached against the unrighteous lifestyle of the clergy, which resulted in his lack of support among religious leaders. Upon his death, the people of his Czech homeland viewed him as a national leader. This church, originally known as the Bohemian Brethren, unified around the theme of rebelling against the Roman See. It survived until the Hapsburgs restored the Catholic Church in 1620.[24]

---

23. Henry S. Lucas, *The Renaissance and the Reformation* (New York: Harper & Brothers, 1934), 569.
24. Tim Dowley, *The Baker Atlas of Christian History* (Grand Rapids: Baker, 1997), 112.

The Lollards

Had the reforming ideas of John Wycliffe, a professor of theology and philosophy at Oxford, been accepted, they would have advanced the starting date of the Protestant Reformation by at least 150 years. Wycliffe believed that the state had supremacy over the papacy and that the Scriptures were the final authority over spiritual matters. He further held the conviction that the measure most desirable for salvation was the complete renunciation of all land ownership both by the church and the laity. The aristocracy and the emerging middle class of London, fearing further damage beyond that which was done in England during the Peasants Revolt of 1381, renounced any support for religious reforms that might have a detrimental impact on their land holdings. Wycliffe was able to flee for his life, but a number of his followers were captured and either hanged or burned at the stake. His followers were referred to as Lollards because of their propensity to mumble during prayer.[25]

The Albigensians

The Albigensians originated in the eleventh century and gained their name from the southern French town of Albi. They viewed themselves as Cathari (pure ones) and criticized the worldly and corrupt lifestyle of the clergy. Because they viewed all material forms as evil, desire for material possessions was tantamount to sin as well. Land ownership, telling falsehoods, and waging war were considered mortal sins. The church often targeted them for persecution.[26]

In 1184, Pope Lucius III delegated the problem of resolving heretical guilt or innocence to his bishops, instituting the Episcopal Inquisition. In 1227, Pope Gregory IX appointed a board of papal inquisitors in direct response to the Albigensian heresy in southwest France. The heresy was related to oriental concepts of mysticism and asceticism and was distinctly anticlerical. It flourished during the twelfth and early thirteenth centuries and was savagely repressed at the instigation of the papacy. The Dominican order of

---

25. E. H. Gwynne-Thomas, *A Concise History of Education to 1900 a.d.* (New York: University Press of America, 1981), 88-89.
26. R. Freeman Butts, *A Cultural History of Education: Reassessing our Educational Traditions* (New York: McGraw Hill, 1947), 147.

friars (the Black Friars) was founded c. 1215 by St. Dominic (1170–1221) for the specific purpose of counteracting the heresy, and this order subsequently was designated to administer the operations of the Inquisition.[27]

The Anabaptists

Zwingli had taught the importance of personal Bible study in his ministry throughout Zurich. Many of his followers were deeply committed to searching the Scriptures for themselves rather than relying on the priest's interpretation. The Anabaptists had their theological birth in the context of these Zurich reforms. Although Zwingli himself advocated a more tolerant and patient timetable for change, his followers were more insistent on a radical break from tradition. These radical reformers took a more conservative position on several important theological issues as a result of their search through the Scriptures. Chief among their theological distinctives was the conviction that an infant should not be baptized because it could not have an understanding of the requisite conditions for baptism (e.g., awareness and accountability for personal sin, ability to appropriate God's grace through a personal decision to accept Christ, or repentance from sinful habits). These individuals, also known as "rebaptizers," viewed the church as comprising the universal and invisible members of God's family apart from the limitations of civil institutions and governments.[28]

Those who preferred the more methodical and diplomatic course of slow reform pressured the radical reformers to leave Zurich. Painted as radicals and heretics, they were expelled from Zurich and forced to travel abroad, looking for a place where their theological views would be accepted. "The growing Anabaptist movement caused, in 1529, the German diet assembled at Speyer to address itself to the problem. It recalled that there was in the books an ancient decree forbidding rebaptism at the penalty of death, and reissued it. Henceforth, the admission of Anabaptist convictions was sufficient to send a man to the stake or at least—in the case of benevolent authorities—to prison."[29]

---

27. Gwynne-Thomas, *A Concise History of Education*, 86.
28. Hans J. Hillerbrand, *The Reformation: A Narrative History Related by Contemporary Observers and Participants* (Grand Rapids: Baker, 1964), 218.
29. Ibid.

The Puritans

When Elizabeth (1533-1603) came to the throne in England, a large number of exiles who had been living on the European continent returned home. Many of these individuals had been fully indoctrinated by Calvin during their sojourn. They rose quickly to positions of influence and exercised their theological convictions over matters of consequence. They described as "idolatrous," "paptistical," and even "satanic" the various practices of the church. They favored a more Presbyterian organizational structure for the church. Because they demanded that the church be "purified" of its ancient Catholic traditions, these people became known as Puritans.[30] Their original intention was not to form a new institution but rather to bring about reform from within the church. Those who were Separatists called for a stronger response, advocating the formation of a new church that aligned itself with practices and customs more closely indicative of the New Testament model.

One of the first Separatists was a ministry leader named Robert Browne of Cambridge. "He developed a congregational theory of the church as the body of those who were 'called out' or 'gathered' from the great mass of men voluntarily associated with each other in the local church. The congregation should elect the pastors, teachers, and elders, not necessarily the well educated, and its worship would follow a very plain order of service. Around 1580 Brown actually gathered such a congregation at Norwich. Alarmed, the government set the wheels of repression in motion."[31]

The Mennonites

Menno Simons (1496-1561) was a peace-minded Anabaptist from Holland. He sought for a church government that was marked by congregational control and characterized by peace, charity, and acts of kindness in the community. He viewed the sacraments as symbolic reminders of Christ's atoning death, and those who were impenitent were excluded from membership. Simons believed that military service was an affront to God because He alone deserved our allegiance. He eschewed taking oaths and participating in any form of civil government. His popular philosophy was summarized in 1539 in a manuscript titled *Book of Fundamentals*. Mennonite

---

30. Lucas, *Renaissance and the Reformation*, 673.
31. Spitz, *Renaissance and Reformation Movements*, 529.

congregations spread from his native East Frisia through the Netherlands, Germany, and Russia.[32]

The vast majority of the groups that we have just sketched, and a few others that we didn't, continued to face harsh criticism and persecution from the civil and religious authorities. Little, if any, freedom existed for individual expression of spiritual formation. Church leaders who held opinions that differed from either the governmental or the ecclesiastical seat of power were quickly identified and persecuted. The climate was ripe for a radical response from these groups. What was needed was the discovery of a new land where religious freedoms would be tolerated and where one's personal faith in Christ would be free from governmental interference. Clearly defined lines of separation were needed between matters that pertained solely to the state (e.g., collection and distribution of taxes, use of natural resources, civil laws, and the military) and matters that were best left to the church to decide (e.g., salvation, worship practices, ordinances, civil morality, and ethical conduct). Without these clearly defined boundaries, conflicts of interest emerged and power struggles ensued.

The last reformer who warrants our investigation is the eminent Moravian bishop John Amos Comenius (1592–1670). Perhaps in his day the most outstanding writer and thinker in the field of educational theory, Comenius was, by all accounts, a prophet ahead of his time. He was appalled by the barbaric methods being employed to teach students in schools. Children were forced to memorize and recite words in a language they neither knew nor understood. He sought to apply the methods of science to educational theory, curriculum design, and instructional methodology. He believed that all education should be carefully graded to follow the natural development of the child. Like Jean Piaget, who would come many years later, Comenius believed that curriculum was best taught sequentially and systematically. He made extensive use of pictures in his teaching to help the student "see" the object that was being learned. Picture books were a mandatory component of Comenius's classrooms.[33]

In *Didactica magma* ("The Great Didactic") he espoused his theory of reforming curriculum and school structure throughout the public school system. Starting when the child was six, he would train the senses of the child and bring about moral, religious, ethical, and social development through

---

32. Ibid., 404.
33. Butts, *Cultural History of Education*, 278.

the use of play, games, storytelling, rhymes, and music. In his vernacular school for ages six to twelve, he would teach reading, writing, and arithmetic. In addition, he would offer studies in music, morals, economics, politics, history, and mechanical arts. In the classical school set aside for those between the ages of twelve and eighteen, he would teach German, Latin, Greek, Hebrew, grammar, rhetoric, logic, mathematics, science, and art. The social dimension of schooling was also considered because, to Comenius, a well-educated child was one that contributed to the betterment of the nation as a whole. Comenius was called upon to consult with the governments of Sweden, Poland, Hungry, and England regarding their educational systems.[34]

THE CATHOLIC COUNTER-REFORMATION

To characterize the Catholic Church as being insensitive to the needs of internal reform would be incorrect. Many of its leaders had attempted to bring reform to the attention of the pope. However, tradition can be difficult to change, and tradition that is also vested in deeply held religious, cultural, and emotional wrappings can be nearly impossible to change. Complicating matters was the relatively short reigns of many of the popes during this time. For example, seven different popes ruled in the half century between 1513 and 1565, from Leo X to Pius IV. "The brevity of papal reigns was here undoubtedly a factor of considerable importance. These seven popes ruled, on the average, for about seven years, all too brief a time to initiate, undertake, and carry out policies."[35] During the Reformation, a number of significant Catholic leaders made strides to bring about reform in the church. We have identified several of them already. Of significance and worthy of some additional attention because of their contributions to religious education are the efforts of Ignatius Loyola (1491–1556) and Francis Xavier (1506–52).

Inigo Lopez de Onaz y Loyola was born into an aristocratic family residing at the castle of Loyola in the Pyrenees. He was the youngest of thirteen children and once served as a page in the courts of Queen Isabella, where he learned to read and write but lacked clear direction. As a result, he seemed

---

34. Ibid., 278–79.
35. Hans J. Hillerbrand, *Christendom Divided: The Protestant Reformation* (New York: Corpus Instrumenttorium, 1971), 274.

to flounder and found himself wasting his early years in idle pursuits of gambling, drinking, reading romance novels, and engaging in various amorous adventures. At one point, he and his brother Pedro Lopez beat up another man and were cast in jail. Inigo Lopez subsequently joined the entourage of the Duke of Najera as a courtier. Courtiers were not actually soldiers but provided assistance to them in much the same way a squire attended to the needs of a knight during the medieval period. During this season of his life, he was injured while defending the citadel of Pamplona when a cannonball passed right between his legs, wounding his left leg and breaking his right leg. The victorious French provided a physician to set his broken limb, and he was released with a handful of Spanish soldiers, who carried him back to Loyola. Once back at the castle, they discovered that the French doctor had not set the bone properly. Inigo insisted that the leg be broken and reset and that a protruding bone be sawn off.[36]

During the subsequent nine-month recuperation, he read Ludolf of Saxony's *Life of Christ* and Jocobo de Voragine's *Lives of the Saints.* These books had a profound impact on his life, whereupon he soon gave his life to Christ and the service of the church. He lived in a cave near Manresa, Spain, where he claimed to have received visions, dreams, and direction for how he would serve the church.

In 1522, he wrote a book titled *Spiritual Exercises,* which became, after its publication in 1548, a handbook for spiritual formation among those who would choose to follow him. He established a Catholic order dedicated to the defense of the papacy and the disciplined service of the church. Although Loyola preferred to call this group the Company of Jesus, or the Society of Jesus, the name *Jesuits* became the lasting label of choice. Having been sanctioned by Pope Paul III, the order was organized along military lines of authority. Loyola was commissioned as the general, and strict obedience was required of everyone who desired to join. After several years of careful reflection, Loyola established a set of general rules to direct the conduct of the fathers in their various duties to God, their superiors, their fellowmen, and themselves. The following nine rules were the educational philosophy of his order and are summarized as follows.[37]

---

36. Richard L. DeMolen, ed., *Leaders of the Reformation* (London: Susquehanna University Press, 1984), 154.
37. Daniel Bartoli, *History of the Life and Institute of St. Ignatius de Loyola* (New York: Edward Dunigan & Brother, 1856), 10–12.

1. The fathers were to endeavor to have their hearts constantly occupied and filled by God.
2. They were to see in their superiors the image of God Himself, to respect their will, and to execute their will with zeal.
3. While conversing with a fellow creature, in hopes of withdrawing him from sin, the same precautions have to be employed as are used to rescue a drowning man, so that he who endeavors to save him may not run the risk of perishing along with him.
4. The fourth rule is that of silence, when our own necessities or those of others do not require it to be broken; but even then, neither proud not haughty language, nor that of curiosity which listens to worldly news, nor the idleness which takes pleasure in vain and jesting remarks, must in any way mingle in the conversation.
5. Whatever great things it may please God to operate through our means, we must count ourselves absolutely nothing, and never usurp a glory which cannot belong to a mere worthless instrument, which (like the jaw-bone of the ass in the hands of Samson) depends solely upon the arm which has directed it.
6. If any of the members shall fall into a public error, likely to injure their reputation, or to diminish the esteem in which they were held, they ought not to feel discouraged; but on the contrary, to render thanks to God for having unveiled the real weakness of their virtue.
7. During the short time set aside for recreation, the Fathers should never lose sight of that modesty which the apostle requires of us at all times.
8. They must never neglect the opportunity of doing good when it presents itself, in the uncertain hope of effecting some still greater good at a future period.
9. Let each member remain firm and unshaken in their vocation, as if its roots were laid in the foundations of the Lord's house.

The hallmark of Jesuit education was the integration of faith and learning. The classroom was marked by stiff competition among learners. The class was divided along military lines with a ratio of one student battalion chief for every ten students. These small groups of students entered into verbal combat with each other through lengthy debate, orations, and exercises of intellectual gymnastics. The instructor identified faulty logic and then applied correct reasoning. The students were rewarded with ribbons and medals for their victories on the academic battlefield. The Jesuit curriculum consisted of religion, languages, the Greek and Roman classics, and strenuous physical exercise. Jesuit education began and ended each day with prayer. Chapel services were mandatory and contributed to the student's ability to live uprightly in this world and to prepare for eternal life with God. The Jesuit system of instruction intended that the student would obtain a wealth of sacred and secular knowledge, think logically through complex issues, and be able to defend the faith (i.e., apologetics) before others both verbally and in writing.[38]

During the remaining fifteen years of Loyola's life, the work of the Jesuits centered on education, preparation of men for service in the church, and evangelism through worldwide missions. The last element would have the most lasting effect on the world. Loyola had a profound impact on the structure and format of education. Jesuit instructors were willing to explore new and innovative ways to improve education and employed methods beyond those of their traditional past. The *Jesuits Plan of Studies,* published three years after Loyola's death in 1596, set forth a model for the structure and substance of Jesuit educational institutions. This pattern was followed for numerous centuries because of its unequivocal success.

Contributing to their success probably more than any other factor was their approach to faculty development and supervision. No teacher was hired without his first having passed their basic university course work, an extensive oral interview, and a rigorous three-year internship. During this time, the novice was placed under the tutelage of a master teacher, who guided his professional development. Those who excelled in teaching undergraduate levels of university students were sent to university for further studies and brought back to instruct in the advanced levels of instruction. Jesuit teachers were head and shoulders above their secular contemporaries in scholarship. They had a reputation for excellence in scholarship, methodical and systematic classroom delivery, the ability to use contemporary instructional methodologies, and a caring and nurturing attitude toward their students. They were model teachers in every respect.

By 1584, the Jesuit Order had established more than 160 colleges. The number of colleges continued to grow at a healthy rate until 1749, when 800 Jesuit colleges existed with a combined student population of 22,589.[39] "Catho-

---

38. Reed and Prevost, *History of Christian Education,* 205.
39. Tim Dowley, *Eerdmans' Handbook to the History of Christianity* (Grand Rapids: Eerdmans, 1977), 414; as cited in Reed and Prevost, *History of Christian Education,* 207.

lic and Protestant historians agree in saying that it was the educational work of the Jesuit Order that checked the advance of Protestantism and saved much of Europe for Catholicism."[40]

The second Catholic educator of note was a fervent Jesuit missionary named Francis Xavier (1506–52). He, like Loyola, was born into a wealthy family with the necessary means to finance his studies in philosophy at the College de Sainte Barbe in Paris. One of the early disciples of Loyola, Xavier swore an oath dedicating himself to the conversion of the Moors. While the older Catholic orders of the Franciscans, the Dominicans, and the Augustinians were actively evangelizing Mexico, Peru, and other Latin American countries, Xavier traveled to India and the East Indies in pursuit of the lost. He was relentless in his efforts to convert the lost and earned a reputation as the "apostle to the Indies and Japan." Traveling through southern India, Xavier met with remarkable success, preaching for three years in the Portuguese colonies at Goa, Cochin, and San Thome and along the coast of Travancore. From there, he traveled to the Portuguese colonies of Malaya, Malacca, Moluccas, and other islands of the East Indies, where he remained for two and a half years. His most prosperous years were spent on a missionary journey to Japan from 1549 to 1551. There he was successful in his efforts to convert people at Kogoshima, Yamagutsi, and elsewhere. He would have continued his Asian tour and moved into China had he not contracted a fever and died at the age of only forty-six.[41]

The Protestant Reformation required a serious and well-orchestrated response from the Catholic Church. The papacy was loath to convene a council because to do so would grant those who participated a platform for criticism and complaint. It was also seen as a means by which to challenge the authority of the pope, who preferred simply to issue a decree and move on. Establishing a venue for the airing of doctrinal differences within the church by the various bishops was the last thing that the pope desired. However, Pope Paul III was forced to call for such an assembly in the *Bull of the Convocation of the Holy Ecumenical Council of Trent* (1545–63). The Council of Trent was the most important council since that of Nicea in A.D. 325. After the adjournment of the Council of Trent, no other council was held for three hundred years, until the First Vatican

---

40. Charles B. Eavey, *History of Christian Education* (Chicago: Moody, 1964), 153.
41. Spitz, *Renaissance and Reformation Movements,* 482–83.

Council in the nineteenth century—the longest span between councils in the history of the church.[42]

The Council of Trent was established with a twofold purpose: to address the heretical doctrines that were circulating throughout Europe and to examine the abusive practices of the clergy. Upon deliberation, they clearly defined the Catholic Church's position on all important doctrinal issues. "All the main points of dispute between Protestants and Catholics were defined in an uncompromising and clear way, and all the distinctive Protestant beliefs were bluntly condemned."[43] During this council, Jerome's Latin Vulgate translation was declared authoritative. The council did not go far enough for most Protestants in that it did not call for the translation of the Scriptures into the vernacular. On this issue and numerous others, however, the Italian representatives at the council held a firm majority of the votes and were determined to preserve papal control over the outcome.

The Council of Trent: An Executive Summary

The grand reforming council of the church was at Trent (1545–63), held strategically in northwest Italy near France. Through a series of gatherings the modern Roman Catholic Church forged its creed. Cardinal Gasparo Contarini (1483–1542) and his supporters still hoped to avoid a final schism in the church. Council action, however, formally made Roman Catholic doctrines nonnegotiable. Protestant teachings were condemned, and the church alone was recognized as having the authority to interpret the Scriptures. Tradition was granted an authoritative status, seven sacraments were defined as the means of reclaiming the grace of salvation, and justification was seen as a gradual process of becoming righteous (righteous as infused, not imputed). Christ's death was a sacrifice that only made salvation possible; it then had to be received through the offices and sacraments of the Roman Church. Further, it was deemed that the actions of Trent were the direct will of the Holy Spirit for the church, giving council decisions the authority of infallible dogma.[44]

---

42. Ibid., 482.
43. Nauert, *Age of Renaissance and Reformation*, 193.
44. Hannah, *Kregel Pictorial Guide to Church History*, 15.

By reading this chapter the reader has probably concluded that the Reformation was a bit more confusing than originally thought. If one considered the Reformation to be the creation of national churches, one would date it from 1517-1648. However, because only Holland was won to Protestantism after the Council of Trent, it might be more accurate to date the Reformation as being between 1517 and 1545. In this way, the Reformation is best explained as that movement of religious reforms that resulted in the creation of the national Protestant churches. The Catholic Reformation may be defined a little differently because its desire was to bring about renewed doctrinal purity and refocus their missionary efforts. Taken this way, the Catholic Reformation may be defined as that movement within the Catholic Church to bring about renewal between 1545 and 1563.[45]

So What? Lessons from the Past for Twenty-first-century Christian Education

"The Reformation, in short, was a coat of many colors. It took many reforms, many meanings, many expressions. It meant different things at different times to different people. It was simple as well as complex, pure as well as adulterated. In such ability to absorb such diversity of roles and meanings may well lie the secret of its historical success—defined rather modestly as its establishment as an institution and an idea that lasted beyond its own time."[46] Yet, in spite of this lack of clarity, several specific principles for application exist within the bounds of twenty-first-century ministry.

1. **God's purposes are often accomplished by people whom we would least expect.**

Looking back through the lens of hindsight, of all of the lessons we can learn from the Reformation, it is a message that is consistent with the earliest dealings between God and humanity. Those upon whom God lays His mantle of mission are not always the individuals whom the world would have chosen. We saw this truth in the Old Testament with the selection of Moses, Gideon,

---

45. Cairns, *Christianity Through the Centuries,* 271.
46. Hans J. Hillerbrand, *The World of the Reformation* (Grand Rapids: Baker, 1981), 31.

Ehud, Saul, David, and many of the prophets. Such was also the case with the selection of many of the apostles, Paul, and Timothy. We see this familiar pattern in the selection of those whom God anointed to bring about change during the Reformation as well.

Many of the men whom God called for Reformation service were young and inexperienced, given the size of the task that they were expected to fulfill.

> The common characteristic of the advocates of the new theology was youth. Luther was thirty-four at the outbreak of the controversy, and Huldriech Zwingli just a few months younger; Melanchthon was twenty. Other reformers were equally young: Wenzesles Link was born in 1483; Friedrich Myconius, in 1491; Jacob Strauss, in 1485; Andreas Osiander, in 1498; Johann Brenz, in 1499; Johann Oecolampadius, in 1482; Martin Bucer, in 1491; Wolfgang Capito, in 1478; Bugenhagen, in 1495; Urban Rhegius, in 1489; Thomas Muntzer, in 1490. Virtually all were young men in their twenties and thirties when controversy broke out, a fact that helps to explain the vitality of the new faith. The Reformation was a movement of youth.[47]

Much can be said about the enthusiastic passions of youth. Youth was not made to be squandered on self-abasement. It was created for valor, courage, and great causes. If the Great Commission is ever going to be brought to completion, it will require the harnessing of youthful energy and channeling it toward the accomplishment of great and noble causes for the sake of Christ's kingdom.

2. The separation of church and state is a principle upon which the United States was established.

Judging by some of the abuses that we have seen thus far in history, when a state and a church become so closely aligned that the decision of one entity conflicts with the interests of the other, abuse of power is usually not far behind. The problem comes when we try to decide who will have the final authority to interpret Scripture. This individual, or governing body, is susceptible to the weaknesses associated with a fallen human nature. The

---

47. Ibid., 41.

saying "Power tends to corrupt, and absolute power corrupts absolutely" is true. We have seen such abuse throughout history on the part of both Catholics and Protestants.

Perhaps in an ideal world we could enjoy having church and state blended. Certainly that will be the case once we arrive in heaven. However, until that time when we enjoy a just and impartial ruler, we will have to provide certain safeguards to ensure freedom of religious expression and to allow for a divers set of opinions about how the Word of God is to be applied in our social systems. Such a system might not be the ideal, but, given the historical pattern of abuse, it is the wisest safeguard that we have.

3. Publicly funded education is the ideal approach to educating our children.

We have seen thus far in history that many countries did not provide for their children's education. It cost too much, and the structural supports were not set up to accommodate the needed resources. A child received an education only if they were fortunate enough to be born into an aristocratic family, able to afford private tutors, pedagogues, or instructors who could provide the child with an education. The majority of children were not so fortunate.

Even in many parts of the world today, the government does little to provide for the educational development of its children. The church should view this problem as a strategic opportunity to send educational missionaries into these countries to provide a basic educational foundation for these children. The North American church has significant resources to provide for this purpose. A simple college degree in almost any field would be more than enough required training to provide basic instruction to children in many Third World countries.

Advanced programs such as Teaching English to Speakers of Other Languages (TESOL) are received with open arms in many countries around the world. This would make for wonderful short-term missions opportunities around the world for churches who are alert to the challenge. Retired adults with years of wisdom and experience have all of the resources they need to teach young children overseas. Single adults who have a background in business, science, mathematics, or social ecology are invaluable assets on the mission field school campus, even if only for a month or more at a time. Many mission organizations have already developed programs for short-term professionals who are able to provide only a few weeks of service. A little education can go a long way toward shaping and influencing a child (and a country) in the name of Jesus.

4. The church must remain relevant.

Ministry programs within the church must change and stay abreast of cultural transitions. Programs that worked with one generation might not—in fact, probably will not—be effective for reaching the next generation. The church must stay relevant and current in its ability to understand changing cultural patterns. Tradition must not be the most important principle or guideline to follow in ministry today.

This task is hard for many ministry leaders because they get set in their ways and prefer not to have to revise and update their materials regularly. Many youth pastors prefer to do what they did before and see if they can get just a little more mileage out of that existing message, game, or song. But culture changes and requires us to change our old worn lesson plans. The game or joke might not be as much fun the second time around. Styles of music and song preferences change as well. Sometimes change is good and even necessary for ministry's ongoing effectiveness.

FOR ADDITIONAL READING

Aland, Kurt. *Four Reformers.* Translated by James L. Schaaf. Minneapolis: Augsburg, 1979.

Bangs, Carl. *Arminius: A Study in the Dutch Reformation.* New York: Abingdon, 1971.

Bartoli, Daniel. *History of the Life and Institute of Ignatius Loyola.* New York: Edward Dunigan & Brother, 1856.

Butts, R. Freeman. *A Cultural History of Education.* New York: McGraw Hill, 1947.

Christopher, Steven. "Martin Luther." In *The Evangelical Dictionary of Christian Education.* Edited by Michael J. Anthony. Grand Rapids: Baker, 2001.

Creighton, M. *A History of the Papacy.* Vol. 6. New York: Longmans' Gren & Company, 1897.

Cunningham, Shelly. "Ulrich Zwingli." In *The Evangelical Dictionary of Christian Education.* Edited by Michael J. Anthony. Grand Rapids: Baker, 2001.

D'Aubigne, J. H. Merle. *The Life and Times of Martin Luther.* Chicago: Moody, 1978.

Davies, James A. "John Calvin." In *The Evangelical Dictionary of Christian Education.* Edited by Michael J. Anthony. Grand Rapids: Baker, 2001.

DeMolen, Richard L., ed. *Leaders of the Reformation.* Toronto: Associated University Press, 1984.

Gough, David. "Philip Melanchthon." In *The Evangelical Dictionary of Christian Education.* Edited by Michael J. Anthony. Grand Rapids: Baker, 2001.

Green, V. H. H. *Renaissance and the Reformation.* London: Edward Arnold, 1952.

Grimm, Harold J. *The Reformation Era.* New York: Macmillan, 1973.

Gutek, Gerald L. *Historical and Philosophical Foundations of Education: A Biographical Introduction.* Upper Saddle River, N.J.: Merrill Prentice-Hall, 2001.

Gwynne-Thomas, E. H. *A Concise History of Education to 1900 a.d.* New York: University Press of America, 1981.

Hillerbrand, Hans J. *Christendom Divided: The Protestant Reformation.* New York: Corpus Instrumentorium, 1971.

———. *The World of the Reformation.* Grand Rapids: Baker, 1981.

Hillerbrand, Hans J., ed. *The Reformation: A Narrative History by Contemporary Observers and Participants.* Grand Rapids: Baker, 1978.

Konig, Gustav. *The Life of Martin Luther: The German Reformer.* London: Nathaniel Cooke, Milford House, Strand, 1585.

Lamb, Robert L. "The Reformation." In *The Evangelical Dictionary of Christian Education.* Edited by Michael J. Anthony. Grand Rapids: Baker, 2001.

Lilje, Hanns. *Luther and the Reformation.* Philadelphia: Fortress, 1967.

Lucas, Henry. *The Renaissance and the Reformation.* New York: Harper & Brothers, 1934.

Martyn, Carlos W. *The Life and Times of Martin Luther.* New York: American Tract Society, 1866.

Monroe, Paul. *A Text-Book in the History of Education.* New York: Macmillan, 1915.

Nauert, Charles G. *The Age of Renaissance and Reformation.* New York: University Press of America, 1981.

Penley, David. "Brethren of the Common Life." In *The Evangelical Dictionary of Christian Education*. Edited by Michael J. Anthony. Grand Rapids: Baker, 2001.

Reisner, Edward H. *Historical Foundations of Modern Education*. New York: Macmillan, 1928.

Richard, James W. *Philip Melanchthon: The Protestant Precepter of Germany*. New York: Lenox Hill, 1898.

Rogness, Michael. *Philip Melanchthon: Reformer Without Honor*. Minneapolis: Augsburg, 1969.

Spitz, Lewis. *The Renaissance and Reformation Movements*. Chicago: Rand McNally, 1971.

Steinmetz, David C. *Reformers in the Wings*. Philadelphia: Fortress, 1971.

Workman, Herbert. *The Dawn of the Reformation*. London: Charles H. Kelly, 1902.

What in the World?

➤ The first Romanov becomes tsar in Russia in 1613.

➤ Personal rule of Louis XIV begins in France in 1661.

➤ Catherine the Great, foremost Russian leader, is born in 1729.

➤ Wolfgang Amadeus Mozart, one of the greatest composers in musical history, is born in 1756 in Salzburg, Austria.

➤ Battle of Waterloo ends the Napoleonic wars in 1815.

Chapter 8

EUROPEAN ORIGINS OF
MODERN CHRISTIAN EDUCATION

THE ENLIGHTENMENT IS DESIGNATED AS THE period between the Peace of Westphalia in 1648 and the French Revolution in 1789. This era was characterized by a continuation of Reformation humanism, whereby man was put at the center of the universe and allowed to be the supreme artisan of his destiny. It is marked by an emphasis upon the concepts of reason, science, progress, personal happiness, scientific inquiry, and the endowed rights of all mankind. Whereas the philosophies intrinsic to the Middle Ages were predicated upon the works of Aristotle and Aquinas's integration of theology and philosophy (faith and reason), the Enlightenment brought about a separation of these entities.

> The worldview of the Middle Ages, the Medieval synthesis, rested on a dualistic conception of reality in which the natural order was viewed as somewhat inferior to the supernatural. The Reformation saw a reawakening of human interest in the awe of the supernatural order. The Enlightenment era saw theorists looking to nature to find clues on how life should be lived. Education was important in that, in the minds of the Enlightenment *philosophes* (philosophers), it prepared people to live according to the principles of nature.[1]

---

1. Gerald L. Gutek, *Historical and Philosophical Foundations of Education: A Biographical Introduction* (Upper Saddle River, N.J.: Merrill Prentice-Hall, 2001), 110.

The theme of the Reformation was developing a new paradigm for thinking about God's relationship with His creation. No longer limited by the dysfunctional theology of unregenerate clergy, constricted by multiple layers of bureaucratic ecclesiastical hierarchy, or confined by the bonds of tradition, the reformed church was free to enjoy a relationship with God typified by renewed vigor and vitality. The Enlightenment took this freedom one step further; it encouraged man to explore the world apart from God.

> For many of the thinkers of the Enlightenment . . . it was important that human beings stopped gazing upward to heaven and begin looking at the natural world about them. They should observe and study natural phenomena and from their observations extract the principles needed to operate in the "real world." The principles of the natural universe could be discovered, the Enlightenment theorists believed, by means of science and use of the scientific method.[2]

Newfound freedoms to think and act according to one's personal beliefs, as opposed to the prescribed expectations of the church, created an environment ripe for new discoveries about the universe. Man was free to ask questions that a few years earlier would have been used against him in a court of inquisition. All across Europe, men were testing new hypotheses about how things worked, how to make society better, and whether the church played a necessary role in the shaping of government and culture.

EUROPEAN CULTURAL CONTEXT OF THE ENLIGHTENMENT

Disillusioned by a thousand years of religious intolerance and man-centered ecclesiastical institutionalism, society was left with two choices: reform the church with a focus on returning to the efficacy of the New Testament model (the intent of the Reformation theologians), or reject God altogether and establish a new worldview totally devoid of God (the intent of the Enlightenment philosophes). Indicative of this attitude, the Enlightenment philosophe Voltaire stated in *Candide,* "Let's eat some Jesuit." Although to state that all Enlightenment philosophes were atheists would be incorrect, their perspective would be more accurately described as agnostic. They believed in a higher power or universal force of some kind, but, they viewed

---

2. Ibid.

this force as unknowable and impersonal. To them, whoever (or whatever) created the universe got the whole thing started and then simply left it to its own devices.

Enlightenment thinkers preferred the world of facts. Facts were drawn from observable behavior that could be tested and measured in controlled environments. The *scientific method* that we take for granted in our schools and laboratories today had its beginnings in this period. "In their investigations of the natural world, the *philosophes* were vitally preoccupied in collecting scientific information about the world. Their enthusiasm for scientific research led them to develop such natural sciences as geology, chemistry, botany, zoology, and physics."[3]

The Enlightenment had profound sociological implications for countries all across the European continent. It threatened the monarchial reigns of national governments with its emphasis on free thinking. "Voltaire and Hume saw an intimate relation between politics, commerce, and religion. Freedom of trade and freedom of opinion, they said, were inextricably linked with civil freedom, and religious tolerance appeared to be linked to commercial prosperity."[4] These new ways of thinking influenced not only the European continent but also many of the Founding Fathers of the American Revolution. We will return to this theme in chapter 10, our discussion of "Christian Education in Colonial America."

The Enlightenment offered a serious challenge to the theologians and Christian educators of its day as well. The Enlightenment philosophes were highly critical of the established church. By proposing that knowledge came from the senses, experience, reason, and feelings rather than from history, tradition, or a universal authority, the Enlightenment thinkers tended to undermine the theological and philosophical presuppositions of seventeenth- and eighteenth-century Christians. The response of many of those believers was to become overly defensive and argumentative. The Roman Catholic Church became particularly embroiled in debate with these philosophes and issued numerous declarations and condemnations of Enlightenment writings. Eventually, however, the smoke cleared, and the church was able to look for the kernel of truth in their criticisms. In time, Christian scholars and church educators accepted some of the educational theories and practices of the Enlightenment thinkers. The most renowned of these pre-Enlightenment

---

3. Ibid., 151.
4. Peter Gay, *Age of Enlightenment* (New York: Time, 1966), 103.

and Enlightenment thinkers included the French philosophes Montesquieu, Voltaire, and Rousseau; the English scholars Newton, Locke, and Hobbes; the German philosophers Kant and Lessing; the Scottish philosopher David Hume; and, in the United States, Thomas Jefferson and Benjamin Franklin.[5] Time and space will not allow a detailed examination of each of these individuals, but a brief overview of the most predominant philosophers will provide the reader a general feeling of what the Enlightenment period was all about. We will consider them in chronological order (as opposed to geographic proximity) to illustrate how the thoughts and impressions of one influenced those who came later.

Glossary of Philosophies

The Enlightenment is known for its emphasis upon the study of philosophy. To help the student grasp a basic understanding of some of the most dominant philosophies that were prevalent before and during this time, the following brief glossary might be helpful.[6]

Empiricism. Man's source of knowledge comes from experience. This experience has two sources: our senses (through interacting with our world) and our reflections (our mind's operations upon our senses).

Existentialism. In a philosophical context, it refers to an atheistic worldview wherein man is pessimistic and without hope. All reality is centered in the individual. In a theological context, man is in complete dependence upon God, and religious expression is personal and highly subjective.

Humanism. Humanity is viewed as the highest order of life. Mankind is seen as the artisan of his universe, and he is in final control of life events.

---

5. John L. Elias, *A History of Christian Education: Protestant, Catholic, and Orthodox Perspectives* (Malabar, Fla.: Krieger, 2002), 127-28.

6. These terms have been defined in countless philosophy texts. Some of these specific definitions have been extrapolated from a variety of sources. Included among them are the following: James M. Baldwin, *Dictionary of Philosophy and Psychology* (Gloucester: Peter Smith, 1957); Nicholas Horvath, *Essentials of Philosophy* (Woodbury: Barron's Educational Series, 1974); Jack Terry, *Educational Philosophy* (Dallas: Maple Springs, 1982); and Warren Young, *A Christian Approach to Philosophy* (Grand Rapids: Baker, 1954).

Idealism. The view that all basic reality resides in the realm of ideas, rather than in the realm of the material world. It does not deny the existence of a physical universe but contends that the highest order of reality is to be found in the observed rather than in the world being observed.

Naturalism. The belief that the whole of the universe or of one's experience may be explained only through means similar to those employed by the physical sciences. Unless it can be measured and/or examined within the confines of the stipulations agreed upon by the physical sciences, it is not real and therefore is unworthy of discussion and debate.

Neo-Thomism. This philosophical position was made famous by Thomas Aquinas. Also known as traditionalism, it is a view that all reason and being are rooted in an immutable existence or a supreme whatness. Aquinas believed in the harmony of faith and reason and in the integration of philosophy and theology.

Pragmatism. A theory that the meaning of an idea expresses itself in its practical application or consequence. Truth is best understood in terms of its practicality and ability to bring satisfaction in everyday life.

Realism. A metaphysical theory that things have existence apart from our ability to recognize or understand them. Plato believed that the idea, or universal, was more real than the individual thing. For example, the concept of "man" has a higher state of reality than an individual man, such as "John Doe."[7]

Scholasticism. A prominent philosophical theory during the medieval era whereby philosophy was examined through the predominant lens of theology. The ultimate aim was the explanation and exposition of Christian teachings in relation to reason.

Theism. From a philosophical (as opposed to a theological) point of reference, theism is defined as a belief that the universe was created by one Supreme Being. This can be viewed through *pantheism* (God is impersonal and does not distinguish Himself from the world), *deism* (God created the universe but does not interfere with its natural laws), and *theism* (God is personal and engaged in the affairs of both the world and those who live in it).

---

7. The concept of realism has undergone conceptual changes over the centuries. For example, Platonic or conceptual realism is actually closer to modern idealism than to modern realism. It assumes that the "real" is the permanent or unchanging. See Harold H. Titus, *Living Issues in Philosophy* (New York: Van Nostrand Reinhold, 1970), 243.

European Enlightenment Philosophers

In England, the transition from respect for religion to skepticism began with a group of Cambridge Platonists. In response to the contentious bickering of various denominational sects that had developed (e.g., Waldensians, Hussites, Lollards, Albigensians, Puritans, and Anabaptists), they proposed to reduce the essential teachings of Christianity to its basic fundamentals. According to these rationalists, Christianity was essentially the practice of reason, the demonstration of virtue, and mystical contemplation. Reason and faith were not seen as contradictory but rather complementary. Reason was viewed as the road to faith; faith enhanced reason. Toward the end of the seventeenth century, this rationalist theology was continued by a larger community known as Latitudinarians. Some of the most prominent British clergymen of that time were associated with this movement. Latitudinarians denounced the use of unbridled emotion, which was being advocated by revivalist preachers. Instead, they espoused and defended the use of reason. They stressed the ethical conduct of man, which would be demonstrated by good deeds, moral behavior, and civic contributions.[8]

Chief among these British Latitudinarians was a philosopher named John Locke (1632–1704). Although he is known more for his contributions to the field of educational psychology, Locke was considered one of the Enlightenment's major predecessors. As a seventeenth-century philosopher born in Somersetshire, England, he experienced the embryonic start of the Enlightenment soon after the Glorious Revolution, in which the Catholic monarch James II was unseated from the throne, thereby allowing a Protestant succession. Locke's *Reasonableness of Christianity* encouraged a more tolerant attitude toward the many religious sects that had emerged from the Reformation, except for atheists and Roman Catholics. According to Locke, miracles were simply natural occurrences that only seemed to be supernatural because they lay outside the bounds of human understanding. Although he did not deny that Christianity was a viable religion, he did argue that Christianity could be reduced to one essential tenet: Jesus Christ was the Messiah. Everything else was, in the words of Locke, "fiction, merely the invention of superstitious or power-hungry priests."[9] His philosophical per-

---

8. Gay, *Age of Enlightenment*, 32.
9. Ibid.

spectives set the tone for the theological beliefs of the Church of England throughout the eighteenth century.[10]

Philosophers of the Enlightenment

CARTESIANS	SKEPTICS
CAMBRIDGE PLATONISTS	UTILITARIANS
DEISTS	ATHEISTS

CARTESIANS. Disciples of Descartes; discarded authoritarianism and argued that only that which is clearly perceived is true.

CAMBRIDGE PLATONISTS. Revived the Platonic theory of ideas, particularly the belief that moral ideas are innate in man.

DEISTS. Argued that the course of nature was sufficient to demonstrate God's existence. Regarded formal religion as superfluous.

SKEPTICS. Denied the ability of man to know all and the capacity of his reason to penetrate everything.

UTILITARIANS. Held that the happiness of the greatest number is the greatest good.

ATHEISTS. Flatly denied God's existence.[11]

As applied to education, Locke's ideology espoused a philosophical empiricism that held to the supremacy of reason over religious faith, revelation, and tradition. His basic assumption was that human nature was not innate at birth but was the result of environmental influences that came about throughout one's life. Virtue was not endowed but communicated through various experiences along life's path. At birth, a child possessed what Locke called *tabula rasa,* or blank slate. Impressions were put on this slate as a result of one's interaction with the environment. Although Locke has been credited with popularizing the concept of *tabula rasa,* it was first used by Plato in a

---

10. Ibid.
11. Ibid., 37.

metaphorical sense as a waxed tablet. Aristotle used the metaphor of a piece of writing paper to express the relation of potential to actual reason. Descartes used the phrase but only in passing and not with the same meaning that Locke later espoused. Interestingly, Locke himself did not use the phrase, although he speaks of the mind as being a white sheet of paper upon which "imprinting" sensations on the mind were made.[12]

Locke began by rejecting the idea of innate ideas. He thought that all knowledge came from *experience*. By experience, Locke meant two things: *sensations,* which come from man's interaction with the material world around him/her; and *reflections,* which result from the mind's operations upon the sensations. To Locke, nothing entered the intellect that did not first come through the senses. Sensation and reflection are the sources of all ideas from which subsequent human thought originates. From his suggestion that thought was merely the putting together of ideas came the Association-Connectionist school, which became a dominant force in psychology for many years.[13]

Much of the intellectual life of the Enlightenment grew out of investigations and discoveries made in the natural sciences. Sir Isaac Newton (1642–1727) probably typified this perspective more than anyone else of his day. He published *Mathematical Principles of Natural Philosophy* in 1687, building upon the monumental advances made by the sciences during the Reformation. In it, he postulated the "laws of nature," which became the scientific gospel until the late nineteenth century. Among these "laws" were the law of gravitation and the law of cause and effect. As a result, the universe became known as an orderly system immune from supernatural intervention. To Newton, the world was, for all intents and purposes, a well-oiled machine running on autopilot and immune from divine intervention. This view later evolved into philosophical materialism, which stated that nothing existed apart from atoms, which operated according to mechanical and mathematical natural laws. The opposite viewpoint, held by such idealists as Bishop George Berkeley of the Church of England, held that the world was purely spiritual and mental. As such, material substances were merely a figment of our imagination and changed their qualities as our ability to understand

---

12. James M. Baldwin, *Dictionary of Philosophy and Psychology* (Gloucester: Peter Smith, 1957), 660.
13. Warren Young, *A Christian Approach to Philosophy* (Grand Rapids: Baker, 1954), 108-9.

them changed.[14] What was needed during this time of public scientific debate was someone who could bring together these two opposing sides in one coherent dialogue. The man who would do this was a French philosopher named François Marie Arouet de Voltaire (1694–1778).

Voltaire held to a deist worldview, which taught that God was the Supreme Creator of the universe, but once He set the universe in motion, He stepped back and remained aloof from the daily operations of His creation. It wasn't that He was incapable of intervening but that He chose not to do so. To intercede in the affairs of the world would be to conclude that God had made a mistake and needed somehow to improve or correct His error. Deism held no room for miracles, prophecy, the deity of Christ, or the Bible as God's revelation to man. Although Voltaire broke from the viewpoint of traditional Christianity and embraced Newtonian science, he did not wander as far as materialism.[15] For this reason, he was viewed as a moderating voice between Newtonian science and materialism.

In France, Voltaire was concerned about the injustices he had observed among the masses. He rejected forms of government led by perverted kings and priests and believed that education was the key to releasing man from the bondage of his intellectual ignorance. He championed the cause of the destitute and worked tirelessly to advance the cause of social justice and equality of rights. He was known for his wit and took advantage of opportunities to share it with those around him. A sample of such would include the following quotes:[16]

> In general, the art of government consists in taking as much money as possible from one class of citizens and giving it to the other.

> Marriage is the only adventure open to a coward.

> I have never made but one prayer to God: "O Lord, make my enemies ridiculous." And God granted it.

> If God did not exist, it would be necessary to invent Him.

---

14. R. Freeman Butts, *A Cultural History of Education: Reassessing our Educational Traditions* (New York: McGraw Hill, 1947), 319.

15. Ibid.

16. Gay, *Age of Enlightenment,* 59.

All the reasoning of men is not worth one sentiment of women.

Men use thought only to justify their wrong doing, and employ their speech only to conceal their thoughts.

Voltaire had strong personal opinions about the need for educational and political reform. Because education would free the masses to enjoy their pitiful existence, he wanted education to be more accessible to them. Voltaire would not have advocated a Christian education per se because he was a deist and did not believe in a personal deity but rather one marked by scientific methods of inquiry and characterized by justice and equality for all of its participants. His personal philosophy had a profound impact on the Founding Fathers of the American Revolution across the Atlantic.

In England, David Hume (1711–76) carried the banner of deism although he was viewed as being more temperate than Voltaire. Born into a Scottish family living in Edinburgh, Hume published numerous articles on the subjects of philosophy, ethics, economics, and politics in a three-volume work titled *Treatise* (1739 and 1740). Although that work "fell dead-born from the presses," as Hume lamented, it became a popular text soon after his death. Expanding on the views expressed in *Treatise,* he subsequently wrote *An Enquiry Concerning the Human Understanding* (1748), *An Enquiry Concerning the Principles of Morals* (1752), and *Dissertations on the Passions* (1757). Although Hume never won much acclaim for his writings in the field of philosophy, much to his personal disillusionment, he did win a great deal of respect and admiration for his writings in the field of history. His *History of England* (1754) allowed him to enjoy a good deal of financial gain. With his newfound wealth, he traveled to France where he acquainted himself with the French philosophes. After a season of interaction with Voltaire, Diderot, and Helvetius, Hume returned to Edinburgh, where he busied himself writing the controversial *Dialogues Concerning Natural Religions.* He completed that work but chose not to have it published until after his death in 1776. Hume arranged in his will for its publication, and his nephew published it in 1779.[17]

Hume is viewed as one of the most influential philosophers of modern times. He rejected the world-machine concept of Newton and the theologi-

---

17. Sterling P. Lamprecht, *Our Philosophical Traditions* (New York: Appleton-Century-Crofts, 1955), 325–26.

cal explanations of biblical creation. He was an open-minded inquirer into the world around him and uncommitted to any particular viewpoint. He was even known to argue against his own conclusions in part because he did not want to offend his reader and because he himself was somewhat uncertain about them. In the three volumes that he published between 1748 and 1751, he openly criticized his earlier material found in *Treatise*. He was open to criticism and was even willing to take the lead in discrediting his own thinking. "Hume's unorthodox views in religion and politics gained him great notoriety, so that by the time he retired he was generally known as 'the gentle sceptic' and the 'great infidel.'"[18]

Perhaps no other individual so personifies the philosophes of the Enlightenment as does Jean-Jacques Rousseau (1712-78). He was born in Geneva to a watchmaker, Isaac Rousseau. His mother died when he was just nine days old. His father preferred to educate his son outside the bounds of traditional schooling and chose rather to guide him through the reading of numerous classical books such as Ovid's *Metamorphoses*, Plutarch's *Lives of Famous Men*, and Plato's *Republic*. As a result of an altercation with the law, his father abandoned him, and he spent the rest of his childhood years being shuffled between foster homes. Perhaps that was why he chose an orphan boy as the principal character in his novel *Émile*. In his early adolescent years, he sought employment under the tutelage of the town clerk, to whom he was apprenticed as a notary. After being fired for lack of attention to the finer details of the job, he began an apprenticeship as an engraver. Rousseau claims he was mistreated at the hands of his supervisor so at the age of sixteen, he ventured off to begin life on his own.

He wandered through Europe trying to determine how best to spend his life. After a brief pilgrimage in Italy, he ventured to Savoy, where he became the beneficiary of a wealthy widow named Madame de Warens, who converted him to Roman Catholicism. For a brief time he seriously considered becoming a priest. Soon after venturing to France, he tested the waters in the fine arts. Skilled in music, which he had learned while living with his benefactress, he wrote several operas and ballets and began a career as a music teacher. He never seemed to find personal fulfillment in this vocation, however, so he accepted a position as secretary to the French ambassador in Venice. He was dismissed from that job as a result of quarreling with his

---

18. Richard H. Popkin and Avrum Stroll, *Philosophy Made Simple* (New York: Made Simple Books, 1956).

superiors. With no place to go, he returned to Paris and lived a life of reckless abandon, leaving behind several illegitimate children. In addition to those children, he fathered five children through a mistress named Therese Levasseur, an illiterate servant girl. Each child was subsequently deposited in a local orphanage.

During this period of his life, he became friends with several prominent French philosophes, chief among them being Diderot. In 1750, the Academy of Dijon awarded Rousseau a prize for his essay on the question of whether the development of the sciences and the arts had contributed to the improvement of morals. Rousseau's position on the subject was that man, in fact, deteriorates as civilization advances. He believed that the soul of man actually became more corrupt as a result of the advances of science and the arts. He advocated a return to more primitive methods of social order and civil development.

> In this climate of self-criticism Jean Jacques Rousseau worked out his ideas for a better society—ideas that were widely misunderstood in his own time and continue to be so today. Partly this was Rousseau's own fault. Morbid and suspicious, he turned against all his friends and turned his friends against him. Also it was partly the fault of his prose, which is lively and epigrammatic in style, and invites quotation out of context. Thus he got the reputation for being a utopian dreamer who wanted to do away with organized society and go "back to nature" and the state of the "noble savage."[19]

Although Rousseau wrote a number of significant works covering a wide range of topics, most noteworthy for our emphasis on educational philosophy was a novel titled *Émile*. Some people have viewed this work as a discourse on child development, whereas others dismiss it as an unrealistic attempt to espouse a utopian model for restructuring society. Émile was a young orphan who grew under the care of a tutor. Removed from the potentially damaging effects of society, the child was exposed to nature, where his natural inclination toward moral behavior could be cultivated. The book begins by revealing its philosophical intentions: "Everything is good as it leaves the hands of the Author of Things; everything degenerates in the

---

19. Gay, *Age of Enlightenment,* 62.

hands of man." In making this statement, Rousseau was ridiculing the Calvinist doctrine of the depravity of man and the spiritual deprivation caused by original sin. To Rousseau, man is not born in a state of depravity but assumes this state as a result of his existence in a morally corrupt society. To prevent this damaging influence, Émile is to be raised with as much interaction with nature as possible. Metaphorically, this new Adam of the Enlightenment will be the father of a new, naturally educated race of men and women. In this context, it might be possible for an entire race of men and women to create a radical world order in which social, political, economic, and educational institutions can function naturally.[20]

The challenge comes for Rousseau when he tries to find a way to educate the children living in this new utopian realm. The schools that he had witnessed during his journeys across Europe held little hope for the future. Indeed, these corrupt bastions of learning were counterproductive for developing educated children. Their harsh, authoritative instructional methods displayed a philosophy of education that was antithetical to Rousseau's because the children spent far too much time in structured classrooms hunched over books and listening to lectures, rather than being allowed to run free in nature.

The four stages of Rousseau's model of education revolve around a belief that educational methods should take into consideration the natural stages of development through which a child goes: infancy, childhood, early adolescence, and late adolescence. This theme would later serve as a foundational element of the Swiss educational theorist Jean Piaget. To Rousseau, each stage had its own set of physical, social, emotional, and educational considerations that had to be addressed in the development of curriculum, discipline, instructional methods, etc.

During infancy (birth to five), the child is viewed as an animal in terms of his/her need for physical activity, reliance on feelings, and social interactions. Education at this level is primarily concerned with giving the child enough time to play and for exploring the world through the senses. The child should be given freedom to explore the world without restrictions and authority. During childhood (ages five to twelve), the individual is still viewed as an animal that is primarily interested in activity and exploration. The teacher should eschew the study of books and language development, preferring games, sports, constructive play, and the manual arts.[21]

---

20. Gutek, *Historical and Philosophical Foundations of Education*, 5.
21. Butts, *Cultural History of Education*, 344.

During early adolescence (twelve to fifteen), when reason and self-consciousness appear, the curriculum should gravitate toward stimulating curiosity and useful activity, which are the only real motives for learning. Because the child is largely nonsocial at this stage, Rousseau was a strong advocate of the student reading Daniel Defoe's *Robinson Crusoe.* In this classic, Crusoe learns how to survive in a natural setting using his independent resources devoid of society's authority or input from others. He should learn by observing nature. At this juncture, Rousseau's educational philosophy of learning by doing as opposed to learning through words is promulgated. It is only in later adolescence that the youth should come to terms with the problems associated in society. That's when the sexual drives and impulses of young people come to the surface and they struggle to find constructive ways to integrate their budding sexuality with socially acceptable activities. At this level of education, the young people are introduced to the study of society, economics, politics, history, and religion. At this point, the youth are encouraged to develop in their moral, aesthetic, and spiritual dimensions.[22]

The final chapter of *Émile* discusses the educational development of girls. Rousseau taught that girls needed religious instruction more than boys did and thought that the best setting for instructing girls was in a convent, where they would offer short prayers to what seems to be a deist's concept of God.[23] After *Émile,* Rousseau wrote a book titled *Social Contract,* in which he continued his theme of a utopian society in which education played a major role in the training of its populace.

To say that Rousseau's views were controversial would be a gross under-statement. His wholesale rejection of culture's influence on the educational development of the child was clearly underestimated. His view of man as being innately good contradicts biblical teaching, and believing that a child is basically amoral and unreasonable until the age of twelve minimizes the influence that teachers, coaches, and other adult role models can have on the constructive development of children. Although he emphasized strongly the role that parents play in the child's early growth, he forbade common forms of discipline that Christian parents must demonstrate if they are to abide by the biblical injunction to "discipline your son while there is hope"

---

22. Ibid.

23. Elias, *History of Christian Education,* 137.

(Prov. 19:18) because discipline is indeed evidence of a parent's love and commitment to their child's healthy growth and development (Heb. 12:4–11). Rousseau's philosophy of education helps us understand the role that exists between the child's personal academic development and the contribution that he or she is expected to make in becoming a contributing member of society. Educational philosopher John Dewey would take up this charge years later and develop his democratic ideals of the learner based on Rousseau's foundational thinking.

The writings of David Hume and Jean-Jacques Rousseau had a profound impact on the thinking of a German philosopher named Immanuel Kant (1724–1804). Hume taught him that the law of cause and effect could only be assumed, never proven. "Kant set out to give a defense of common sense notions about the world, which had been undermined by Hume. Kant felt that empiricists failed to acknowledge that the human mind makes its own contributions to sense-based knowledge and imposes its subjective categories upon the world. This reorientation of epistemology, or the theory of knowledge, had its effect upon the philosophy of education."[24] He also embraced Rousseau's belief in the ultimate goodness of man and came to believe that ethical and moral values were not something to be acquired through classroom instruction but rather were intrinsically imbedded in man's nature.[25]

Kant is best known for his critical analysis of human knowledge, which he saw as a "philosophy of philosophy." His trilogy of criticism, *Pure Reason* (1781), *Practical Reason* (1788), and *Judgment* (1790), sought to examine the three most important aspects of philosophy: metaphysics, ethics, and aesthetics. "Beginning at age sixteen and continuing for a lifetime, Kant was insatiably interested in the scientific realm and in its epistemology. His defense of a priori concepts were applied to the disciplines of math, physics, morality, and everyday experiences. Time, space, number, and cause and effect were among his a priori givens."[26]

Perhaps one of the more lasting influences of Kant's thinking is the development of moral law as a basis for ethical behavior. In his *Metaphysics of*

---

24. Kenneth O. Gangel and Warren S. Benson, *Christian Education: Its History and Philosophy* (Chicago: Moody, 1983), 196.
25. Gay, *Age of Enlightenment*, 147.
26. Cheryl L. Fawcett, *The Evangelical Dictionary of Christian Education*, ed. Michael J. Anthony (Grand Rapids: Baker, 2001), s.v. "Immanuel Kant."

Morals and his *Critique of Practical Reason,* Kant put forth the philosophical position that came to be known as *formalism,* by which he sought to discover moral principles that were inherently right or wrong apart from any particular circumstance (as opposed to situational ethics). In other words, he wanted to know if a common set of moral standards governed thinking and behavior that were somewhat universal in origin. In this point, he inherited the Christian reverence for a divine "natural" law that transcended culture or geopolitical boundaries. He blended this divine law with an esteem for the individual self and developed a school of moral philosophy that was concerned with what ought to be. According to Kant, in man is found a sense of duty, the "I ought," or moral law, that comes about before experience and is found in the deepest core of man's existence. As such, these laws of nature and reason are essentially one. Kant proposed three criteria, or formulations, of this moral law: the Principle of Universality, the Principle of Humanity as an End, and the Principle of Autonomy.[27]

Reacting to Rousseau's views on childhood discipline, Kant sought to bring a more balanced perspective to bear. In his book *On Education,* he supported many of Rousseau's views on education with a stronger philosophical foundation in German idealism. He took issue with Rousseau by arguing for a moral education that gave the child more freedom through discipline. Children were awarded freedom in their early years provided they did not impinge on the rights of others. To Kant, the value of discipline was in its ability to help children learn to be independent of others. He wanted children to learn how to do the right things not because of habit but for their own reasons. This teaching of critical thinking skills at such an early age was a significant contribution to the system of education in its day.[28] It also ran counter to the traditional philosophy that viewed children as incapable of developing critical reasoning abilities. To this point, most educators saw children as repositories of information and the teaching-learning process as simply the transmission of information from one repository to another. Kant challenged all of that and paved the way for Swiss psychologist Jean Piaget's groundbreaking work in the early twentieth century.

To this point, most of the philosophes of the Enlightenment emphasized espousing philosophical and educational theories but were deficient

---

27. Titus, *Living Issues in Philosophy,* 364–65.
28. Elias, *History of Christian Education,* 141.

in their ability to apply these theories practically. It was much easier to proclaim boldly how things ought to be than to risk actually being proved a failure by taking one's views into the classroom. Few Enlightenment philosophes were willing to demonstrate their beliefs by creating schools in which their theories had to stand the test of praxis. Most notable among those who actually developed experimental schools to examine their educational philosophies was a Swiss educator named Johann Heinrich Pestalozzi (1746–1827).

His childhood was marked by sadness because of the early death of his father. His grandfather was a minister, and Pestalozzi frequently accompanied him to the countryside when he visited families in his parish. At this time in his young life, he developed a heartfelt compassion for the impoverished and destitute conditions that characterized Switzerland at the end of the eighteenth century as a result of the French wars. Pestalozzi believed that society could be improved by empowering individuals toward achievement, security, and self-respect. With this end in mind, he created at Neuhof and Stans orphanages for poor children whose fathers had been killed in the wars. Later, he established boarding schools for boys at Burgdorf and Yverdon, where he received his greatest acclaim for the manner in which he integrated his educational philosophy with praxis.[29]

Pestalozzi was a man of tremendous forethought and vision. He dared to view education for what it could become rather than lamenting all that it wasn't. He conducted his schools with sympathy and gentleness. Through his orphanages and boarding schools, he provided a living and learning environment in which children received mild discipline and moral and religious instruction in addition to a comprehensive curriculum consisting of drawing, music, reading, writing, geography, arithmetic, and nature studies. Through his curriculum, he emphasized the development of sense perceptions by associating models and actual objects with the various symbols and symbols that those models represented. Using this form of sense realism, Pestalozzi modeled a much more liberal approach to elementary education than was common at that time.[30]

---

29. Butts, *Cultural History of Education*, 426.
30. Ibid.

Pestalozzi's Classroom Reformation

Pestalozzi's principles of instruction can be divided into two categories, the "general" and the "special." The general method involved teachers providing an emotionally warm and secure climate in which the student could feel safe. Once this predisposition was established, the special method was employed. This involved sensory learning through the use of natural objects, in what Pestalozzi called the "object lesson." Like Rousseau, he urged that lessons be based on the sensory experiences with which the child was familiar. As students progressed in their learning, Pestalozzi further employed a set of learning strategies that summed up his approach. Instruction, he urged, should (1) begin with the concrete before introducing abstract concepts; (2) begin with the learner's immediate environment before dealing with what is distant and remote; (3) begin with easy exercises before introducing complex ones; and (4) always proceed gradually, cumulatively and slowly. He believed strongly that all children had an equal right to education and possessed the inherent capacity to profit from it.

In attacking conventional educational forms as excessively verbal and lifeless, he held that the innate faculties of a child were best developed in accordance with natural principles. Such an educational pattern would be successful only to the extent that teachers were adequately prepared to carry it out. Thus, to Pestalozzi, training teachers in naturalistic principles was of primary importance. The schoolmaster, he argued, should be one of the most important persons in the community. He was to be a person of strong emotional and ethical character and capable of loving children from every strata of society.

Frequently criticized and considered revolutionary in his day, the educational concepts of Pestalozzi subsequently exerted great influence on the development of progressive pedagogy in Europe and the United States in the twentieth century. His emphasis upon learning by natural principles and human emotions paralleled the earlier thought of Rousseau. But whereas Rousseau proposed abandoning the school concept, Pestalozzi sought to reform it. Ever the champion of the underprivileged, when he died on February 17, 1827, his grave was marked only by a rough stone and a single rosebush. On the one hundredth anniversary of his birth, a monument was erected at his burial site, which read in part, "All for others, nothing for himself."[31]

---

31. David Gough, *The Evangelical Dictionary of Christian Education*, ed. Michael J. Anthony (Grand Rapids: Baker, 2001), s.v. "Johann Heinrich Pestalozzi."

As an educational realist, Pestalozzi believed that truth was gained through sensory perception. Instructional methodologies that employed the senses were developed to facilitate these experiences. He called for the use of object lessons in the classroom because he believed that a student would learn best if he/she could smell, touch, taste, or hear an object in addition to seeing it. In addition to object lessons, teachers employed field trips, audio-visual aids, and classroom demonstrations/experiments. Realist teachers are concerned about the mastery of facts as a means of appropriating naturalism (e.g., the natural law that governs the universe). They desire for their students to comprehend the universal laws of nature. They rely heavily on inductive logic as they move from particular facts gleaned through the use of sensory perception to the more general laws that can be inferred from those data.[32]

In 1781, Pestalozzi published a novel, much like Rousseau's *Émile,* titled *Leonard and Gertrude.* In this manuscript, he promoted his views concerning the social good and revealed his desire for changes in the educational system that would contribute to social, political, and moral reforms. Because that book was so widely received, he published two additional novels with similar themes: *How Gertrude Teaches Her Children* (1801) and *Epochs* (1803).

One of the most enduring contributions of Pestalozzi was the value that he placed on the teaching profession. Because his view of the learning process was defined in terms of a drawing out more than the traditional pouring in, it required a new paradigm in teacher training. The teacher must not only know the subject matter but also be able to organize it in terms of the nature of the learner and to direct the student such as to facilitate content mastery.[33] Pestalozzi developed a school for training teachers and taught them the importance of fostering a nurturing classroom environment. He believed that the environment most conducive for learning was marked by a loving and caring instructor. The teacher and the parents were viewed as partners; the educational process was best fostered in a symbiotic relationship between home and school.

Soon teachers and school administrators came from all across Europe to

---

32. George R. Knight, *Philosophy and Education* (Berrien Springs, Mich.: Andrews University Press, 1998), 50.
33. Charles B. Eavey, *History of Christian Education* (Chicago: Moody, 1964), 402.

witness the applied philosophy of Pestalozzi. Chief among those who were influenced by his views were Johann Herbart and Friedrich Froebel. Pestalozzi's views were taken into consideration during the various educational reforms that occurred in Prussia during the early nineteenth century. Years later in America, his concept of teaching as a distinct profession gave impetus to the formation of some of North America's greatest teachers colleges.

Picking up the torch that Pestalozzi passed to him was a German educator named Johann Friedrick Herbart (1776–1841). Like others before him, he endured a difficult childhood because of the divorce of his parents at an early age. He was reared by an overprotective mother, who arranged for him to be schooled at home by tutors. One of these tutors was a university student named Uelzen. Because Uelzen had a deep and abiding love for theology and philosophy, he instilled in his young student the love of these disciplines early in his academic development. At age twelve, Herbart began formal schooling at the local Latin school, and in 1794 he entered the University of Jena with his mother, who chose to attend classes with him. Herbart continued his love for the study of philosophy and was heavily influenced in the study of idealism by Professor Johann Gottlieb Ficthe. Ficthe was a follower of Kant, but in time Herbart gravitated more toward his own form of realism. At the University of Jena, Herbart joined a student literary club named the Association of Free Men. Students in this society immersed themselves in the profound readings and discourses of philosophes who had gone before them.[34]

Upon graduation, Herbart secured employment as a tutor at a school directed by Friedrich von Steiger. He had also traveled to see firsthand the school system developed by Pestalozzi. After receiving his doctorate in psychology from the University of Gottingen in 1802, he remained as a professor of philosophy for the next seven years. During this season of his life, he began to write books that brought together his own version of philosophical realism and the educational practice that he had observed under von Steiger and Pestalozzi. It was a prolific season for Herbart as he published numerous books on the topics of pedagogy, educational reform, childhood development, general psychology, and educational psychology.

A depiction of Herbart's model of education can be summarized as a five-step process:

---

34. James E. Reed and Ronnie Prevost, *A History of Christian Education* (Nashville: Broadman & Holman, 1993), 248.

1. *Preparation:* the student is prepared for learning by recalling past experiences and concepts that have been learned before arriving in the classroom.
2. *Presentation:* the new information to be learned is presented and explained to the student.
3. *Association:* the student seeks to determine the relationship between past experiences and the new material to be learned.
4. *Generalization:* the student seeks to discover principles or general concepts from the previous step.
5. *Application:* the student explores ways whereby the principles can be applied to real-life situations.[35]

Herbart was one of the few Enlightenment thinkers who did not have contempt for the contributions of religion on educational development. For this reason, Christian educators of the nineteenth and twentieth centuries found it more palatable to integrate the theories of Herbart into their own philosophy of education. "Herbart insisted that an adequate educational theory must include a comprehensive analysis of the aims, intended outcomes, and means of education. This is a balance that contemporary Christian educators have discovered and appreciated in the analytic educational philosophy of William Frankena."[36]

The final Enlightenment philosophe who will be discussed is a German educator who was also heavily influenced by Pestalozzi. Friedrich Wilhelm Froebel (1782–1852) is best known as the father of the kindergarten. Froebel was the son of a Lutheran pastor in Oberweissbach, Germany. His mother died when he was just nine months old, and he grew up a lonely, dejected, and introverted child. Upon completing his academic preparation in the field of forestry, he was unable to find employment in that field, so he secured a position as a tutor. He was sent to observe the instructional methodologies that Pestalozzi was using at his school in Yverdon. This experience had a profound impact on him, resulting in a new career emphasis. He found fulfillment in teaching, and after receiving further formal training in the field at the University of Berlin, he opened a kindergarten for young children in Keilhau in 1817. There he furthered the instructional emphasis

---

35. Ibid., 250.
36. Daniel C. Stevens, *The Evangelical Dictionary of Christian Education,* ed. Michael J. Anthony (Grand Rapids: Baker, 2001), s.v. "Johann Friedrich Herbart."

that he had observed in Yverdon, but he added his own educational philosophy to the curriculum. He believed that play was an important component in the learning process and invited children as young as three years old to attend his school.[37]

That he tried to integrate his love for natural creation with his educational philosophy should be surprising to no one who understands Froebel's love for nature, as evidenced by his original career plans. "For him, education enabled persons to realize their essence by living in tune with the Creator's purposes. In Froebel's mystical philosophy children were to identify with this goal by seeing themselves as part of the unity of the world, developing freedom and self-determination."[38] Froebel's highest educational goal was to enable the child to see God clearly revealed in all of His creation.[39] He compared the development of the child with a plant that was growing in a garden; the nature of the child could not be changed, but he or she could grow healthy with the oversight of a good teacher. From this "child's garden" concept he developed the idea for kindergarten.

Froebel believed that children should be encouraged to play as part of their educational development. During this playtime, children manifested significance through symbolic representation with objects around them. For example, as a child played with a ball, he was reminded of the spherical nature of our planet and of the Supreme Creator of the universe. Froebel viewed objects such as cylinders, cubes, balls, and spheres as *gifts* that had special symbolic potential. Other play materials such as clay, wood, and sand were called *occupations* because they were the raw materials that a child used to reveal his inner thoughts and feelings. Children were encouraged to use these materials in conjunction with their imagination to express themselves and to interact socially. The object lesson was also an important element in his instructional methodology.

In *The Education of Man,* which he published in 1826, Froebel expressed his educational philosophy regarding the nature of the child, basic theology, and educational psychology. Written in prose, it sought to weave philosophical idealism with romanticism, science, and Christian mysticism. His Lutheran roots were exposed as he proclaimed God as the ultimate Creator of the universe and mankind as His created work. To Froebel, man possessed a

---

37. Reed and Prevost, *History of Christian Education,* 252.
38. Elias, *History of Christian Education,* 144.
39. Ibid.

spiritual dimension as well as the more obvious physical body. God's intent was that the two would be developed simultaneously and that neither would be ignored at the expense of the other. The role of the teacher was to facilitate the process of each in a timely manner without force or constraint. His blending of theology and educational philosophy make Froebel a leading contributor to modern Christian education.

The Enlightenment was a turbulent time in many respects. Although it represented a general sense of freedom and release from the highly restrictive paradigms of traditional church education, its emphasis on humanistic explanations of the universe, ultimate truth, and mankind's reason for being made it a challenging time for religious educators. New theories about the universe were being communicated by scientists in the fields of astronomy, biology, medicine, geology, mathematics, etc. These new views, validated by the scientific method, were instrumental in creating new paradigms about the world. Resulting applications were found for politics, government, law, economics, education, and society as a whole.

While many religious educators of the time remained distant from these developments in educational theory and practice, in time they came to see value in some of the components of the Enlightenment educational theory. The greatest stumbling block for most educators was the Enlightenment's somewhat naive view of the human person that did not include an adequate recognition of the doctrine of original sin and human inclination to evil. What irked many a moralist was the negative attitude of some of these theorists to the teachings of the Bible and the catechism to young children. Enlightenment theories tended to minimize the role of religion in education, especially in the education of the young. In the perspective of many church educators these theories permitted too much freedom to the child and too little control to teachers and parents in moral and religious formation. Many of these criticisms were leveled against twentieth-century progressive education, which drew in part on the educational ideas and experiments of Enlightenment educators.[40]

---

40. Ibid., 145.

So What? Lessons from the Past for Twenty-first-century Christian Education

The period known as the Enlightenment represented a significant shift in how man viewed God. Moving away from a God-centered orientation of the world, man had begun to place himself at the center. This trend would continue in the future. This period of human history has a number of important principles to guide and shape the way we do ministry with people today. Following are a few suggestions for your reflective consideration.

1. The Christian should not feel threatened by a discussion of philosophy and its integration into the Christian life.

Because believers of many different faiths accept that all truth is God's truth, then it seems reasonable that the discovery of truth by people in the field of science is not necessarily undermining our rational faith. However, that is not to say that Christians must accept as fact the hypotheses espoused by science; even the casual observer can see that science obviously is constantly making new discoveries about the universe around us. The results of these new discoveries often invalidate the discoveries that were once held as fact just a few years earlier. For this reason, although Christians do not feel threatened by people who are involved in the scientific quest for knowledge, we also realize that the quest is anything but conclusive. Today's discoveries make yesterday's "facts" obsolete. Therefore, tomorrow's discoveries will do the same for many of the things that we hold as true today.

Many believers are involved in this search for scientific knowledge and seek to find ways to bring together science and biblical faith. The Christian scientist, a term that some people view as an oxymoron, works to reconcile the manner in which God created and controls the universe in light of the limited degree to which we know and understand it. Seen in the light of the Word of God, God being the sustainer of the universe, the Christian scientist can provide a more rationale explanation for the workings of the universe. Although it is true that a great many scientists and philosophers find no comfort in this theistic worldview, the Christian realist finds in this perspective an answer that is both rational and sufficient.

---

41. Young, *Christian Approach to Philosophy*, 80.

2. One of the fundamental roles of education in a culture is to prepare children to play a contributing role in society.

One should not assume that this will take place through some form of osmosis as the child grows up in the context of his or her peers. Intentional training and instruction as to what is socially acceptable behavior and what is not should take place throughout the child's development. The French and German Enlightenment philosophes spoke passionately about the contribution that education should have in the formation of those people within its citizenry. Educating a child about what is or is not normative should be intentional. Some people today take a reactionary approach and revolt against any form of instruction about responsibilities toward their country and local community. The goals of becoming law-abiding citizens and giving back to their community when appropriate should be ingrained in every child's consciousness early in their development. The classroom is an ideal location to demonstrate and test these ideals of democracy, tolerance, and volunteerism.

Christian educators can learn much from the Enlightenment thinkers about the values of tolerance, freedom, liberty, individual rights, and giving back to one's community. Each of these values serves as a foundation stone for our country's establishment and are to be found throughout the Scriptures as well. Without these core values at the heart of our national psyche, we would have little hope for our future.

3. The professionalism of childhood education comes of age.

During the Enlightenment, we begin to see some glimmer of hope for children's education that went beyond the mere transmission of data. For thousands of years, children were told to sit down and be quiet so they could "learn" from their teacher. In most cases, children were forbidden to talk in the classroom because doing so was a sign of disrespect. The child, teachers thought, had no basis for thinking critically about the subject matter because he or she did not possess the cognitive capacity for such reasoning. Kant and Pestalozzi began to change all of that with their philosophical presuppositions about childhood development. Pestalozzi, in particular, was willing to take the supreme risk of allowing others to come into his experimental classrooms and challenge his findings. Where he was wrong, he reassessed and developed new hypotheses about the mind of the child. The scope and sequence of curriculum and the structure of the learning environment took into consideration the child's developmental stage.

One's philosophical presuppositions about childhood development have a great deal to do with how the children's ministry of the church will look. For example, if the children's ministry director has a view that the child is incapable of thinking deeply about what they are being taught, then the programs for children will be plebian and "caretaking" in nature. Instruction will be directed toward rote memorization with little, if any, emphasis on understanding or application. Bible memory activities that have only the accumulation of stickers in books and patches on jackets without advancing to higher levels of reasoning will be evident in such churches.

If, however, the children's ministry director views the child as one who is capable of rational thought, critical thinking, and reasoning—at least to some age-appropriate degree—then the program will be characterized by (1) instruction that is geared toward the higher domains of the learning taxonomies, (2) worship that takes into consideration multidimensional creative arts (as opposed to mindless repetition of trite sayings and phrases), and (3) leadership opportunities for children that allow the child to have input regarding the manner in which children's programs are implemented.

Enlightenment philosophes began a new trend in our understanding of childhood development. It would not come to fruition for about another hundred years, but, as is so often the case, although the seeds of change take a long time to blossom, once they do, they reap a harvest of radical discovery and transformation.

FOR FURTHER READING

Butts, Robert F. *A Cultural History of Education.* New York: McGraw Hill, 1947.

Eavey, Charles B. *History of Christian Education.* Chicago: Moody, 1964.

Elias, John L. *A History of Christian Education: Protestant, Catholic, and Orthodox Perspectives.* Malabar, Fla.: Krieger, 2002.

Gangel, Kenneth O., and Warren S. Benson. *Christian Education: Its History and Philosophy.* Chicago: Moody, 1983.

Gay, Peter. *Age of Enlightenment.* New York: Time, 1966.

Gutek, Gerald L. *Historical and Philosophical Foundations of Education: A Biographical Introduction.* Upper Saddle River, N.J.: Merrill Prentice-Hall, 2001.

Harvey, David. *The Condition of Postmodernity.* Cambridge: Blackwell, 1990.

Horvath, Nicholas S. *Philosophy.* New York: Barron's Educational Series, 1974.

Kelly, William L., and Andrew Tallon. *Readings in the Philosophy of Man.* New York: McGraw Hill, 1967.

Knight, George R. *Philosophy and Education: An Introduction in Christian Perspective.* Berrien Springs, Mich.: Andrews University Press, 1998.

Lamprecht, Sterling P. *Our Philosophical Traditions.* New York: Appleton-Century-Crofts, 1955.

Porter, Burton F. *Philosophy: A Literary and Conceptual Approach.* New York: Harcourt Brace Jovanovich, 1974.

Reed, James E., and Ronnie Prevost. *A History of Christian Education.* Nashville: Broadman & Holman, 1993.

Smith, Peter. *Dictionary of Philosophy and Psychology.* Glouchester: Macmillan, 1957.

Titus, Harold H. *Living Issues in Philosophy.* New York: Van Nostrand Reinhold, 1970.

Young, Warren C. *A Christian Approach to Philosophy.* Wheaton: Van Kempen Press, 1954.

What in the World?

➤ Tokugawa Shogunate is in power in Japan in 1603–1867.

➤ Galileo's telescope is invented in 1610.

➤ Execution of Charles I occurs; climax of English revolution in 1649.

➤ Height of the first Great Awakening revival movement comes to the North American colonies in 1740.

➤ Ludwig Van Beethoven is born in Germany in 1770.

Chapter 9

EARLY ORIGINS OF THE
SUNDAY SCHOOL MOVEMENT

IN THE AFTERMATH OF THE FRENCH REVOLUTION in Europe, many of the church-sponsored schools were forced to relinquish their monopoly over the educational institutions they had labored so hard to establish. The Jesuits, in particular, had created secondary and college-level schools that had become well entrenched throughout Europe. However, the history of the Catholic Church and its form of religious instruction via catechetical indoctrination had left a bad taste in the mouth of many Europeans. They desired the benefits of the church-sponsored schools but rejected the church's strict control over the curriculum. If one central theme was coming from the Enlightenment, it was that God had been minimized and man's efforts to control his destiny had become paramount.

The Enlightenment philosophes whom we described in the preceding chapter had paved the way for a remaking of the educational system across the European continent. No longer would education be limited to only what the church could provide. Now, with the educational breakthroughs of Rousseau, Pestalozzi, and Froebel, federal and local governments were beginning to see the benefits of tax-sponsored forms of public education. Froebel's groundbreaking work on the creation of the kindergarten had stirred the hearts of people who desired more for their children than they themselves had received growing up. As a result, many church-sponsored schools were ordered to close, and state-sponsored schools came in their place.

Napoleon placed all French schools under the control of the Imperial University, making it difficult for church-oriented schools to continue to exist. During the reign of Napoleon's successor, Louis XVIII (d. 1824), the church pressed for control of all education, arguing that religion should permeate all areas of the curriculum. At this time freedom was also granted to Protestants and Jews to establish their own schools.[1]

In addition to the new thinking on state-sponsored education that was coming from the Enlightenment was a growing desire to expand further mankind's knowledge of the universe. This task required schools that were committed to the exploration of the liberal arts. Beginning at the elementary levels of education, children were instructed in basic curricular components of reading, writing, grammar, mathematics, and social studies among other subjects. In this geopolitical climate, public education heavily emphasized rationalism and secular philosophical thought. Religious instruction, especially outside the Roman Catholic Church, was minimal at best in many countries. Religious education that had at one time been a focal point of education had now become virtually extinct from these state-sponsored public schools.

"While Enlightenment political ideas did not succeed in establishing a republic in regal England, they did serve to loosen education from the control of the Anglican church and the middle classes and to extend education to the poor children throughout the country. Education in early nineteenth-century England was caught in a crossfire between the defense of ecclesiastical and bourgeois privilege and the liberal, Enlightenment-inspired programs of mass schooling."[2] The problem was that in the midst of such tensions and political infighting, children of the poorer classes were being ignored and left without educational opportunities. The result was catastrophic for an entire generation of children living in the throes of the Industrial Revolution.

It was a time when people left their agrarian heritage and migrated to the mills and factories available in the larger cities of London, Birmingham, and Manchester. Jobs were more plentiful because the demand for factory-made

---

1. John L. Elias, *A History of Christian Education: Protestant, Catholic, and Orthodox Perspectives* (Malabar, Fla.: Krieger, 2002), 146.
2. Ibid., 149.

products was growing. However, the twelve to fifteen hours of work each day were long and hard. Life was anything but hopeful and encouraging for the masses. Those who owned the mills and factories ruled them with the hand of an imperial magistrate. Working conditions were harsh, and laws allowed the people who were in control to maintain their domination over the workforce. Child labor laws had not been developed, so factories, seizing on this large pool of low-wage employees, put many young children to work for long hours each day. Some of them were employed in mills, whereas others worked in assembly and manufacturing plants. One popular job had them sorting pins because their small fingers were more adept at this particular job. Working eight to ten hours a day, six days a week, left little time for attending schools. It's little wonder that the juvenile crime rate was astoundingly high.

What was needed was an impassioned reformer who could integrate the educational possibilities that Froebel and other Enlightenment educational reformers brought to light with the biblical teachings of Protestant theology. This individual came in the unlikely figure of an English newspaper owner named Robert Raikes Jr. Upon the death of Robert Raikes Sr. in 1757, the younger Raikes inherited the *Glouchester Journal,* a newspaper that his father had started.

Raikes used his influence in the community to draw his readers' attention to the plight of individuals who were imprisoned and in desperate need of assistance. Over a span of twenty-five years, he set out to make Glouchester a better place for its citizens to live through his numerous philanthropic interests. He was also interested in bringing about some measure of reform to the English penal system. However, his efforts failed because many people who had been released from incarceration showed little interest in long-term rehabilitation. Realizing that any hope of rectifying the situation was going to require reaching the prison population *before* they entered it in the first place, Raikes set about to address the needs of the many juvenile delinquents who were running wild in the streets after work and on Sunday.

Born and bred in abject poverty and sometimes the unhappy victims of a child labor situation, boys and girls roamed the streets, ragged, quarreling, undisciplined, fighting, cursing, mouthing the foulest and most obscene speech. In particular, he pitied the plight of chimney sweeps, whose debased existence was to be described in a novel in the next century, written by Charles Kingsley, a Church of England clergyman, and titled *Water Babies*.[3]

In the midst of such depravity, Raikes rented the kitchen of Mrs. Meridith in her home on Sooty Alley. There a motley collection of young juvenile delinquents assembled in her makeshift classroom on Sundays when they were not working. They were the most illiterate and undisciplined children whom anyone could ever hope to gather in one location. The rules that governed them in this classroom were strict. No one was allowed to enter who had not first washed themselves thoroughly. They had to wear clean clothes and have shoes on their feet. If they didn't possess such basic commodities, Raikes would provide for the children from his own financial resources. He believed in the biblical admonition not to spare the rod, so corporal punishment was applied when necessary.

One day in 1781, Raikes described how he felt when the need for a Sunday school for these young children came to him:

> I was walking into the suburbs of the city, where the lowest of the people (who were principally employed in the pin factory) chiefly reside (where) I was struck with concern at seeing a group of children wretchedly ragged, at play in the street. I asked an inhabitant whether those children belonged to that part of town, and lamented their misery and idleness. "Ah! Sir," said the woman to whom I was speaking, "could you take a view of this part of town on Sunday, you would be shocked and indeed; for then the street is filled with multitudes of these wretches who, released on that day from their employment, spend their time in noise and riot and playing at chuck, and cursing and swearing in a manner so horrid, as to convey to any serious mind an idea of hell, rather than any other place. . . ."
>
> This conversation suggested to me, that it would be at least a harmless attempt, if it were productive of no good, should some little plan be formed to check this deplorable profanity of the Sabbath. I then inquired of the woman, if there were any decent, well-disposed women in the neighborhood, who kept schools for teaching to read. I presently was directed to four: to these I applied, and made an agreement

---

3. Galbraith H. Todd, *The Torch and the Flag* (Philadelphia: American Sunday School Union, 1996), 1.

with them, to receive as many children as I should send upon Sunday, whom they were to instruct in reading and the church catechism. For this I engaged to pay them each a shilling for their day's employment. The women seemed pleased with the proposal. I then waited on the clergyman before-mentioned, and imparted to him my plan; he was so much satisfied with the idea, that he engaged to lend his assistance, by going round to the schools on Sunday afternoon, to examine the progress being made, and to enforce order and decorum among such a set of little heathens.

This, Sir, was the commencement of the plan.[4]

No doubt, Mrs. Meridith meant well, but one can only imagine what the educational conditions must have been like in actual practice. It wasn't long before she could no longer handle the stress and resigned, thus forcing Raikes to find alternative accommodations in the home of Mrs. Critchley, a neighbor of Raikes who lived across the street from St. Mary de Crypt Church. In the first school that Raikes developed, he gathered about ninety children who were employed in one of the local pin factories and paid each of the four teachers about twenty-five cents to teach the children in their homes. Classes were conducted from 10:00 A.M. until noon, then after a lunch break they resumed again from 1:00 to 5:00 P.M. Undoubtedly, the ladies who served as teachers and described the children as "miserable little wretches" earned their twenty-five cents!

Interestingly, Raikes himself was not a trained theologian or clergyman. In addition, those whom he recruited to teach in this educational enterprise were also untrained in professional ministry. They were laypeople who simply had a love for children in need and a desire to see the Great Commission fulfilled in their own neighborhoods. Although they were untrained by the world's standards and ill equipped by anyone's valuation, these servants set themselves to the task of winning the poorest of the poor for Christ. "When it is recognized that inadequately trained teachers often serve under poor

---

4. Robert Raikes, *Gentleman's Magazine* 54, pt. 1 (1784): 410–11; the letter had been written to Colonel Townley of Bolton on November 25, 1783; the earliest reference to Sunday schools in this influential journal occurs on page 377. This is cited in Thomas W. Laqueur, *Religion and Respectability: Sunday Schools and Working Class Culture, 1780–1850* (New Haven: Yale University Press, 1976), 23.

physical conditions, inefficient administrative arrangements, and with content not well adapted to the needs of pupils, the marvel is that so much good has been accomplished by the Sunday school. So great has been its contribution to the world that it has been called 'the university of the people.'"[5]

The curriculum of the Sunday school was pretty basic by today's standards. The children could not be expected to read the Bible if they had no ability to read at all. So the first priority was to teach basic reading and writing skills. The Bible became the textbook to teach these curricular matters, and soon the gospel was being presented. The Sunday school was always intended to have two purposes: first, to instruct the children in the basic educational aims of reading, writing, morals, and manners; and second, to evangelize those who were in desperate need of new life within. Transformation of morals, values, and ethics came about as a natural consequence of spiritual conversion. At first, Raikes's friends ridiculed his efforts, but the dramatic decline of juvenile crime in the city forced the civil authorities to take notice. Even Raikes himself was reluctant to publish a progress report on the program. In a brief article published in the *Glouchester Journal* on November 13, 1783, however, he wrote,

> Farmers and other inhabitants of the town and villages complain that they receive more injury to their property on the Sabbath than all the week besides. This is in great measure, proceeds from the lawless state of the younger class, who are allowed to run wild on that day, free from every restraint. To remedy this evil, persons duly qualified are employed to instruct those that can not read, and those that may have learned to read are taught the catechism and conducted to church. In those parishes where this plan has been adopted, we are assured that the behavior of the children is greatly civilized.[6]

Eventually, the success of the Sunday school program gained international acclaim. People came from all across Europe to study the methods and practices used in Raikes's experiment in social, civil, and spiritual reform. It would be nice to report that the church caught the vision of this evangelistic zeal, but such was not the case. In fact, many officials in the Anglican Church

---

5. Charles B. Eavey, *History of Christian Education* (Chicago: Moody, 1964), 215.

6. Wesley R. Willis, *200 Years—and Still Counting!* (Wheaton: Victor, 1980), 22.

were opposed to his efforts. The Archbishop of Canterbury even went so far as to gather a group of church leaders to see what they could do to prevent the Sunday school movement from continuing in England. Some people were concerned that because the teachers were being paid a small stipend for their efforts that such work constituted a violation of working on the Sabbath. Others didn't want the poor to receive any form of education for fear that a rebellion would be the natural consequence. Then, too, some people didn't want the Sunday school to continue because they didn't want their worldly amusements curtailed on Sunday.[7]

In spite of the church's efforts to oppose Raikes's work, the Sunday school became a popular means of Christian education throughout England and Europe. Within four years of Raikes's newspaper article, enrollment grew to an estimated 250,000 children! By 1835 (after just fifty years), as many as 1,500,000 people reportedly attended Sunday schools in England alone. For many of these students, the Sunday school was the only means of educational input in their lives. Over 160,000 volunteer teachers were involved in this ministry program. Historians have identified at least five major contributions of the Sunday school movement in England, including the following.

1. It triggered and supported across England a nationwide revival led by John and Charles Wesley and George Whitefield.
2. It stimulated people to recognize the need for public education for all classes of society.
3. It awakened the middle and upper classes to their responsibility to make meaningful contributions to society. This awakening, in turn, triggered dramatic social reforms throughout the country in other areas as well.
4. It stimulated the production and distribution of quality religious education curriculum materials that were needed to keep the movement moving. These materials were developed such that the average untrained layman could understand them.
5. It aroused a desire for adult education. Although children were the original focus of the Sunday school, adults soon came to recognize their need for improved schooling as well.[8]

---

7. Ibid.
8. Wesley R. Willis, *The Evangelical Dictionary of Christian Education,* ed. Michael J. Anthony (Grand Rapids: Baker, 2001), s.v. "History of the Sunday School."

The Sunday School Movement in England

The Sunday school was fundamentally a volunteer-based organization. As such, it had little, if any, formal authority or structure. In time, however, a number of distinct entities came into existence that brought organizational strength and support to the program. The following chart provides a brief overview of these efforts.

Name	Date	Denomination
Sunday School Society	1785	Interdenominational
Sunday School Union	1803	Interdenominational but predominantly Dissenting
Sunday School Association	1833	Interdenominational but predominantly Unitarian
Methodist Sunday School Union	1837	Wesleyan
Sunday School Institute	1843	Church of England
Society of Friends First Day School Association	1847	Quaker

The Society for the Support and Encouragement of the Sunday School (or, as it was usually called, the Sunday School Society) was formed in London in 1785 under the leadership of a Baptist merchant named William Fox. Its purposes were to prevent vice, encourage moral education, promote evangelism among the lost, and advance the peace and civility of the nation. The society was expressly ecumenical in structure, comprising twelve volunteer church leaders and twelve Dissenters. Within ten years of its founding, the society had given away 94,000 spelling books, 24,000 testaments, and more than 5,000 Bibles. By 1804, each of these figures had doubled.[9]

The Sunday School Union was quite different in composition because it was established by several young Sunday school activists whose vision was for the creation of new schools and the publication of materials to support the Sunday school movement. One such publication, the *Youth's Magazine,* helped

---

9. Laqueur, *Religion and Respectability,* 34.

young people understand their unique worldview and find ways to integrate Christian values into their contemporary lifestyle. The Sunday School Union was nondenominational in scope and made a conscious effort to reach across denominational boundaries for the sake of reaching young people for Christ. The harmony was short-lived, however, and eventually various denominations preferred to start their own associations rather than join the efforts of others.[10]

Growing out of the revival movement of the late eighteenth century, the Sunday school movement had a profound impact upon the face of England. Reaching out across the country to the uneducated masses of the working population, the Sunday school movement provided the only means of public education that most poor families would ever experience. Not only was it effective in producing a basic level of literacy among the populace, but it also made significant inroads into the spiritual renewal of the country as a whole.

Much like the church across the rest of Europe, the Church of England had grown accustomed to its grip on the people and had lost its passion for evangelism and religious instruction. The Sunday school movement changed all of that and forced the established church to reexamine its efforts at reaching the lost for Christ. Lay leaders who didn't know they couldn't accomplish great things for Christ without the requisite formal university education ventured into a noble cause with only the faith that they were obeying God. Surely with God's resources the challenge of reaching such a large population with unskilled workers and meager educational facilities would only serve God's purposes for revealing His sovereign hand over the program. It was an evangelical foray that pressed the Sunday school forward toward a Protestant "benevolent empire." William Wilberforce and other Anglican evangelicals spearheaded what has been described as an "immense reform movement, well organized and superbly directed . . . and using agencies and resources of a size, number and power not yet fully recognized."[11]

THE SUNDAY SCHOOL MOVEMENT IN AMERICA

In the years between 1780 and 1830, the Sunday school crossed the Atlantic and was involved in the early nineteenth-century North American awareness

---

10. Ibid., 38.
11. Ford K. Brown, *Father of the Victorians* (Cambridge: Cambridge University Press, 1961), 4; as cited in Robert W. Lynn and Elliott Wright, *The Big Little School*, rev. ed. (Birmingham, Ala.: Religious Education Press, 1980), 28.

of children and childhood as a stage of life. Canada and the United States were evolving from a rural and agricultural economy into urban and industrial economies. Whereas children of lower class urban families remained as significant economic contributors in their homes, the role of middle-class children and youth was changing rapidly. Now free of adult concerns, youth entered their teen years faced with vocational choices never before encountered by adolescents.[12]

A firm date for the first American school is difficult to establish, but the widely held belief is that William Elliot founded the first school in Virginia in 1785. The great Methodist leader Francis Asbury is credited with the second school a year later. The teaching of slaves was the central purpose of Asbury's school. In fact, this whole movement, both British and American, should be viewed as evangelicals' commitment to social concerns. By 1790, the Methodist Conference in Charleston, South Carolina, advocated the establishment of such schools for all children. They were under way in Philadelphia, New York, and Boston by 1791.[13]

In 1790 or 1791, a group of prominent Philadelphians founded the First Day Society. The Philadelphia Sunday and Adult School Union, founded in 1817, changed its name to American Sunday School Union (ASSU) in 1824.[14] The ASSU (now the American Missionary Fellowship) was evangelistic and missionary in its emphasis, organizing Sunday schools on the frontier west of the Appalachian Mountains; it was sometimes designated the Mississippi Valley Enterprise.

In 1830, the first national Sunday school conference in the United States was held with people attending from fourteen of the twenty-four states of the Union. These conferences continued sporadically into the 1960s, with the Sunday school continuing to be the central agency of most churches, especially those on the evangelical end of the theological spectrum. The National Sunday School Association was founded in 1945 as churches of a

---

12. Kenneth O. Gangel and Warren S. Benson, *Christian Education: Its History and Philosophy* (Chicago: Moody, 1983), 263.

13. Eavey, *History of Christian Education*, 231–32.

14. Anne M. Boylan, *Sunday School: The Formation of an American Institution, 1790–1880* (New Haven: Yale University Press, 1988), 61. See also James C. Wilhoit, "The Illusion of Change in Curriculum," *The Christian Education Journal* 8, no. 1 (autumn 1987): 25–30; and also Ronald H. Cram, "The Origins and Purposes of the Philadelphia Sunday and Adult School Union," *The Christian Education Journal* 10, no. 3 (spring 1990): 47–56.

more conservative theological tradition became aligned under the aegis of the National Association of Evangelicals.[15]

The growth of the Sunday school movement in North America was similar to that in England. In Canada, for instance, Sunday schools had formed in seven of the country's provinces. In 1887, Canada reportedly had 418,243 Sunday school students with 50,956 teachers and officers. In the United States, the Sunday school had been extended across the land as a result of the pioneering efforts of the ASSU. As a result of the national conventions that they sponsored, the movement enjoyed amazing momentum and growth. By 1832, 8,268 Sunday schools were affiliated with the ASSU. They were spread across twenty-seven states and also the District of Columbia. By 1875, the number of ASSU schools had grown to approximately 65,000 in thirty-six states and the District of Columbia. In 1889, approximately ten million people were enrolled in Sunday schools across the United States. With a U.S. population at the time of sixty million, Sunday school enrollment accounted for one-sixth of the entire population![16] Indeed, the Sunday school movement had a profound impact on the face of North America during its early years of inception.

During this period of unprecedented growth, the Sunday school curriculum became a focal point of concern. Denominational distinctives crept into some programs as a result of the sponsorship of a particular church denomination. By the mid-1800s, a major drive took place to bring many of these programs under one doctrinal tent. Sunday school conventions had become popular venues for the sharing of ideas about supplies, curriculum, instructional methodologies, and organizational structure. At the 1872 Sunday school convention, a Baptist layman named Benjamin Jacobs led the assembled diverse denominational groups to accept the International Uniform Lesson Plan, by which everyone would teach from the same biblical passages on given Sundays while making different emphases in light of the students' ages and developmental considerations. A Methodist pastor named John Vincent was highly motivated to use the best pedagogical concepts developed by the public schools and the teachers colleges (then called normal schools). He added his support while also advocating the seminar method of instruction.

---

15. Donald W. Dayton and Robert K. Johnston, eds., *The Variety of Evangelicalism* (Knoxville: University of Tennessee Press, 1981), 248–50.

16. Gerald E. Knoff, *The World Sunday School Movement: The Story of a Broadening Mission* (New York: Seabury, 1979), 3–5.

Vincent was aware that instructing the teachers in good methodology was the most powerful motivation for them to attend the conventions. However, despite Vincent's desire for high-caliber instruction in the Sunday school movement, the converse was often the reality.

Dark clouds were forming over the future of the American Sunday school movement, as evidenced at the worldwide Sixth Sunday School Convention held in Washington, D.C., in 1910. President William Taft gave a stirring address, and Congress even adjourned to march in the festive parade. Although world and North American Sunday school conventions would continue for many decades, in 1910 a dream was fading. It was the end of an era.[17]

With the emergence of the International Council of Religious Education (ICRE) at the Sixteenth International Convention in 1922, evangelicals became further disaffiliated with the direction the Sunday school movement had taken. The ICRE was forced to "counterbalance the American Sunday School Union," which had remained evangelical even over its lengthy yet imperfect history.[18] For evangelicals, the American Missionary Fellowship (formerly the ASSU) had long since lost its leadership role. However, the missionaries of the American Missionary Fellowship continue to the present to proclaim faithfully the good news in Jesus Christ in the rural areas and more recently in the inner cities of the United States.

The normative interpretation of Sunday school history has been that six periods existed, three before 1900 and three after 1900. In 1888, Henry Clay Trumbull outlined the first three periods; Jack L. Seymour suggested periods after 1900.

1. 1780–1830   The Sunday school as missionary and philanthropic agency.
2. 1830–1860   An extra-church agency to a church institution concerned with the evangelization and nurture of the young.
3. 1870–1900   Period of expansion when the evangelical spirit of revival became rooted in the Sunday school as the primary agent of church growth.

---

17. Lynn and Wright, *Big Little School*, 115.
18. Gerald E. Knopf, "The Sunday School Movement," in *Harper's Encyclopedia of Religious Education*, ed. Iris V. Cully and Kendig Brubaker Cully (San Francisco: Harper & Row), 626.

4. 1903–1929   An allegiance to liberal Protestant thought and Progressive religious education.

5. 1929–mid-1960s   Rise of neo-orthodox thought and the partial demise of liberal religious education.

6. Mid-1960s–1990   Decline in mainline church schools; evangelicals remain stable and strong.[19]

CURRICULAR ISSUES OF THE SUNDAY SCHOOL MOVEMENT

Early efforts at teaching biblical truth through the Sunday school lesson were largely developed by unskilled lay leaders. This fact was part of the concern of local church leaders. Without some degree of assurance that the biblical doctrines were being interpreted and taught accurately, church leaders were reluctant to reach out to the ministry endeavors of the Sunday school movement. The International Uniform Lesson, which Benjamin Jacobs had developed, was an attempt to bring some measure of theological integrity and consistency to the curriculum of Sunday schools.

Using some form of uniform plan was the topic of conversation at frequent Sunday school conventions in both England and North America. At the first convention, a worldwide International Lessons Committee was formed with both British and American representatives. As a result of complications brought about by World War I, the British thought that it was necessary to separate, and a different curriculum was written for each entity. These lessons were divided according to age appropriateness with designations for beginner, primary, and junior departments and advanced materials for adults. Although these lessons were being used throughout the world, differences in cultural distinctives were making it unrealistic for the same lesson to be taught to so wide an audience. Eventually, the strain of trying to appeal to such a diverse body of learners made the Uniform Lesson Plan unrealistic for worldwide distribution. By the time of the Glasgow convention, which convened in 1924, the chorus of dissatisfaction with the curriculum was almost universal.[20]

---

19. Jack Seymour, *From Sunday School to Church School: Communities on Protestant Church Education in the United States, 1860–1929* (Washington, D.C.: University Press of America, 1982), viii–x.

20. Knoff, *World Sunday School Movement,* 66–67

The Nineteenth Century in Review

The Sunday school has had a fascinating yet turbulent history. Initially, it was an attempt to teach poor children to read, write, count, and receive moral instruction. As it inexorably made its way into the life of the church, it was a lay-led Bible-teaching agency that adopted the twin aims of evangelism and edification. For a full century, it maintained a buoyant enthusiasm for the conversion of children and youth. As the twentieth century opened, two philosophies of the Sunday school were in place: first, those with educational goals particularly focused on reading, writing, arithmetic, and manners; and second, those with more evangelical directives.

> Although all Sunday schools provided an education centered on Christian belief, the founders of the evangelical schools placed paramount emphasis on the religious aspects of teaching, which they defined in a specifically evangelical Protestant manner. For them, teaching reading and writing was only a means to a greater end, not an end in itself. That greater end—an evangelical interpretation of the Bible—was to be achieved by teaching students to read the Bible, familiarizing them with its contents, and leading them to interpret it as their teachers did.
>
> Thus, the religion that these Sunday school founders hoped to impart was much more specific than the mere teaching of belief in God, the immortality of the soul, and the need for religious practice. It encompassed the evangelical doctrines of innate depravity, future punishment, and, most important, the need for a personal experience of regeneration.[21]

The evangelical schools grew in number, and the inherent drive in such a message created a desire to evangelize in wider and broader geographic areas. They had "different origins, purposes, organization, and appeal." Three major reasons for activism existed. First, it was a response to the Second Great Awakening. Second, the changing status of the child as new approaches to child psychology, combined with the growth of all types of schooling, convinced adults that children represented a vast untapped potential. Third,

---

21. Boylan, *Sunday School*, 9–10.

significantly more families were coming to church regularly and were bringing their children with them. Therefore, by 1830, the Sunday school was "becoming a permanent fixture in American life."[22]

The Sunday school actually accomplished a valuable task in keeping the churches and the public schools together. The teachers in the public schools/common schools and Sunday schools had become drillmasters in their teaching style. However, by the middle of the century, the public schools were beginning to move away from that pedagogy as the teachers colleges matured. With the encouragement of John Vincent and others, the Sunday school desired to follow these emerging teaching styles.

Horace Mann, the father of the common schools, attempted to reduce the religious ethos of the public school system. Having himself departed from Christianity to Unitarianism, Mann insisted that the schools not remain sectarian in their approach although still retaining a high moral tone. A "lowest-common-denominator reductionism" was actualized.[23]

By 1830, the movement was becoming more denominational. H. Shelton Smith, Robert T. Handy, and Lefferts A. Loetscher contend that by 1860 "spokesmen for all of the more churchly Protestant traditions—Lutheran, Reformed and Presbyterian, Anglican—arose to challenge the nondenominational unity which was forming. They advocated that each denomination conduct its own educational and missionary enterprises."[24]

THE DAWN OF THE RELIGIOUS EDUCATION ASSOCIATION

The Sunday school was in transition. Departmental and closely graded lessons were coming to the forefront of its design, and underlying each was the thinking and research of John Dewey, William James, Edward L. Thorndike, and G. Stanley Hall. Concepts derived from the field of psychology such as interest, motivation, experience, stages of maturity, and ability

22. Ibid., 12, 14, 16, 20.
23. William B. Kennedy, *The Shaping of Protestant Education: An Interpretation of the Sunday School and the Development of Protestant Educational Strategy in the United States, 1789-1860* (New York: Association Press, 1963), 72.
24. H. Shelton Smith, Robert T. Handy, and Lefferts A. Loetscher, *American Christianity: An Historical Interpretation with Representative Documents* (New York: Scribner's, 1963), 67-68; as cited in Kennedy, *Shaping of Protestant Education*, 74.

levels in learning became foundational. The Uniform Lessons seemed outdated and in need of extensive reworking. However, the excitement that existed in the golden days of the Sunday school in the latter half of the nineteenth century was gone. The emphasis on the conversion of the student was diminishing in most of the mainline churches. Denominationalism was strangling evangelical zeal. It was a new day.

The first president of the University of Chicago, William Rainey Harper, founded the Religious Education Association (REA) in 1903. A gifted Old Testament scholar, Harper retained an enthusiasm for popularizing the expositional study of Scripture. "His pioneering work on biblical correspondence courses, was, in part, a flank attack on the Uniform Lessons. So, too, was the creation of the REA. This small agency developed into a 'brain trust' for the reformers who hoped to transform the Sunday school into a thoroughly modern institution."[25]

If the Association was the "brain trust," the International Council of Religious Education was the organizing center. The Council, founded in 1922, was a single expression of both the Sunday school convention heritage and the concerns of powerful denominational boards of education.[26]

Henry Frederick Cope served the REA from 1905 until his death at fifty-three in August 1923. In 1907, he became its general secretary. Theodore Soares indicates that Cope was not an original thinker, but his skills were in organizing and popularizing the REA. He edited the journal *Religious Education* through the first one hundred issues. Cope encouraged research and integrated what different thinkers and church workers were developing. His enthusiasm was contagious, and his editing kept the flow of scholarship focused.[27]

Another influential voice of this era was an educator named George Albert Coe. He was a prolific writer and a fresh and innovative thinker. He was a psychologist of religion, and that background shaped his understandings of religious education. His address at the first REA conference established him

---

25. Lynn and Wright, *Big Little School*, 125.
26. Ibid.
27. Theodore Soares, "Henry Frederick Cope: His Life and Work," *Religious Education* (October 1923): 317–24.

as one of the principal leaders in the field. Coe stated that the turning point in his religious development was "an early turning away from dogmatic method to scientific method."[28]

Coe taught at the University of Southern California, Northwestern University, and Union Theological Seminary. Finally, after a fractious dispute with the Union administrators, he went across the street to Teachers College at Columbia University. Coe was influenced immensely by John Dewey. Coe was not only the academician's academician but also the liberal's liberal. What Dewey was to the progressive religious education movement as a philosopher, Coe was to the movement as a psychologist. To Coe, people should trust contemporary knowledge because God is present in our search for understanding. He espoused that no differentiation should be made between religion and education. Like Horace Bushnell, whose ideas he would share, Coe believed that together, the church, the home, and the public schools shared a common purpose, namely, to have "every child grow up Christian and never know themselves as being otherwise."[29] The term *religious education* was now in vogue, and a new movement had begun. The church and the world were to be seen as one, not separate. The Sunday school movement had, whether by design or by default, transitioned into an organization that had, in turn, morphed into a passionless program of mainline denominationalism. By the middle of the twentieth century, little remained of what Robert Raikes had begun. Starting out with an emphasis on social justice and public education of the poor, it had evolved into a dynamic and critical program for reaching the lost and fulfilling the Great Commission. As liberal theologians moved into prominent roles of decision making, however, the mantle of God's anointing and miraculous power was lifted. This is not to say that the Sunday school ceased to exist, for indeed it is still very much alive in many parts of North America. However, it has changed radically from what it was in the beginning and has gone through countless seasons of ups and downs. It is anything but dead; it continues to live in a variety of different and more relevant forms. We highlight one such example in the next section.

---

28. George A. Coe, "My Search for What Is Most Important," *Religious Education* 47 (March-April 1952): 176; as quoted in Seymour, *From Sunday School to Church School,* 12.

29. John Westerhoff III, *Who Are We? The Quest for a Religious Education* (Birmingham, Ala.: Religious Education Press, 1978), 14.

SUNDAY SCHOOL IN A NEW PARADIGM

Of all of the possible examples of contemporary Sunday school programs—and many across North America exist in reconfigured form—perhaps no other program illustrates the potency of the Sunday school in the twenty-first century as well as Metro Ministries in Brooklyn, New York. Known around the world as the "Sidewalk Sunday School," the program was the brainchild of a visionary leader named Bill Wilson.

In 1988, Wilson was struck by the New Testament parables beckoning people to come and hear the gospel message. Living in the metropolitan region of New York, with millions of people within driving distance from his church, he felt a deep sense of accountability for the lost within his community. "If they came," he pondered, "where would they fit?" His response to the need was to establish a ministry the mission of which was, sending people into the ghettos of New York to bring them the gospel message of hope in the midst of a hopeless environment. If the children of New York could not come to his church for Sunday school, then he would bring the Sunday school to the children of New York. His vision for this program grew out of his own experience as a homeless child. Describing the events that so profoundly influenced his life as a young child, he writes:

> My mother and I were walking down the street on the block where we lived in Pinellas Park, Florida—just north of St. Petersburg. It was near the Welcome Inn on Park Boulevard, where she worked as a barmaid.
>
> We stopped and sat down on a concrete culvert that was built over a little drainage ditch. She was very quiet that day. After a few minutes she stood up and said, "I can't do this anymore. You wait here."
>
> I did exactly what my mom said. I sat there waiting for her to return. The sun went down, and she still wasn't back.
>
> For three days I sat in the Florida sun on that concrete culvert. I didn't know where to turn. If I had known how to pray, I would have done it, but religion had no place in our home.
>
> All I could do was try to be brave and choke back the tears that would fill up my eyes.
>
> Mom never came back. . . .[30]

---

30. All of the materials related to the description of Metro Ministries come from their Web site located at www.metroministries.org.

Sending people into the community with the Sunday school message of evangelism and redemption, Wilson's team interprets literally the passage "Go out into the highways and along the hedges, and compel them to come in, so that my house may be filled" (Luke 14:23). "Unfortunately," according to Wilson, "most in church leadership have rationalized themselves off the streets. They say, 'Well, that was then, this is now, and things are different.' But by and large in the American church we put such an emphasis on 'the coming in' that we forget that there's actually someone who went out and compelled. More often than not, the emphasis is put on what they will see and hear on the inside, not on getting them there in the first place. After a while, no one is coming because no one is going out and compelling anybody to come and do anything."[31]

The kind of Sunday school program that operates out of Metro Ministries would probably shock Robert Raikes if he were alive to see it today. Wilson had packed his church to overflowing. No more people could come in, yet the need to reach the unsaved around his church was still there. He needed a creative solution to his space problem. Then one day an idea came to him. "I saw a trailer with a stage hitched to the back of the truck. I thought about its possibilities. Though I knew it wouldn't be practical for the streets of New York, I realized we were on the right track. Soon we were thinking about trucks. We converted an old fourteen-foot cube truck, cutting out and hinging one side of the truck panel so that it lowered down to make a stage. We outfitted it with a sound system and everything else needed for Sunday School—whether it was indoors or not."[32]

His first Sunday school site in 1988 was located in the inner city of Brooklyn, New York. They laid out tarps on the sidewalk for kids to come and hear Bible stories and play some games. And come they did. That first week, they had one hundred children in attendance. Once they used trucks that could scatter across New York and into other nearby communities, the attendance grew at an almost alarming rate. The programs and multiple ministries offered by Metro would be impossible to implement without the dedicated service of hundreds of volunteers from their church and community. Nearly 450 people volunteer regularly with their ministry.

Today, his "Sidewalk Sunday School" program has a weekly attendance of more than twenty thousand children, making it the largest Sunday school

31. Ibid.
32. Ibid.

program in the world. So popular has it been that churches from all around the world have come to study its methods and replicate them in cities where they live. Now Sidewalk Sunday School programs exist all over the world.

The Sidewalk Sunday School

PURPOSE . . .
Metro's ultimate purpose is to provide the children, youth and adults of the inner city the means to find salvation through Jesus Christ.

VISION . . .
Our vision is to see leaders, teachers and pastors raised up out of the streets of the cities worldwide. Then, they in turn will minister to the next generations.

OBJECTIVE . . .
Our objective is to see families and neighborhoods changed as we reach children through the power of Sunday School and Personal Visitation.

CORE VALUES . . .
- To aspire to Christian maturity through prayer and study of the Word
- To be committed to our families
- To maintain a high standard of integrity
- To promote Sunday School, Sidewalk Sunday School, and visitation as a means to fulfill our call to the Great Commission[33]

The Sidewalk Sunday School developed by Metro Ministries is an example of how the Sunday school movement that was started in England more than 250 years ago still lives in North America. Sure, it might look different from what Raikes began, but it is still fulfilling many of the same reasons for existence. Surely Raikes would be pleased to see that the Sunday school movement that he began in the mid-1700s to provide basic biblical instruction to inner-city street children is still at work reaching the same kinds of children these many years later.

---

33. Ibid.

So What? Lessons from the Past for Twenty-first-century Christian Education

Looking back over the years of the Sunday school movement, we see the hand of God at work in humanity. Man had come out of the Enlightenment with a sense of self-sufficiency and self-reliance. Fortunately, God recognized our folly and stirred the heart of a man who was obedient to His calling, a common businessman by trade, but a willing heart was all that was required. Robert Raikes, although trained as a newspaper editor, became responsible for countless millions of souls being brought into the kingdom of Christ through the efforts of the Sunday school. His movement spread throughout the world as a means of helping the needy receive some basic level of education and instruction. In addition to the guidance that the students received in reading, writing, moral development, and spiritual formation, they also gained the mentoring of a caring adult. These children who had come into the world with so little discovered that they were blessed beyond their understanding. Those who served in the Sunday school movement did so out of love and devotion to their Savior. Sure, they might have received some small financial remuneration to compensate them, the early pioneers of the movement, but who could believe that twenty-five cents a day could possibly motivate one for all that was required of them. Indeed, it was a labor of love.

1. Lay leadership ignites a spiritual renewal and international fire.

The first Sunday school program, which began in 1780, depended on the passion and perseverance of volunteers. Formal theological training for those in charge was nonexistent. Those who provided the direction and weekly instruction were qualified only by virtue of their desire to see the fulfillment of the Great Commission. Some of the greatest and most lasting movements in Christianity have been founded by volunteers. Eventually, they transitioned to the auspices of paid professionals once the organization had grown beyond that which could be supervised by volunteers. The Holy Spirit of God seems to enjoy watching and blessing the efforts of those whose theological training is lacking in the eyes of the world. He delights in confounding the wise and thrives on blessing those who have a heart and passion for ministry.

History is replete with examples of ministries that were established by volunteers and were transitioned to paid professionals only to find that years later they no longer resemble much of what the original visionaries had expected. Years of organizational bureaucracy had in turn created layers of institutional structure resulting in an organization that had a lot of activity but no longer served the original purposes of the founder.

The Sunday school is an excellent example of an organization that started under the tutelage of laymen with a simple desire to reach the poor inner-city children of larger British cities with the gospel message. It grew far beyond what any of its founders could have envisioned. However, with that growth came the tendency to lose its evangelical passion. If we can learn any lessons from the history of the Sunday school, the first must be that God is still about the business of reaching the lost and that He is capable of reaching His objectives through volunteers. As more and more of the ministry is transitioned to paid professionals, a tendency arises to lose sight of the original passion and calling of the organization. When that happens, God seems to lift His mantle of blessing and provision from the original organizations and to call for someone else in whom He can begin a new work. Soon after the Sunday school movement lost its passion for evangelistic drive in the 1940s, new organizations such as Youth For Christ, Young Life, and a host of other mission-related organizations were begun. Many of these new organizations were also founded by people who had a passion to reach the lost with the unchanging message of hope in Jesus Christ alone.

2. Curriculum development was essential to preserve the doctrinal purity of the Sunday school movement.

That a unifying curriculum be established was essential to ensure that untrained Bible teachers were not teaching aberrant doctrines. However, looking back through the lens of hindsight, we now see that it is critical that those who controlled the development of "unifying" curriculum needed to use their influence to steer away from doctrinal and denominational splintering.

> These union lessons were widely used but never held complete sway. They were followed by lessons which put special emphasis on denominational distinctions in doctrine. Each denomination issued lessons of its own, stressing its creed. Independent publishers planned lessons to suit their particular constituencies. Writers and publishers competed to provide means to help teachers. Quarterlies and Sunday

school materials took the place of the use of the Bible. Semi-Biblical commentaries were produced for the use of teachers in the Sunday school. Extra-Biblical materials introduced in the Sunday school began to compete with Biblical materials. The period from 1840 to 1870 was a period of turmoil known as the "Babel era."[34]

As long as the curriculum focused on fundamental elements of the Christian faith—such as salvation in Christ alone, the Bible is God's Word, the Scriptures contain historical stories, miracles are possible under God's power, etc.—then the Sunday school movement prospered. Once the curriculum writers began to steer away from these and other fundamental topics and appropriated a less conservative interpretation of these doctrinal issues, however, the evangelical community lost trust in the movement, and support declined. It wasn't that they lost trust in the Sunday school mission or program itself—they incorporated many of the basic elements of the Sunday school program into their own denomination's ministry programming—it's that they lost faith in that into which the organization had evolved.

In many respects, the decentralization of the curriculum allowed more flexibility across denominational, geographical, and philosophical boundaries. We shall explore the development of the Christian curriculum publishing companies in chapter 12, but suffice it to say at this point that many of the publishing companies that would later be established for the purpose of publishing Sunday school curriculum had their beginnings as a direct result of the influence of the Uniform Lesson Plan.

3. Two hundred fifty years of Sunday schools have taught us that the strongest programs were those that remained faithful to the original message of evangelism, instruction in God's Word, and responsiveness to social need.

The Sunday school movement was not a church effort toward catechetical indoctrination. In addition to teaching the lost about how to receive a saving faith in Christ, it sought to meet a significant social need.

The Sunday school movement was a blending of the best of both worlds. It identified both spiritual and social needs and tried to find a way to bring the two together. How could young children be taught to read the Scriptures

---

34. Eavey, *History of Christian Education,* 279.

if they could not read at all? How could they be expected to sit still and receive instruction if they lacked the basic human needs of food, hygiene, and clothing. In its earliest form, the Sunday school movement sought to find a way to provide basic educational skills to children who fell through the socioeconomic cracks of their society. In addition to providing religious instruction, the Sunday school movement helped provide these basic needs.

Sometimes in our zeal and passion to reach the lost for Christ, we neglect to recognize the importance of the basic human needs of safety, shelter, security, belonging, etc. It's not that we neglect the physical realities that exist, but we are so overly focused on the end goal of saving the lost that we minimize the means by which we are accomplishing the end. If Raikes had only gathered the children into the homes of caring women for religious instruction in the late 1700s, the program would have been limited in scope and effectiveness. It was the dramatic impact that the program had on juvenile street crime that garnered so much public acclaim and notoriety. That, in turn, started a groundswell of support for the program as a whole. In a sense, it was the social agenda that it incorporated that validated the effectiveness of the spiritual transformation that it accomplished. Both emphases were intertwined and essential for success. No reason existed for the objectives of one emphasis to conflict with the objectives of the other emphasis. A blending of the two was not only possible but also expedient. In a very real sense, the synergy created by the blending of the two emphases ensured greater success for each.

We stand on the threshold of a new generation in need. No one could possibly believe that our society has evolved into such a highly structured enterprise that we no longer have evident needs. Juvenile crime is still rampant across our country, and young people still wander the streets in lost isolation. Their minds and souls cry out for someone to take an interest in them and provide some form of mentoring. Although the original program elements of the Sunday school movement might have changed since its inception, the need for the program remains the same. What we need is for people to think outside the box and create ministries that accomplish the same objectives as the Sunday school but perhaps in a different venue. Programs such as the "Sidewalk Sunday School" sponsored by Metro Ministries is one such enterprise. May God continue to raise up people who have the courage to take new risks and accept new challenges in the name of reaching the lost for Christ.

For Further Reading

Boyland, Anne M. *Sunday School: The Formation of an American Institution, 1790–1880.* New Haven: Yale University Press, 1988.

Eavey, Charles B. *History of Christian Education.* Chicago: Moody, 1964.

Elias, John L. *A History of Christian Education: Protestant, Catholic, and Orthodox Perspectives.* Malabar, Fla.: Krieger, 2002.

Fergusson, E. Morris. *Historic Chapters in Christian Education in America: A Brief History of the American Sunday School Movement and the Rise of the Modern Church School.* London: Revell, 1935.

Gangel, Kenneth O., and Warren S. Benson. *Christian Education: Its History and Philosophy.* Chicago: Moody, 1983.

Graendorf, Werner C. *Introduction to Biblical Christian Education.* Chicago: Moody, 1981.

Knoff, Gerald E. *The World Sunday School Movement.* New York: Seabury, 1979.

Laqueur, Thomas W. *Religion and Respectability: Sunday Schools and Working Class Culture, 1780–1850.* New Haven: Yale University Press, 1976.

Poehler, William A. *Religious Education Through the Ages.* Minneapolis: Masters Church & School Supply, 1966.

Reed, James, and Ronnie Prevost. *A History of Christian Education.* Nashville: Broadman & Holman, 1993.

Todd, Galbraith H. *The Torch and the Flag.* Philadelphia: American Sunday School Union, 1966.

Willis, Wesley R. *200 Years and Still Counting!* Wheaton: Victor, 1980.

What in the World?

➤ First permanent English colony is established in Jamestown, Virginia, in 1607.

➤ The Manchu rule China as the Qing Dynasty in 1644–1912.

➤ Slave trade from West Africa booms in 1680.

➤ The French and the British wage four consecutive wars over territory in the New World, 1689–1763.

➤ The French Revolution begins in 1789.

➤ The Latin-American wars of independence are fought in 1791–1824.

Chapter 10

CHRISTIAN EDUCATION
IN COLONIAL AMERICA

EUROPE AT THE END OF THE EIGHTEENTH century had become known as a land of enlightenment because of its focus on new ways of thinking about society and the surrounding world. It was an era marked by revolution and reformation. The Enlightenment was a reaction against the absolutist and authoritarian ways of those in control during the Reformation. "It was a protest against absolute monarchy, against authoritarian economic systems, against rigid social stratification, against religious totalitarianism, against an unscientific world, against the doctrine of original sin in human nature, and against the domination of intellectual life by ancient and medieval conceptions of truth and knowledge. Underlying these protests was a growing faith in the common man, in science, and in human reason."[1]

Many historians refer to the Enlightenment as the "age of reason" because of man's increased emphasis upon the scientific method for explaining the world. Whether it pertained to explanations concerning scientific inquiry, economic expansion, political ideology, or social stratification, man sought to use rational thought to understand his world. This emphasis resulted in the marginalization of theology and discussions about God's influence in the world. The deists had won the day and rationalized away man's ability to have a

---

1. R. Freeman Butts, *A Cultural View of History: Reassessing Our Educational Traditions* (New York: McGraw Hill, 1947), 316.

personal relationship with his Creator. According to the deist, God had abandoned His creation and gone on a very long vacation. Man was clearly on the throne of his own universal destiny. These effects of humanistic thinking brought about during the Reformation were well established and had pretty well permeated thinking in all academic disciplines and social systems.

REASONS FOR LEAVING EUROPE

Many people living in Europe at that time dreamed of a new society in which all people, not just the fortunate aristocrats, would be free to pursue their personal dreams of a better way of life. People who had kindled a relationship with God desired a place where they would be able to develop that relationship free from the constraints of an overbearing church. In addition to those who desired religious freedom, many other people in the merchant class across Europe had come to experience the taste of middle-class living. New modes of transportation and communication brought about through expanded trade routes and political treaties had provided for those who possessed an entrepreneurial spirit the opportunity for economic gain.

However, those in power viewed this freedom as a threat to their ongoing control. Although they enjoyed the revenue from increased taxation of this growing portion of the population, they also recognized that this growing middle class, left unchecked, represented a threat to their long-term stability. The result of these fears was a form of economic constraint that choked the spirit from those who sought a better way of life for themselves and their families. These European citizens envisioned a new world characterized by the pursuit of political liberty, religious freedom, and economic entrepreneurism. We explore each in greater detail in this chapter.

The Pursuit of Political Liberty

People living in Europe during the late seventeenth century came to realize that to expect those in power to give up control and authority was relatively futile. They had hoped for a system of political governance whereby their needs of health, education, security, and life happiness were considered important. The monarchical system, however, did not lend itself to democratic ideals, and by that point many of the growing middle class were realizing that those in control were only paying lip service to change. A new system was needed whereby the taxpayers had some say about where and how those taxes would be spent. That simply wasn't going to happen in any of the European countries.

Enlightenment philosophes were speaking of new ideals upon which such a governing system would be developed, a system in which personal freedoms and life pursuits would not be in conflict with the people in authority. But how could this grand experiment ever be confirmed as viable if no monarch was willing to cede his/her authority to a parliamentary system in which the common people elected their representatives? As explorers returned from their journeys across the Atlantic, they brought back stories of a vast frontier of undeveloped land, a region that was rich in natural resources and had no formal system of government that required change. They could develop a new approach from scratch, if only they could get there first. Soon France, Spain, Great Britain, and a host of other countries would seek to lay claim to that land and set up their own systems of government over its inhabitants. Until then, it seemed plausible to the early settlers to go and see if this new approach to civil government could actually be established. It would take time and certainly a good many risks. But if it could be accomplished, the world would have an example of a nation governed by its own people through a system of temporarily elected representatives from among its own populace. Such was the rationale of some people who came to the shores of North America in the early seventeenth century.

The Pursuit of Religious Freedom

Those who sought religious changes during Europe's Reformation received instead large measures of persecution. The Hussites, Waldensians, Moravians, Puritans, Lollards, and others discovered that the authorities of the Roman Church would never grant religious liberties. What was needed and dreamed about was a land in which these religious freedoms could be experienced free of the constraints and autocratic methods of church authorities.

The Roman Church had developed such a highly structured system of bureaucracy that reform seemed almost beyond the realm of possibility. Even leading Catholic theologians who had called for reforms after the excesses that had been exposed during the Reformation lacked the ability to see their ideas come to fruition. The system had grown too powerful and had largely ignored calls for substantive change.

Believers were now able to read the Scriptures for themselves and soon discovered the erroneous teachings of the church. They rejected many of the traditional teachings of the church and favored the approach of "solo scriptura," which had been heralded during the Reformation. The church, realizing its eroding influence, responded by persecuting these sects. Persecution was harsh and punitive. With few places to protect them, the victims were faced with few alternatives other than to flee to a land where they could practice their biblical faith without fear of retribution. When the invitation came for them to travel to a new land, they had little to lose, and they accepted the challenge.

Integrating biblical values into the structure of America was what the Founding Fathers intended from the beginning. They crafted the Declaration of Independence and the Constitution such as to establish a Christian order. In the 1892 Supreme Court decision of *Church of the Holy Trinity v. United States,* the Justices wrote as follows:

> Our laws and our institutions must necessarily be based upon and embody the teachings of the Redeemer of mankind. It is impossible that it should be otherwise; and in this sense and to this extent our civilization and our institutions are emphatically Christian.
>
> This is a religious people. This is historically true. From the discovery of this continent to the present hour, there is a single voice making this affirmation . . . we find everywhere a clear recognition of the same truth. . . . These, and many other matters which might be noticed, add a volume of unofficial declarations to the mass of organic utterances that this is a Christian nation.

The Passions of Our Founding Fathers

It is impossible to rightly govern the world without God or the Bible.
—President George Washington

We've staked the whole future of American civilization not on the power of government, far from it. We have staked the future of all our political institutions upon the capacity of each and all of us . . . to govern ourselves according to the commandments of God. The future and success of America is not in this Constitution, but in the laws upon which this Constitution is founded.

—President James Madison

The highest story of the American Revolution is this: it connected in one indissoluble bond the principles of civil government with the principles of Christianity.

—President John Adams

A Bible and a newspaper in every house, a good school in every district—all studied and appreciated as they merit—are the principle support of virtue, morality, and civil liberty.

—Benjamin Franklin, March 1778

Four score and seven years ago our fathers brought forth on this continent a new nation, conceived in liberty, and dedicated to the proposition that all men are created equal.

—President Abraham Lincoln,
"The Gettysburg Address," November 1863

It cannot be emphasized too strongly or too often that this great nation was founded, not by religionists, but by Christians; not by religions, but on the gospel of Jesus Christ. For this very reason peoples of other faiths have been afforded asylum, prosperity, and freedom of worship here.

—Patrick Henry

In no other way can this republic become a world power in the noblest sense of the word than by putting into her life and the lives of her citizens the spirit and principles of the great founder of Christianity.

—David J. Brewer,
Associate Justice of the U.S. Supreme Court, 1889–1910

The Pursuit of Economic Entrepreneurialism

To this point, the average citizen had few opportunities for economic prosperity. Although many European societies had developed a middle class, they were exploited and taxed beyond reason. Being in the middle class simply meant that a heavier tax was levied upon them by the civil authorities. In time, a growing resentment of this treatment was a natural consequence. After all, if one was willing to take a risk and venture into a new economic enterprise, why shouldn't they be allowed to share in the spoils of the venture if it proved financially successful? Unfortunately, most governmental leaders did not share this ideology, and as a result middle-class merchants and businessmen harbored resentment in their hearts. They grew in their resolve to enact changes that would benefit their risk taking.

According to the Enlightenment philosophes, the human mind was motivated by an economic desire for profit. To them, for man to seek ways to better himself financially was human nature.

> The conception of the "economic man" was also basic to other "natural laws" of economics, most important of which was the law of supply and demand. According to this law of laissez-faire economics, prices will always reach their natural level when goods are bought and sold in an unrestricted market kept open for free competition. A seller tries to get the highest price possible, and the buyer tries to get the lowest price. Competition among sellers tends to force prices down, and competition among buyers tends to force prices up: the greater the demand for goods, the higher the price. In order to allow this natural process to operate the government must let business alone hence laissez-faire capitalism.[2]

The desire for reform was strong throughout Europe, but it was not always well received among those who held firm control of their power. What was needed was a new world in which the ideals of the Enlightenment could be tested. To that point, much of those ideals were held to be true and reliable, but they lacked the ultimate test of pragmatic application on a grand scale.

Venturing to the New World to apply the philosophical ideals preached during the Enlightenment was a risk. But without taking such a daring venture,

---

2. Ibid., 318.

how would anyone know if the ideas were plausible? The rewards of obtaining political liberty, religious freedom, and economic entrepreneurism were too great from which to walk away, so venture the people did. New inventions led the way for new methods of manufacturing, distribution, commerce, and agricultural production. A new world awaited those who were daring enough to cross the Atlantic and plant their dreams in the fertile soil of colonial America.

The Inventive Urge

The industrial and agricultural revolutions of the eighteenth century produced a variety of devices and processes, some trivial, others of lasting importance. They ranged from the deep-cutting plow, invented by the agrarian farmer Jethro Tull, to the modern water closet and the recipe for mayonnaise. Some of those inventions are listed as follows, with the names of their creators and the dates of their invention.[3]

Date	Invention	Inventor
1701	Seed-planting drill	Jethro Tull
1708	Hard paste porcelain	Johann Bottger
1709	Iron smelting with coke	Abraham Darby
1712	Steam pump	Thomas Newcomen
1732	Mill-rolled iron	Michael Menzies
1733	Flying shuttle (weaving)	John Kay
1742	Sheffield silver plate	Thomas Bolsover
1747	Beet sugar extraction	Andreas Marrgraf
1756	Mayonnaise	Duc de Richelieu
1768	Spinning jenny	James Hargreaves
1769	Steam engine	James Watt
1774	Improved cannon borer	John Wilinson
1777	Winnowing machine	James Sharp
1778	Modern water closet	Joseph Bramah
1784	Threshing machine	Henry Cort
1785	Chlorine bleach	C. L. Berthollet
1787	Power loom	Edmund Cartwright
1793	Cotton gin	Eli Whitney
1800	Improved lathe	Henry Maudslay

---

3. Peter Gay, *Age of Enlightenment* (New York: Time, 1966), 103.

NEW HORIZONS OF OPPORTUNITY

From the very beginning of the first settlement in Jamestown on April 26, 1607, ideas of government, economics, religion, education, class structure, and the legal system were inherently of English origin. The new thirteen "plantations" were transplanted from English soil, and they reflected their English ancestry. From the religious turmoil of the period came the Lutherans with their insistence upon believers' ability to read and interpret the Scriptures for themselves; the Calvinists with their conviction of the inherent depravity of man and their corresponding quest for education; and the English with their Church of England, Puritans, and Separatists. The Puritans who landed at Plymouth Rock in 1620 were Protestants who brought their faith and theories of government with them. Although some Catholics and Jews were among the early settlers, the vast majority of those who made their home in the new land of the American colonies were Protestants.[4]

In contrast to what they had known on the European continent, America was a land of freedom and opportunity. They now had the freedom to dream new dreams about political liberties, religious freedoms, and economic opportunities. Then, as never before, fate provided them rich potential for prosperity and independence. Freedom from both domestic tyranny and foreign interference infused these settlers with hope for the future.

EDUCATION IN THE NEW ENGLAND COLONIES

The Northern Colonies consisted of Massachusetts, Connecticut, New Hampshire, and Rhode Island. These early colonies were structured around towns or townships in which homes were built in proximity to each other. Towns also consisted of a church, a jail, essential stores, and a schoolhouse. These early settlers understood the importance of education for their children and quickly set about making legal and curricular provisions for that education.

The Common School

The legal basis upon which general education was conducted in these

---

4. S. E. Frost, *Historical and Philosophical Foundations of Western Education* (Columbus: Charles E. Merrill, 1966), 246.

colonies was known as the Mayflower Compact of 1620. In 1642, Massachusetts passed a law asserting its right to force apprenticeship training upon children in all towns and villages within its sphere of influence. In addition to this stipulation, the law also required parents and masters to carry out their obligations to the young so that children would be instructed how to read and understand the principles of Scripture and the laws of the country. Those who ignored this state-imposed regulation would be fined. This law is significant because it was the first time the state had passed a law requiring that all children receive instruction in reading. It did not, however, require townships to establish schools for this purpose. Such a provision came about shortly thereafter; in 1647, the General Court of the Massachusetts Bay Colony passed a law requiring the creation of schools and the employment of teachers in each township. What is significant about that law was the manner in which it left the support of schools to local communities.[5] It became widely known as the "Old Deluder Satan law" because of the law's preamble, which reads,

> It being one chief project of that old deluder Satan to keep men from the knowledge of the Scriptures, as in former times by keeping them in an unknown tongue, so in these later times by persuading from the use of tongues (that so at least the true sense and meaning of the original might be clouded by false glosses of saint-seeming deceivers)—[to the end] that learning may not by buried in the grave of our fathers in church and commonwealth, the Lord assisting our endeavors.

The law, then, was formulated to establish the creation of schools within each township to provide instruction to the children living within its jurisdiction. The law reads:

> IT IS THEREFORE ORDERED, that every township in this Jurisdiction, after the Lord has increased them to the number of 50 households, shall forwith appoint one within their own to teach all such children as shall resort to him, to write and read, [a teacher] whose wages shall be paid either by the parents or masters of such

---

5. Ibid., 286.

children, or by the inhabitants in general by way of supply [general tax] as the major part of those that order the prudential [government] of the town shall appoint: *provided*, [that] those that send their children be not oppressed by paying more than they can have them taught for in other towns. AND IT IS FURTHER ORDERED, that where any town shall increased to the number of 100 families or householders, they shall set up a grammar [i.e., Latin] school, the master thereof being able to instruct youth so far as [i.e., that] they may be fitted for university [Harvard]. *Provided* that, if any town neglect the performance hereof above one year, that every town shall pay $5 to the next school until they shall perform this order.

The primary textbooks for these early schools included the Bible and the English catechism. Consistent with the Puritans' reason for coming to America in the first place, religious freedom and the ability to study the Scriptures were hallmarks of elementary education in the early colonies. Children were taught from an early age the contents of the Scriptures and its application to life. Four other textbooks also were used for instructional purposes: the hornbook, the *New England Primer*, the Psalter, and a book titled *Spiritual Milk*.

The hornbook was an educational resource that came about of necessity. Although the Bible was an ideal textbook for the English reading classes used in colonial schools, it was hardly an appropriate text for the elementary school child who did not yet know the alphabet or how to pronounce the sounds of letters. Parents were expected to teach these fundamental skills to their children before sending them to school. For this reason, the hornbook was invented. Actually, it wasn't a book at all but rather a slate that the child held in one hand. It consisted of a think board, sometimes shaped such that the bottom was cut in the shape of a handle that could easily be held in one hand. On this board was fixed a thin printed leaf with text on it. The text might be the alphabet for young learners, the Lord's Prayer, or a passage of Scripture. The entire board was then covered by a thin sheet of transparent horn, which protected the letters underneath from finger marks and the wear and tear of being handled by young children.[6]

After the Bible, the Psalter, and the hornbook, the next most popular

---

6. William A. Poehler, *Religious Education Through the Ages* (Minneapolis: Masters Church & School Supply, 1966), 280.

educational resource for young learners was the *New England Primer,* which came on the scene in 1690. It included the contents of *Spiritual Milk* and the *Westminster Catechism.* It was popular among not only the New England Puritans but also the English-speaking Lutherans. Its total sales are estimated to have been three million copies. It comprised a mere eighty-eight pages and was 3½ by 4½ inches and bound with a wooden cover.[7] A rhyme just inside the cover reads,

Good Boys at Their Books
He who ne'er learns his A, B, C,
Forever will a Blockhead be;
But he who to his book's inclin'd,
Will soon a golden Treasure find.

In addition to these public schools, private schools also were available for children. Because not everyone who came to America came to avoid religious persecution, some parents preferred that their children receive a more secular education than what was available in the public school. In those days, particularly in the New England and Middle Colonies, public school was synonymous with religious education by virtue of the curriculum, textbooks, social values, and school board policies.

The Dame School

Another form of education was available for children in the New England colonies: the dame school was established for girls almost as soon as the first settlers arrived. Because girls generally were not admitted into the town schools, dame schools gave young women their entire education. The dame school curriculum was basic reading, writing, and arithmetic. Some towns helped finance dame schools, but because they were less esteemed than the town schools, they were generally poorly funded and the quality of both the teachers and the instruction was often lacking.

In addition to the dame school, some forms of private tutoring were available from skilled and trained teachers, who provided their services for a fee. In some instances, when a township was unable to fund a complete school for its children, they would point to one of these tutors as proof that

---

7. Ibid., 281.

education was available for their children when, in actuality, few could afford the tutor's services. In a few cases, private tutors grew in popularity, and their schools competed with the publicly funded town school for students.[8]

Latin Grammar Schools

The Latin grammar school was another provision of the Act of 1647. It was designed to continue the education that had begun in the common school. Families who desired that their children get an education in the classics enrolled them in the Latin grammar school, in which the curriculum consisted of a seven-year sequence of studies designed to provide students a more comprehensive education in Greek, Latin, and many of the classics. It was designed for families who wanted their children to be trained in the humanities, which were valued during the Reformation. The Latin grammar school became the secondary school system of its day and remained so until the creation of the academies a hundred years later.[9]

The curriculum of the Latin grammar school began with several years of language studies to prepare the students for subjects to follow. Once the students mastered Greek and Latin, they began reading such classics as Cato's *Distichs*, Aesop's *Fables*, and Corderius's *Colloquies*. In their second year, they read the works of Horace, Erasmus, Ovid, Cicero, Virgil, Homer, Isocrates, and selected Hebrew writings.[10] It was a vigorous form of education that for obvious reasons appealed more to the elite members of colonial society than to the common folk. It was beneficial for its time but soon lost much of its following as the need for more practical instruction rose in priority among the masses.

EDUCATION IN THE MIDDLE COLONIES

The Middle Colonies consisted of New York, New Jersey, Pennsylvania, and Delaware. The colony of New Netherland was settled primarily by the Dutch, but it also included persecuted Huguenots, Waldensians, Moravians,

---

8. Frost, *Historical and Philosophical Foundations*, 258–59.
9. Kenneth O. Gangel and Warren S. Benson, *Christian Education: Its History and Philosophy* (Chicago: Moody, 1983), 236.
10. Samuel Elliot Morison, *The Puritan Pronaos: Studies in the Intellectual Life of New England in the Seventeenth Century* (New York: New York University Press, 1936), 102–3; as cited in Gangel and Benson, *Christian Education*, 237.

Baptists, Quakers, and Jews. In 1675, reportedly no fewer than fifteen languages were spoken in that colony. New Amsterdam, Brooklyn, and New Amstel (now Newcastle) in Delaware had charters that provided for the establishment of schools. In New Amstel, the charter read "that the city of New Amstel shall send thither a proper person for schoolmaster, who shall also read the Holy Scriptures and set the psalms."[11] In New Netherland, as in New England, the schools was closely associated with the church in the community. Not only was religious instruction included in the school curriculum, but also the teacher was viewed as an assistant to the pastor. In some cases, the teacher's services went beyond the confines of the classroom. In addition to his school duties, the teacher also rang the bell for church each Sunday morning, read the Ten Commandments (along with other selected passages) in the services, served as the choir director, taught the catechism to the children, provided a basin of water for people who were being baptized, served the bread and wine during the communion service, and performed other similar duties as needed by the local pastor.[12]

In Pennsylvania, the church had a significant degree of authority over public education. The Quakers were not as enamored by education as were the Puritans in New England. The Quakers did not believe that a knowledge of the classics was appropriate preparation for ministry leadership. Neither did they highly value knowledge of Hebrew, Greek, or Latin. To the Quakers, spiritual understanding came to the believer through an inner illumination, and a college education actually got in the way of ministry preparation. George Fox, the founder of the Quakers, once said, "God stood in no need of learning, and that Oxford and Cambridge could not make a minister."[13] Fox did, however, value schools as important agencies for the transference of values, traditions, and biblical morals, all of which were critical for raising children to become effective community citizens. Pennsylvania adopted a law requiring all parents to have their children educated in reading and writing. By the end of the eighteenth century, approximately sixty to seventy schools had been established according to this Quaker standard. Most famous among them was the Penn Charter School, founded in 1689.[14]

---

11. Ibid., 265.
12. Oliver Perry Chitwood, *A History of Colonial America* (New York: Harper & Row, 1961), 459.
13. Ibid., 459–60.
14. Ibid.

EDUCATION IN THE SOUTHERN COLONIES

The Southern Colonies consisted of Virginia, Maryland, North Carolina, South Carolina, and Georgia. Schools in this region of the country were somewhat different from those in the Northern and Middle Colonies. Settlers in the Southern Colonies came to America not so much to avoid religious persecution at the hands of the Catholic and Anglican churches as for commercial and financial incentives. Wealthy people in England saw America as a land of opportunity. Many of them came to purchase large sections of land that could be farmed for tobacco production. The middle class followed to ply their trades among those who could afford to pay for their services. Likewise, the servant class went where jobs were plentiful. All came to continue the English culture and the class societal structure. Because society as a whole was more rural, it stands to reason that the educational system would be more family oriented and less structured. Formal education was not emphasized, and large landowners saw the benefit of not providing education beyond basic apprenticeship for the children of indentured servants and slaves.[15] The lower the level of education provided, the fewer questions were asked about how things could be changed for the better.

Private schools were provided for the children of the wealthy upper-class land barons because they could afford to pay the high tuition rates for their children. Such schools were referred to as "old field" schools because they were built on tobacco fields that had been abandoned because of overfarming. The teacher was a local minister who was not currently employed by a local parish. As for the quality of the instruction provided for these children, they received an education not unlike what they would have received in England. The curriculum was determined by the parents and often included Greek, Latin, and French. The young child was also expected to learn manners and protocol commensurate with their standing in society. Many parents in the Southern Colonies sent their children back home in England to stay with relatives while they received their education.[16]

Summary of Colonial Elementary Education

The revolution of 1776 was fought in the belief that government should have as its chief concern the welfare of its citizens. Colonial leaders such as

---

15. Frost, *Historical and Philosophical Foundations,* 268.
16. Ibid., 270.

Jefferson and Washington were concerned with the problem of education because they realized that the very future of democracy depended on a rational and educated citizenry. Jefferson played a large role in developing a public educational system that would serve the needs of the populace. While serving in the Virginia legislature, he introduced a bill that would have established free education for the children residing in the state. Although he was ahead of his time and the bill was defeated, he was relentless in his commitment to public education of the masses. Jefferson tried to establish that the objectives of elementary education is sixfold:

1. To give every citizen the information he needs to transact his own business.
2. To enable him to calculate for himself and to express and preserve his ideas, contracts and accounts in writing.
3. To improve, by reading, his faculties and morals.
4. To understand his duties to his neighbors and his country, and to discharge with competence the functions confided to him by either.
5. To know his rights; to exercise with order and justice those he retains; to choose with discretion, candor and judgement the fiduciary of those he delegates.
6. And, in general, to observe with intelligence and faithfulness all the social relations under which he shall be placed.[17]

"Although the new republic's political foundations had been laid with the Constitution, it still needed the institutions and processes to educate its citizens. Still in place but in disrepair were the inherited schools and colleges of the pre-Revolutionary colonial period. In New England were the locally controlled town and district schools and Latin grammar schools that still reflected much control by religious denominations."[18] The colonies in the South lacked even more educational resources than the Middle or Northern Colonies because the large plantation owners were less concerned about educating their citizens than they were about maintaining control over their large land holdings. Each region had its own unique concerns.

---

17. Fredrick Mayer, *A History of Educational Thought* (Columbus: Charles E. Merrill 1966), 372.
18. Gerald L. Gutek, *Historical and Philosophical Foundations of Education: A Biographical Introduction* (Upper Saddle River, N.J.: Merrill Prentice-Hall, 2001), 155.

During the eighteenth century, the greatest growth in attendance occurred in elementary education, where enrollment was about sixteen million students by 1900. At that time, however, only about 10 percent of the eligible age group was attending secondary education.[19] America had a long way to go to discourage students from dropping out after receiving an elementary level of education. More effort was required to move students from elementary to secondary levels. Some of this resistance was due to the philosophy, curriculum, and administration of secondary education as conducted in America at that time.

Secondary Education in Colonial America

The provision for including the Latin grammar school in the "Old Deluder Satan law" of 1647 was the colonists' attempt to keep the British preparatory school alive in America. Few American children would have desired an education comprised primarily of Greek, Latin, and the liberal arts. That was a curriculum for upper-class British children whose parents desired a more comprehensive preparation for their children so they would be prepared for roles in church or civil leadership. Although the law of 1647 sought to provide for maintaining such a school, it was a futile effort.

As we stated earlier, the secondary school that originated in the New England colonies was designed as a college preparation school for the children of wealthy citizens. Its purpose was to educate young men in Latin grammar. Because relatively few youths attended this form of school, two newer approaches to secondary education came to the forefront of public education.

Private Schools

The private English secondary school responded to the needs of the commercial and trading classes of citizens. It was more vocational in direction and sought to equip young students in practical subjects rather than in the traditional classics. The basic language of instruction was English rather than Latin, which was the traditional language of secondary instruction. Young

---

19. James W. Noll and Sam P. Kelly, *Foundations of Education in America: An Anthology of Major Thoughts and Significant Actions* (New York: Harper & Row, 1970), 180.

women were allowed to attend these schools as well. Students took whatever courses they thought were important to their future, so they inaugurated a type of elective system. Some classes convened after the evening meal so that those who worked during the day could attend classes in the evening to further their careers. Curricular offerings included bookkeeping, accounting, penmanship, and mathematics. Such courses were designed to further the middle-class professions of banking, accounting, merchandising, engineering, and navigation. Students who sought more intensive instruction in mathematics could also take advanced courses in algebra, geometry, astronomy, trigonometry, calculus, and surveying.[20]

Academies

"About the same time that the academy was superseding the Latin school in New England it was also playing an important role in Southern education. This new type of school had a place between the small private school and the college. There was no sharp line separating it from the 'old field school' below or the college above, for in its curriculum it overlapped both."[21] Its curriculum included subjects in Greek, Latin, science, mathematics, and other important topics.

The academy form of secondary instruction was first proposed as early as 1743 by Benjamin Franklin in Philadelphia. In his widely circulated pamphlet titled *Proposals Relating to the Education of Youth in Pennsylvania,* he set out to prescribe a rationale for the collection of funds leading to the establishment of an academy. The state legislature authorized it in 1753 and in 1755 added a charter for a college. From that institution came the University of Pennsylvania. Franklin proposed that the new academy should have three departments: English, Latin, and mathematics. It had far more subjects than the Latin secondary school and allowed the student to choose from what seemed to be a limitless array of course offerings. The academy would be surrounded by lawns, gardens, reflection pools, meadows, and orchards. It would also house an extensive library, science labs, and other essential academic resources. Judging from this list of academy offerings, Franklin seemed to represent the influences of European empiricism, sense realism, and other utilitarian interests. Because he had a well-known love for scientific

20. Butts, *Cultural View of History,* 375.
21. Chitwood, *History of Colonial America,* 463.

experimentation, it is not surprising that his academy would also favor empirical forms of inquiry. He made no reference to either religious or sectarian instruction, except for a class in the history of religion, which would have been well within his personal deistic philosophy.[22]

The Life of Benjamin Franklin

More commonly known as an inventor, Franklin made significant contributions in a variety of areas affecting colonial America. Born in Boston, Massachusetts, on January 17, 1706, he is also known for his exploits as a statesman, diplomat, editor, and scientist.

He attended school for a short time before going to work in his father's tallow shop and then later in his brother's print shop. In 1723, he took a job as a printer in Philadelphia, where he later secured a partnership in the *Pennsylvania Gazette,* of which he served as editor until 1748. He also edited *Poor Richard's Almanac* from 1732 to 1757. As a leader in various cultural movements of his day, in 1727 he founded the Junto, a debating club that later became the American Philosophical Society. He also established a circulating library (1731); Philadelphia's first fire department (1736); and an academy (1751), which would later become the University of Pennsylvania.

His acclaim as an inventor started with the creation of the Franklin stove (1742). The identity of lightning was demonstrated in France in 1752 using methods that he first suggested, and they were later confirmed with a kite experiment. He served as the deputy postmaster at Philadelphia (1737–53), and jointly with William Hunter, the postmaster general for the colonies (1753–74).

Politically, he was a delegate to the Albany Congress (1754), where he drafted a Plan of Union that was adopted by the colonies but was later rejected by both Great Britain and the colonies for opposing reasons. He went to England to represent the colonies and, upon returning to Philadelphia in 1775, was elected to the Second Continental Congress, in which he was also elected as Postmaster General (1775–76). He was one of three commissioners sent to secure the assistance of Canada (1776) and helped

---

22. Ibid., 376.

draft the Declaration of Independence (1776). He traveled to France and later to England, where he negotiated the peace treaty with Great Britain (1783). He also served as president of the Executive Council of Philadelphia (1785–1788) and was a member of the Constitutional Convention (1787), in which he was influential in helping to frame the composition of the House of Representatives.[23]

HIGHER EDUCATION IN COLONIAL AMERICA

In effect, Christians founded the Ivy League. Harvard in 1636, Yale in 1701, Princeton in 1769, and Dartmouth in 1754 all had significantly Christian roots. The first president of Columbia University (then King's College) was a missionary to America under Great Britain's "Society for the Propagation of the Gospel in Foreign Parts." The College of William and Mary was established in 1693 as a seminary for ministers of the gospel. The founding of Yale was for the "upholding and propagating of the Christian Protestant religion by a succession of learned and orthodox men."[24] Harvard was brought into existence by a legislative body, itself less than eight years old, in a colony less than ten years old, through the following community commitment: "After God had carried us safe to New England and we built our houses, provided necessaries for our livelihood, reared convenient places for God's worship, and settled the civil government: one of the next things we longed for, and looked after was to advance learning and perpetuate it for posterity."[25]

In time, however, perspectives change and not all change is good. War for independence from England had a profound impact upon the Christian vibrancy of many of these leading institutions of higher education.

A state of war is peculiarly unfriendly to religion. It dissipates the mind, diminishes the degree of instruction, removes great numbers almost wholly from it, connects them with the most dangerous company, and presents them with the worst examples. It hardens and

---

23. Richard B. Morris, ed., *Encyclopedia of American History* (New York: Harper & Brothers, 1961), 709-10.
24. Lawrence A. Cremin, *American Education: The Colonial Experience 1607-1783* (New York: Harper and Row, 1970), 321.
25. Ibid., 210.

emboldens men in sin; is productive of profaneness, intemperance, disregard for property, violence and all licentious living.

The Revolution had loosened the bonds of Christian piety. . . . Churches had been burned; loyalist ministers had fled their pulpits; schism had rent several of the leading denominations; clergymen had been ordained under the most dubious circumstances; and congregations had fallen to new lows in size and fervency . . . the war had unhinged the principles, the morality, and the religion of the country.[26]

Harvard, Yale, the College of New Jersey (now Princeton University), Columbia, and the College of William and Mary felt the interruption, and even the destruction, that war brings. It was a pivotal moment in American educational history. The ties with England, which had given form and substance to American education, were cut. Educators, now open to rethinking and recasting, were even more free to try new structures and consider fresh content.

For the first two hundred years of American higher education, people made a concerted effort to include biblical studies as part of the curricular offerings. With the expansion of society, a broadening of the curriculum occurred that brought about a decline in the number of graduates entering the ministry. As a result of this displacement of biblical and theological students, many denominations began shortly after 1800 to develop their own colleges and seminaries to train leaders for their churches.[27]

The curriculum in these higher education schools consisted of Greek, Latin, Hebrew, and elementary Chaldee and Syriac. In addition to these language studies, they offered courses in arithmetic, geometry, history, politics, logic, ethics, Bible, rhetoric, composition, oratory, astronomy, physics, and botany. Discipline was strict, and standards of conduct were clearly communicated. Students were expected to rise early, attend all classes, and be respectful of their teachers and staff supervisors. At Harvard, discipline was enforced by flogging until 1734, when the system was changed and

---

26. Benjamin Trumbull, *A Complete History of Connecticut,* 2 vols. (New Haven: Maltby, Goldsmith & Co., and Samuel Wadsworth, 1818), 2:18; as cited in Cremin, *American Education,* 564.

27. Charles B. Eavey, *History of Christian Education* (Chicago: Moody, 1964), 335.

Higher Education Institutions in Colonial America

Institution	Date	Colony	Denominamtion
Harvard	1636	Massachusetts	Puritans
William and Mary College	1693	Virginia	Anglicans
Yale	1701	Connecticut	Congregational
College of New Jersey (Princeton)	1746	New Jersey	Presbyterian
University of Pennsylvania	1751	Pennsylvania	None
King's College (Brown University)	1754	New York	Anglican
College of Rhode Island (Columbia University)	1764	Rhode Island	Baptist
Queen's College (Rutger's University)	1766	New Jersey	Reformed
Dartmouth	1769	New Hampshire	Dutch Congregational

student infractions were punished by monetary fines instead. Such standards grew out of the theological belief that man was naturally depraved and needed such restrictions to curb his natural bent toward sinfulness and to help facilitate the development of virtue. One course noticeably absent from the curriculum was athletics. Athletic competition was looked down upon and viewed as sinful indulgence.[28]

THE GREAT AWAKENING

The first Great Awakening to affect America took place at the beginning of the eighteenth century, specifically between 1730 and 1760. In time, the

---

28. Chitwood, *History of American Education*, 470-71.

fervency of the first-generation Puritans began to subside, and a spiritual malaise had begun to settle over the hearts of this new generation. Revival began to spread throughout the Eastern seaboard, however, as prominent traveling preachers visited towns, heralding a call to repentance. Congregationalist preacher Jonathan Edwards (1703-58), Presbyterian Gilbert Tennent (1703-64), and itinerant George Whitefield (1714-70) traveled extensively, calling colonial citizens to return to their spiritual roots. Reminding Protestant Americans of their unique place in the world as a divinely instituted country, these religious leaders were passionate about purifying American culture and calling their audiences to righteous living and genuine faith.

Jonathan Edwards was disappointed by what he saw as a significant moral decline in American culture. Educated at Yale College, he was ordained to the ministry in the Congregational Church. In addition to traveling across Europe, he spent a considerable amount of time traversing America, preaching a Calvinist message of mandatory new birth. His sermon "Sinners in the Hands of an Angry God" tore at the heart of Americans and brought many of them to their knees in repentance. "Edward's [sic] evocations of the tortures of the damned made his hearers roll on the floor in physical agonies, but he thrilled them with hope that they might yet be saved, and the experience of conversion became the core of revivalist religion."[29] Although people did not view Edwards as a particularly gifted orator, they highly esteemed him for his intellect, which his writings clearly demonstrated. His book *Treatise Concerning Religious Affections* (1746) presented his views concerning the role of one's will and intellect in shaping his or her religious life. To Edwards, each element played a unique role in a person's spiritual life.

After being dismissed from his church, Edwards became a missionary to the Indians in Stockbridge, Massachusetts. During that time, he wrote *Freedom of the Will* (1754), in which he laid out his perspective on the controversy over the issues of man's free will and the election of God. Toward the end of his life, he became the president of the College of New Jersey.[30]

The Great Awakening added new churches across all denominations. This growth of churches resulted in a movement to provide educa-

---

29. Dumas Malone and Basil Rauch, *American Origins to 1789* (New York: Appleton-Century-Crofts, 1960), 98.
30. Michael J. Anthony, *The Evangelical Dictionary of Christian Education*, ed. Michael J. Anthony (Grand Rapids: Baker, 2001), s.v. "Jonathan Edwards."

tional opportunities for the growing number of ministerial recruits. The forerunners of many present day eastern universities were born during this period of time, with William Tennent's *"Log College,"* representative of the educational initiative begun in this period. Basic schools also emerged for Indians, Negroes, and the children of indentured servants.[31]

After the leadership of Jonathan Edwards, a lull occurred in the spirit of religious revival until the preaching of George Whitefield. An eloquent preacher from England, Whitefield visited the colonies and preached emotionally charged messages that stirred the hearts of his audiences. Although he was less intellectual than Edwards, Whitefield's reputation for personal piety made a deep impression on America. His preaching was often punctuated with dynamic gestures and unconventional antics. He attracted such large crowds that the churches that had invited him often were unable to accommodate those who came to witness his message. As a result, he would convene his assembly outside. At times, the house would be so full of people that they would have to lift him over their heads as they transported him to the pulpit. The increase in colleges such as Princeton (Presbyterian), Brown (Baptist), Dartmouth (Congregational), and Rutgers (Dutch Reformed) can be considered direct results of this colonial revival movement.[32]

POLITICAL DREAMS BECOME REALITY FOR COLONIAL AMERICA

Many of the dreams that had come across the Atlantic with the early settlers had taken root and grown to fruition. However, they did not come without cost. A series of repressive economic and political acts by the British crown forced many of the early colonists into decisive action. In 1775, representatives of these discontented Americans met as a Continental Congress to formulate their response. Individuals such as John Adams, Patrick Henry, Richard Lee, and George Washington held firm to their resolve that the British monarch should not be allowed to repress American liberties.

On July 2, 1776, the Continental Congress voted to separate from British

---

31. Byron D. Klaus, *The Evangelical Dictionary of Christian Education*, ed. Michael J. Anthony (Grand Rapids: Baker, 2001), s.v. "Great Awakenings."
32. Chitwood, *History of Colonial America*, 447.

rule and commissioned Thomas Jefferson to draft the Declaration of Independence. The president of the Congress, John Hancock, and other delegates signed it on July 4. For the next five years, the colonies and their motherland would be engulfed in war as each side sought to maintain control over their sovereign rights. The war continued until October 19, 1781, when British General Cornwallis surrendered at Yorktown to the victorious colonists. In 1783, a peace treaty was signed, and America was free and independent of monarchial interference. Over the next few decades, the colonies would organize, coordinate activities, and create a more solidified nation.

At the beginning of the eighteenth century, the door of democratic thinking had been opened through the writings of John Locke (see chap. 8). In his *Treatise on Civil Government,* he espoused a "contract theory" by which he advocated that the middle-class parliament strip the monarch of his authority. In this contractual arrangement, the people delegated authority to a representative government in exchange for protecting their natural rights as citizens. These natural rights included the rights of life, liberty, and land ownership. According to this constitutional perspective, the government would exercise its authority through those who were selected as citizen representatives.[33]

Locke concluded that the best way to organize the government was around three entities of shared power: first, the legislative branch, which would be entrusted with the responsibility of making laws; second, the law-enforcing executive branch; and third, the adjudicative or legal branch. Members of the government would be elected by the people and, once having served their terms, would return to the way of life from which they originated. To protect property rights, taxes would be levied only with the consent of those who were being governed. These principles are very Lockean. Locke's philosophical viewpoint was particularly influential on Thomas Jefferson (1743–1826) and shaped both his views as expressed in the Declaration of Independence in 1776 and those of the framers of the Constitution in 1788 and 1789.[34]

On September 13, 1778, the Continental Congress passed a resolution that would bring an end to the current system of governance. They established dates for the selection of electors who in turn would vote on presiden-

33. Butts, *Cultural View of History,* 316
34. Gutek, *Historical and Philosophical Foundations,* 153.

tial candidates. Thus, the Continental Congress was signing its own death warrant; their action signified the passing of the Confederation and marked the beginning of the Second Republic.[35] This date also signified the end of the colonial period of American life and ushered in a new era of American history.

So What? Lessons from the Past for Twenty-first-century Christian Education

Canada and the United States have a rich heritage of Christian values. Mennonites fled Russia and Germany and settled across Canada, bringing with them the desire to spread the gospel message. Soon, churches, Bible schools, and Sunday school camps were formed. In the United States, numerous groups brought the message of hope and salvation in Christ. As they settled, they helped establish new laws, churches, and schools that reinforced their biblical ideals of religious freedom.

1. The primary characteristic of education during the colonial period of American history was its adherence to religious ideals and values.

Because the colonial educational system clearly was founded upon biblical teaching, no debate occurred between "secular versus religious" education for the first several decades in the American educational system. "Though education in Colonial days, whether tax supported or not, commonly included religious education, the very multiplicity of religions in a given community, soon watered down the content of the religious instruction to include basically only Protestant ethos, culture and tradition, without teaching specific doctrines."[36]

But the desire to accommodate the countless immigrants that came to the shores of America took its toll on the "Christian" component of Christian education. *Christian* education gave way to *religious* education, which was more broad based and inclusive. Not wanting to offend those who had recently arrived from other cultures, schools were reticent to require

---

35. Chitwood, *History of Colonial America*, 640.
36. Peohler, *Religious Education Through the Ages*, 294.

instruction in topics that were fundamentally religious in nature. In an effort not to offend, public education in colonial America lost its spiritual component. Moral education, values-based learning, and spiritual instruction were omitted from the curriculum, lesson plans, and textbooks. Soon, educational learning materials became amoral and vague. What was *true* for one group of immigrants might not be *true* for another group, so materials had to sink to the lowest common denominator. What began as freedom *of* religion slowly evolved into a freedom *from* religion.

The result of this series of compromises and accommodations is that American public school education is valueless and spiritually bankrupt. Perhaps it would make us feel a bit more satisfied if we could point to a particular event or person that caused this decline, but history is not so precise. In fact, in many cases, it was the church itself that facilitated the decline by refusing to take a definitive stand for ethics, morality, and religious values. Liberal theologians, pastors, and educators in positions of authority and decision-making power allowed these changes to occur. Hindsight has shown us that the steep slippery slope of moral and religious descent occurs one step at a time over a prolonged period. Rarely can we point to one individual or momentous event that caused the final decline.

Twenty-first-century Christian educators must remain alert and vigilant for continuing erosions of ethics, morals, and biblical values from our society. Without this level of watchfulness, it might not be long before North Americans experience a form of persecution similar to what overcame our European ancestors. Persecution, rather than coming from a monarchy or a state government, might come from an increasingly secular society that has grown increasingly intolerant of our biblical convictions and moral judgments.

2. The family abdicated its role.

A second lesson to be learned from the colonial period is found in the changing view of the role of the family in the Christian upbringing of our children. Colonial Americans had a deep conviction about the role of the family and its foundation in the religious instruction of its children. The earliest tax-supported schools indicated that their purpose was to train students to read and study the Bible. Indeed, the "Old Deluder Law" of 1647 and other laws from New England clearly substantiate this belief. In time, however, the church and the state took over for the family and assumed the role of chief religious instructor for the parents. With the introduction of the Sunday school after the Revolutionary War, the home was simply left to provide food and shelter.[37]

For obvious reasons, it is time for American families to wake up to the consequences of abdicating their parental responsibilities. The two-parent working home and the alarming divorce rate in America throughout the latter half of the twentieth century have had and will continue to have a devastating effect on children and youth. Studying history gives us the ability to regain some perspective and learn some valuable lessons. One of the most valuable lessons from the colonial period of American Christian education is the realization that parents must continue to be the focal point of religious instruction for their children. Whether it be through a dramatic conversion experience (as espoused by Finney) or through a consistent nurturing in a Christian family environment (as espoused by Bushnell), whatever means and/or method is applied, the end result is the true litmus test of whether this task has been accomplished. The question that must be answered is simply this: "Do my children evidence a genuine faith in Christ, and do I see ongoing and consistent evidence of that vital relationship?"

3. Our nation's founders had a high regard for one's personal religious convictions.

Freedom of personal faith was a foundation stone of both the Declaration of Independence and the Constitution. It was always the desire of America's Founding Fathers to grant its citizens the right to pursue (or not) their own religious education without governmental interference. That right included the selection of the educational process for our children.

The Constitution grants us the freedom not to send our children to public schools, provided we can and do make some provision for their education by some other means. Thus, some of the Lutherans in Pennsylvania; the Roman Catholics, who protested the Protestant's seeming monopoly on education during the common school movement; and others continued to establish private schools for the express purpose of educating their children within the religious traditions of the parents.[38] People living in America are indeed blessed with freedoms and privileges that many people all over the world only dream of having in their land. We who live in the United States and Canada have much for which to be grateful!

---

37. Ibid.
38. Ibid.

For Further Reading

Butts, R. Freeman. *A Cultural History of Education.* New York: McGraw Hill, 1947.

Chitwood, Oliver P. *A History of Colonial America.* New York: Harper & Row, 1961.

Cremin, Lawrence A. *American Education: The Colonial Experience 1607–1783.* New York: Harper & Row, 1970.

Eavey, Charles B. *History of Christian Education.* Chicago: Moody, 1964.

Elias, John L. *A History of Christian Education: Protestant, Catholic, and Orthodox Perspectives.* Malabar, Fla.: Krieger, 2002.

Frost, S. E. *Historical and Philosophical Foundations of Western Education.* Columbus: Charles E. Merrill, 1966.

Gangel, Kenneth O., and Warren S. Benson. *Christian Education: Its History and Philosophy.* Chicago: Moody, 1983.

Graendorf, Werner C. *Introduction to Biblical Christian Education.* Chicago: Moody, 1981.

Gutek, Gerald L. *Historical and Philosophical Foundations of Education: A Biographical Introduction.* Upper Saddle River, N.J.: Merrill Prentice-Hall, 2001.

Malone, Dumas, and Basil Rauch. *American Origins to 1789.* New York: Appleton-Century-Crofts, 1960.

Mayer, Fredrick. *A History of Educational Thought.* Columbus: Charles E. Merrill, 1960.

Noll, James William, and Sam P. Kelly. *Foundations of Education in America: An Anthology of Major Thoughts and Significant Actions.* New York: Harper & Row, 1970.

Poehler, William A. *Religious Education Through the Ages.* Minneapolis: Masters Church & School Supply, 1966.

Reed, James E., and Ronnie Prevost. *A History of Christian Education.* Nashville: Broadman & Holman, 1993.

Simpson, Mark E. "Colonial Education." In *The Evangelical Dictionary of Christian Education.* Edited by Michael J. Anthony. Grand Rapids: Baker, 2001.

What in the World?

➤ Thomas Jefferson purchases the Louisiana Territory from France for $15 million in 1803.

➤ Adoniram and Ann Judson sail for India in 1812.

➤ Napoleon Bonaparte is defeated in the Battle of Waterloo, ending his attempt to rule Europe in 1815.

➤ Darwin returns from the Galapagos Islands and begins to record his observations of natural selection in 1836.

➤ Numerous violent political revolutions shock central Europe in 1848.

➤ Southern states secede from the United States to form the Confederate States of America, part of a chain of events leading to civil war in 1861.

➤ William Booth founds the Salvation Army in London in 1865.

➤ Japan opens its doors in 1868.

➤ The Transcontinental Railroad is completed at Promontory, Utah, in 1869.

➤ European nations expand in Africa and Asia in 1870–1914.

➤ Alexander Graham Bell sends his voice across a wire to his assistant Thomas Watson in 1876.

➤ Freud publishes his first work, *On Aphasia,* in 1891.

Chapter 11

CHRISTIAN EDUCATION IN THE NINETEENTH CENTURY

AMERICA AT THE BRINK OF THE NINETEENTH century was experiencing a virtual population explosion. In the thirty years between 1840 and 1870, the population doubled. It doubled again from 1870 to 1900. The primary factor contributing to this growth was a vast migration from Europe. Of the seventy-six million people living in America at the turn of the century, ten million were foreign born. In many of the larger industrial cities, the population of immigrants was nearly 50 percent of the population.[1]

Capitalism was reaching its zenith during the onset of the nineteenth century. America was gradually shifting from a commercial type of capitalism to a form of industrial capitalism. The shift meant the development of large factories and the creation of large business corporations. In fact, corporations grew so large during this period that they had almost exclusive control over many of the natural resources across the land. This situation resulted in a corresponding concentration of wealth among those who owned or controlled the large corporations. In 1900, approximately 90 percent of the country's wealth was controlled by one-tenth of the population. As the country changed from an agrarian society to an industrial society, the capitalist methods had a profound impact on the face of America.[2]

---

1. R. Freeman Butts, *A Cultural History of Education* (New York: McGraw Hill, 1947), 449.
2. Ibid., 450.

The nineteenth century was marked by progress in a number of important areas besides commerce. Obviously, significant changes occurred in America as the political climate built upon the progress that was made since the ratification of the Constitution. In addition, progress was made in the development of labor unions, the Civil War brought about considerable change regarding one's views on slavery and social justice, and the Great Awakening that was evident in the eighteenth century returned for another manifestation in the nineteenth century. Coming out of this second national revival was the birth of the Bible college movement, which, in turn, sparked the beginning of Christian higher education as we know it today. Many of the colleges that were established in the 1800s had lost their passion for preparing men and women for ministry service and altered their mission statements. A number of important figures in Christian education—including Horace Bushnell, Charles Finney, John Wesley, and D. L. Moody—made a lasting impact on America during the nineteenth century. We explore these and other themes in this chapter.

The Second Great Awakening

The second great awakening to influence America occurred between 1800 and 1830 and was a response to a growing secularization of American society. Many of the influences that we described in the introduction to this chapter had negative consequences on the nation's spiritual values. Some religious groups decided to retreat into a form of spiritual seclusion rather than remain in the forefront of the battle for religious ideals. "Pietists, Dunkers, Moravians, and others from Europe maintained themselves in groups apart. The Mormons under Joseph Smith and Brigham Young traveled most of the width of the continent until they found haven in Utah."[3] Those who chose to confront culture with the teachings of Christ were rewarded for their efforts but the battle was by no means easy.

This nineteenth-century revivalist movement was spearheaded by Presbyterian James McGready (1758-1817); Timothy Dwight (1752-1817) was the president of Yale College and the grandson of Jonathan Edwards; and Lyman Beecher. Beecher sought to identify the relationship between education and settling the new western frontier of America. In his book *A Plea for the West*

---

3. Ibid., 452.

(1835), he expressed his belief that settling this new region would best be accomplished by establishing new schools, churches, colleges, seminaries, and other religious institutions. Through this approach, the West would be won for Protestantism.[4]

Another leading preacher of the second awakening was Charles Finney (1792-1875), who has been acclaimed as one of North America's greatest nineteenth-century evangelical preachers.[5] Finney was a prominent figure in many tent revivals and church gatherings in America at this time. Although he traveled extensively, Finney was for forty years associated with Oberlin College, and in some respects that institution became the embodiment of his vision of producing "an army of inspired evangelists" and the "evangelical Christian community."[6] "When Finney died in 1875, evangelicalism had become the characteristic form of Protestant Christianity in America, and surely the most pervasive version of the Protestant American *paideia*."[7]

Charles G. Finney

Revivalism did not end with the end of the Second Great Awakening. A lawyer named Charles G. Finney was converted in 1821 and became a revivalist preacher. His campaigns in Rockchester, New York, in 1830 and 1831 received wide acclaim, in part, because of his unique methods. He conducted lengthy meetings during unseasonable hours, used colloquial language in his preaching, named specific individuals in his public prayers, and employed an "anxious bench" to which people who were under spiritual conviction could come. He became a pastor in New York City and eventually moved to Oberlin, Ohio. In 1851, he became the president of Oberlin College, where he lectured in systematic theology and revivalism. Under

4. John L. Elias, *A History of Christian Education: Protestant, Catholic, and Orthodox Perspectives* (Malabar, Fla.: Krieger, 2002), 162.

5. Martin E. Marty, *The Irony of It All, 1893-1919*, vol. 1 of *Modern American Religion* (Chicago: University of Chicago Press, 1986), 200.

6. Lawrence A. Cremin, *American Education: The Colonial Experience, 1607-1783* (New York: Harper & Row, 1970) 43.

7. Ibid.

Finney's leadership, Oberlin admitted African-American students, and Finney was influential in the abolition of slavery movement. An African-American woman named Antoinette (Brown) Blackwell (1825–1921) was the first woman to complete her theological training in 1850, and three years later became the first woman to be ordained in the United States. Evangelical feminists trace their origins to Finney's second wife, Lydia, whom he allowed to pray and speak in public while she conducted women's revival meetings.[8]

"These early religious awakenings had a major impact in the development of Christian education in Protestant churches. The awakenings themselves were educational experiences for adults and to a lesser degree for children. In their tent meetings religious awakenings took to task not only the quality of religious observance but also the existing educational methods of producing so-called committed Christians."[9] From these revival movements came a thirst for biblical knowledge and understanding. They inspired the formation of Bible schools, colleges, and seminaries by the Presbyterians, Congregationalists, Baptists, and Methodists.

Dwight L. Moody (1837–1899) came on the evangelical scene at a time when Americans were searching for meaningful existence. Born in Northfield, Massachusetts, Moody grew up in a rough home. His father was an alcoholic and died when Dwight was just four years old. At seventeen, his contempt for farm living motivated him to go to live with his uncle in Boston, where he obtained a job as a shoe salesman. Shortly thereafter, he heard the gospel message while attending a local Sunday school and gave his life to Christ. He later moved to Chicago, where his outgoing personality led to his great success as a salesman. However, God had begun a new work in Moody's heart that made increasing his own bank account less of an interest to him than introducing souls to God's kingdom. Moody left his secure job to become the director of a local YMCA, where he had the opportunity to teach the Bible and preach the gospel message of salvation. His success as a Bible teacher soon flourished, and although Moody lacked any significant formal

---

8. Earle E. Cairns, *Christianity Through the Centuries: A History of the Christian Church*, 3d ed. (Grand Rapids: Zondervan, 1996), 431.

9. William G. McLoughlin, *Revivals, Awakenings, and Reform: An Essay on Religion and Social Change in America, 1607-1977* (Chicago: University of Chicago Press, 1978); as cited in Elias, *History of Christian Education*, 161

education, God richly blessed him with a spiritual harvest of souls. His popularity in the pulpit soon attracted a large following; people from all across Chicago came to hear him preach. He established a church, which, after his death, was named the Moody Memorial Church.[10]

During this period, Moody accepted invitations from churches and ministry leaders in Canada, England, Scotland, and Ireland to come travel there to conduct evangelistic crusades. His popularity increased at a phenomenal rate, and people came to faith in Christ in unheard of numbers. This caused Moody great concern, however, because he understood that spiritual conversion was only the beginning of the road toward spiritual maturity. He realized that conversion without any responsible follow-up would have little lasting effect on the church. As a result, he began to consider ways whereby the spiritual growth of these new converts could be strengthened. What was needed was a school to train these new believers in the basic elements of the Christian faith and to help stir their missionary zeal for reaching the world for Christ.

Moody's perceived need for formal instruction in Bible training led him to found a secondary school known as Mount Hermon School for Boys and later Northfield Seminary. Both institutions were committed to training men and women in Bible study and Christian ministry. However, the big city was what had ahold of Moody's heart, and he wanted to develop an educational institution that would make a more significant impact on America. In January 1886, Moody preached a sermon in which he said, "I believe we have got to have 'gap men'—men who are trained to fill the gap between the common people and the ministers."[11] One month later, he established the Chicago Evangelization Society. Growing out of this agency would be Moody Bible Institute and Moody Press.

D. L. Moody was one of the nineteenth century's greatest American evangelicals. Committed to the work of the church and especially the Sunday school, Moody saw the need for the transforming work of the Holy Spirit in American life. His vision for Christian education was instrumental in establishing Moody Bible Institute, which today continues its mission of training

---

10. Michael J. Anthony, *The Evangelical Dictionary of Christian Education*, ed. Michael J. Anthony (Grand Rapids: Baker, 2001), s.v. "D. L. Moody."
11. Richard Ellsworth Day, *Bush Aglow* (Philadelphia: Judson, 1936), 264; as cited in Charles B. Eavey, *History of Christian Education* (Chicago: Moody, 1964), 340.

men and women for Christian service all over the world. Moody was also a catalyst for the founding of the Fleming H. Revell Company and Moody Press, two popular publishers of Christian educational materials.[12]

The Bible School Movement

The Bible school movement that swept across North America in the nineteenth century had its impetus in Great Britain. The best known of these British counterparts were the East London Institute for Home and Foreign Missions, established in 1872 by H. Grattan Guinness, and the Pastors College, founded in London in the 1850s by Charles Haddon Spurgeon. Spurgeon's college was designed "for dedicated and devout young men who had been preaching for less than two years, but who had not had adequate opportunities for schooling or sufficient money to make up their educational deficiencies."[13] He accepted even the semiliterate and the indigent.

In North America, the Bible institute/college came into being in part to provide a biblical education for lay workers. Courses were offered in urban areas in both daytime and evening programs, by correspondence, and at off-campus locations. Because they were not degree-granting institutions initially, they admitted a wide circle of applicants. They particularly "welcomed older students who found their vocations late in life."[14] Their curricula centered on the study of the Bible and evangelistic methodology. The founders of these schools were aware of their European counterparts who served as models for what they were attempting in North America. "At the heart of the fundamentalist configuration of education was the Bible institute, which became one of the most influential types of Christian school of the twentieth century."[15]

The Bible school movement in America was influenced significantly by revivalism. Charles G. Finney, Dwight L. Moody, Billy Sunday, and J. Gresham

---

12. James E. Reed and Ronnie Prevost, *A History of Christian Education* (Nashville: Broadman & Holman, 1993), 305.

13. Wendell G. Johnston, "Bible College," in *Harper's Encyclopedia of Religious Education*, ed. Iris V. Cully and Kendig Brubaker Cully (San Francisco: Harper & Row, 1990), 56.

14. Virginia Lieson Brereton, *Training God's Army: The American Bible School, 1880-1940* (Bloomington: Indiana University Press, 1990), 162.

15. Cremin, *American Education*, 97.

Machen were dominant figures in this reawakening movement. Moody was a cofounder with Miss Emma Dryer of the Moody Bible Institute. Dryer had conducted a school of "Bible work" by 1873 in the church that later bore Moody's name.[16] A. B. Simpson's Missionary Training Institute commenced in New York City in 1882 and subsequently moved to Nyack, New York. So effective was this movement that one hundred years later, five hundred Bible colleges were functioning in Canada and the United States.

Many of these schools had the word *missionary* in their name (e.g., Simpson's Missionary Training Institute and A. J. Gordon's Boston Missionary Training School). Simpson described missionary training schools as "institutions less technical and elaborate than the ordinary theological seminary, and designed to afford the same specific preparation for direct missionary work, and to meet the wants of that large class, both men and women, who do not wish formal ministerial preparation, but an immediate equipment for usefulness as lay workers."[17]

The missionary training schools in America shared the following particular characteristics:

1. They were designed to equip workers for home and overseas missions.
2. They wanted to provide a thorough acquaintance with the Bible as the central focus of the curriculum.
3. Women were welcomed on "equal terms with men" and constituted the majority of the students.

The Bible institute/college has had a profound impact on the face of the United States and Canada since the nineteenth century. Many of these schools morphed into Christian colleges and universities during the twentieth century and have changed the shape of Christian higher education for generations of believers. The concept of Christian scholarship, which was viewed as an oxymoron during the nineteenth century, has developed in contemporary evangelical institutions to such a degree that Christians are now influencing the agendas of secular institutions all over North America.

---

16. Ibid.
17. Brereton, *Training God's Army,* 55.

HORACE MANN AND THE COMMON SCHOOL MOVEMENT

Horace Mann (1796–1859) descended from a community named after Benjamin Franklin in Massachusetts. Raised in a large farming family, he took advantage of the local library and became an avid reader at a young age. His family attended church regularly, and the biblical values that were instilled in him as a child while he listened to the itinerate "fire and brimstone" preachers of his day influenced his thinking as an adult educator and lawyer. Mann sought to reconcile the strict Calvinist theology to which he had been exposed as a child with a more moderate humanitarianism. He was convinced that America had been divinely favored by God and was destined for greatness.[18]

Mann's own education as a child was not very extensive. He thought that his teachers did their best but fell far short of reaching their potential with the students. Like most teachers of their day, Mann's teachers were paid about one hundred dollars annually to instruct their students in the basic fundamentals of reading, writing, and arithmetic. Soon after the death of his father, he enrolled in Brown University and became a truly gifted orator. His presentations, in both writing and oral debate, were highly skilled and eloquent. He graduated as the valedictorian and by 1823 had passed the Massachusetts bar and had become a lawyer. A few short years later, he was elected to the House of Representatives and subsequently became a state senator. He never lost sight of his desire for serving the greater needs of the public, and this goal would become a focal point of his drive toward public education for all members of society.[19]

Mann, like Jefferson, was a staunch supporter of public education. As a leader of the common school movement, which was a precursor to the public school system in America today, he championed the cause of education for all members of society, including the rich and the poor, men and women. He was successful in both his political life and his educational initiatives.

The ideas of the republic's founding statesmen, especially those of Benjamin Franklin and Thomas Jefferson, were part of the optimistic philosophical outlook of the eighteenth century's Age of Reason.

---

18. Gerald L. Gutek, *Historical and Philosophical Foundations of Education: A Biographical Introduction* (Upper Saddle River, N.J.: Merrill Prentice-Hall, 2001), 193–95.
19. Ibid., 196–97.

Reflecting the milieu of political and scientific enlightenment present at the republic's birth, a new kind of education was needed to create a sense of American cultural identity and to apply scientific knowledge to develop the continent's vast natural resources. Benjamin Franklin, proponent of practicality and invention; Thomas Jefferson, proponent of an enlightened and scientific citizenship; and Noah Webster, proponent of American language and cultural identity, each contributed to ideas that formed the bedrock of Horace Mann's philosophy of education.[20]

Mann's twelve reports, which he published while serving in his post as secretary of the Board of Education for the state of Massachusetts, revealed his educational philosophy, which was based upon five ideals that he highly valued:[21]

1. Education was to be available to both the rich and the poor.
2. Education was to be free for those who attended.
3. Education is best overseen and administered by the state.
4. Education requires competently trained teachers.
5. Education should be available for both men and women.

Although Mann is identified as the father of America's public school system, he also made significant contributions to the field of national politics and higher education. As a Northern abolitionist, he fought against slavery and worked hard to get African-Americans admitted to both common and normal schools. When an African-American student named Cloe Lee could not find housing to attend normal school at West Newton, he made room for her in his own house. As a skilled attorney, he represented several clients who had been charged with aiding the escape of fugitive slaves. Having retired from public office, he became the president of Antioch College in Yellow Springs, Ohio. As the institution's first president, he was instrumental in developing its curriculum, which included studies in Greek, Latin, mathematics, English, history, philosophy, and natural sciences.[22] This broad-based

---

20. Ibid., 189.
21. Frederick Mayer, A History of Educational Thought (Columbus: Charles E. Merrill, 1966), 373.
22. Gutek, Historical and Philosophical Foundations of Education, 200.

education in liberal studies would provide the graduates with a well-rounded education and equip them for various avenues of public service regardless of their chosen profession. To Mann, the best American citizen was one who was well educated and could make a reasonable contribution to society.

HORACE BUSHNELL ON CHRISTIAN NURTURE

Whereas Finney called for a clear, concrete, identifiable conversion experience, other preachers disagreed and were willing to challenge these theological viewpoints in public debate. One such leader in criticizing the revivalist theology was Horace Bushnell (1802–76). Viewed as the father of both American theological liberalism and modern religious education, he believed that the child should grow up a Christian and never know oneself as being otherwise. Bushnell's desire was to have Christian parents rear their children such that the child could never remember not having been a Christian. From the child's earliest days, he/she should be taught to respond to God in faith and love to do His will. As a result of this type of training in the home, the child would never have to experience a radical conversion of any kind. Following is the foundational reasoning behind Bushnell's thinking:

> What is the true idea of Christian education? I answer in the following proposition, which it will be the aim of my argument to establish, viz.: That the child is to grow up a Christian. In other words, the aim, effort, and expectation should be, not, as is commonly assumed, that the child is to grow up in sin, to be converted after he comes to a mature age; but that he is to open on the world as one that is spiritually renewed, not remembering the time when he went through a technical experience, but seeming rather to have loved what is good from his earliest years.[23]

Bushnell was a Congregational pastor who served the North Church in Hartford, Connecticut, from 1833 to 1859, when he had to retire because of poor health. His major writing was a volume published three times under three different titles: *Discourses on Christian Nurture* (April 1847), *Views of*

---

23. Horace Bushnell, *Views of Christian Nurture and Subjects Thereto* (Hartford, Conn.: E. Hunt; reprint, Delmar, N.Y.: Scholars Facsimiles & Reprints, 1975), 6.

Christian Nurture and Subjects Adjacent Thereto (October 1847), and *Christian Nurture* (1861).

Revivalist theologians believed that the Christian life began with the conversion experience that resulted in a change of heart. Bushnell, however, continued to believe that it came through the nurture process and that conversion was "confirmed in an 'inward discovery' of God's infinite spirit, a discovery that was intuitive, direct, and immediate."[24]

Bushnell was writing and preaching in very unsettled theological times. The majority viewpoint was a revivalism centered on a strong Calvinistic theology. In this historical context, three theological controversies raged in New England. One controversy was focused at Harvard, where liberal and conservative groups tangled, with the result that Unitarianism became the dominant position. The second controversy raged within Congregationalism in Connecticut, pitting liberal Calvinist Nathaniel Taylor of Yale Divinity School against the more conservative Calvinist Bennet Tyler. The result of their theological disagreement left the denomination permanently fractured. Unitarianism was the locus of the third controversy, which accented the ideas of Ralph Waldo Emerson and Theodore Parker.[25]

To Bushnell, nurture was an integral role of the human experience and was a natural process. It seemed logical for Bushnell to conclude that if one's values, ethics, and morality could be passed between parent and child, why could not the parent's faith be transmitted as well? This idea, according to Bushnell, was at the very heart of the nurturing process.

> How different the kind of life that is necessary to bring them up in conversion and beget them anew in the spirit of loving obedience to God, at a point even prior to all definite recollection. This is Christian nurture, because it nurtures Christians and because it makes an element of Christian grace in the house. It invites it, nourishes hope, it breathes in love, it forms the new life as a holy, though beautiful prejudice in the soul, before its opening and full flowering of intelligence arrives.[26]

---

24. Horace Bushnell, *Sermons on Living Subjects* (New York: Scribner's, 1908), 127; as cited in Cremin, *The National Experience,* 44.
25. H. Shelton Smith, *Horace Bushnell* (New York: Oxford University Press, 1965), 3.
26. Bushnell, *Views of Christian Nurture,* 61.

Once more, if we narrowly examine the relation of the parent and child we shall not fail to discover something like a law of organic connection, as regards character, subsisting between them. Such a connection as makes it easy to believe, and natural to expect that the faith of one will be propagated in the other. Perhaps I should rather say, such a connection as induces the conviction that the character of one is actually included in that of the other as a seed is formed in the capsule.[27]

Many of Bushnell's concepts were years ahead of their time. His writings were only superficially accepted in his lifetime. After his death, and particularly in the twentieth century, Bushnell was, and is, considered one of the dominant figures in the development of Christian education. Although his theological basis remains questionable, his thesis that "a child should grow up a Christian" continues to be one of the most critical and most criticized notions in Christian education.

Horace Mann, the "father of the common school," and Horace Bushnell, the "father of modern religious education," both struggled with the theological descendents of Jonathan Edwards and their strong commitment to Calvinistic orthodoxy. Mann became a Unitarian; Bushnell never embraced evangelical theology. Bushnell had a remarkable impact and influence on the field of Christian religious education. His critique of the revivalist movement would establish the agenda for theological debate for the next one hundred years.

Educational Philosophies of the Nineteenth Century

During the nineteenth century, America struggled with an increasing degree of material prosperity. This, in turn, caused Americans to focus more on their resources than on their Creator. The Industrial Revolution had provided Americans with a degree of wealth of which their ancestors in Europe had only dreamed. In addition, several influential movements appeared that threatened the faith of many people. Biblical criticism grew out of the European obsession with Renaissance humanism. This development was also strengthened by the historical outlook of the Romantic movement

---

27. Ibid., 18.

and German idealistic philosophy. In addition, America's infatuation with the scientific method of inquiry was undermining supernaturalism's influence in Christian education. The result was a denial of biblical authority for establishing moral absolutes and ethical decision making.[28] Scientists, philosophers, and educators all played a part in the erosion of the church's influence on society.

Pragmatism

Early in the nineteenth century, a philosophy known as pragmatism became the dominant force in American education. America could little afford the mind-numbing exploits of traditional philosophizing. Real-life struggles required real-life solutions, and anything that did not contribute to the ability of Americans settling the new frontiers of science, education, commerce, politics, and society was of little benefit. What they valued was utilitarian application. Scientific inquiry prevailed and pragmatic thought reigned supreme in all walks of American life.

Chief among the people who espoused this new paradigm was a Harvard-trained mathematician named Charles S. Peirce (1839–1914). While at Harvard, Peirce studied mathematics, science, and philosophy and upon graduation began a thirty-year career as a physicist with the U.S. Coast Guard. Peirce described his philosophy as the attempts of a physicist, using the scientific method of inquiry, to explore and explain the composition of the universe. Peirce was mesmerized by the meaning of words and sought to understand how words received their meanings. He insisted that unless a word referred to an object or a quality about which practical evidence could be viewed, the word had no meaning. He coined the word *pragmatism* to describe his theory of logical analysis because he believed that words should derive their meaning from some form of action or effect. Peirce's approach to the definition of meaning, expanded later into a formalized theory of truth, became the basis for a physiological science of mind and a philosophy of radical empiricism.[29]

Peirce delineated his pragmatic theory of meaning in an article titled "How to Make Our Ideas Clear" in 1878. This article went largely unnoticed for

---

28. Cairns, *Christianity Through the Centuries*, 418.
29. Carlton H. Bowyer, *Philosophical Perspectives for Education* (Glenview, Ill.: Scott, Foresman & Co., 1970), 274–76.

twenty years until a philosopher named William James (1842–1910) quoted from it during one of his conference lectures. Although Peirce vehemently claimed that he had been misquoted and misunderstood, pragmatism became a prominent force on the American philosophical landscape.

Born in New York City in 1842, James traveled extensively throughout Europe and eventually earned the M.D. degree from Harvard in 1869. He was appointed to their faculty as an instructor of physiology in 1872 and remained there for the next thirty-seven years. By the time of his death in 1910, he had published numerous works, including a two-volume series titled *Principles of Psychology,* which became a required staple for students in the field of psychology.[30]

James detailed his theory of pragmatism in his books *Pragmatism: A New Name for Some Old Way of Thinking* (1907) and *The Meaning of Truth: A Sequel to Pragmatism* (1909). He defined *pragmatism* as "the attitude of looking away from first things, principles, 'categories,' supposed necessities; and of looking toward last things, fruits, consequences, facts."[31] He viewed pragmatism as a method for analyzing philosophical questions and also as a theory of truth. "He further saw it as an extension of empiricist thinking in that it departed from abstract theory with absolute principles to concrete theory with relative principles. . . . Theories, James would contend, were useful only so far as their utilitarian value was determined. But, he would add, as human experience changes, truth may also change."[32]

In a lecture titled "What Pragmatism Means," James explained what he saw as the value of pragmatism. He stated,

> It is astonishing to see how many philosophical disputes collapse into insignificance the moment you subject them to this simple test of tracing a concrete consequence. There can be no difference anywhere that doesn't make a difference elsewhere—no difference in abstract truth that doesn't express itself in a difference in concrete fact and in conduct consequent upon that fact, imposed in somebody, somehow, somewhere, and somewhen. The whole function of

---

30. Ibid., 276.
31. William James, *Pragmatism: A New Name for Some Old Way of Thinking* (New York: Longmans, Green & Co., 1907), 54–55.
32. David Gough, *The Evangelical Dictionary of Christian Education,* ed. Michael J. Anthony (Grand Rapids: Baker, 2001), s.v. "William James."

philosophy ought to be to find out what definite difference it will make to you and me, at definite instants of our life, if this world-formula or that world-formula be the true one.[33]

To James, truth was not based upon a set of absolutes to be applied in any given circumstance but was situational and relied on the context to determine its truthfulness. According to James, "Truth is subject to change whenever better methods of acting and thinking are devised to meet exigencies of life."[34] This form of relativism began to spread across the moral fabric of the country. Dewey would later pick up on this tenet of pragmatism and become one of the founders of the American Civil Liberties Union, a bastion of American liberalism and relativism.

Two of James's students, Edward L. Thorndike (1874–1949) and G. Stanley Hall (1844–1924), subsequently became influential in the field of education. Thorndike concentrated his research in the application of the stimulus-response theory to education, whereas Hall is known as the father of the child development movement.

Instrumentalism and Progressive Education

Building on the foundation of pragmatic philosophical thought beyond Peirce and James was another nineteenth-century philosopher named John Dewey (1859–1952). Born into a rural family in Burlington, Vermont, he was the son of a Civil War veteran and a churchgoing mother. Dewey grew up attending Burlington's Congregational Church. After progressing through grade school, he attended the University of Vermont where he earned his bachelor's degree in 1879. A few years later, he entered Johns Hopkins University, where he majored in philosophy and psychology. There he first encountered the seminar method of instruction as opposed to the more traditional information-dictation approach. He was intrigued by this method of instruction, and it soon shaped his thinking about the process of learning. To Dewey, education became student-centered knowledge through inquiry

---

33. James, *Pragmatism,* from Lecture II, "What Pragmatism Means," 45–46, 49–52, 53–55, 67–68, quoted in James Wm. Noll and Sam P. Kelly, *Foundations of Education in America: An Anthology of Major Thoughts and Significant Actions* (New York: Harper & Row, 1970), 304.
34. Butts, *Cultural History of Education,* 459.

and exploration rather than teacher-centered dictation. Dewey enrolled in several courses taught by the renowned philosopher Charles S. Peirce, who was developing a new method of understanding philosophy called pragmatism, which, unlike the more popular Hegelian approach, stressed the consequences of one's thoughts once they were acted upon. In addition to the courses taught by Peirce, Dewey studied psychology with G. Stanley Hall, one of the founders of child and adolescent psychology. Dewey received his Ph.D. degree from Johns Hopkins in 1884 after having successfully defended his dissertation on the topic of Kant's psychology. Interestingly, Charles Darwin published his earth-shattering book *Origin of Species* in the year John Dewey was born. Years after the publication of that book, Darwin's theory of evolution would have a profound effect on Dewey's thinking.[35] The year Dewey was born also happened to be the year when Horace Mann died. Interestingly, Dewey would later take up Mann's charge as an advocate of public education.

We present Dewey among nineteenth-century educators because of his immense influence on almost everyone who has attempted to develop an educational philosophy in North America during this century. As a philosophical pragmatist, Dewey saw philosophy as being viable when it engaged not so much the issues postulated by philosophers as a philosophical method that confronted the real-life issues facing humanity. During the span of Dewey's life, America had experienced the Industrial Revolution, the Civil War, World War I, War War II, the Great Depression, and the Korean War. America was exploring new geopolitical frontiers, developing transglobal commercial opportunities, and testing new social contracts with its ever-increasing immigrant population. These ventures produced a seemingly endless list of social, moral, ethical, and political dilemmas. To Dewey, real-life dilemmas of such proportions required real-life solutions.

Ever the pragmatist, he had little patience with people who majored in absolutes and abstract ideas. He fostered the American proclivity to discard purely speculative philosophy as metaphysical meandering. He identified philosophy's raw materials as social and educational—people, social problems, economics, and environmental changes. He believed in humankind's creative capacities to bring about a more progressive society. He believed that much of this would be accomplished through education.

---

35. Gutek, *Historical and Philosophical Foundations of Education*, 308.

Pragmatic education is unequivocally a philosophy of democratic education, whereas other educational theories might apply with equal effectiveness to aristocratic and totalitarian ways of life. Its social mission is the liberation of human intelligence, which is understood to be realizable in and through the social medium. Whereas closed societies must resort to fixed systems of thought for their perpetuation, the free society requires a public philosophy, that is, one that is open-ended, amendable, open to criticism of all who would question, and within the power of the people to control. If education is to support the idea of a free, open-ended society, then it cannot at the same time be hemmed in by a closed system of thought. It becomes a unique purpose of education, therefore, to keep all avenues to truth open, free, and accessible, as well as to point up the irreconcilable conflict between democracy and all forms of absolutism.[36]

To Dewey, human control of one's circumstances through the use of creative intelligence was a central focus of life. Adaptation to environment that requires a change in our intellectual orientation is a given. His view of ideas as instruments in the change process led to his philosophy's being known as instrumentalism.

Instrumentalism—or experimentalism, as it is also known in the literature—gave theoretical expression to the later American frontier experience. A mobile population migrated westward and faced a plethora of environments. Americans came to measure success in terms of the consequences that accrued from harnessing the environment, which was charged by the dynamics of constant flux, change, and movement.

Dewey's books *The School and Society* (1898) and *Democracy and Education* (1910) were socially transforming for the American educational system. Taking into consideration the Social Darwinists of his day, Dewey saw the public school as being an educational community, a sort of embryonic and miniature society, in which children shared experiences and solved mutual problems. The school was the enculturator, the sociological transformer, so it took on an almost messianic role.

---

36. Hobert W. Burns and Charles J. Brauner, *Philosophy of Education* (New York: Ronald Press, 1962), 318.

Principles of Instrumentalism in the Educational Process

In keeping with the concepts that he learned from Charles S. Peirce, Dewey rejected the traditional methods of classroom instruction that focused on the primacy of tradition, external authority, and on reason alone as a final means of determining one's beliefs. Dewey believed such approaches to instruction were inferior to his experimental approach. This latter method allowed for ongoing self-corrective processes. Dewey detailed this preference in his book titled *How We Think* (1910) wherein he described a five-step method of inquiry.

The first step for the inquirer is the experience of a "felt difficulty" or a confusion that demands resolution. The second step is an intellectual response made in an attempt to formulate and articulate the nature of the problem. Thirdly, a testable hypothesis is presented, which, if proven true, will resolve the problem. Fourthly, this hypothesis is tested through what Dewey called "experiments," which were reflective thought processes and reasoning as well as possible quantification. The final stage of inquiry is a testing that involves overt action in the "real world" to determine if the problem that precipitated the original inquiry is resolved.[37]

Dewey was a careful student of educational philosophy and was eminently aware of good thinkers and their contributions. Initially, these thinkers included John Comenius (1592–1670) and his pansophic empiricism, Jean Jacques Rousseau (1712–78) and his romanticism and naturalism, and Johann Pestalozzi and his natural method of education that so influenced Europe and North America.

When most people speak of Dewey's educational views, they generally associate them with progressive education. Although a few of the original elements of this movement can indeed be traced to his philosophy, many more of them have their origin in Rousseau's idealistic views of child nature. Popular clichés such as "learning by doing," "child-centered learning," and "meeting the needs of pupils" don't begin to represent accurately the full orb

---

37. Richard Leyda, *The Evangelical Dictionary of Christian Education*, ed. Michael J. Anthony (Grand Rapids: Baker, 2001), s.v. "John Dewey."

of Dewey's educational ideas. To Dewey, not so much *what* was done in the act of learning as much as *how* it was done represented the true value of the learning process. He argued that the basis upon which pupil needs are decided was every bit as important as actually meeting them. Perhaps the best differentiation between pragmatism and progressive education is that the former is concerned with a theory of child nature, whereas the latter is based upon a theory of knowledge acquisition.[38]

Progressive educational principles involve putting the child's interests foremost in the learning process. Education would no longer be teacher centered but would now place the child as the school's fundamental reason for being. As it affected the classroom environment, progressive education looked significantly different from the model that had been brought over from Europe.

> Rather than relying on teacher directed recitations, curricular progressives introduced such innovations as relating instruction to children's experience and needs; using the laboratory or experimental method as an instructional strategy; using field trips and excursions that involved visits to zoos, art galleries, parks and museums; creating learning situations that encouraged collaborative social interaction; and relating instruction to broad social, political, and economic issues and problems. These progressive innovations were embodied in Dewey's educational philosophy and practice.[39]

Dewey could not accept an orthodox religious faith. Even as a collegian teaching Sunday school in the Congregational Church, he espoused the social tenets of his pastor, who stated, "No man finds completeness in himself. We come to the perfect man, to the perfect stature in Christ, only in our associate life. Men must be won to a common life and built together in it." Indeed, the central concept of Dewey's philosophy was that fulfillment for a person "is found in and through wholehearted participation in those relationships that make up the life of the community."[40]

---

38. Burns and Brauner, *Philosophy of Education*, 318.
39. Gutek, *Historical and Philosophical Foundations of Education*, 307.
40. Lewis A. Brastow, *The Work of the Preacher* (Boston: Pilgrim, 1914), 25; as cited in Steven C. Rockefeller, *John Dewey: Religious Faith and Democratic Humanism* (New York: Columbia University Press, 1991), 446.

In essence, Dewey applied to education the tenets of several of the then fashionable schools of thought—pragmatism, thoroughgoing empiricism, and Darwinian evolutionism. Dewey himself was an open antagonist of supernaturalism. While he considered himself to be religious, his understanding of religion and divinity was vastly different from an orthodox understanding of the Christian faith. He dabbled in religion and religious education throughout his life and in the end developed his own peculiar and thoroughly "scientific" faith. His educational philosophy, however, is only incidentally connected to his religious views.[41]

It would be difficult to find someone in the nineteenth century who had a more profound impact on the educational system of America as a whole and on Christian education indirectly as John Dewey. His emphasis upon pupil needs, a collaborative learning environment between the teacher and student, and activity-centered learning have shaped modern Christian education in numerous ways. "The magnitude of his writings is so great that just the bibliography, beginning with his first article in 1882 and including posthumous notes that appeared as late as 1960, is a one-hundred-and-forty-three page listing in a volume that devotes another one-hundred-and-forty-three pages to the bibliography of dissertations, criticisms, and commentaries of his works."[42] Dewey espoused many of the priorities that we first saw in classical humanism with its emphasis on student-centered learning. He built upon that theme a "man-centered universe" with practical methods for curriculum design, instructional methodologies, diverse means of evaluation, and active learning. We will return to some of these themes again in the next chapter because other philosophers gladly picked up where Dewey left off when he died.

THE CHAUTAUGUA MOVEMENT

Cambridge University in England sponsored lectures that, in turn, gave birth to an extension form of education. Along this line, the Methodist

---

41. Jim Wilhoit, *Christian Education and the Search for Meaning* (Grand Rapids: Baker, 1991), 89.
42. Bowyer, *Philosophical Perspectives for Education*, 280. This bibliographic listing is M. Halsey Thomas, *John Dewey: A Centennial Bibliography* (Chicago: University of Chicago Press, 1962).

Church in America developed a program that became known as the Chautaugua Movement during the last quarter of the nineteenth century. It began in 1874 with the development of a normal school on Lake Chautaugua in western New York State.[43]

The purpose of that school was to provide further training and education to teachers during the summer months when they were away from their classes. In addition to the in-service aspect of the instruction, the program also spread biblical instruction and popular education using many of the same methods that became popular in the Sunday school movement, which was also prominent at this time. The program originated under the auspices of Lewis Miller and Bishop John H. Vincent of the Methodist Episcopal Church. The Chautaugua Assembly was organized as a summer training course for religious leaders and soon spread to hundreds of communities. In 1878, the Chautaugua Literary and Scientific Circle developed reading courses in literary, social, scientific, and religious studies. Flowing out of this movement with an emphasis for youth in America were the Young Men's Christian Association (YMCA) and the Young Women's Christian Association (YWCA). Directed more for children at younger ages was the Boy Scouts of America, which soon became a popular out-of-school education program.[44]

America was enthralled with education and responded to a variety of nontraditional forms of education. William Rainey Harper (1856–1906) was a teacher and administrator at Chautaugua Lake. He later became the first president of Chicago University in 1891. There he popularized the correspondence method of extension education and within ten years of operation had ten thousand students from every state in America enrolled in the program. Eighty-seven percent of the students were teachers in schools and/or churches. Harper considered the scientific method of Bible study to be the best method for a detailed examination of the Scriptures. By using methods commonly used in "higher criticism," he did not always espouse the literal interpretation of the passage. For this, and other less conservative methods of biblical hermeneutics, he was the object of widespread contempt among

---

43. Joseph E. Gould, *The Chautaugua Movement: An Episode in the Continuing American Revolution* (New York: State University of New York Press, 1961), 5; as cited in Elias, *History of Christian Education*, 305.
44. Butts, *Cultural History of Education*, 496.

conservative Christians.[45] Harper was one of the founders of the Religious Education Association (1903), to which we referred in chapter 9.

Numerous philosophies and ideologies converged in America during the nineteenth century. As we have indicated in this chapter, America was undergoing an enormous expansion and a virtual explosion in immigrant population. Accommodating this massive influx of people was no small feat either. Whether it was a concern for where all of these people would live or about where their children would be educated, America had a good many things to consider during that progressive century. American culture had to make necessary adjustments to facilitate these accommodations. Compromise in national religious convictions and acceptance of European humanism, relativism, naturalism, and progressivism all took place during this period. Add to this mix America's own contribution of democracy, pragmatism, industrialism, scientific methods of inquiry, and a new psychology, and one has the ingredients of a truly monumental century.

So What? Lessons from the Past for Twenty-first-century Christian Education

A century with such an impact is bound to provide a number of important lessons for those of us who are serving as ministry leaders. Some of the residual effects of the changes that occurred in this century are still reverberating through North America today. Following are a few of these lessons that are applicable for us today.

1. Dewey's pragmatism joins the church.

The nineteenth-century philosophy of pragmatism created a great deal of tension for believers from its inception. Commenting on this dilemma, Gangel and Benson write,

> How much of Dewey's educational philosophy can the evangelical educator consciously adopt? That there are theological perversions in Dewey, no Christian can deny. . . . That Dewey's influence has extended itself throughout all of American education, even though

---

45. Reed and Prevost, *History of Christian Education*, 305–6.

> progressivism as a movement died some years ago, must be recognized by anyone cognizant of the total scene today. . . . Is it legitimate to separate Dewey's educational theory from his philosophy? In philosophy Dewey was an avowed naturalist who for all practical purposes classified man with the animals. He rejected absolute truth and values . . . and had an inadequate view of metaphysics and allowed for no supernaturalism in the universe. . . . All of the above are totally alien to biblical Christianity; and as a philosophy, Dewey's work can never be acceptable to evangelical educators.[46]

Although all of the preceding charges about Dewey and philosophical pragmatism as it was handed down to us through Peirce, James, and Dewey are true, one must confess that the majority of churches across North America use many of pragmatism's methods and practices in their Christian education programs every week. Progressive and pragmatic methodologies include, but are not limited to, group dynamics, creative cognition exercises, active Bible learning, understanding student needs and motivations before deciding on curriculum, being student centered in classroom management, and emphasizing the social relevance of the material. These emphases are all aspects of our modern Sunday school system that can be traced back to Dewey et al.

The twenty-first-century Christian educator should educate himself/herself regarding these important philosophies of the nineteenth century and critique their relevance for contemporary ministry application. As believers, we can reject the moral relativism of pragmatism and insert biblical authority. Where instrumentalism places a higher value on scientific methods of inquiry, the believer has no problem with rejecting such shortsighted thinking for one steeped in supernaturalism. Likewise, where pragmatism lacks moral absolutes, the believer has plenty of them in the pages of Scripture.

Sunday school classrooms that employ discussion-oriented learning, activity-based instruction, problem-solving methods, and relevant Bible teaching with clear application to life demonstrate what is best about instrumentalism, progressivism, and pragmatism. Much like our earlier

---

46. Kenneth O. Gangel and Warren S. Benson, *Christian Education: Its History and Philosophy* (Chicago: Moody, 1983), 302–3.

discussion about humanism (see chap. 6), the believer is called to analyze these educational philosophies critically. We must realize that they might offer some beneficial elements for ministry application, and we must be cautious not to reject all of the outcomes as unacceptable.

2. Tension builds between the home and the Sunday school over religious instruction.

The nineteenth-century Christian educator Horace Bushnell speaks to us of the importance of Christian nurturing within the context of the family. As we stated earlier, Bushnell's influence was far greater in the twentieth century than in his own time. We have had more time to process the theological consequences of his thinking and haven't always liked the conclusions that we reach, particularly when the family is losing its Christian distinctive as a result of society's secularizing influence.

Note that Bushnell, although not a strong supporter of the Sunday school movement, stirred a debate among evangelicals regarding the validity of ministry to children. "Bushnell contributed little to the Sunday school movement in his day, 1802–1876, for his contention that children should be raised as if they had always been Christians flew in the face of Sunday school ideology in mid-twentieth century when youngsters were treated as 'little adults needing conversion.' By appealing to Bushnell within a Sunday school context, religious educators gave their reforming ideas an undeserved appearance of maturity. They also created the impression, which too few historians have bothered to correct, that Bushnellian Christian nurture was an integral part of popular Protestant education."[47]

Although we can now see Bushnell more accurately through the lens of hindsight as a prominent liberal in terms of his theological and philosophical thinking; nevertheless, he provides us with a deeper sense of value that is to be placed on family ministries within the church. Although we reject Bushnell's notion that conversion is unnecessary for a child who grows up in a Christian home, he does help us see the importance of providing a deeply spiritual environment in which a young child is to be nurtured. Nothing is wrong with knowing only a godly Christian family. A dramatic "fire from the heavens" testimony is certainly not to be preferred over one in which a child is nurtured in the faith from his/her earliest recollections. Once again,

---

47. Robert W. Lynn and Elliott Wright, *The Big Little School,* rev. ed. (Birmingham, Ala.: Religious Education Press, 1980), 121-22.

a degree of discernment is needed in rejecting those elements of Bushnell's theology from some of its potential ministry application today.

No children's ministry in the twenty-first century would stand alone in the church and separate from family ministry. The two areas are inseparably linked, not merely because of the obvious parent-child connection but more importantly in that no church could possibly replicate the most beneficial environment for a child's faith—the home. If the church is going to accomplish the Great Commission, it must exert a more concerted effort toward bridging the gap between the children's ministry and family ministry programs in the local church.

3. The value of democracy and its implications for classroom application also has beneficial implications for us today.

Dewey was on to something when he saw the connection between the democratic ideals of the American political system and the integration of those ideals into the classroom. In some respects, Dewey's desire to see the classroom replicate life outside the school campus has implications for the way we conduct ministry in the twenty-first century. Our ministries should involve our members and look for ways to engage them in the shared decision-making processes of goal setting, budget development, and leadership training.

The apostle Paul spoke of this matter with strong conviction in Ephesians 4:11–16 when he called on ministers to train and equip the members of the church for works of service and ministry. Although the church is ruled in the context of a theocracy in which God is the ultimate authority, He has chosen to involve the members of each local body in the programs of ministry. Throughout the pages of Scripture we see the selection of ministry leaders and their sharing of power and authority for the mutual benefit of the body of Christ. These democratic ideals should be seen in ministry today as well. Dewey certainly didn't invent these power-sharing ideals, but he did remind us of the need to incorporate democratic ideals in the governance of the local church as well.

FOR FURTHER READING

Bowyer, Carlton H. *Philosophical Perspectives for Education*. Glenview, Ill.: Scott, Foresman & Company, 1970.

Burns, Hobert W., and Charles J. Brauner. *Philosophy of Education: Essays and Commentaries.* New York: Ronald Press, 1962.

Bushnell, Horace. *Views of Christian Nurture and Subjects Adjacent Thereto.* Hartford, Conn.: E. Hunt, n.d.; reprint, Delmar, N.Y.: Scholars Facsimilies & Reprints, 1975.

Butts, R. Freeman. *A Cultural History of Education.* New York: McGraw Hill, 1947.

Cahn, Steven M. *The Philosophical Foundations of Education.* New York: Harper & Row, 1970.

Cremin, Lawrence A. *American Education: The Colonial Experience, 1607–1783.* New York: Harper & Row, 1970.

Dewey, John. *Democracy and Education.* New York: Macmillan, 1916.

——. *Experience and Education.* New York: Macmillan, 1938.

Dupuis, Adrian M. *Philosophy of Education in Historical Perspective.* Chicago: Rand McNally, 1966.

Eavey, Charles B. *History of Christian Education.* Chicago: Moody, 1964.

Elias, John L. *A History of Christian Education: Protestant, Catholic, and Orthodox Perspectives.* Malabar, Fla.: Krieger, 2002.

Gangel, Kenneth O., and Warren S. Benson. *Christian Education: Its History and Philosophy.* Chicago: Moody, 1983.

Gutek, Gerald L. *Historical and Philosophical Foundations of Education: A Biographical Introduction.* Upper Saddle River, N.J.: Merrill Prentice-Hall, 2001.

Mayer, Frederick. *A History of Educational Thought.* Columbus: Charles E. Merrill, 1966.

McLoughlin, William G. *Revivals, Awakenings, and Reform: An Essay on Religion and Social Change in America, 1607–1977.* Chicago: University of Chicago Press, 1978.

Noll, James W., and Sam P. Kelly. *Foundations of Education in America: An Anthology of Major Thoughts and Significant Actions.* New York: Harper & Row, 1970.

Reed, James E., and Ronnie Prevost. *A History of Christian Education.* Nashville: Broadman & Holman, 1993.

What in the World?

➤ The "unsinkable" ship, H.M.S. *Titanic*, strikes an iceberg in the North Atlantic and sinks in 1912.

➤ World War I starts when Austria declares war on Serbia in 1914.

➤ Russian Bolsheviks murder Czar Nicholas II, and begin a three-year civil war in 1918 that ends in the formation of the Marxist USSR government over Eastern Europe.

➤ The U.S. stock market crashes in October, contributing to a worldwide economic depression in 1929.

➤ Adolf Hitler becomes chancellor in Germany in 1933.

➤ Hitler launches his first attacks against Europe, starting World War II in 1939.

➤ The Japanese attack Pearl Harbor, and the United States enters World War II in 1941.

➤ The Chinese Communists defeat nationalist forces and assume power in China in 1949.

➤ The Korean War rages in 1950–1953.

➤ The Soviet Union launches the first satellite into space in 1957.

➤ JFK confronts the Russians in Cuba and commits troops to Vietnam in 1962, and U.S. troops are embroiled there for twelve years.

➤ Neil Armstrong is the first man on the moon in 1969.

➤ Soviet troops invade Afghanistan to support its leftist government in 1979.

Chapter 12

CHRISTIAN EDUCATION
IN THE TWENTIETH CENTURY

As WE NOTED IN THE PRECEDING CHAPTER, the nineteenth century brought about profound changes in the social, political, and economic conditions of Europe and North America. The harnessing of science and engineering in England and Europe brought unparalleled growth in the textile- and steel-producing industries. In North America, people migrated from their farms and began new careers in factories and manufacturing plants. In many of these plants the workers formed labor unions, which, in turn, forced concessions from the wealthy mine and factory owners. Sociologists mark this period as the beginning of a new class of workers. The nineteenth century had a significant impact on the conditions that led to even further changes that would emerge in the twentieth century.

Radical seeds of change had been sown throughout the nineteenth century, and a monumental harvest was about to begin. The world was in motion in every corner. Social migration, the emergence of large industrial corporations, new discoveries in medicine, science, and industry were having their effect on the world. Education was the recipient of new ways of thinking, and those who influenced America's thinking about how to educate the next generation also were having an indirect influence on religious education. Public education in North America was experimenting with new ways of instruction, and there was simply no way to prevent some of these new approaches to learning from spilling over into the way education was conducted in the church as well.

Beyond these larger societal changes, the nineteenth century brought about radical new paradigms for thinking about education. Educational philosophers Pestalozzi, Froebel, Herbart, and Dewey had left prominent marks on education across Europe and North America. A summary of these principles would include the following statement.

1. Children are naturally good.
2. The source of evil lies in a distorted and corrupt society rather than in human nature.
3. The right kind of education can curb the contagion of a malfunctioning society and stimulate children to develop according to the good impulses of their nature.
4. Human growth proceeds gradually according to well-defined stages.
5. Sensation rather than verbalism is the true source of ideas, and healthy emotional experience rather than moral preachment is the true source of morality.
6. The natural environment is a fruitful scene of educative experiences.[1]

However, neither Pestalozzi, Froebel, or Herbart embraced a completely naturalistic religion as did Rousseau and Dewey. Dewey's educational philosophy had a significant impact on the shaping of religious values throughout this century.

> In essence, Dewey applied to education the tenets of several of the then fashionable schools of thought—pragmatism, thoroughgoing empiricism, and Darwinian evolutionism. Dewey himself was an open antagonist of supernaturalism. While he considered himself to be religious, his understanding of religion and divinity was vastly different from an orthodox understanding of the Christian faith. He dabbled in religion and religious education throughout his life and in the end developed his own peculiar and thoroughly "scientific" faith. His educational philosophy, however, is only incidentally connected to his religious views.[2]

---

1. Gerald Gutek, *Cultural Foundations of Education: A Biographical Introduction* (New York: Macmillan, 1991), 112-13.
2. James Wilhoit, *Christian Education and the Search for Meaning*, 2d ed. (Grand Rapids: Baker, 1991), 89.

Dewey could not accept an orthodox religious faith, even as a collegian teaching Sunday school in the Congregational Church. Indeed, the central concept of Dewey's philosophy was that fulfillment for a person "is found in and through wholehearted participation in those relationships that make up the life of the community."[3] Dewey picked up the charge of liberal religious educator Horace Bushnell, who repudiated a conversion experience for children and preferred that they simply grow up in a religious environment where they would never know anything other than religious values. "He emphasized divine love at the expense of divine justice and bitterly opposed the revivalism of his day."[4]

TWENTIETH-CENTURY CHRISTIAN EDUCATION THOUGHT

Christian education in thought and practice can be divided into three periods during the twentieth century, each of which is influenced by several prominent personalities who helped to shape and direct its practice. This chapter will provide a brief biographical overview of each of these personalities and describe the differences in practice that came about during this formative century of historical development. The following chart will provide the reader an advanced organizer of the significant personalities depicted in this period. Because time and space will not allow a detailed exposé of each individual, we will discuss in greater detail the names in italics.[5]

Early Twentieth Century: Liberal Dominance (1900–1940)

The turn of the century brought changes in the way people thought about the application of their faith to the complicated issues facing society. Revivalism, which was a prominent means of religious expression in the latter half of the nineteenth century, was being challenged by those who advocated a

---

3. Lewis A. Brastow, *The Work of the Preacher* (Boston: Pilgrim, 1914), 25.
4. Earle E. Cairns, *Christianity Through the Centuries: A History of the Christian Church*, 3d ed. (Grand Rapids: Zondervan 1996), 439.
5. I am indebted to Dr. Kevin Lawson for his research in this era. He, perhaps more than any other contemporary Christian educator, has researched the works of twentieth-century Christian educators. The reader is encouraged to review the biographical overview of the twentieth century, which was developed under his editorial leadership. This can be viewed at www.talbot.edu/ceacademic.

Periods	Mainline Denominations	Evangelicals
Early Twentieth Century: Liberal Dominance (1900-1940)	*George Albert Coe* *George Herbert Betts* *William Clayton Bowyer* Adelaide Teague Case Ernest Chave *Harrison S. Elliott*	*J. M. Price*
Mid-Twentieth Century: Neoorthodox Response (1940-1970)	*H. Shelton Smith* Paul Vieth *Randolph Crump Miller* D. Campbell Wyckoff Sara Little Rachel Henderlite *James D. Smart* C. Ellis Nelson	Gaines S. Dobbins *Frank Gaebelein* Lois LeBar Herbert Byrne *Henrietta Mears*
Late Twentieth-Century Developments (1970-1999)	*John Westerhoff III* *Paulo Freire* Maria Harris *Thomas Groome*	*Lawrence Richards* *Kenneth Gangel* Robert Pazmino

more balanced approach to spiritual formation. Rejecting what they saw as radical conversion and transformation methods of revivalism, this new breed of religious educators embraced the teaching of social Darwinism and sought to apply the tenets of the Christian faith to the more challenging issues facing America at the beginning of a new century.

Rejecting the doctrines of evangelical theology and embracing both Protestant liberal theology and many of the features of progressive education, the religious education movement attacked revivalist piety and education provided by the traditional Sunday school. The religious education movement did not try to replace the Sunday school but rather attempted to bring to it a new approach to the teaching of religion. The movement also added other educational efforts to traditional Protestant religious education: adult education, religion in public schools, research in religious education, and the religious education of the public.[6]

The religious education movement held an evolutionary viewpoint of the world and embraced the application of modern historical methods to Bible study. These modern forms of higher criticism undermined the authority of Scripture and rejected the notion of a degenerative human nature. To these liberals, the world was changing, and biblical passages written thousands of years earlier could not possibly have foreseen the kinds of issues facing society at the time. For this reason, ethical decisions were based more on the situation involved rather than on a dogmatic application of biblical teaching. Liberal religious educators were absorbed with making the world a better place and had misplaced their passion for reaching the lost for Christ. These liberals tended to provide humanistic or social interpretations to Christianity's doctrines about God, mankind, salvation, redemption, Jesus Christ, the role of the church, the authority of the Scriptures, and the future of mankind.[7]

Two of the leading figures of this new religious thinking were George Albert Coe (1862-1951) and William Clayton Bowyer (1878-1982). Coe was born into a minister's family in Mendon, New York. He attended the University of Rochester, Boston University, and the University of Berlin. His teaching career included appointments at the University of Southern California (1888-91), Northwestern University (1891-1909), Union Theological Seminary (1909-21), and the Teachers College of Columbia, from which he retired in 1927. With William Rainey Harper, Coe established the Religious Education Association (REA) in 1903 to advance the study of religion and apply it to public education.[8]

Coe's views regarding religious education were based upon two theological assumptions: the existence of God and the infinite value of the individual. He recognized the differing viewpoints that people held regarding their religious convictions and thought that it was inappropriate to force a particular theological position on another person. Instead, he preferred open dialogue and debate. He sought to bridge the gap between religion and psychology in a book titled *The Spiritual Life: Studies in the Science of*

---

6. John L. Elias, *A History of Christian Education: Protestant, Catholic, and Orthodox Perspectives* (Malabar, Fla.: Krieger, 2002), 167.

7. Ibid.

8. James E. Reed and Ronnie Prevost, *A History of Christian Education* (Nashville: Broadman & Holman 1993), 334.

Religion (1901).[9] Coe vehemently repudiated revivalism. Concerning the contribution of religious education to early childhood development, he wrote, "The constant aim of elementary religious education should be to make conversion unnecessary."[10] Likewise, he spoke of evangelism of adolescents as being "uneducational evangelism."[11]

In a 1937 work, Coe reviewed his own pilgrimage and determined when he departed from any possible identification with evangelicalism. He had been reading Charles Darwin's *Origins of Species* and *The Descent of Man* and stated reflectively, "I settled the question, as far as I was concerned, on a Sunday morning by solemnly espousing the scientific method, including it within my religion, and resolving to follow it wherever it should lead."[12] Shortly before his death in 1951, Coe wrote, "I judge that the most significant turning point in my life, religiously considered, was this early turning away from dogmatic method to scientific method."[13]

He had a significant influence in shaping religious education in the early twentieth century through his prolific writing and frequent guest lectures. When Coe had a dispute with the administration at Union Theological Seminary thirteen years into his teaching career there, Dewey invited him to join the Teachers College faculty at Columbia across the street. Even before that invitation, Dewey's terminology had become part of Coe's terminology. Terms such as *scientific method, democracy, reconstruction,* and *relationships* already permeated his vocabulary.

> He redefined certain key concepts of Christianity, removing their supernatural layer of meaning and casting them in characteristically progressive terms. He understood incarnation as the supreme instance of sharing life, the way by which an incomplete life unfolded or attained education. In a similar vein, Coe considered atonement as the achieve-

9. David Gough, *The Evangelical Dictionary of Christian Education,* ed. Michael J. Anthony (Grand Rapids: Baker, 2001) s.v. "George A. Coe."

10. George Albert Coe, *A Social Theory of Religious Education* (New York: Scribner's, 1917), 181-83.

11. Ibid.

12. Coe, "My Own Little Theatre," in *Religion in Transition,* ed. Vergilius Ferm (New York: Macmillan, 1937), 95.

13. Coe, "My Search for What Is Most Meaningful," *Religious Education* 47 (1952): 176.

ment of education. For Coe, atonement translated to a oneness with the human race. A clue to his "low" Christology lies in his reference to Jesus as the "Supreme Educator" rather than as the Redeemer.[14]

In Coe's later work *What Is Christian Education?* (1929), he defines *Christian education* as an attempt to reconstruct relations between persons based on Jesus' teachings concerning the value of the individual. It also involved bringing about social justice and equality in society. This "social gospel" approach of ministry strategy influenced a number of church denominations and parachurch movements across much of North America and Europe.

Although Coe was the principal advocate of the social gospel approach to ministry in the field of religious education, he was by no means the only proponent of it. William Clayton Bowyer (1878-1982) also provided substance to the movement. Born on a farm in Wolcottville, Indiana, he preached his first sermon at the early age of sixteen in Green's Chapel, a local Wesleyan Methodist Church. During his college years at Tri-State College in Angola, Indiana, he preached in both a Wesleyan Church near campus and a Christian Church (Disciples of Christ). Charles S. Medbury, the senior pastor of the Christian Church, had a profound impact on his spiritual development. He continued with his education by earning both master's and doctoral degrees from Columbia University. Among his professors at Columbia at that time were the renown William H. Kilpatrick, Edward L. Thorndike, and George Albert Coe. In 1912, he began his teaching career by accepting an appointment at the College of the Bible (now Lexington Theological Seminary), where he remained until 1926, whereupon he accepted an appointment to teach at the University of Chicago. His academic work was greatly influenced there by the process theology of Alfred North Whitehead and the educational theories of John Dewey.[15]

It was during his tenure at Chicago University that he served as a director and vice president of the REA. He also served as a member of the International Lesson Committee for the REA and was a member and secretary of the Educational Commission of the International Council of Religious Education until its merger with the International Lesson Committee in 1928.

---

14. Mary C. Boys, *Educating in Faith* (San Francisco: Harper & Row, 1980), 51.
15. W. Alan Smith, "William Clayton Bowyer," the Christian Educators of the twentieth-century web-based database. Located at www/talbot.edu/ceacademic, ed. Kevin Lawson, 2003.

From these influential positions of leadership, Bowyer had a significant impact on the field of religious education. He was one of the foremost advocates for the progressive school of education.[16]

Bowyer wrote a book titled *The Curriculum of Religious Education* (1925), in which he spelled out the agenda for a sociocultural approach to religious education in the local church. The emphasis was not so much on evangelism through a personal relationship to God through Christ as it was an approach that sought to revitalize society as a whole through the efforts of cultural renewal and societal revitalization. "He saw religion as inseparable from the cultural experience of persons, and advocated the inclusion of religion within the development of values in public education."[17] Evangelical methods of conversion that were indicative of the revivalism in the nineteenth century were discouraged because they were seen as being socioculturally intrusive and did not respect the culture of those people who were being converted. To Bowyer, what was needed was not a one-on-one approach to spiritual reconciliation as much as efforts toward greater societal transformation brought about through "social conversion."

Following the influence of Coe and Bowyer was a disciple named Harrison Elliott (1882-1951) who, like Coe, also taught at Union Theological Seminary. In his work *Can Religious Education Be Christian?* Elliott sought to defend religious education based upon liberal theological principles. He viewed the evangelical position of Bible teaching as nothing more than mindless indoctrination. He saw it as an anti-intellectual exercise that failed to develop critical thinking skills. He rejected the Bible as being authoritative, contending rather that for religious education to be truly Christian it must rest intrinsically on human experience.[18]

In addition to the influences of Coe, Bowyer, and Elliott, other liberal educators such as George Herbert Betts, Adeline Teague Case, Arenest Chave, Henry F. Cope, and Sophia Lyon Fahs left their mark on the religious education movement during the early decades of twentieth century.

Tucked into the historical context of this era was the research and practice of Maria Montessori (1870-1952). Although not viewed as a religious educator per se, she was a devout Catholic who began her career as a medical doctor in Italy. She viewed children as inherently good and believed that

---

16. Ibid.
17. Ibid.
18. Elias, *History of Christian Education,* 171.

they should be allowed more freedom of discovery and self-expression in the classroom. While working with mentally challenged children, she espoused an educational philosophy that placed the child at the heart of the system.

She believed that children possessed a natural inclination toward learning as a result of their inquisitive nature and creative spirit. Too often, the constraints of a traditional learning environment stifle this character trait and cause it to lose its influence on the child. Rather than allowing that to occur, Montessori sought ways to free the child to explore and create in the learning environment. The classroom was set up with learning centers focused on activities such as phonetics, mathematics, science, music, and other curricular emphases. To her, the role of the teacher was to facilitate learning by guiding the child in self-discovery and exploration. The teacher asked questions to challenge the student's thinking. In addition, the teacher guided the child's learning within a climate of social interaction with others.

The Montessori Method

The Montessori educational environment is a wall-to-wall totality in which every object, every piece of furniture, even the decor itself, is the product of careful preparation and thought-out design. Furthermore, the environment provides an open atmosphere of freedom tempered with structure and order. For example, children are free to move about the classroom from one set of specially designed materials to another but knowing that their boundaries of work space will be respected by others. Children also have freedom in selecting and using materials, but there is a sense of order and structure in how the materials are arranged.

The Montessori method of education has been used in thousands of schools around the world, although it has been only mildly accepted in the United States. The first American public Montessori school was opened in 1975, and the number of public schools offering Montessori programs in this country now number about one hundred. The method has been embraced in the United States by private institutions and home school teachers as well.[19]

---

19. Harley Atkinson, *The Evangelical Dictionary of Christian Education*, ed. Michael J. Anthony (Grand Rapids: Baker 2001), s.v. "Maria Montessori."

The Montessori method was not without its critics, chief among them being William Kilpatrick in his book *The Montessori Method Examined* (1914). Because Montessori's academic training was not in the field of either theology or religious education, she is not heralded as a strong religious educator; however, her educational philosophy is guided by deep Catholic convictions, which come out in her writings. The influence of Montessori in Christian education is found in Sonja Stewart and Jerome Berryman's *Young Children and Worship* (1989).

Mid-Twentieth Century: Neoorthodox Transition (1940–1970)

Between the two world wars, a theological movement known as neo-orthodoxy began to sweep across Europe. Before long, its challenge to Protestant liberal theology was being felt in North America as well. "Neoorthodoxy distanced itself from Protestant orthodoxy by its acceptance of modern critical approaches to the study of the Bible. It criticized liberal theology for ignoring fundamental biblical doctrines in its attempt to make Christianity relevant in the modern world."[20]

Neoorthodox Theology

Neoorthodoxy is a twentieth-century theological movement in Europe and North America that rejected classical liberalism and attempted to reaffirm the orthodox teaching of the Christian community (such as those articulated by Paul, Augustine, Luther, and Calvin), but in a new or modern voice. As such, neoorthodoxy drew critics as well as converts from the theological left and right and signaled a fundamental shift from the human-centered theology of classical liberalism to a God-centered theological position.

Existentialism is the philosophical basis for neoorthodoxy. Søren Kierkegaard (1713–1755), the father of existentialism, postulated a "leap of faith," wherein the basis and/or object of faith is not necessarily intellectually or rationally discernable, hence separating faith and reason. This becomes the fundamental assumption in neoorthodox theology.

---

20. Elias, *History of Christian Education*, 171

> Neoorthodoxy's theological position is decisively to the right of the classical liberalism to which it responded. Its major assumptions are fivefold: (1) *God* is viewed as being transcendent from His creation and humanity and consequently possesses the quality of Otherness. Only God can transverse this transcendence, and hence necessitating revelation, intervention in history, and grace. (2) The *Scriptures* are regarded as God's Word and are authoritative. However, the Bible is not the content of God's revelation but regarded as a witness to divine revelation. (3) The *Christ* of faith is the basis and object of faith, as opposed to the historical Jesus of classical liberalism's quest. The miracles surrounding His life are reinterpreted for modern significance ("demythologized") but not affirmed as actual historical events. (4) *Salvation* is viewed as both personal redemption and historical. The atonement is viewed broadly, almost to the point of universalism. (5) *Humanity* is affirmed as being the *imago dei*. Sin is regarded as rebellion against God due to human freedom. This sinfulness is manifest in self-centeredness and alienation from others, and hence is psychological and sociologically understandable.[21]

As neoorthodoxy influenced the church, its doctrinal distinctives were obviously felt in the field of religious education. "The case for reforming religious education according to neoorthodox theology was made in H. Shelton Smith's *Faith and Nurture* (1940). Smith called for a reformulation of Christian education along neoorthodox lines. The term Christian education became the label for writing and speaking about religious education for those who proposed a more theologically oriented religious education."[22] Smith criticized liberal religious educators for their assertion that the social sciences had a seemingly preeminent position over Scripture. He chastised them for not giving God His rightful place as preeminent Creator. To Smith, liberal theologians were wrong in reducing the kingdom of God to the particular social order that happened to be prevalent in the United States at the time. During this time, a distinction developed between the terms *religious education* and *Christian education*. The latter term became the

---

21. James Riley Estep, *The Evangelical Dictionary of Christian Education*, ed. Michael J. Anthony (Grand Rapids: Baker 2001), s.v. "Neoorthodoxy."
22. Elias, *History of Christian Education*, 171–72.

moniker for those who advocated religious instruction with a more substantive foundation of biblical and theological content.[23]

Partnering with Shelton Smith during this period was an educator named Paul Vieth (1895-1978). In his early ministry experience, he was the field secretary for the Missouri Sunday School Association. In addition, he served on the staff of the International Council of Religious Education and then moved to Yale Divinity School, where he accepted an appointment as a professor of religious education and the director of field education from 1931 to 1963. He was later selected as the Horace Bushnell Professor of Christian Nurture.[24]

In 1930, Vieth published two books that came about as a result of his research as the executive director of the curriculum arm of the International Council of Religious Education. *Objectives in Religious Education* and *The Development of Curriculum of Religious Education* sought to delineate the specific goals and objectives requisite for a local church's religious education program. These objectives provided guidelines for the International Lesson Committee of the Council and the much larger community of Christian educators to assess the impact that their efforts were making in the religious education programs of their local churches. Vieth made significant contributions in the area of character development, creative teaching, and measurable outcomes of instruction in the curriculum. He had a passion for using media in the classroom as an instructional supplement to the curriculum. He was one of the first people to advocate the integration of various forms of instructional media such as bulletin boards, chalkboards, charts, diagrams, models, and projected visuals (movies, charts, diagrams, etc.) in church education classrooms.[25]

The neoorthodox position found continuing expression in James D. Smart (1906-82). As a Canadian-born Presbyterian pastor, theologian, and Old Testament professor at Union Theological Seminary, Smart sought to bring about a closer relationship between theology and religious education. He favored a stronger emphasis on the conversion experience as being foundational for Christian education. He became the first editor in chief (1944-50)

---

23. Ibid.
24. Norma Hedin, *The Evangelical Dictionary of Christian Education*, ed. Michael J. Anthony (Grand Rapids: Baker 2001), s.v. "Paul H. Vieth."
25. Reed and Prevost, *History of Christian Education*, 344.

of *Christian Faith and Life Curriculum: A Program for Church and Home,* which the Presbyterian Church, U.S.A., developed. Although he did not support the revivalist perspective of conversion, he did see conversion as the focal point of one's religious experience with God. He challenged theological schools to rethink their curricular offerings to find ways for increased coursework in Christian education.[26] In 1954, Smart published his groundbreaking book *The Teaching Ministry of the Church,* in which he criticized those who fail to take the "essential doctrines" of the Christian faith seriously. From his perspective, neoorthodoxy had come to the kingdom for just this time.

Smart's birthing and guidance of the curriculum was accomplished with considerable expertise even though he had little background in religious education and curricular concerns. He had become, through extensive reading and broad educational conversations, a competent educator. After going back to the pastorate (1950-56), he taught practical theology at Union Theological Seminary, New York City (1957-71) and authored ten books and some fine scholarly articles. In "retirement" he went back to his Toronto church as the associate minister, wrote three more volumes, and lectured periodically on Christian education at several seminaries.

James Smart never lost his touch with the people in the pew. He had spent two years in Germany, broadly accepted the *Formgeschichte* hermeneutical methodology, and brought this thrust in scholarly biblical criticism to his editorial role. He believed that the new curriculum should be totally "up-front" with laypeople regarding critical problems in the text. The final words of *The Teaching Ministry of the Church* are those with which these authors resonate:

> If the arguments of these chapters are sound, they lead to some important practical conclusions. They call for reconsideration of the place of Christian education in the theological curriculum and of the place of basic theological disciplines in the curriculum of schools of education. They raise sharply the question of the unity of the ministry, and the right of those who are teachers rather than preachers to share in the full ministry when they are properly trained. They point to the importance of more thorough training in Bible, history,

---

26. Elias, *History of Christian Education,* 174-75.

and doctrine for church school teachers. They call for a recognition by the congregation as a whole of its responsibility for teaching. Above all, they set a new aim for education, one that is significant for a Church that is interested in regaining its evangelizing power. The call we hear is simply the call to be the Church for which Christ lived and died, a royal priesthood, daring to put itself at his service to be used by him for his conquest of the world.[27]

As we begin to conclude our review of the people in this second period who held to a neoorthodox position, we turn to an Episcopalian religious educator named Randolph Crump Miller (1910-2002). Although he had never taken courses in Christian education, he was invited to teach in the field at Yale Divinity School. He had a keen mind and pen for theology, and Dean Liston Pope and Paul Vieth wanted to bring his expertise to bear in the field of Christian education. Seeing the need for a more rigorous theology of Christian education, they employed him to teach at the seminary and provided him with ample opportunities to write. He studied under the tutelage of Douglas Clyde Macintosh, Luther Weigle, Hugh Hartshorne, and Robert Calhoun. Not surprisingly, he held to a strong position of process theology, which he described as follows in his early writing.

Process thinking provides a metaphysical framework for all of our thinking. It gives us a view of the cosmos that accounts for the working of God, for the development of novelty, chance, and freedom, for the experiences of suffering and evil as well as those of transformation and joy, for the meaning of living in community and for the validity of being an individual, for understanding that all existence is a matter of becoming perishing in the context of a continuity underwritten by God, for grasping the meaning of the past and the present as they point to an open future—open even to God himself.[28]

---

27. James D. Smart, *The Teaching Ministry of the Church* (Philadelphia: Westminster, 1954), 206-7.

28. Randolph Crump Miller, "Empiricism and Process Theology: God Is What God Does," *The Christian Century,* 24 March 1976, 284.

According to Miller, those who had sought to bring a theological foundation to Christian education during this second period had been unsuccessful in their efforts. For example, Smith rejected the liberal positions regarding divine immanence, growth, the goodness of persons, and the historical Jesus. However, Elliott's and Coe's major flaw was their almost total rejection of orthodox theology. They substituted psychology and sociology for theology. From a biblical perspective, their theology was extremely thin. *The Clue to Christian Education* (1950) was R. C. Miller's major contribution to the theological void. Years earlier, Miller had stated, "A theology for Christian education is needed. The objectives, theory, and methods of Christian education need to be undergirded and perhaps altered by a more self-conscious theological reconstruction."[29]

It was also in *The Clue to Christian Education* that Miller made his famous comment: "Someone has to make a Christian out of John Dewey!" Obviously Miller was calling for someone to develop a methodology that embraces both Dewey's profound insights into the concept of experience, what motivates and creates interest on the part of the student, and how this fits theologically. To use Miller's own words, "By this I mean we must show how the fundamental insights of progressive education can be made consistent with the Christian way of life and belief."

Regarding the need to create a bridge between theology and Christian education, Miller wrote,

> The clue to Christian education is the rediscovery of a relevant theology which will bridge the gap between content and method, providing the background and perspective of Christian truth by which the best methods and content will be used as tools to bring the learners into the right relationship with the living God who is revealed to us in Jesus Christ, using the guidance of parents and the fellowship of life in the church as the environment in which Christian nurture will take place.[30]

---

29. Henry H. Shires and Randolph Crump Miller, *Christianity and the Contemporary Scene* (New York: Morehouse-Gorham, 1943), 196-201.
30. Randolph Crump Miller, *The Cue to Christian Education* (New York: Scribner's, 1950), 15.

However, although *The Clue* evidenced a somewhat conservative view in contrast to the liberals who had proceeded him, Miller drifted continually toward the process position of theology. He spelled out his biblical theology in *Biblical Theology and Christian Education,* a theology of the church in *Christian Nurture and the Church,* and a process theology in *The Theory of Christian Education Practice.* Yet, despite his protestations to the contrary, his view of the authority of Scripture and his emphasis on experience prompts him to claim that "the center of the curriculum is a two-fold relationship between God and the learner. The curriculum is both God-centered and experience-centered."[31]

A curriculum cannot be both! His process theology leaves much to be desired from an evangelical critique. However, he accurately challenges all educators to be "aware of their own theological assumptions and be capable of expressing these beliefs as they relate to educational practice."[32]

"The neo-orthodox approaches to Christian education during the end of this second period were also advanced through the writings of Lewis Sherrill, D. Campbell Wykcoff, Sara Little, Iris Cully, and Howard Grimes. Many of these theologically oriented writers were influential in working with their denominations in developing curricula for Christian education. Smart's influence is seen in the Presbyterian *Christian Faith and Life* curriculum; Miller's ideas are reflected in *The Seabury Series* of the Episcopal Church. Sherrill's signature is evident in the development of the curriculum of the United Church of Christ."[33]

Late Twentieth-Century Developments (1970–1999)

During the close of the second period of twentieth-century religious education thought and practice, the neoorthodox movement came to an end, and greater emphasis was placed upon developments within the various mainline denominations (some of which were cited in the preceding para-

---

31. Ibid., 23f. Miller, ed., *Empirical Theology: A Handbook* (Birmingham, Ala.: Religious Education Press, 1962).

32. Norma H. Thompson, "The Role of Theology in Religious Education," in Norma H. Thompson, ed. *Religious Education and Theology* (Birmingham, Ala.: Religious Education Press, 1982), 41.

33. Kendig B. Cully, *The Search for a Christian Education Since 1940* (Philadelphia: Westminster, 1965), 157–58.

graph). Leading the charge along these lines was a religious educator named John Westerhoff III (b. 1933).

Born in Paterson, New Jersey, Westerhoff attended Ursinus College and Harvard Divinity School and completed his education with a doctorate from Columbia University. He was ordained to the ministry in the United Church of Christ (UCC) in 1958. He also served as the editor for the United Church Board of Homeland Ministries from 1966 to 1974 until his appointment as a professor at Duke University. He was the editor of the journal *Religious Education* for ten years and was later ordained in the Episcopal Church in 1978. He continues to make contributions in the REA and the Association of Professors and Researchers in Religious Education (APRRE).[34]

Westerhoff's primary contribution to religious education during this period of the twentieth century is his emphasis on the socialization process within one's spiritual formation. Reviewing his definition of Christian education will reveal his particular emphasis. He states, "Christian education is those deliberate, systematic, and sustained efforts of the community of faith which enable persons and groups to evolve Christian life styles."[35] More than thirty books later, Westerhoff's emphases have sharpened since those early days of editing the *Colloquy* journal and writing *Values for Tomorrow's Children* (1970), *Will Our Children Have Faith?* (1976), *Bringing Up Children in the Christian Faith* (1980), and *Schooling Christians* (1992), which he coedited with Stanley Hauerwas. With time, certain key factors in his philosophy of Christian education have evolved.

In his book *Will Children Have Faith?* (1976), Westerhoff presents the case for a broader emphasis in faith-building dynamics within the local church. His socialization focus in Christian education has been one of his hallmarks. He states, "No one has faith who has not been in part educated to it by others. . . . That was done in the context of participation in a local church."[36] In his many writings, Westerhoff urges the church to reexamine its emphasis on content-driven instruction. He believes that such an approach leads to a myopic view of religiosity rather than a more life-changing, faith-based perspective, which is achieved through a deeper socialization within a faith

---

34. Reed and Prevost, *History of Christian Education*, 357.
35. John H. Westerhoff III, ed., *A Colloquy on Christian Education: A Socialization Model* (Philadelphia: United Church Press, 1972), 66.
36. Ibid., 82; as cited in Reed and Prevost, *History of Christian Education*, 357.

community. The latter approach results in a reorientation of life as opposed to simply accepting propositional knowledge that is of limited lasting value.[37]

The constant torrent of ideas that have flowed from Westerhoff has settled into a very thoughtful and mature series of formulations. Importantly, some definitions provide the contours for his views of catechesis. Catechesis calls for "three deliberate or intentional, systemic or interrelated, sustained or lifelong processes essential to Christian faith and life formation, education and instruction."[38]

Formation, obviously the key concept, generally entails eight facets of communal life. Westerhoff develops these perspectives from the field of vision of intentional assimilation or enculturation that bring Christians to maturity by specific experiences and practices. Following is a brief summary of the eight facets.

1. *Communal Rites.* These include "repetitive, symbolic, and social acts which express and manifest the community's sacred narrative, along with its implied faith and life." They may follow the church year, transitional rites that follow the life cycle, or initiatory rites such as baptism that induct one into the fellowship.

2. *Environment.* Churchill said that we shape our buildings and then our buildings shape us. Our spaces, our artifacts, accompanied by sights, sounds, smells, and tastes, influence our perceptions and understandings. Inevitably these factors matter more than even allegedly nonliturgical communions imagine.

3. *Time.* Events such as Advent, Easter, and Lent encourage Christians in unique ways spiritually, emotionally, and intellectually. They provide direction, meaning, and purpose in our lives.

4. *Communal Life.* This aspect points to the local church and denominational governance or polity, the programs and events, the economics and budgets that encourage certain behaviors and experience. It generates and directs our personal investments of time, energy, and money toward mission and ministry.

5. *Discipline.* Elton Trueblood suggests that absolute freedom is absolute

---

37. Reed and Prevost, *History of Christian Education,* 357-58.
38. Stanley Hauerwas and John H. Westerhoff III, *Schooling Christians: "Holy Experiments" in American Education* (Grand Rapids: Eerdmans, 1992), 266.

nonsense. Individually and corporately we determine our behavioral patterns and the community's restrictions; hopefully, built on a biblical basis. Critical reflection and resistance to non-Christian influences should be examined. We are fully responsible for our own lives.

6. *Social Interaction.* We establish who does what, with whom for what purposes: the natural, normal, unconscious ways in which people relate to and treat each other. We reflect our familial education and church environments.

7. *Role Models.* Who teaches, who sings the solos, who conducts the business aspects of the church carry a greater profundity than we often realize. Do we hold up the wealthy, the athletes, the duly ordained—and on what basis are they critiqued? James speaks powerfully regarding our lives matching the words coming from our lips (James 3:1).

8. *Language.* Westerhoff indicates the importance of both verbal and nonverbal means of communication, our vocabulary and our grammar. . . . One of the functions of the theologian is to teach Christians how to talk so that they might live as Christians.[39]

Additional contributions were made in this latter period by religious educators such as Paulo Freire (1921-27), Brazilian educator and Catholic advocate of liberation theology and literacy development, and Thomas Groome (b. 1945), Irish-American Catholic who proposed a theoretical reflection/ praxis model for undertaking Christian education. Unfortunately, time does not allow for a more detailed exploration of these individuals.[40]

The twentieth century was an explosive century for religious education. It began with the liberals holding a virtual lock on the theological framework of the discipline. By the 1940s, their grip had subsided and was taken up by those of a more neoorthodox and mainline persuasion. At the end of the century, other mainline and international influences were felt. However, we must state unequivocally that evangelical voices were heard throughout the century. Their influence began much like a flickering candle in the midst of a voracious wind. In time, however, their light grew as God gave them strength

---

39. Ibid., 272-78.

40. For a more detailed examination of these important figures in twentieth-century religious education, the reader is encouraged to explore the biographies of Paulo Freire and Thomas Groome in the *Evangelical Dictionary of Christian Education,* ed. Michael J. Anthony (Grand Rapids: Baker, 2001).

until, by the end of the century, they became the dominant force among religious educators. The following section will provide a summary of a few significant evangelical Christian educators who influenced the field in the twentieth century.

EVANGELICAL CONTRIBUTIONS TO CHRISTIAN EDUCATION

Although some people have traced evangelicalism from the days of the New Testament authors to the works of numerous Reformation preachers, it became more clearly delineated in North America, especially within the field of Christian education, during the formative days of colonial America. Revivalist preachers and religious educators in early America were strong advocates of the theological doctrines consistent with evangelicalism. These doctrinal distinctions that grew out of the Reformation included the authoritative view of Scripture for resolving theological disputes (as opposed to church authority or tradition), the absolute sufficiency of the atoning death of Christ for redeeming sinful man, justification by grace through faith alone in the substitutionary death of Christ on the Cross, and the regenerating work of the Holy Spirit, who is the third member of the Godhead. The following chart will help the reader understand some of the theological distinctions between liberal and evangelical positions.[41]

At the dawn of the twentieth century, a young man named John Milburn Price (1884-1975) was preparing to enter the pastoral ministry within an environment of liberal thinking. "Price recalls that he studied Hebrew under a Reformed Jewish Rabbi, who preached on Browning the night I went to hear him at his synagogue, Greek under a liberal Episcopalian, and sociology under a materialistic evolutionist."[42] During these formative years of preparation, Price realized the deadness of liberal theology and its lack of hope for man's condition. He determined to seek a different path, one that would lead him to reliance on the foundation of God's Word for man's needs.

As a pioneer in the field of religious education, he began his academic career by organizing the School of Religious Pedagogy at Southwestern Baptist Theological Seminary. Under his leadership, the school grew from one student in 1915 to the largest school of religious education in the world. At

---

41. Cairns, *Christianity Through the Centuries*, 464.
42. Rick Yount, *The Evangelical Dictionary of Christian Education*, ed. Michael J. Anthony (Grand Rapids: Baker, 2001), s.v. "John Milburn Price."

A Comparison of Liberal and Evangelical Theology

Evangelical Theology	Liberal Theology
Bible is God's Word	Bible contains God's Word
Individual sinful through heredity	Social structures; sin is environment
Evangelism: proclaiming the gospel	Social action to correct evils
Vertical emphasis: relate to God by faith	Horizontal emphasis: relate to others
Justification	Justice
Faith	Works
Church is bride of Christ	Kingdom on earth by man's efforts
Amillennial or premillennial	Postmillennial
God is transcendent	God is immanent
Transform person through new birth	Transform society through education
Otherworld orientation	This-world orientation
Social action through changed people	Social action by church response
Christ centered	Man centered
Renovation	Reconstruction

the school Price established the Diploma of Religious Education (1915), the Bachelor of Religious Education (1919), the Master of Religious Education (1920), and also the Doctor of Religious Education (1923).[43] Price's contributions in the field of religious education at Southwestern are nothing short of monumental, especially given the liberal cultural and theological context of America at this time. Price continued to serve as the dean of the school for forty-one years.[44]

---

43. Reed and Prevost, *History of Christian Education,* 337.
44. For a more detailed accounting of the many accomplishments of Price at Southwestern Baptist Theological Seminary, see the article by Rick Yount, *Evangelical Dictionary of Christian Education,* s.v. "John Milburn Price."

Although a number of noteworthy evangelical religious educators were in the period between 1940 and 1970, including Finley Edge, Lois LeBar, Henrietta Mears, and Gordon Clark, perhaps the most acclaimed educator was a seminal scholar from Yale Divinity School named Frank E. Gaebelein (1889-1984).

In 1944, the International Council of Religious Education began to strategize regarding the problems that they were encountering. Leading theologians and educators were chosen to propose solutions and to look at the entire field of Christian education. Paul Vieth's famous study *Objectives in Religious Education* had appeared in 1930 while Vieth was still the Superintendent of Educational Administration of the ICRE. It provided guidance for the next twenty-five years for this organization and its successor, the Division of Christian Education of the National Council of Churches. The genial and able Vieth, who taught at Yale from 1931 to 1963, played a mediating role in the divisive theological battle.

However, in 1945, a seminal volume appeared known as the *Harvard Report*. It, too, was searching for meaning in education but from a secular vantage point. *General Education in a Free Society* describes their quest: "Thus the search continues for some over-all logic, some strong, not easily broken frame within which both school and college may fulfill their at once diversifying and unifying task." The authors of *General Education* acknowledge that Christianity at one time had given "meaning and ultimate unity" to the curriculum but dismiss religion as a "practical source of intellectual unity."[45] They then turned to society for a source of unifying educational philosophy. Secularists continued to identify society and sociology as the basis of their educational philosophy.

Frank Gaebelein, headmaster of Stoney Brook School in Long Island, New York, and associate editor of *Christian Today,* rejected that option and accepted the invitation of the National Association of Evangelicals to chair the Commission on Education Institutions. Gaebelein developed a comprehensive statement on the philosophy and practice of Christian education as an evangelical response. That statement was published in 1951 under the title *Christian Education in a Democracy.* Although evangelicals had been slow to address these theological arguments,

---

45. *General Education in a Free Society* (Cambridge: Harvard University Press, 1945), 40.

Gaebelein's work had a significant impact on the direction of the debate that followed.

Although Gaebelein did all of the writing of *Christian Education in a Democracy,* the committee comprised prominent evangelical figures, including Carl F. H. Henry, Ruth E. Eckert, Harold L. Kuhn, Emile Caillet, Bernard S. Ramm, and Stephen W. Paine. The committee argued for the revival of a distinctly Christian approach to learning and teaching with a high priority on the liberal and fine arts. The following year, in the W. H. Griffith Thomas lectureship at Dallas Theological Seminary, Gaebelein attempted to spell out how such a revival might be achieved. The lectures were published as *The Pattern of God's Truth: Problems of Integration in Christian Education.*[46] Not by his own choice but by the demand of others, Frank Gaebelein's name became synonymous with the highest ideals in the philosophy of Christian education.

Daily Bible reading and prayer shaped his character. His protégé and longtime colleague at Stony Brook, D. Bruce Lockerbie, claims that Gaebelein prayed for the faculty *and* students by name every day.[47] Having been reared in the home of biblical scholar, pastor, and author Arno C. Gaebelein, and observing the godly lives of his parents, he gained a love for Scripture and the arts. He followed his father in the pursuit of knowledge and aesthetics. He graduated from New York University and Harvard, and his carefully disciplined life enabled him to accomplish amazing quantities of productive work. This unusual breadth of learning provided the richness and depth for extremely competent performance as a distinguished educator, lecturer, and editor.

For a number of years, Gaebelein met with groups of the Wheaton College (Illinois) faculty for two-week sessions in which he led them in the attempt to integrate their disciplines with theology. His sparkling wit, breadth of learning, and insightful analyses of their disciplines brought a fresh interest and acceleration to achieve greater integration. In fact, Gaebelein became known for two words: *integration* and *integrity*—the importance of theology in the *integration* process and the *integrity* of his person.

---

46. Frank E. Gaebelein, *The Pattern of God's Truth: Problems of Integration in Christian Education* (New York: Oxford University Press, 1954).

47. Frank E. Gaebelein and Bruce Lockerbie, eds., *The Christian, the Arts, and Truth: Regaining the Vision of Greatness* (Portland: Multnomah, 1985), 21.

Gaebelein believed that the watershed for the ultimate frame of reference was a high view of Scripture. If God is the Creator of the universe, then naturalism has no place. He believed that all truth is God's truth, and if the disclosure of truth has its deep revelational basis, then the Christian teacher and the Christian student have all they need to ensure an encounter with God. Gaebelein identified the following four principles as mandatory conditions if integration was to be achieved with God's truth.

1. Christian education can only be done by Christian teachers who understand and embrace a Christian worldview.
2. The Bible is to be at the center of the curriculum. The Word of God is the starting point of the integration process. Gaebelein utilizes a suggestion by Emil Brunner. The distortion in our thinking, because of sin, is seen at its greatest in theology, philosophy, and literature, due to their nearness to humankind's relation to God and therefore are "most radically altered through the fall."
3. Through excellence in education the integration process can most readily take place. Gaebelein quotes Jonathan Edwards: "God is the head of the universal system of existence from whom all is perfectly derived and on whom all is most absolutely dependent, whose Being and Beauty is the sum and comprehension of all existence and excellence."
4. Christian education must be democratic in a biblical sense. The danger of the pursuit of excellence in education lies in narrowing opportunity only to the more able of our youth at the risk of a snobbery that looks down upon those who are less gifted.[48]

The foregoing statements make clear by its absence that Gaebelein was not one who became involved in the debate going on between those people who embraced liberalism and those people who chose to follow the neoreformation, neoorthodox claims theologically. He was instrumental in constructing a philosophy of Christian education the principles of which were related first to his comparatively tiny evangelical preparatory school and second to graduate institutions and local churches.

To this point, we have examined the contributions of men who have

---

48. Frank E. Gaebelein, "Toward a Philosophy of Christian Education," in *An Introduction to Evangelical Christian Education,* ed. J. Edward Hakes (Chicago: Moody, 1964), 46–49.

influenced the evangelical scene. However, we would be remiss if we did not mention the strong milestones made by two evangelical women in the field at this time: Henrietta Mears and Lois LeBar.

Henrietta Mears was born in Fargo, North Dakota, in 1890, the youngest of seven children. She came from a rich spiritual heritage that could be traced through five generations on her mother's side. Included in her spiritual lineage were a number of pastors and ministry leaders, including her grandfather, Dr. W. W. Everts, pastor of First Baptist Church of Chicago. Her family often entertained religious leaders who came to visit while ministering in the city. Some of the personalities whom she had the privilege of meeting while in her formative years include W. Graham Scroggie, G. Campbell Morgan, and R. A. Torrey. She became a devoted Christian at the young age of seven shortly after an Easter service at her church. Her pastor, W. B. Riley, was synonymous with the Fundamentalist movement, and his dispensational interpretation of theology as well as his commitment to the inerrancy of Scripture influenced her early understanding of the Scriptures and would later influence her writings as well. At age eleven, she began her teaching ministry as the leader of the new believers Bible study at her church.[49]

Upon completing her college degree in chemistry, she began a career as a science teacher and high school principal. While living in Minneapolis, she also taught a Sunday school class at her church. Her *Fidelis* class, as it was known, comprised young women who desired a closer walk with God through in-depth Bible instruction. In time, her class grew to an enrollment of more than three thousand students! Her ministry was structured around small groups comprised of five girls, including one student leader. In the fall of 1928, she accepted an invitation to serve as the Director of Christian Education under Dr. Stewart P. MacLennan, pastor of the First Presbyterian Church of Hollywood. Under her gifted leadership, the church's educational ministry expanded from four hundred fifty in 1928 to more than six thousand five years later. Shortly thereafter, it expanded to become the largest Presbyterian Sunday school with an attendance of more than sixty-five hundred people.

Mears was gifted in a number of areas, including the ability to organize and administrate such a large educational enterprise, write and produce the curriculum for the classes, teach the materials each Sunday herself in the college

---

49. Richard J. Leyda, "Henrietta C. Mears," The Christian Educators of the twentieth-century web-based database. Located at www.talbot.edu/ceacademic, ed. Kevin Lawson, 2003.

class, and articulate a vision of what Christian education could become in the years ahead. Her vision for the future was nothing short of infectious.[50]

As a result of years of writing curriculum for her classes, the demand for her materials grew, and requests for her resources came in from across the country. With the assistance of three other individuals, Mears founded the Gospel Light Press in 1933, later to become known as Gospel Light Publications. Her biblically based resources were a huge success. In addition to her exploits in curriculum publishing, she was also convinced of the benefits of Christian camping. She often took college-aged students on retreats so they could grow in their spiritual formation away from the distractions of city life. Seizing on the opportunity to solidify a long-term camp ministry program, Mears purchased a sizable piece of land outside of San Bernardino, California. Forest Home Christian Conference Center was founded in 1938. The camp grew rapidly and developed programs for children, families, and collegians. The College Briefing conferences held at the end of each summer in 1947 and 1949 produced revival movements that shaped the agenda of church and parachurch activities across North America for decades to come. She was also instrumental in developing an outreach ministry to the radio and film industries operating in Hollywood. Finally, her passion for international missions led her to found Gospel Literature in National Tongues (GLINT) in 1961. The purpose of this organization was the translation of Gospel Light literature into materials that could be used for Bible study and evangelism overseas.[51] She was a truly remarkable woman, and God used her in the field of Christian education throughout the middle years of the twentieth century.

Likewise, Lois LeBar had a distinguished career at Wheaton College as both a teacher and a writer. Through her many abilities and outstanding productivity as an efficient discipler of hundreds of people who studied under her, she left an indelible mark on lives and churches both domestically and internationally. But her writings indicate no particular theological astuteness as in the case of Sara Little or Henrietta Mears. Yet, she was indeed a discerning and biblically insightful interpreter of ideas, as her *Education That Is Christian* (1958, 1989) testifies.[52] Her keen insights helped to shape

---

50. Ibid.
51. Ibid.
52. Lois LeBar, *Education That Is Christian* (Old Tappan, N.J.: Revell, 1958); idem, *Education That Is Christian: The Classic Bestseller,* updated and rev. James Plueddemann (Wheaton: Victor, 1989).

the understanding of an entire generation of students in the field of Christian education during the 1960s.

The 1960s, a decade of decadence and turbulence, were a defining time for ministers in America. The 1960s formed the context for the development of subsequent ministry paradigms that divided the evangelical church for decades to come. The Jesus People movement brought innovations in our music, preaching, and worship styles. The Pentecostal contingent gained a new prominence and presence as well.

Newsweek described each of the decades from 1930 to 1990 in their January 3, 1994, issue. The article "The 60s: Tornado of Wrath" laid out some of the major themes.

> The 60s split the skies. Only the Civil War and the two World Wars so nearly clove our history into a Before and After. And the 60s were more divisive than World War II, which drew people together for the war effort. The 60s drove people apart—husbands from wives, children from parents, students from teachers, citizens from their government. Authority was strengthened by World War II. It was challenged by the 60s.[53]

Leonard I. Sweet wrote a more evenhanded essay titled "The Crises of Liberal Christianity and the Public Emergence of Evangelicalism."[54] Sweet contends that there were actually "two sixties," one from 1960 to 1967 that was "bursting with belief, fresh hope, and ambition" and a second from 1967 to 1971 "comprised of polar opposites with broken dreams, worn-out emotions, shattered institutions, fragmented selves, and failed communes."[55]

The key issue was authority in the first segment. Among the major old-line denominations, it "led to a profound loss of Protestant identity and consequent evacuation of meaning, confusion of purpose, and frustration of mission in American religious life."[56] Toon concludes that "for the first time the

---

53. Cited in Peter Toon, *The End of Liberal Theology: Contemporary Challenges to Evangelical Orthodoxy* (Wheaton: Crossway, 1995), 112.
54. Leonard Sweet, "The 1960s: The Crises of Liberal Christianity and the Public Emergence of Evangelicalism," in *Evangelicalism and Modern America*, ed. George Marsden (Grand Rapids: Eerdmans, 1984).
55. Cited in Toon, *End of Liberal Theology*, 112-13; Sweet, "The 1960s," 31.
56. Cited in Toon, *End of Liberal Theology*, 113; Sweet, "The 1960s," 31.

authority of the church was widely discredited in American life."[57] Society was setting the standards. Relativism in moral life ushered in Joseph Fletcher's *Situation Ethics* (1966) and Harvey Cox's descriptive *The Secular City: Secularization and Urbanization in Theological Perspective* (1965). John Robinson's radical *Honest to God* (1963) evaluated the British religious scene that was reflective of North America. Thomas Altizer and William Hamilton wrote of *Radical Theology and the Death of God,* and Altizer and his colleagues Hamilton and Paul VanBuren spoke of the *Gospel of Christian Atheism.* It was within this turbulent context that two courageous evangelical educators addressed the needs of Christian education in North America: Lawrence Richards (b. 1931) and Kenneth Gangel (b. 1935).

No North American so dominated evangelical Christian education over the last twenty-five years of the twentieth century as Lawrence Richards. Richards, a Phi Beta Kappa graduate in philosophy at Michigan State University; a student who immersed himself in Greek, Hebrew, and English Bible at Dallas Theological Seminary; and a Ph.D. graduate from Northwestern University-Garrett Seminary with a major in sociology of education, has given only brief respite to his pen, having written more than 120 volumes.

Richards began to capture the attention of evangelical Christian education with his articles in *United Evangelical Action,* the periodical of the National Association of Evangelicals. From the start, he has restlessly trumpeted change in the church. His teaching colleagues at Wheaton College, Drs. Mary and Lois LeBar, encouraged and participated with him in professional seminars designed to look at local church Christian education in fresh, new ways.

A maverick at heart,[58] Richards has written curriculum for a traditional publishing house, written a curriculum of his own that involved parents in an

---

57. Toon, *End of Liberal Theology,* 113.
58. "In 1965 Richards was invited to join the faculty of the Graduate School of Theology of Wheaton College in the department of Christian education. At this time he was also the Associate Pastor of the Wheaton Evangelical Free Church, with specific duties in Christian education. He had been teaching an adult Bible class that had grown from sixteen people to over one hundred in regular attendance, and this had provided the impetus for the church to invite him to join the pastoral team. However, it was at this point in his life that Richards first began to question seriously the practices of the Christian education program of the local church. He perceived such radical differences between the teaching of

intergenerational effort, lectured in a wide variety of contexts, been offered professorships at many evangelical seminaries and colleges, and yet has retained a humble and teachable spirit. He is not easily threatened, and challenging his constructs only brings additional life and passion to his presentations and dialogues.

Richards became a nationally recognized figure among evangelicals when his *New Face for the Church* and *Creative Bible Teaching* appeared in 1970. *New Face* put his radical (for 1970) ideas into the new mix of church life. Deeply committed to the church and to a high view of God's authoritative Word, he catapulted evangelicals into new modes, structures, formats, and educational processes while looking at Scripture from various perspectives.[59] *Creative Bible Teaching* is still used in some schools because of the clarity and succinctness of its pedagogical approaches; however, he has nuanced those approaches greatly since 1970.

His most widely used books are his "theology" series. Although they are not theologies in the pure sense of the term, they were an attempt to give a more theological presence and context to books in Christian education. They include the following titles: *Youth Ministry: Its Renewal in the Church* (1972); *A Theology of Christian Education* (1975; new title–*Christian Education: Seeking to Become Like Jesus Christ*); *A Theology of Church Leadership* (1980, with Clyde Hoeldtke; new title–*Church Leadership: Following the Example of Jesus Christ*); *A Theology of Personal Ministry* (1981, with Gib Martin; new title–*Lay Ministry: Empowering the People of God*); *A Theology of Children's Ministry* (1983; new title–*Nurturing Faith Within the Family of God*).

To Richards, the source of truth or epistemology provides the essence of reality through revelation, as stated in the following:

Scripture regarding the process of nurture and the practice of the local church that he actually removed his own children from the local church program that he was directing because he felt that the process was actually 'destructive to their own faith'! Needless to say, this created certain tensions in his relationship to the church." Cited in Perry G. Downs, "Christian Nurture: A Comparative Analysis of the Theories of Horace Bushnell and Lawrence O. Richards" (Ph.D. diss., New York University, 1982), 117.

59. D. A. Carson, *Exegetical Fallacies* (Grand Rapids: Baker, 1984), 56, 109-110. Carson points out what he feels is Richards's "fallacious reasoning" in regards to headship and authority in the New Testament as it pertains to headship and authority both in the church and in the home.

In this book I take a simple approach. I affirm that God through His written Word both meets us in person and reveals true information not available through other sources. What "no eye has seen, no ear has heard, no mind has conceived" about God's plans and purposes "God has revealed to us by His Spirit" (1 Cor. 2:9–10). To say that such information is "true" is to affirm a belief about reality. God has cut through mankind's conflicting and confusing notions to give us a picture of reality on which we can stake our lives. From Scripture we learn the nature of God, man, and the universe. We also learn about the structure of healthy relationships between God and men, among human beings, and between man and his social and physical environment.[60]

In declaring this, Richards is not stating that truth is available only through Scripture but rather that it is the only trustworthy source of truth in an ultimate sense. He continues,

None of this denies that God speaks to His people by His Spirit in additional ways. He whispers within us, calls out through fellow believers, guides by circumstances. Yet these and other avenues through which God's voice comes are not open to objective verification. They are not a portrait of reality. They themselves demand some external revelation against which they can be tested for trustworthiness. And so we are always driven back to Scripture.[61]

Although an authoritative Bible underlies all considerations about theology and Christian education and that Christian education is indeed a theological discipline, Richards does not use the traditional categories of dogmatics or systematic theology but rather approaches Christian education questions from the discipline of biblical theology. Furthermore, Richards places a weighty emphasis on creedal statements rather than on doctrinal statements. Therein he becomes more difficult to classify and a bit enigmatic. In addition, in time Richards became more open to a social science/theological approach. He remains a prominent evangelical Christian educator because of his ability to

---

60. Lawrence Richards and Gib Martin, *Lay Ministry: Empowering the People of God* (Grand Rapids: Zondervan 1981), 9.
61. Ibid.

integrate theoretical constructs from the combined fields of theology, philosophy, and education.

Another leading Christian educator during the latter half of the twentieth century was Kenneth O. Gangel. Few contemporary Christian educators can match the voluminous works of Gangel. Having received his undergraduate degree from Taylor University, M.Div. degree from Grace Theological Seminary, M.A. degree in Christian education from Fuller Theological Seminary, STM degree from Concordia Seminary, and Ph.D. from the University of Missouri at Kansas City, Gangel began his teaching career at Calvary Bible College in 1960. He served a variety of administrative roles at this institution over a ten-year period before founding the Christian education department at Trinity Evangelical Divinity School (1970-74). He accepted an invitation from Miami Christian College to serve as the institution's president (1974-79) and later as a professor of Christian education (1979-82). He then moved to Dallas Theological Seminary, where he taught Christian education (1982-92) and served as their vice president of Academic Affairs and Academic Dean (1992-97). In his retirement years, he has remained active in his teaching and administration by serving as the Executive Director of Graduate Studies at Toccoa Falls College (1997-2000) and Scholar in Residence (2000-). He maintains a travel and writing schedule that would make men half his age grow weary. Gangel has lectured and ministered in colleges, seminaries, and churches across all fifty states, all of the Canadian provinces, and in twenty-one countries around the world. He has authored several hundred articles and more than forty books. Few evangelical Christian educators of the latter twentieth century can compare with the contributions made in the field by Gangel.

In addition to works in the field of Christian education, Gangel has also written numerous Bible commentaries. His commitment to biblical theology and his ability to integrate a solid theological foundation with his Christian education materials sets him apart from his peers. Perhaps the best example of this strength is his article titled "Biblical Theology of Leadership," which first appeared in the *Christian Education Journal*.[62] It is indicative of the thoroughness with which Gangel approaches the discipline. His career is a role model for those who serve in the field of Christian education and

---

62. Kenneth O. Gangel, "Biblical Theology of Leadership," *Christian Education Journal* 12, no. 1 (1991): 13-33.

challenges other authors to provide clearly articulated and solidly biblical foundations for their theories as well.

The middle and latter half of the twentieth century also brought about a major influx of evangelical movements. Chief among them was the National Association of Evangelicals (NAE), founded in 1942. This organization was established to provide an alternative to the liberal-controlled Federal Council of Churches (now the National Council of Churches). The mission of the NAE is "to extend the kingdom of God through a fellowship of member denominations, churches, organizations, and individuals, demonstrating the unity of the body of Christ by standing for Biblical truth, speaking with a representative voice, and serving the evangelical community through united action, cooperative ministry, and strategic planning."[63] From its inception with only 147 delegates, it has grown to comprise more than 50 denominations (totaling 43,000 congregations), local churches from an additional 27 denominations, several hundred independent churches, and about 250 parachurch organizations. They have since started several subsidiary organizations such as the National Religious Broadcasters and World Relief.[64]

In addition to the formation of the NAE, the twentieth century brought about a plethora of parachurch organizations such as Youth For Christ (1944), Young Life (1940), AWANA (1950), Youth With a Mission (YWAM) (1960), Christian Camping International (CCI) (1961), Youth Specialties (1970), Group Publishing (1974), Walk Through the Bible Ministries (1976), the Christian Broadcasting Network (CBN) (1960), Promise Keepers (1990), Concerned Women of America (1978), The International Network of Children's Ministry (1980), and Teen Mania Ministries (1986).

So What? Lessons from the Past for Twenty-first-century Christian Education

The twentieth century was a revolutionary period in the history of Christian education. The century began with a liberal dominance as Enlightenment thinkers with a naturalistic worldview controlled the agenda of theological

---

63. As cited in the National Association of Evangelicals (NAE) web site: (www.nae.net).
64. Ibid.

education. Countless Bible colleges and seminaries that had begun as schools for the training of denominational leaders had long since lost their spiritual vitality and exuberance. Liberal theologians had moved into the faculty offices on many of these campuses, bringing with them an emphasis on relativism, rationalism, and scientific empiricism.

During the middle half of the century, neoorthodox thinkers began to question the veracity of these religious leaders as they observed the atrocities of two global wars and the Great Depression. The guidance and instruction of liberal theologians and religious educators seemed inadequate and naive. Man's inhumanity to man was simply too self-evident to believe in the inherent goodness of man. Neoorthodox theologians and educators began to challenge the views of their liberal colleagues in spirited debates across North America.

Toward the end of the century, religious education received a name change to Christian education as a result of a shift in emphasis. Evangelicals preferred the latter name because of their insistence on the inerrancy of Scripture and the supremacy of biblical authority for solving the dilemmas facing society. To this new breed of church leaders, a true conversion experience was necessary for spiritual birth. These Christian educators embraced their revivalist roots once they realized how perilously far their liberal forefathers had drifted from their origins.

Their passion and fervency resulted in the formation of numerous positions, church ministry programs, and parachurch organizations. Indeed, the twentieth century was an exciting period for those who claimed religious or Christian education as their own. But what of the lessons that were learned? We can learn several important lessons from the overview presented in this chapter.

1. The authority of the Scriptures is foundational for life.

Twenty-first-century Christian educators must never lose their grip on the authority of Scripture. The inerrancy of God's Word is once again the theme of the century. History is replete with examples from generation to generation regarding misdirection and social waywardness as a result of losing the authority of Scripture as a guiding principle for life.

The lessons of the past few centuries remind us that we are not new to this phenomenon. Generations dating back to the children of Israel in the wilderness had a natural inclination toward independent thinking. By nature, man does not like to admit that he is inadequate in authority and influence. To the evangelical believer, however, one's authority is never found in man-made answers that are crafted with human reason and explanation. God's Word is our final authority. Anytime we wander from that mooring, as evidenced by the liberal thinkers at the beginning of the twentieth century, trouble is never far behind. On the banner of every evangelical Christian educator should read the testimony of Isaiah 40:8: "The word of our God stands forever."

2. A well-rounded education provides the best foundation for influencing the world in Christian education.

Some of the most profound thinkers of the twentieth century were people who were deeply grounded in the Scriptures. They had formal training in both biblical studies and theology. In addition, they had a background in philosophy and related fields in the social sciences. Today, we seem to have an emphasis toward praxis without a clear understanding of theology and philosophy. We see a need and craft a response. If things go well, we assume that because it works it must be the right course of action (pragmatism). We seldom take the time to develop a plan that is informed by theology and sound philosophical reasoning (i.e., metaphysics, ontology, and axiology).

Two examples of this latter approach were seen in Richards and Gangel. Their contributions of teaching, writing, consulting, conference speaking has influenced a wide audience around the world, in part because they took the time to examine social and ecclesiastical problems from an informed theological foundation, a clear philosophical perspective, and only then developed a program for implementation. Part of the reason why Richards has drawn criticism over the years is because he has not shied away from confronting praxis that is not biblically informed. It is hard to argue with success unless the basis of success uses nonbiblical methods. Richards and Gangel often have been the lone voices in the pragmatic wilderness, seeking a different (i.e., biblical) way to solve ministerial dilemmas.

3. The parachurch organization has become an enigma to the church.

Obviously, to find a great deal of support for the creation of parachurch ministries in the Scriptures is difficult if one is looking for precise verses. Numerous principles do lend their support to such ministries. If these parachurch ministries are going to continue to thrive in the twenty-first century, however, they will have to overcome a number of important challenges that will be posed in the future. Jonathon Thigpen, the former executive director of the Evangelical Training Association (ETA), has articulated clearly a summary of these challenges. They include the following.

Challenge 1: The challenge of leadership. Many of the parachurch organizations that were founded in the twentieth century are now facing the transfer of leadership. Can the next generation of Christian leaders assume the mantle of leadership and fill the void created by a retiring wave of senior statesman? In essence, who will rise up and fill the shoes of Billy Graham, Bill Bright, and many other dynamic leaders in the twenty-first century?

Challenge 2: The challenge of funding. George Barna recently reported that only about 54 percent of Americans make financial donations to their church. Baby Busters (ages seventeen to thirty-four) are less likely to give (35 percent on average) than are their parents (61 percent on average), thus creating a potential problem once the Busters become the predominant members of their local church.

Challenge 3: The challenge of the growth and influence of the megachurch. Defined as a church with a membership of one thousand people or more, megachurch ministries are continuing to grow across North America. As such, they will be retaining resources that otherwise would have gone to parachurch organizations. In essence, because of their size, these large churches no longer need the resources that until now have been available only through parachurch ministries.

Challenge 4: The challenge of emerging technologies. Because many of the resources that once were available only through parachurch organizations are now available online via the Internet, parachurch organizations face the challenge of staying relevant and up-to-date in the areas of cutting edge technologies in the years ahead. Those who cannot keep pace will be sidelined and destined for extinction. For example, entire degree programs are now available online, thereby decreasing the demand for some Bible college and seminary institutions.

Challenge 5: The challenge of parachurch organizations and their relationship to government entities. Although a peaceful working relationship seems to be in place between parachurch organizations and local, state, and federal governmental entities, no guarantee exists that this situation will continue in the years ahead. As we grow into an increasing secular and postmodern society, the ability to deduct charitable contributions may be threatened in the future.[65]

---

65. For a more detailed explanation of these challenges and other insights regarding parachurch organizations, see Johnathon Thigpen, "Parachurch Perspectives," in *Introducing Christian Education: Foundations for the Twenty-first Century*, ed. Michael J. Anthony (Grand Rapids: Baker, 2001), 283–89.

The church has faced challenges throughout history. Whether the challenges came from opposing armies during the Crusades; stagnation resulting from autocratic hierarchical church structure, as in the Middle Ages; or the onslaughts of secular humanistic philosophies in the present, the church will prevail. One must never forget that the ultimate battle for effective church ministry rests in the resources of God, not in human wisdom. We are commanded to do our best as we identify and develop our areas of spiritual giftedness. Then, in partnership with the Holy Spirit, we employ those gifts to equip the saints for the work of service and to build up the body of Christ for His eternal honor and glory. We need not fear what either spiritual darkness or fallen man can throw in our way in their efforts to thwart us because we know that the final battle has already been won. The church will one day be victorious. However, until that day, let us make every effort to be diligent and faithful to teach the Word of God with accuracy and to remain faithful to our calling as Christian educators, conducting ourselves in a manner that is worthy of the high calling with which we have been called. Being servants of Christ through the various ministries of Christian education in the twenty-first century is a calling worthy of our attention and excellence.

For Further Reading

Anthony, Michael J., ed. *Introducing Christian Education: Foundations for the Twenty-first Century.* Grand Rapids: Baker, 2001.

Bowyer, Carlton H. *Philosophical Perspectives for Education.* Glenview, Ill.: Scott, Foresman & Company, 1970.

Butts, R. Freeman. *A Cultural History of Education.* New York: McGraw Hill, 1947.

Cahn, Steven M. *The Philosophical Foundations of Education.* New York: Harper & Row, 1970.

Cairns, Earle E. *Christianity Through the Centuries: A History of the Christian Church.* 3d ed. Grand Rapids: Zondervan, 1996.

Dupuis, Adrian M. *Philosophy of Education in Historical Perspective.* Chicago: Rand McNally, 1966.

Eavey, Charles B. *History of Christian Education.* Chicago: Moody, 1964.

Elias, John L. *A History of Christian Education: Protestant, Catholic, and Orthodox Perspectives.* Malabar, Fla.: Krieger, 2002.

Frost, S. E. *Historical and Philosophical Foundations of Western Education.* Columbus: Charles E. Merrill, 1966.

Gangel, Kenneth O., and Warren S. Benson. *Christian Education: Its History and Philosophy.* Chicago: Moody, 1983.

Graendorf, Werner C. *Introduction to Biblical Christian Education.* Chicago: Moody, 1981.

Gutek, Gerald L. *Historical and Philosophical Foundations of Education: A Biographical Introduction.* Upper Saddle River, N.J.: Merrill Prentice-Hall, 2001.

Mayer, Fredrick. *A History of Educational Thought.* Columbus: Charles E. Merrill, 1960.

Noll, James W., and Sam P. Kelly. *Foundations of Education in America: An Anthology of Major Thoughts and Significant Actions.* New York: Harper & Row, 1970.

Reed, James E., and Ronnie Prevost. *A History of Christian Education.* Nashville: Broadman & Holman, 1993.

What in the World?

➤ Communism falls in Eastern Europe in 1989.

➤ World Wide Web is introduced in 1989.

➤ Iraqi forces invade Kuwait; President Bush wages the Gulf War in 1990.

➤ Federal building is bombed in Oklahoma City in 1995.

➤ Dolly the sheep becomes the first mammal to be cloned successfully in 1997.

➤ September 11, 2001, terrorist attacks become the worst terrorist activity on U.S. soil.

Chapter 13

PHILOSOPHICAL FOUNDATIONS OF CHRISTIAN EDUCATION

DURING THE MANY YEARS THAT WE HAVE both been teaching Christian education in Bible colleges, Christian universities, and evangelical seminaries, we have noticed among students an aversion to discussing educational philosophy. Many undergraduate Christian education students are more concerned with the realities of surviving the next math exam, writing the fifteen-page research paper that is due tomorrow morning, or what they are going to teach next Wednesday night at their youth group meeting. Delving into the heady arena of deciding the epistemological presuppositions of idealism as applied to the twenty-first-century youth group is not at the top of their list of personal priorities.

Likewise, seldom does one find his or her graduate student peers sitting around the local coffee shop examining the ramifications of Dewey's concept of a free society. To them, life is simply too complex and demanding for these seemingly deeper elements of philosophic reasoning. Such matters will have to wait until after graduation, when time allows more freedom to pursue such esoteric matters. However, seldom after graduation does life allow these matters to come back on the table for discussion.

The time to examine such philosophic patterns of reasoning is now. One will never have as much time available for considering the philosophical foundations of his or her ministry as while a student. Life has a way of pushing these topics off the daily schedule. Somehow the pressures associated with submitting the next budget, interviewing a new youth intern, transitioning to a new job, or getting the kids out the door for school in the morning pushes matters of philosophy beyond our reach. That's unfortunate because unless we spend the time immersing ourselves in the issues of philosophical thought, we might be destined to repeat past failures over and over without realizing why we get stuck in programmatic ruts. If we don't spend the time asking why we just got terminated from our recent ministry position, we might be destined to repeat the same mistakes and fall into a repetitive pattern of short-lived ministry experiences. Philosophy has everything to do with our career longevity and professional satisfaction.

Although we might not be so bold as to ask our professor what is really on our minds, if we could muster the courage, we would stand in class and ask, "What really is the value of philosophy? What role does it play in life?" or "What relationship does philosophy have to the way I do ministry at my church?"

Perhaps a better way to phrase the earlier question of "What is philosophy?" would be to ask, "What is the subject matter of philosophy?" Traditionally, the common stereotype of philosophers is that they are wandering intellectual troubadours who ask piercing questions and seldom give answers with any degree of practical relevance. They answer questions with another question, and lengthy discussions with them tend to leave one feeling as though he or she has just consumed a meal but that it provided little, if any, lasting nutritional benefit.

> Philosophers, wanderers as well as wonderers that they are, are like the cattlemen of the Old West when it comes to fencing in their ranges. Those not so in love with their own forty-acre spread they'd shoot anyone who set foot on it or look upon anyone who would define philosophy narrowly as a smelly sheepherder come to fence them in (or out), and an intellectual fence is something to be torn down and destroyed, or at least crept through, for the grass of inquiry may be greener on the other side. Sheriffs, sheepherders, or shootin' irons notwithstanding, most philosophers are not content until they have the right gaze over their academic land. Indeed, they demand the right even if they do not plan to use it.[1]

---

1. Charles J. Brauner and Hobert W. Burns, *Problems in Education and Philosophy* (Englewood Cliffs, N.J.: Prentice-Hall, 1965), 7

The academic turf of philosophy has changed substantially over the years. The academic boundaries that it held a few hundred years ago are no longer the same today. In a very real sense, philosophy has lost a good deal of acreage over its imperial days of glory. The territory has shrunk as new disciplines established clearly defined boundaries. For example, from the time of the early Greeks to the Middle Ages, philosophers held sway over the masses in terms of understanding and defining what was real, true, and of lasting value. However, the Renaissance and the subsequent Enlightenment redefined their ability to speak with authority on such philosophical matters. "Territorial expansion, however, was halted first by the secession of the developing areas in the physical sciences (e.g., astronomy and physics) and, more recently, by the declaration of independence of the behavioral sciences (e.g., psychology and sociology)."[2]

In its narrowest scope, *philosophy* is simply translated from the Greek to mean "lover of wisdom." To explore the reasons behind man's behavior and conduct has long been considered a virtue. Philosophers took the time to stop and ask the question, "Why?" From their observations of human experience, they challenged mankind to explain their mental reasoning, rationale for conduct, or raison d'être. Wisdom came as they collected these musing about life and sought to find ways to provide answers to some of life's deepest questions.

It's important to understand that we cannot escape philosophy because it provides the foundation for all that we do in life. Philosophy is the reason we think, speak, and act the way we do. Our thought patterns reveal our philosophy about the world. The way we treat those around us indicates our philosophy of life. Likewise, the way we conduct ourselves at church, design our ministry programs, and set priorities for the use of our resources are all reflections of our personal philosophy of ministry. There is no escaping philosophy.

To Christian educators, only one true source of philosophic thought exists because only one origin of wisdom exists. Ultimately, we know that source to be God Himself. This source of Eternal Wisdom reveals Himself to humanity in a couple of ways: first, through the works of His visible creation, and second, by His supernatural revelation, particularly through His incarnate Son, Jesus Christ.[3]

---

2. Ibid.
3. John S. Brubacher, *Eclectic Philosophy of Education* (New York: Prentice-Hall, 1951), 7.

Where science seeks explanation of separate facts, their relationship to one another, and the laws that govern their operation, philosophy goes to first principles. Philosophy is concerned with the *ultimate* meaning of all reality, and may be defined as *the methodological investigation of the whole reality through its ultimate causes* in so far as those causes can be known through natural reason unaided by divine revelation.[4]

Some people might define *philosophy* differently, depending on the particular worldview that they bring to bear in its application. By and large, however, we have agreed on a working definition of several critical terms associated with philosophy. A brief summary of these terms might be helpful for further discussion.

Glossary of Philosophical Terms

Aesthetics. A subset of axiology that concerns itself with the study of creation, value, and one's experiential perception of art and beauty.

Anthropology. A subset of metaphysics that has as its concern the nature, meaning, and existence of mankind.

Axiology. The study of value. It is that aspect of philosophy that is concerned with right and wrong, good and evil, means and ends. It tries to formulate a consistent theory to govern ethical conduct. This branch of philosophic thoughts asks the question, "What is good?"

Cosmology. A subset of metaphysics that has as its concern the meaning and purpose of the universe.

Epistemology. The study of the nature of knowledge and what can be known.

---

4. Ibid.

5. Morris L. Bigge, *Educational Philosophies for Teachers* (Columbus: Charles E. Merrill, 1982), 207.

6. Brauner and Burns, *Problems in Education and Philosophy,* 9.

Ethics. A subset of axiology that concerns itself with proper behavior and conduct.

Logic. Logic is concerned with the ability of one to understand premising information and to process that data in such a way as to come to reasonable findings about the information. It is the science of examining correct principles of thought that allow for the insurance of sound conclusions.[7]

Metaphysics. The study of what is real. Aristotle saw this as examining the principles of Being. It proposes to study the principles common to a variety of existence: physical, mental, necessary, and contingent. In metaphysics we explore the meaning of self, matter, mind, body, God, reality, appearance, etc.[8] This branch of philosophic thought asks the question, "What is real?"

Ontology. A subset of metaphysics that has as its concern the question of being. The ontological task is to determine whether or not an object has existence and being.

Theology. A subset of metaphysics that has as its concern the existence of God.

The integration of philosophy and education is the result of one discipline asking questions of the other. In truth, philosophy and education cannot be separated because each relies on the other for illumination. Blending the two results in taking the problems associated with human learning and understanding (i.e., education) and postulating methods of inquiry (i.e., philosophy) as to how these problems should be addressed and subsequently solved.

THE NATURE OF EDUCATIONAL PHILOSOPHY

One might be asking, "Just what are the activities associated with developing a philosophy of education?" If establishing a philosophical foundation for what we do is so important, how is it accomplished? Clive Beck has postulated nine characteristic tenants of philosophical inquiry

---

7. Carlton H. Bowyer, *Philosophical Perspectives for Education* (Glenview, Ill.: Scott, Foresman & Co., 1970), 15.

8. Harry S. Broudy, *Building a Philosophy of Education* (New York: Prentice-Hall, 1954), 17.

that bear repeating in an abridged form here.[9] Although his purpose in writing is not prescriptive for church leaders, he nevertheless offers interesting insights into the means by which philosophical inquiry is produced by ministry leaders.

1. The philosopher typically is concerned with developing and employing strategies of cogitation rather than strategies of observation.
2. Philosophy typically is concerned with "higher order" problems, that is, problems that do not have to do directly with the answering of substantive questions, but rather have to do with the work of clarifying meaning, developing concepts, establishing frames of reference, and generally providing the intellectual tools for the thought and observation involved in answering substantive questions.
3. Philosophy typically is concerned with what might be called "intellectual puzzles": peculiarly baffling problems that are such that one "does not know one's way about."
4. Associated with the development of strategies of cogitation, but often gaining considerable autonomy of its own, is the typical philosophical concern with the nature of conceptual thought: the nature of concepts, criteria, judgments, inferences, beliefs, theories, etc.
5. The philosopher typically is preoccupied with the study of language— terms, sentences, speech acts of various kinds, and whole languages.
6. The philosopher typically is concerned with the search for generality and perspective.
7. Philosophy typically is viewed as a "helping discipline" because the other side of the coin of drawing data for other disciplines is contributing to those disciplines.
8. The typical activity of philosophers is a preoccupation with what is going on in other disciplines.

Knowing these characteristics helps lift the veil of mystery that many people associate with philosophers. Their activities are not restricted to an isolated desert retreat where they hum an endless mantra of unintelligible babblings. Contemporary Christian educators who take time to philosophize about

---

9. Clive Beck, *Educational Philosophy and Theory: An Introduction* (Boston: Little, Brown & Co., 1974), 285–88. The reader is encouraged to examine a more detailed discussion of each of these tenants presented in this work.

their thought process, ministry activities, and rationale for action is neither capable of walking on water nor calling down fire from heaven. They are neither mystical nor magical. They simply take the time to examine the "why" of their life and ministry. The result is a more reasoned response and intentionality toward their life and ministry endeavors. They know how to adjust their methods to meet changing social conditions and can articulate why a particular instructional methodology works in one location but not in another. They understand how to remain relevant and do not feel threatened when unplanned circumstances force them to change their plans. They will have a strategic plan laid out that explains why they do what they do, and they will know what resources they will need to arrive at their destination successfully. They don't get carried away with every new seminar or tangent that comes through town because they can determine whether the new idea is needed or useful in their ministry setting.

TRADITIONAL CATEGORIES OF PHILOSOPHIC INQUIRY

To develop this critical philosophy of ministry, one must first gain a basic understanding of some basic philosophical concepts and key terms. Having done that, the student is able to begin to articulate the definitions of terms, describe the rationale for activities, and formulate an understanding for what is done in the ministry context. From a traditional point of view, philosophy has been classified into three main categories of thought: metaphysics, epistemology, and axiology. We will explore each in greater detail to help the readers formulate their own personal philosophy of ministry at the end of this chapter.

Metaphysics

Literally defined as "after physics," metaphysics is the branch of philosophic inquiry that asks, "What is real?" It is concerned with examining the essence of existence. Metaphysical questions can be divided further into four subcategories of inquiry. *Ontology* deals with seeking an answer to the problem of being. The ontological task is to determine whether an object has existence and being. Questions central to this form of inquiry include the following: "Is its reality found in matter or physical energy (e.g., the world we can experience through the use of our senses), or is its realness found in transcendent matter?" "Is its realness limited to one realm (monism), such as physical matter, or does it exist in two forms (dualism) such as matter and spirit?" "Is its reality limited to a finite existence, or does it transcend time as we know it?"

Cosmology is the second subcategory, and it is concerned with the origins of the universe. Cosmological inquiry asks such questions as "Is the universe orderly and systematic or random and dynamic?" "Do universal laws govern its operation, or do things occur without preliminary sequence?" Beyond the existence of the universe, cosmology also investigates issues relevant to its purpose by asking such questions as "What is the ultimate meaning or purpose of the universe?" As Christians, we believe that the universe was created for a distinct purpose and that it exists toward fulfilling this purpose. This belief is referred to as teleological because the Bible speaks of God's created purpose for the world as reflecting His glory. However, some people in the realm of science disagree with a teleological perspective and hold to a random (e.g., Big Bang theory) or circulative (i.e., it repeats itself) philosophy. Two other popular discussions regarding the cosmological argument involve the realm of time and space.[10]

Two additional subsets of metaphysics are anthropology and theology. *Anthropology* deals with a philosophical understanding of the existence, meaning, and purpose of humanity. Anthropological questions that a philosopher ponders include "What is the essence of human nature?" "Is man inherently good or evil?" "What is the relationship between body and mind, and which one operates or controls the other?" "Does man have a soul; if so, how does it function in relation to the other components of body and mind?" *Theology* is the philosophical understanding of the existence, nature, and character of God. Metaphysical questions concerning God include such inquiries as "Does God exist?" "Can God be known?" "What are the character qualities of God?" "Do other spirit beings besides God—such as angels, demons, or other entities—exist?" "Do these other entities interact with mankind; if so, under what conditions or limitations do they exist?"[11]

In summary, the philosophical concept of metaphysics deals with the issue of realness and existence. It is further subdivided into categories of

---

10. George R. Knight, *Philosophy and Education* (Berrien Springs, Mich.: Andrews University Press, 1998), 16.

11. Ibid., 15.

inquiry to determine the meaning and purpose of the universe (cosmology), the nature and purpose of humanity (anthropology), the existence of a spirit realm (theology), and whether an object has existence and being (ontology). Metaphysical reality is concerned with knowing what lies beyond the realm of the observable world; it is a reality that is the foundation for physical objects.

Epistemology

Epistemology refers to the investigation of the origin, structure, methods, and validity of knowledge. Over the years, considerable debate has occurred regarding the importance of epistemology in relation to metaphysics. The most popular view—held by Descartes, Locke, Kant, and Dewey—was that an investigation of the sources and validity of knowledge must come *before* metaphysical speculation. The opposite view was espoused by philosophers who placed a higher priority on metaphysics, including Spinoza and Hegel. A compromised view allows both views to have equal importance.[12]

Epistemology is philosophy's attempt to determine whether what we know is credible. Stated simply, epistemology asks two critical questions about knowledge:

1. "Can we know?" (i.e., "Is the knowledge we receive really valid?").
2. "How do we know?" (i.e., "What is the best means for obtaining knowledge?").

The first question is answered by one of four means: *skepticism* (knowledge and truth is not knowable by the mind), *relativism* (knowledge and truth is relative to the human mind), *dogmatism* (accepting knowledge and truth without any substantiating proof), and *positivism* (knowledge and truth are valid once they have been proven by the sciences).[13]

The second question ("How do we know?") is really concerned with the means by which we know that something is true. For example, "Is this newly acquired knowledge valid?" We can know if it is valid through four means of

---

12. Bowyer, *Philosophical Perspectives for Education,* 14.
13. Arnold Griese, *Your Philosophy of Education: What Is It* (Santa Monica, Calif.: Goodyear Publishing, 1981), 136.

analysis. The first test of its validity is *empiricism;* the new knowledge comes to us through the senses but also involves some degree of intellectual processing. *Sensationalism* allows us to test this knowledge when it comes to us through our sensory receptors. *Rationalism* allows us to test this knowledge when we apply our human reasoning abilities. Finally, *transcendentalism* is the means by which we verify knowledge when it comes to us from a source beyond either the sensory receptors or the human intellect. From a historical point of view, the two most popular means of determining its validity have been empiricism and rationalism. For obvious reasons, scientists have been reluctant over the years to wander far from that which can be replicated under the strict confines of a laboratory environment.[14]

Axiology

Axiology is the theory and science of value. It asks questions related to what is right and wrong in a given circumstance. It is also concerned with determining what is of natural or man-made beauty. For that reason, axiology is subdivided into two subsets of study: ethics—the study of right and wrong behavior, and aesthetics—the study of art and beauty. "Axiology is the modern term for search into: (1) the nature of value; (2) the types of value; (3) the criterion of value; and (4) the metaphysical status of value."[15]

Coming to a concise definition and conceptualization of what determines value depends to a large degree on one's philosophical perspective. For example, noted idealist J. Donald Butler makes a strong case for two generic types of values: *ultimate values,* which are God-based (God alone has absolute existence), and *social values,* which are rooted in man's interpersonal and societal relations. Noted pragmatic empiricist John Dewey outlined a theory of valuation based upon man's human experience. Charles L. Stevenson, a noted logical empiricist, analyzes ethical arguments from the perspective of attitudinal differences. For this reason and others, the study of value has been difficult for philosophy students because valuation is heavily influence by personal philosophical bias.[16]

---

14. Ibid., 137.
15. Bowyer, *Philosophical Perspectives for Education,* 14.
16. Hobart W. Burns and Charles J. Brauner, *Philosophy of Education* (New York: Ronald Press, 1962), 196.

We see this influence every day in our own world of value ladened terms. When we declare a person to be a theologically "liberal," "moderate," or "conservative," we are placing a degree of value on each term and the person whom we are describing. These terms make statements about our personal values. In some cases, they make statements about the societal groups to which we belong. To say that one is a "Democrat," a "Republican," or an "Independent" identifies him as being a member of a particular political group that has certain established patterns of value regarding such issues as education, labor, defense, and fiscal policy. Value and language are inseparable and remind us that we must choose our words carefully because one misspoken word in the wrong place or the wrong context can have devastating consequences; they reveal, or assume to reveal, our values about a particular position.

To summarize this section, philosophy comprises three major categories: metaphysics, epistemology, and axiology. Each of these categories helps us determine our basis of reality, truth, and values. Perhaps the simplest way to look at philosophy is to see it as an answer to a series of questions that mankind has posed over the years. The following chart illustrates the categories of philosophy and the questions that philosophers ask.

CATEGORY OF PHILOSOPHY	QUESTION POSED
Metaphysics	What is real?
Epistemology	What is true?
Axiology	What is of value?
Ethics	What is right?
Aesthetics	What is beautiful?

A SUMMARY OF FIVE EDUCATIONAL PHILOSOPHIES

Over thousands of years of inquiry, philosophers have tried to understand the issues relevant to the subject of education. Once having identified the relevant questions, they endeavored to organize solutions to these educational problems while still remaining true to their particular philosophical outlook. In some cases, their particular philosophy had specific application to the field of education. Philosophically, neo-Thomist philosophers applied their presuppositions to the field of education, and their educational philosophy has become known as perennialism. In some cases, several philosophies blended to suggest answers to some of education's questions. For example, idealist and realist philosophers who lived during the Greek period explored education's problems and provided answers based upon their combined metaphysical, epistemological, and axiological biases. When it is applied to education, this blending of philosophies is known as the educational philosophy of essentialism. Quite a number of variations have been developed over the years. In addition, beginning educational philosophy students have had some difficulty understanding it because different terms have been used over the years to describe the same educational philosophy. Neo-Thomism has also been called neoscholasticism and dualistic theism. These differing labels for the same educational philosophy have contributed to the challenge of understanding educational philosophy over the years.

Because idealism, realism, and neo-Thomism are founded on more classical arguments and philosophers, educational philosophy texts often refer to them as tradition oriented. Because the philosophies of pragmatism, existentialism, and postmodernism were developed more recently, they are often separated from their traditional counterparts and referred to as modern oriented. The following charts might help the reader see the various philosophies that have been developed and their corresponding educational applications according to the traditional or modern classification.

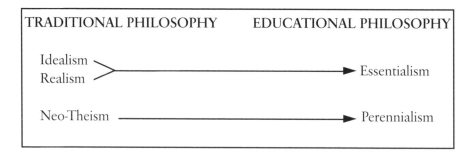

Although space does not allow an exhaustive overview of all of the major educational philosophies that have been developed, a brief overview of five of them will help the reader understand what a particular philosophical position looks like once it is applied to education. We will examine essential-

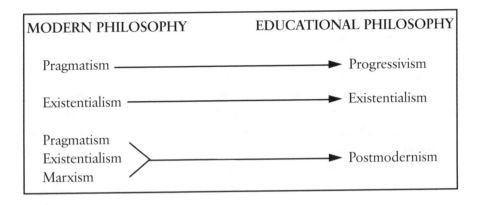

ism, perennialism, progressivism, existentialism, and postmodernism.[17] Although each of the original philosophies have been discussed in greater detail within the various historical chapters that deal with their origins (e.g., idealism and realism in chapter 2 and pragmatism in chapter 11), we will provide the reader with a brief reminder of each view before describing its application to education.

Essentialism as a Philosophy

As applied to the field of education, essentialism is a combination of the philosophical assumptions of both idealism and realism. Idealism is a philosophical position that believes that reality consists exclusively of the realm of ideas, thoughts, and mental images. Matter, or the material realm, is merely a reflection of reality. The universe is defined in terms of a God who is basically mind, or self. Described by some people as *idea-ism*, it holds to the view that a book receives its identity because it is a replica of "bookness." Things may exist but ideas subsist. Mental ideas, minds, or selves are the ultimate form of reality in the universe. People who hold to this perspective would concur with the seventeenth-century philosopher Rene Descartes, who declared, "I think; therefore, I am." Philosophers and educators included in the philosophic camp of idealism include Socrates (469-399 B.C.), Plato (427-347 B.C.), Descartes (1596-1650), Immanuel Kant (1724-1804), Georg Hegel

---

17. The reader is encouraged to examine the text by George Knight, *Philosophy and Education*, as it represents one of the finest resources on the subject of integrating philosophy with education from an evangelical perspective.

(1770-1831), Fredrich Froebel (1782-1852), Ralph Waldo Emerson (1803-82), and Herman Horne (1874-1946).[18]

Realism claims that reality transcends our reasoning ability. It believes that physical matter exists regardless of our ability to know or understand it. Realism is a belief in the ultimate reality of physical matter, that objects such as trees, rocks, or water exist universally. Human reasoning is supreme.

Trees, stars, chairs, people, and so forth exist regardless of our ability to understand all that they entail. They are not mere ideas in the minds of those who observe them, but they exist regardless of our ideas about them. They exist in their own right, independent of the mind. From an epistemological point of view, the realist asserts that the things we know exist independently of any human act of knowledge. In essence, the mind (idealism) no longer dictates reality; reality (realism) now dictates to it. The realist views the world through an uncomplicated mystical construct of ideas, or transcendent persons or selves, and prefers to base reality on three means, including knowing based upon direct sensing of an object (e.g., taste, touch, smell, hearing, sight). In other words, if I can sit in the chair, it exists as real. Second, scientific inquiry assists us in determining what is real because the scientific method employs rigorous methods of investigation and reporting that can be replicated with a high level of certainty (e.g., if I can measure it and observe its existence and can confirm that through repeated experiments, it must exist and be real). The third mode of arriving at truth is referred to as epistemology of essences, that is, when the idea in our mind corresponds perfectly with the thing being known, the correspondence theory comes to full application. The idea of the thing is what is called the "essence" of the object.[19]

Those who have held to a philosophy of realism in history include Aristotle (384-322 B.C.), Thomas Aquinas (1225-74), John Amos Comenius (1592-1670), Baruch Spinoza (1632-77), John Locke (1632-1704), Imanuel Kant (1724-1804), and Johann Herbart (1776-1841).

Essentialism in Educational Context

The philosophies of idealism and realism, when applied to an educational context, form an opinion that the curriculum of a school should emphasize the "essentials." By that, they mean the tried-and-true heritage of skills, facts,

---

18. Bigge, *Educational Philosophies for Teachers*, 25-27.
19. Jack Terry, *Educational Philosophy* (Dallas: Maple Springs, 1975), 90-91.

and laws of knowledge acquisition. Centuries of classroom examples of essentialism exist because it probably formed the basis of educational development more than any other system of philosophical thought. Essentialists select their curricular offerings based upon the "classical curriculum." Students are viewed as a cognitive receptacle. The role of the teacher is simply to fill that receptacle each day with new insights, facts, and figures. Evaluation is determined by how much of what the teacher presented is returned in its exact form on a test or some other means of measurement. For obvious reasons, essentialist educators are hesitant to experiment with any other philosophical methods because history has validated their method as reliable. It is, in essence, education through absorption.[20]

Essentialist educators prefer the lecture method whereby the teacher assumes the role of authoritative master of cognitive data and transmitter of information. Learning in the classroom is defined in terms of transmission, memorization, and presentation. The degree to which this information is processed or critically analyzed is minimally valued. In this traditional classroom, the student is assigned a chair for the duration of his experience and most, if not all, details of the day are mapped out well in advance on the teacher's detailed lesson plan. Rarely will the teacher vary from that plan. The classroom is highly structured and rigid. Methodologies are few and limited beyond lecture. Students sit in prescribed seats and are not allowed to talk among themselves.

For essentialist educators, the ideal teacher would demonstrate the following characteristic behaviors in the classroom:

1. A coworker with God in perfecting man
2. The personification of reality for students to emulate
3. A specialist in knowledge about students
4. An excellent professional technician
5. An exemplar of propriety
6. A personal good friend to each student
7. One who awakens the desire to learn in students
8. A master of the art of mature living
9. One who capably communicates his subjects
10. One who appreciates and enjoys the subjects he teaches

---

20. Theodore Brameld, *Education for the Emerging Age* (New York: Harper & Row: 1950), 23–24.

11. One who is always learning as he teaches
12. A conservative apostle of progress
13. A promoter of democratic living
14. An example of self-elimination—losing oneself in helping one's students grow to a higher life.[21]

In the context of ministry, the pastors who adhere to the philosophy of essentialism use time-honored methods. For example, they will still be using the Bible quiz seats from the 1960s and remain committed to the use of an "afterglow" service on Sunday evening. They follow the curriculum to the letter. The denomination or publishing company authors are viewed as authoritative sources, and although some minor modification in the curriculum would make the material more relevant and meaningful to their students, the modifications are rarely made. New ideas are seldom invited and are usually rejected. What works is what's been done in the past. The mantra for these pastors is "tried-and-true." If it's tried and proven effective, it becomes the basis for continued use. They are constantly remembering "the good old days" of ministry and remain transfixed on developing students who are retrospective rather than futuristic in their thinking.

Essentialist pastors who enter the ministry as new graduates look back to the methods they remembered while progressing through childhood and adolescence. If those methods were effective in bringing them to faith in Christ, why shouldn't they work on a new generation as well? Essentialists value long hours of Bible instruction (from the King James Version), Scripture memorization, and pastor-led programs. These are the tried-and-true methods that built the church, so it stands to reason that because they worked so well for nearly two thousand years, this isn't the time to make radical changes. "Let's stick with the essentials" is their rallying cry.

Perennialism as a Philosophy

Also known by such labels as neoscholasticism, traditionalism, and neo-Thomism, perennialism holds to the view that the universe as a whole is moving toward some prescribed end. Its origins date back to Aristotle,

---

21. J. Donald Butler, *Idealism in Education* (New York: Harper & Row, 1966), 94–102; as cited in Bigge, *Educational Philosophies for Teachers*, 33.

who established the philosophy of realism. Years later, Thomas Aquinas, who also started out as a realist, championed the cause and added a more significant spiritual dimension to its discussion. "The problem, or question for Aristotle, was 'What do all things have in common?' Aristotle's answer was that everything had its own peculiar 'whatness' or essence. But Thomas Aquinas was not so much interested in what things are as in the fact that they are. How is it that things even exist? The problem of what things are will depend on what it means for things to exist."[22] Perennialism dates back nearly seven centuries, and the Catholic Church has been its foremost advocate.

> In a sense, neo-Thomism navigates between two extremes of idealism and naturalism. Whereas idealism recognizes only the mind as the basis of reality and naturalism recognizes only matter, neo-Thomism affirms the dual aspects of reality. This is largely due to Aquinas' adoption of the Aristotelian system which conceives of particular unions of form and matter. Aquinas' Christian views, then, shape his explanation of the theistic dimension of reality.[23]

"The metaphysics of neo-scholastics is a two-sided coin. On the one side is the natural world that is open to reason. On the other side is the subrealm, which is understood through intuition, revelation, and faith. Scientists deal with the natural aspect, but the spiritual side is beyond their reach. Neoscholastics hold the nature of the universe to be permanent and unchanging."[24] When this view is applied to the field of education, the perennialist believes that God has revealed Himself to us through the intellect. We can come to know what is real through three primary means: the scientific method, intuition, and revelation. Intuition is to be valued because it leads us to ultimate Truth. Schooling should include a component that facilitates the development of intuition.[25]

---

22. Terry, *Educational Philosophy*, 99.
23. Michael L. Peterson, *Philosophy of Education* (Downers Grove, Ill.: InterVarsity, 1986), 47.
24. Knight, *Philosophy and Education*, 52–53.
25. Ibid., 99

Perennialism in Educational Context

In the context of the classroom, the perennialist teacher advocates exercising and disciplining the mind as one of the highest contributions of education. It is of paramount importance in higher education because without it critical thinking is not possible. Study of the liberal arts is held in higher esteem than vocational skills development. This belief exposes their perception of the fundamental purpose of education—to liberate man by helping him become an essential self, a rational individual with superior reasoning capabilities. Reasoning requires the ability to use words wisely, so the use of language, vocabulary acquisition, and rhetoric are highly valued. Schooling is seen as preparation for future life. Curricular offerings include the three Rs: reading, 'riting, and 'rithmatic. Reading the classics is preferred to more contemporary materials. Schools that are designed around a perennialist philosophy might employ the great books curriculum. The study of foreign language (e.g., Greek, French, and Latin), even among young elementary school-aged children, provides a valuable base for future educational processing although the students might never actually be able to speak those languages in their social interactions. Study of sciences is deemed valuable to the degree that they confirm and replicate the classic discoveries of Lavoiser or Galileo.[26]

To the perennialist, the student functions as a natural being in the quest for truth and knowledge, but at the same time he/she does so as a spiritual being. In this latter dimension, the student can come to know God in relationship. One of the primary objectives of a school is to bring these two desires together through an integrated blend of curricular and cocurricular activities. The teacher is viewed as a mental disciplinarian who determines what is best for the student (although it would be preferred if the perennialist teacher were to consider student need to some degree). The objective of the teacher is to train the student's mind in rational thought. Education is to sharpen the intellect and quicken the mind because only through such mental discipline can one gain an understanding of the source of ultimate truth. Mathematics is held as a primary venue of instruction because it employs pure reasoning and is not influenced by the transcendent affairs of life.[27]

---

26. Beck, *Educational Philosophy and Theory*, 313–30.
27. Knight, *Philosophy and Education*, 56–57.

As seen in the context of ministry, the Christian educator who holds to the philosophical position of perennialism views the source of authority and discipline as coming exclusively from God. Democratic methods of curriculum selection and programmatic input are not considered important because that should come from ecclesiastical leaders who know what is best.[28] One of the key verses to support ministry for the perennialist is Luke 2:52, "And Jesus kept increasing in wisdom and stature, and in favor with God and men." This verse speaks of the importance of living the balanced life. The goal in ministry would be to create disciples who were strong in wisdom (cognitive) and stature (physical), and in favor with God (spiritual) and men (social). The perennialist sees the need for students to grow in a balanced perspective within each of these important areas. Salvation is not the end result of ministry but a means to the end of discipleship.

Progressivism as a Philosophy

Also known as pragmatism or experimentalism, this theory believes that the most effective means of gaining knowledge is through experimental methods and reflective observations. Depending on the psychological approach that is being applied, pragmatism can be manifested as behaviorism (also known as association/connectionist theory) or as cognitivism (also known as cognitive-field theory). During the twentieth century, it emerged as a reaction against the absolutistic system of thinking. Using this later philosophy, facts are absolute and eternal, never changing regardless of context or culture. Educators who hold to a progressive, or pragmatic, philosophy would hold to a more relative value base, preferring to let the context and setting determine the degree of truth involved. It is basically an epistemological philosophy because it is focused on the nature of knowledge. The goal of a progressive philosopher is to make philosophy functional for mankind generally and, more specifically, during the dealings of daily life.[29]

The progressive educator thrives on the problem-solving method of instruction. This process of learning is indicative of real life, so it stands to reason that it would also be viewed as the supreme method of instruction. This problem-solving method has five components: problem, diagnosis, brainstorming, analysis, and implementation. In the first step, problems are

---

28. Beck, *Educational Philosophy and Theory*, 343–46.
29. Bigge, *Educational Philosophies for Teachers*, 13–14.

identified through interaction with life experience. It might be as simple as how to fix a flat tire on my car or as complex as how to find a cure for AIDS.

Having come upon a problem, the teacher assists the student in diagnosing the problem with more precision and clarity. This step involves trying to get at the heart of the problem as opposed to the often more apparent surface issue. For example, a high school student might view his parent as the problem because he has been placed under an 11 P.M. curfew. In reality, the deeper issue might be the lack of trust that exists between the parent and the teenager. Arguing about getting the curfew extended to 11:30 P.M. does not get at the real heart of developing a deeper trust in the decision-making ability of the youth.

The third step in the problem-solving process is brainstorming. This step involves trying to identify all of the various resources available to the student to solve the problem. A thirteen-year-old adolescent girl might feel despondent and suicidal, having discovered that she is pregnant by her boyfriend. She might be feeling all alone and without any hope until someone is able to help her identify other resources for assistance and support. An extended support system to help her address this problem might be found in her coach, youth pastor, teacher, school counselor, and/or friend.

The fourth step is analysis, which involves rank ordering the various resources and potential solutions. Questions are asked such as "If go to my coach, will she tell my parents?" "If I tell my school counselor, will I get kicked out of school?" "Can I trust my youth pastor to give me accurate advice?" Equipped with answers to these and other questions, the student develops a strategy for solving the problem. The danger at this point is that the teacher will prescribe the "correct" course of action for the student. That would be destructive to the final outcome because the student must be allowed to think outside the box to find her own solution.

The student is now able to progress to the final step of implementing the strategy. If the first approach fails, then the student moves ahead to the next possible solution. This process of implementation continues until the right solution is found. The teacher's role at this step is encouragement so the student doesn't quit after the first failed attempt. Failure is inevitable, and each failure brings the student that much closer to finding the answer that will work. Once the student has achieved a successful outcome, the teacher guides the student through some constructive reflection so that life lessons can be learned and applied to future problems that come along.

Progressivism in Educational Context

Schools that are operated through the lens of progressivism are democratic in their decision making regarding the rules, regulations, procedures, curriculum, and classroom management techniques. They are centers of problem solving, applying the mind to the resolution of life's great dilemmas. Teachers are viewed as sources of authority and direction but also are seen as fellow participants along the road of lifelong learning. In their role as learning facilitators, they achieve the respect of their students by virtue of the fact that they have already traveled down the road of life a little farther and have a valuable contribution to make to others on a similar journey.

In the context of ministry, a youth pastor would form a student council of peers to share in the choices about the program elements of the ministry. This leadership council would determine what camps they would attend, what topics they will study during the year, how fellow students will be disciplined when necessary, where they will go for a spring break missions trip, what policies or procedures will govern their behavior while on youth events, and other programming details. The youth pastor would have the final say on important matters by virtue of his/her additional life experience and spiritual maturity, but he/she would never exert that authority in a coercive or manipulative manner. They are constantly on the lookout for the latest teachable moment that can be brought out of the life of a student or staff member or from their own experience. They use these teachable moments as springboards into the Scripture, from which biblical principles can be brought to bear on real-life contemporary problems.

The mantra for the pragmatic children's ministry leader is "What's working out there with other children's pastors?" Such a utilitarian perspective streamlines decision making and conserves valuable resources. They love to attend new conferences and seminars where they can network with other ministry leaders and find out what is "working" in other ministries. They are concrete thinkers and generally "fly by the seat of their pants." They don't stop to consider why they are using a particular approach or method in their ministry. They only know that it works and, ultimately, that's what counts. They are numbers driven, and anything that produces an increase in numbers is worthy of consideration and practice.

Existentialism as a Philosophy

This philosophy arose in the early eighteenth century and has its origins in the Danish philosopher Søren Kierkegaard (1813-55), although its prominence is almost exclusively seen in the nineteenth century. Epistemologically speaking, truth is what the person defines it to be. Truth is rarely, if ever, spelled with a capital *T* because it is relative to the person defining it. Truth is only true to that person; we must all find our own truth. What you have found to be true in your experience might not be true for me so it is defined contextually.

Likewise, defining what is real (ontology) and what is of value (axiology) are also relative to the person defining them. Reality and values are centered in the individual and are not universal. The statement "Beauty is in the eye of the beholder" is an existential statement because it reveals the position that no one person can dictate what is of universal beauty. Ethics are based on the situation and are rarely prescriptive for others. Freedom is a value esteemed highly to the existentialist because everyone must be free to choose meaning for themselves. Individualism is the flagship of existentialism.

As a philosophy, existentialism has had a relatively new birth because most existential philosophers are prominent twentieth-century thinkers. Some examples of existentialists include Friedrich Nietzsche (1844-1900), Franz Kafka (1883-1924), Karl Jaspers (1883-1969), Martin Heidegger (1889-1976), Jean-Paul Satre (1905-80), and Albert Camus (1913-60).

One of the difficulties in defining existentialism is that existential philosophers find it difficult to agree on much of anything that applies to their philosophical presuppositions. Coming to any definitive conclusion regarding key terms, theoretical constructs, and applications has been nearly impossible to solidify. What's more, existential philosophers don't seem to care much about their contradictory explanations concerning their beliefs. They do not look for ultimate meaning or purpose in the world because that is for each person to decide for themselves.

Existentialism became prominent in American philosophy in the 1950s as philosophers looked back at the dehumanization of life that occurred during the Industrial Revolution, World War I, the Great Depression, and World War II. The existentialist, looking back at these low points of human existence, struggles to find any meaning and purpose from these epics of human suffering.

Existentialism in Educational Context

Existentialism has been applied primarily to the field of literature over the years. Although existentialism has not been applied to education in as concerted a manner as the other educational philosophies that we have discussed thus far, it has had an effect on education as a result of its attitude and influence. "The usual themes of education, one may readily understand, differ widely from the usual themes of existentialism. It is not possible, therefore, to talk about the connection between the two in the same way that one would in the case of a traditional philosophy and education."[30]

Existential educators do not prescribe any particular form of curriculum because to do so would be a violation of their philosophical value of discovering individual meaning. They decry most forms of traditional instruction as coercive and manipulative because traditional education tends to prescribe what is essential and necessary for life. How could anyone be so audacious as to presume what will unfold in my life and then prescribe curricular content to anticipate that need? To the existential educator, life determines curriculum. Until then, freedom of choice must be the rule of the school. Obviously, however, some basic content such as reading, writing, arithmetic, history, music, art, literature, and science is needed. Vocational training is discouraged because any career can be used as a means of discovering truth and reality for themselves. But beyond that, it is difficult to get existentialists to agree on what should be included in academic content.

> The primary purpose of the school is neither intellectual nor social; it is to develop free, moral individuals. The subjects contained in the curriculum are not as important as the approaches to these subjects. It is the personal involvement of the student in whatever subject he is taking that makes it worthy of his time. Every subject and activity (even vocational training) must be studied in the context of the total human situation. There is no such thing as the detached study of science, or mathematics, or history. In the use of teaching methods and evaluational techniques, the teacher must respect the freedom and individuality of the student. In methodology, the existential expresses the greatest preference for the Socratic method. Most traditional and progressive methods need major modification before they

---

30. Burns and Brauner, *Philosophy of Education*, 294.

can be acceptable to the existentialist. Even though personal freedom is the highest good for the existentialist, he offers little advice on how to maintain order in the classroom; he merely asserts that individual freedom must not be violated. Pupil freedom can be honored by allowing free choice of students, activities, and especially, freedom of expression in written and oral composition.[31]

Existential pastors (an oxymoron to the evangelical) would never dictate absolute truth because all truth is relative to the hearer. "Thus saith the Lord" might have meaning to one person but have nothing of value to say to another. As a youth leader, he/she would never conclude an answer as "correct" because that would be relative to the person speaking. They have a high regard for the individual learner because each is created uniquely by God. They guide students to find meaning and purpose in life as each of them defines it. If a young adult can speak with confidence that they love their live-in partner and that love is an expression of a created being, then they are free to live together without the formality of marriage. To say otherwise would be to force one person's belief on another, and that would be a violation of existential theology.

The existential ministry leader is a facilitator of ministry rather than a director of it. Students are free to come and go as they please and can choose from the options provided as to what activities they want to participate. No expectation exists that all (or any) will want to attend the event that is planned. Nevertheless, it is planned and presented for those who choose to attend. Ministry is quite open-ended and free. Choices are optional, and ministry occurs without mission, vision, or strategic planning. They just live one day at a time and go with the flow.

Postmodernism as a Philosophy

Postmodernism is a reaction to Enlightenment thought and philosophical reasoning. Specifically, it rejects the notion of the autonomy of the individual, tradition and authority as sources of societal influence, and the belief that reason can be pure and objective (although one might not always reason objectively, objective reason is nonetheless an achievable goal). Postmodernism

---

31. Adrain M. Dupuis, *Philosophy of Education in Historical Perspective* (Chicago: Rand McNally, 1996), 241.

declares that many different ways exist by which to view the world and that no one perspective should be considered authoritative and final. The postmodernist holds to a progressive worldview in that no one metaphysical presupposition is absolutely true or false. The postmodernist respects other viewpoints and acknowledges the possibility that each one reveals a certain degree of truth (some perhaps being more true than others). Truth is therefore seen as the sum total of differing metaphysical perspectives.[32]

Sources of knowledge are variable to postmodern thinkers. Likewise, neither do moral absolutes exist. Ethics, which are based upon one's axiological presuppositions, are also relative because no one value system can be applied across the board to all other cultures, genders, or socioeconomic groups. Simply too many variations exist in life as a whole to espouse one viewpoint as being more important than another. For this reason, postmoderns value a multicultural worldview. They also see great virtue in trying to hear opposing views. Where there is a significant social problem such as poverty, racism, or injustice, postmodernist thinkers prefer to gather everyone together to hear opposing views in the quest of a solution. Those who hold the dominant social role are not always correct in their position; just because the majority rules doesn't mean that the majority is right.

Postmodernism in Educational Context

When brought into the educational context, postmodern philosophy is seen as relative to the needs of the students. Obviously, no one system fits all needs. Therefore, it is difficult, if not impossible, for one curriculum to be prescribed for all students. The seven liberal arts of the Enlightenment would never be taught to all students. Such a notion implies an authoritative value judgment regarding the nature of curriculum and the needs of students. The purpose of education is far more than the transmission of knowledge from one source to another. Education should meet a social need and broaden a student's worldview. Postmodern educators are concerned about the social ramifications of their classroom content and instructional environment. One of the major aims of postmodern education involves developing an awareness of how one dominant culture has used its power to subjugate and control a powerless culture.[33]

---

32. Bruce Benson, *The Evangelical Dictionary of Christian Education*, ed. Michael J. Anthony (Grand Rapids: Baker, 2001), s.v. "Postmodernism."
33. Knight, *Philosophy and Education*, 90-92.

As applied to the classroom, the teacher asserts his/her influence to enable students of differing ethnic backgrounds to voice their opinions and feelings about current issues affecting their lives. Applied in this manner, the classroom becomes a microcosm of life and is able to provide students of the dominant culture with a broader worldview of their own personal biases. Discussions in the classroom focus on becoming aware of the need for diversity in society. The emphasis is not so much on instructional methods and techniques as on developing an open mind and a broad worldview to allow other cultures and opinions to have equal weight with their own. For this reason, the postmodern classroom is more process driven than product driven. Experiences are explored and feelings about those experiences are discussed openly. Motives for actions are debated openly, and spirited dialogue among students is encouraged.

EDUCATIONAL PHILOSOPHIES IN SUMMARY

Philosophy of education is simply the application of philosophy to the issues and questions posed by education. It does not need to be complicated or mystical. The various philosophies that have been postulated from classical periods of history include idealism, realism, and neo-Thomism. When applied to the field of education, they become known as essentialism and perennialism. From a more modern perspective, the philosophies of pragmatism, existentialism, and postmodernism, once applied to education, become known as progressivism, existentialism, and postmodernism. Each position has its own view about epistemology (knowledge), ontology (reality), and axiology (ethics and aesthetics). Each also has its own opinion about the critical elements of education (e.g., teacher, learner, curriculum, methods, and social policy). The charts at the end of this chapter are helpful ways of demonstrating the relationship between philosophy and its application to education.[34]

This chapter has been focused specifically on the relationship between philosophy and its application to education. We have also sought to draw, where reasonable, a relationship between philosophy and ministry. However, trying to make that distinction is not always realistic and responsible. How often, for instance, is existentialism really going to be applied in the context of a local church ministry where the purpose of ministry in the first

---

34. Terry, *Educational Philosophy,* 23

place is to apply the teaching of Christ (an authoritative source of information) to the fallen state of mankind? Making disciples is in and of itself a violation of much of that for which existentialism stands in the first place. Rather than trying to build bridges where bridges have no business being, we would prefer to discuss the application of philosophy to ministry in the specific context of ecclesiology (the nature and purpose of the church). That will be the focus of the final chapter.

FOR FURTHER READING

Beck, Clive. *Educational Philosophy and Theory: An Introduction.* Boston: Little, Brown & Company, 1974.

Bigge, Morris L. *Educational Philosophies for Teachers.* Columbus: Charles E. Merrill, 1982.

Bowyer, Carlton H. *Philosophical Perspectives for Education.* Glenview, Ill.: Scott, Forseman & Company, 1970.

Brameld, Theodore. *Education for the Emerging Age.* New York: Harper & Row, 1950.

Brent, Allen. *Philosophical Foundations for the Curriculum.* Boston: George Allen & Unwin, 1978.

Broudy, Harry S. *Building a Philosophy of Education.* New York: Prentice-Hall, 1954.

Brubacher, John S. *Eclectic Philosophy of Education.* New York: Prentice-Hall, 1951.

———. *Modern Philosophies of Education.* New York: McGraw Hill, 1939.

Burns, Hobert W., and Charles J. Brauner. *Philosophy of Education.* New York: Ronald Press, 1962.

Butler, J. Donald. *Idealism in Education.* New York: Harper & Row, 1966.

Dupuis, Adrian M. *Philosophy of Education in Historical Perspective.* Chicago: Rand McNally, 1966.

Griese, Arnold A. *Your Philosophy of Education: What Is It?* Santa Monica, Calif.: Goodyear Publishing, 1981.

Terry, Jack. *Educational Philosophy.* Dallas: Maple Springs, 1975.

Philosophical Concepts

	ONTOLOGY	EPISTEMOLOGY	AXIOLOGY
IDEALISM	Reality is found in the realm of ideas, spirit, and mental images.	Truth is defined as an idea or consciousness.	What is of value is the idea.
REALISM	Reality is found in the realm of things and material objects. It exists beyond our ability to know and understand it.	Truth is defined as that which is observable and often measurable.	What is of value is natural law (nature).
NEO-THOMISM	Reality is found in the physical realm but also includes a supernatural dimension.	Truth is defined as both rational and intuitive.	What is of value is that which integrates the physical world with the spiritual world.
PRAGMATISM	Reality is utilitarian and found in what works. It is discovered through experience.	Truth is defined as being relative and contextually applied.	What is of value is that which solves a problem for the person or society.
EXISTENTIALISM	Reality is individualistic in nature and concept.	Truth is defined by one's personal choice, where existence precedes essence.	What is of value depends on the perspective of the individual.
POSTMODERNISM	Reality is found in one's personal choice.	Truth is defined as being open-ended and relative.	What is of value is culturally defined; serves to broaden one's worldview.

Educational Application

	TEACHER	STUDENT	CURRICULUM	METHODS	SOCIAL POLICY
ESSENTIALISM	Source of authority who determines curriculum, aims, methods, and environment for learning.	Receptacle of information, data, facts, and figures.	Emphasis on the classics such as literature, history, science, and mathematics.	Lecture, recitation, memorization. Learning process viewed as lacking freedom and creativity.	Review the past; transmit societal heritage.
PERENNIALISM	Authoritative and firm; structured, viewed as mental disciplinarian.	Able to interact in both rational thought and a spiritual intuition.	Traditional subjects but may also include material for student's spiritual growth.	Rote memory, drills, personal reflection, and contemplation.	Develop well-balanced citizens who contribute to their society.
PROGRESSIVISM	Guide, consultant, and fellow discoverer of information about life.	Participates in selection of curriculum; joint participant in the learning process.	Mostly elective, determined by felt needs of the student or society.	Problem solving, case studies, etc. Utilizes problem-solving techniques: problem, diagnosis, brainstorming, analysis, and implementation.	To solve societal problems and dilemmas.
EXISTENTIALISM	Indirect facilitator.	Subjective and emotionally involved.	Based on questions about good and evil, right and wrong, etc.	Intense personal inquiry; highly subjective and introspective.	None established or agreed upon.
POSTMODERNISM	Challenge existing student paradigms of personal, social, and cultural norms.	Personal awareness, challenge the status quo, asks questions, personal reflection.	History, music, art, literature, and social sciences.	Interaction with multicultural perspectives and values. Confirms data through life experience.	In a mild sense: help broaden one's worldview. In a more extreme sense: to reconstruct society.

Chapter 14

DEVELOPING A PERSONAL
PHILOSOPHY OF MINISTRY

NOT SURPRISINGLY, THE STUDENT OF Christian education who is immersed in the practice of ministry might have a difficult time seeing the connection between the study of philosophy and the practice of ministry. This tension does not exist just in the field of ministry. All through the ages, dating back to Aristotle, a tension has existed between theory and practice. An overemphasis on either element can lead to a dangerous outcome. Put too much emphasis on philosophy, and the individual is "so philosophically minded that he is of no earthly good." Likewise with the minister who knows only practice; an overemphasis here can lead to a reliance on gimmicks and methods without an understanding of why they are being used or why they work (or don't work). Without this awareness, the minister begins his ministry by accumulating a "bag of tricks" filled with teaching methods, messages, and games. However, once this bag runs out, it leaves him with no other alternative but to quit and go looking for another ministry location.

The children's ministry director or youth pastor who has only enough ministry resources to last eighteen months will be caught in an endless cycle of career rotation because he or she has never taken the time to analyze the philosophy of ministry. Without this understanding, the ministry leader is unable to determine how and when changes in methodology should take place and is therefore unable to make the necessary adjustments. No ministry setting remains fixed, so at some point this inability to apply theory to practice leads to frustration and stagnation. Understanding the philosophical presuppositions upon which ministry is based can reduce a lifestyle of endless transition.

The most difficult part of the process is convincing the young student that he/she needs to spend some concerted effort developing a personal philosophy of ministry. When students lose sight of this connection between theory and practice, they protest that theory is vague, too esoteric, and a waste of time. Practice is more fun and requires less motivation.

Generally, we have plenty of practice. But practice is often confused and contradictory, a circumstance already seen to have been almost the continual state of affairs since the time of Aristotle. What we need is not more practical remedies but, as Aristotle pointed out, some theory to guide practice. On this note, the defenders of philosophy have stated that theory is, in the end, the most practical of expedients.[1]

To use the familiar analogy of a man crossing a lake in a boat, he needs to use both oars to keep the boat moving in the desired direction. In this case, long-term successful ministry requires both theory and practice. Without one or the other, the boater is destined to an endless life of paddling in circles wondering why he never arrives at his destination.

While writing this chapter, I received a call from one of my former students. He had been serving as a youth pastor at a local church for the past fourteen months. He received a phone call from his senior pastor this week and was asked to come into his office for a meeting. The outcome of the meeting was that the pastor requested the youth minister's resignation. It seems that the youth pastor just wasn't a "fit" for the type of ministry that the senior pastor wanted. Pain etched my former student's face as he tried to figure out what had happened.

As I explored below the surface, asking questions about the senior pastor's philosophy of ministry, I came to realize that the fellow was trying to transition his church from a traditional, denominationally bound church to a "seeker sensitive" model that required a radical paradigm shift for everyone in the church, including the staff. My former student came with his ministry style made up and was not willing to make the necessary adjustments. In essence, his personal philosophy of ministry did not fit that of the senior pastor's, and it was time for a parting of ways.

---

1. John S. Brubacher, *Eclectic Philosophy of Education* (New York: Prentice-Hall, 1951), 14.

Developing a personal philosophy of ministry while in school and taking the time to review it periodically while in ministry is essential for long-term vitality and happiness in ministry. The purposes of this chapter are to identify the critical components of a personal philosophy of ministry and to assist the young minister in his/her ability to formulate a personal philosophy of ministry that will stand the test of time and ensure a successful career for years to come.

COMPONENTS OF A PERSONAL PHILOSOPHY

What goes into a personal philosophy of ministry is broad and varied. In its broadest format, it entails three components: theology, philosophy, and praxis. This comprehensive approach involves first, detailing one's theological position on important doctrinal issues; second, a description of their philosophical presuppositions in matters pertaining to metaphysics (reality), epistemology (knowledge), and axiology (values); and last, an articulation of their preferences regarding the essential functions of ministry (e.g., worship, evangelism, edification, and service). Although this approach to describing a personal philosophy is time-consuming to develop, it is the preferred document for churches looking into the background of ministry leadership candidates.

Most professors who teach the history and philosophy of Christian education courses in universities and seminaries opt for a more manageable document that details the student's personal philosophy of ministry as it relates to seven important areas: the role of the teacher, the role of the learner, the learning environment, purposes and objectives of the lesson, methods that will be employed, the curriculum that will be used, and the outcomes that will be assessed.

Although you might not be required to provide the more comprehensive document for your class, we will detail the components of the larger document so that you will be better prepared to interview for a position of leadership after graduation. This larger document is identical to the smaller version, except that it also includes a section on theology, philosophy, and praxis. Following are some suggestions regarding each area.

Theological Matters

The kinds of theological issues that need to be included in a comprehensive philosophy of ministry include (but are not limited to) such matters as

1. Your perspective regarding the nature of God as Creator
2. The nature of Jesus Christ as His Son and Savior
3. The nature of the Holy Spirit as a member of the Godhead
4. Your position regarding the authority of Scripture
5. The purpose of the local church
6. Your denominational distinctives
7. Where you stand on matters pertaining to social issues such as abortion, racism, social equality, gender roles, sexuality, etc.
8. The nature and purpose of spiritual gifts
9. The role of women in ministry leadership
10. The place of missions and how it should be conducted

Obviously, this list is only partial, but it represents a few of the many items that should be articulated in advance of pursuing a career in ministry. When students of Christian education fail to examine where they stand on these important issues, they risk entering a ministry that might not be the right theological "fit" for them. In such cases, the outcome is often quite predictable and painful—for both the church and the ministry leader.

Philosophical Matters

The second area that should be included in a comprehensive philosophy of ministry includes a discussion of your philosophical foundations. The preceding chapter detailed these important components (metaphysics, epistemology, and axiology) as applied to an educational and/or ministry context. Ministry leaders who are going into a full-time career in Christian education should take time to examine their positions on important matters pertaining to the source of knowledge (e.g., general and/or special revelation), the meaning of reality and who determines what is (and is not) real and trustworthy, and the degree of value that will be placed on matters of ethical and aesthetical consideration. If one enters ministry without having considered these issues, convictions are not set and decisions are as shifting as the tide, and the ministry will be based on each passing whim and fad.

For example, if your source of authority is God's Word alone and you are not open to other influences, then you had better not take a position in a church with strong ties to its denomination's publishing company. If you reject curriculum from all sources other than God's Word, your ministry at most churches will probably be short-lived. Taking the other extreme view, some people have jumped on the bandwagon of every new seminar and workshop that has come through town and tried each new approach right out of the workshop binder without ever stopping to consider whether the material was relevant for the people in their church. The results have been equally disastrous. Thinking through these three major issues of philosophy is critical to long-term ministry success.

Praxis Matters

Praxis gets at the heart of ministry action. It is the final outcome of our theological positions and philosophical foundations. This is where ministry happens. Praxis begins after we have answered the questions that are foundational to our faith. At this point, we have put to rest questions regarding God's nature and purpose in the world and have joined His efforts to win the lost for Christ. This doesn't mean that we no longer have theological questions, but we have peace about what we believe concerning the essentials of the faith.

Praxis also takes up after we have decided our philosophical positions. We know our source of authority and have come to terms with how it affects the way we do business in the church. We have an established view regarding the nature of the teacher, the nature of the learner, the purpose of our instruction, the environment that works best for us, the methods we will employ, the curriculum we will use, and how we will measure our teaching effectiveness. This final aspect is all that some professors require for their philosophy-of-ministry assignment. That being the case, let's look at how to format the document and detail the components of the material.

DESCRIBING YOUR PERSONAL PHILOSOPHY OF MINISTRY

Your own personal philosophy of ministry is just that—it's personal and unique to you. It comes in the context of your own life experiences. Obviously, it will look different from those of other students in the class. The reason for the variation involves the pilgrimage of your life. For example, if you became a Christian in your late adolescent years as a result of a parachurch camp ministry, you might have a deep appreciation for their efforts and see a higher value for outreach and in contrast to someone who grew up in a

Christian home and within the influence of a traditional church ministry. Likewise, those who were born outside North America and became Christians through the efforts of a local missionary will naturally have a different point of view regarding the need for international missions in contrast to someone who has never seen or heard much about missions while growing up. One's personal life experience, spiritual pilgrimage, ethnic variance, and a host of other factors will make each person's philosophy of ministry unique and distinct from those around them. One last important reason for such variation resides in the identification of your spiritual gift. If you have the spiritual gift of evangelism, your philosophy of ministry should reflect a passion for outreach and ministry to the lost. It's only natural and to be expected. Praise God for such wonderful diversity!

With that fact in mind, following are the seven components of a personal philosophy of ministry. Divide your own personal philosophy into these seven categories, and discuss your perspective regarding each component. Try to support your view with Scripture where appropriate, but try to avoid the tendency to read into Scripture that for which you are looking. That approach to biblical interpretation, known as eisegesis, is man's effort to prove his own biases by making a passage fit his own desire rather than reflecting accurately the meaning of the author. Take some time to consult some Bible commentaries to ensure that the passage means what you are saying it does. Where possible, try to find several verses to support your position because the more passages you find, the safer you will be in supporting your argument with Scripture.

1. Role and Nature of the Teacher

What is the role of the teacher? How do you envision the role of the teacher affecting his or her students? How should the teacher motivate his or her students to accomplish what the Bible is teaching? How would you describe the relationship that would exist between the teacher and the student? How what kind of training and preparation is required of the ideal teacher? What is the nature of the relationship that the teacher should have with God? What qualities should a spiritually mature teacher possess? How should the teacher relate to the students, and to what degree is the teacher a role model, mentor, or coach to the students? What metaphor best describes your view of a Christian teacher?

2. Role and Nature of the Learner

What are some of the different kinds of learners who would be the focus of a Christian education (CE) ministry? Should the emphasis of a CE ministry be the spiritual growth and development of the believer so he/she is trained and equipped to do the work of the ministry, or should the focus be on the nonbelievers so they can be brought into the fellowship of believers first? What are the capacities and responsibilities of the learner to listen and receive the message? What is the nature of the relationship between the learner and the teacher? What principles do you think are critical to a student's being able to grasp biblical truth? What is the moral nature of the learner? From where does the drive and motivation to learn come? Does any difference exist between a nonbeliever and a believer in terms of the learning process? In view of your understanding about the learning process, how do you view each student's personality in relation to their personal learning style? What metaphor best describes your view of a Christian student?

3. Purpose and Goals of the Lesson

What should be the major learning aims and objectives for teaching a Bible lesson? What are the secondary aims of the lesson? To what degree is the ultimate lesson aim outside the parameter of the teacher? Do any priorities exist that are maintained by the Christian teacher? What are your opinions about how God works to guide the goals of your lesson? When Christian education has had its final effect on a person's life, describe what that person would be like. How would you know when they were spiritually mature and complete in Christ? What are your long-term (i.e., five-year) goals and objectives for your ministry group? What are your more immediate (i.e., one-year) group goals and objectives?

4. The Curriculum

How does the Bible influence one's spiritual formation? What role does curriculum from a publishing company play in the content of the lesson? In light of the goals and objectives that you have for your group, what are the long-range and short-range curricula needs of your group? What curricular resources will you use to achieve your goals and objectives? Does the Scripture identify any particular priorities that you will follow in terms of your curriculum?

5. *Instructional Methodology*

What are the essential components that should be included in the teaching-learning process? How does the student's individual learning style influence the methods that are chosen for the lesson? What methods, techniques, and devices will be used in the lesson? How do the Bible teachers begin and end their lessons? What part does the Holy Spirit play in selecting the methods? What part does the Bible play in the teaching-learning process? How should teaching occur to accomplish the goals and objectives of the lesson? What age-appropriate accommodations will be used in the selection of instructional methodologies?

6. *Learning Environment*

What were the predominant learning environments used in the Bible? How does this variety influence the manner in which you will select your environment? What should the climate or atmosphere of teaching be to maximize the experience? Under what circumstances does the environment become a hindrance to learning?

7. *Outcomes Assessment*

How will you know that learning has occurred as opposed to your simply having taught the lesson? What criteria will you use to measure your teaching effectiveness? How is this learning outcome related to the instructional objective (goals and aims) of the lesson? How will you measure spiritual formation? Is all learning measurable? Does it always need to be? Under what circumstances would it not be necessary to measure learning? What is the value in measuring whether learning has occurred?

So What? Lessons from the Past for Twenty-first-century Christian Education

These helpful guidelines are designed to assist you in the important task of developing your own personal philosophy of Christian education. Whether you choose to use the more comprehensive format, which includes a detailed discussion regarding your theological and/or philosophical presuppositions, or you select the more abbreviated format, either will provide you an opportunity to think through and reflect on just what you believe about your personal faith (theology); what you hold to be real (ontology), knowable (epistemology), and of value (axiology) for life and learning; and how faith (theology) and reason (education) are integrated in a learning environment. These are the essence of your calling in Christian education.

1. Your philosophy isn't set in stone.

This personal philosophy of ministry should be revisited from time to time to update and modify previous understandings. Although Scripture is complete and no longer open to change, our understanding of how God created us certainly isn't complete. The fields within the social sciences (e.g., education, sociology, psychology, and anthropology) are constantly making new discoveries about human personality, learning styles, social dynamics that influence instruction, learning styles, the relationship between body chemistry and learning, how one's family of origin affects learning, and a host of other important considerations.

New discoveries are constantly unfolding, and these new discoveries help us understand the complexity of our human composition. The wise Christian educator will take the time to stay abreast of new insights brought about through the efforts of these fields so we, in turn, can become more effective in our ability to communicate biblical truth to a needy world. We suggest that you review and modify your personal philosophy of ministry at least once every five years.

2. Reflect critically on the contributions of the social sciences.

We're well aware of those who believe that the only thing necessary to be an effective classroom communicator is a Bible and a class of students. However, we now know beyond any reasonable doubt that not all students learn in the same manner. Some students respond better to verbal and social collaboration (collaborative learners), other students prefer to learn through lecture (analytic learners), some students prefer more of a hands-on methodology (commonsense learners), and still other students learn only when they are allowed to involve themselves in some creative expression (dynamic learners). Standing in front of a classroom of students and lecturing for an hour might work for about one-third of the students in a class (i.e., the analytic learners), but very little learning is taking place for the other two-thirds of the class.

Being an effective communicator of biblical truth requires some adjustment in one's instructional methodologies to accommodate the lesson to each of the learning styles represented in the class. These observations and discoveries were made fairly recently and have been groundbreaking in Christian education ministries across North America. Our admonition is to remain open to the discoveries of the social sciences and learn from their observations. Become a critical reader of their journals, and look for ways to take their insights and become more effective in your ministry.

This is not to say that you should accept all of their findings because history is replete with findings based on faulty data, inaccurate presuppositions, personal biases, and poorly designed research methodologies. A good deal of wisdom and skepticism might be in order. However, once a healthy measure of critical thinking is applied to the findings, and once enough data reveal a preponderance of evidence, then Christian educators have a responsibility to stay abreast in their application of new information in the field of education and make any necessary adjustments. We should lead the way in terms of applying these new insights to the efforts of evangelism and discipleship. As we do, we will see the church grow in its health and vitality and thereby help fulfill the Great Commission.

EPILOGUE

WE HAVE TAKEN A JOURNEY BACK NEARLY six thousand years in the history of God's dealings with humanity. Along the way, we have stopped to examine some of the means by which God has intervened in world events. Sometimes, it was apparent that God was active in His relationship with mankind, whereas at other times it didn't seem as apparent. Obviously, He was still there playing a behind-the-scenes role.

So in looking back over this span of time, we have the opportunity, through the advantage of hindsight, to pull together some valuable lessons. Perhaps you will recall that in the introduction we stated that those who refuse to examine history and learn its lessons are destined to repeat them. For this reason, it is incumbent upon us to spend a few moments reviewing and summarizing the important lessons gleaned from history.

So What? Cumulative Lessons from the Past for Twenty-first-century Christian Education

1. The family is a high priority.
Clearly from the beginning of God's dealings with mankind, He wanted the family to be the primary means of spiritual formation. Through the example of a righteous father and mother, God expected them to pass on the heritage of their faith to their children. He intended the passing of the

spiritual baton to be replicated throughout the community. The result of this process would be an entire nation committed to walking with God. When other nations saw the result of this national righteousness, they would come with inquisitive hearts, searching for the same kind of relationship.

The unfortunate part of this plan was the lack of spiritual vitality on the part of Israel. They never lived up to their end of the agreement; consequently, other nations were never attracted to what Israel possessed. In fact, those Jews who did enjoy a close walk with God kept it to themselves rather than sharing it with people from other nations. Some families passed on their spiritual heritage to further generations, but the majority clearly did not.

This plan to reach the family gives us a glimpse at the heart of God. God understands the power of a family that is living a vibrant walk with Him. As members of a neighborhood, a family can have a significant impact on the people who live around them. Just yesterday, for example, my wife had the opportunity to lead a neighbor to faith in Christ. The lady came down to our house and asked what was different about the way we were raising our children. She had been watching us for the past couple of years and knew that we operated with a different set of values. She wanted them for her family as well. What's interesting about this situation is that my nine-year-old son had the opportunity to lead this lady's eight-year-old son to faith in Christ last year. We are reaching the family for Christ through the context of family-to-family evangelism. This should come as no surprise because this is how God intended it to be from the beginning.

Churches can learn a great deal from this lesson. How ministry leaders design programs at the church can either support or fracture the family. When different programs operate on different nights of the week, the church can actually hinder healthy family life. For example, having AWANA on Monday night, adult choirs on Tuesday night, the midweek service on Wednesday night, the middle school meeting on Thursday night, and senior high activities on Friday night can divide the family throughout the week. Is it any wonder why our church families feel fragmented and exhausted at the end of a week? The church should consider ways to provide enrichment activities for the family and strategize methods to support family evangelism. Ministry to and with our families should be seen as one of the highest priorities of the church.

2. Ministry leaders should lead the way in demonstrating servant leadership.

Another important lesson that can be learned from this examination of history is that people have a propensity toward the abuse of power. Although the church was born and advanced with a desire to provide spiritual resources to assist men and women in their walk with God, it failed in efforts to provide these resources because of its longing for power, authority, and material gain. The Middle Ages, particularly during the eight Crusades, represented a low point in the life of the church. Rather than being focused on ways to help humanity out of a dark season of existence, the church furthered man's pain by taking advantage of his illiteracy. The organized church lost sight of its mission and sought to fulfill its own wants instead. Jesus stated clearly, "For even the Son of Man did not come to be served, but to serve, and to give His life a ransom for many" (Mark 10:45). The church had sunk to a remarkable low in just a few short centuries!

The lesson for the church to learn today is to avoid endeavors that have the potential for a conflict of interest and to be careful in the use of its power. It is critical for the church to realize that its mission in the world is to provide spiritual insight, direction, and support. The church must never again return to the days when its reason for being is to be served by its membership. Wisdom and a good deal of spiritual discernment are necessary to prevent that from happening again.

Some ministry leaders forget this lesson once they rise in prominence. Being popular leaders with respect and admiration, their temptation to take advantage of this influential power can sometimes be great. Pastors can succumb to this temptation by gaining undue control and power over their congregations. They can demand preferential treatment in the community and in the church. They can take literally the verse that states that a servant of God is worthy of double honor and begin demanding special treatment.

One important lesson that we learn from the Middle Ages is that power can be a corrupting influence, even for people in ministry. In the words of Chuck Colson, special counsel to former President Nixon, "Power corrupts and more power corrupts more." Remember that your calling is to serve the church, not to be served by it. Effective servants know how to use their power with grace and wisdom. Humility, grace, and servanthood are character qualities that are both admired and rewarded by God. Look for ways to serve the needs of the members in your church and community, thereby following the example set by Jesus Christ Himself, who, after washing the feet of His disciples, turned to them and said, "I gave you an example that you also should do as I did to you" (John 13:15).

3. God's Word is preeminent.

Throughout the ages, we have seen the disadvantages of people not having access to God's Word in their own language. Where people were prevented from learning and studying the Bible, they were at the mercy of people who chose to manipulate and distort God's instructions. The efforts of Huss, Wycliffe, Luther, and a host of other Christian leaders clearly demonstrates the importance of putting God's Word into the vernacular and getting it into the lives of people. These Renaissance and Reformation leaders paid a steep price for their efforts, but it was a major turning point in the life of the church. Without such knowledge, the people would have remained hopelessly ignorant and biblically illiterate.

The lesson for our application is clear. Although God's Word has been and continues every year to be the most published book in the history of the world, countless millions of people ignore its implications for their lives because no one makes the effort to present the claims of the Scriptures such as to command their attention. God's Word must be allowed to penetrate the hearts of people. To do this requires intentional training and thoughtful presentations.

God's Word is powerful and able to stand the test of time. It does not need our defense because it is God's Word, and He is capable of defending it Himself. What is needed are teachers who can put forth the declarations of God such as to make them applicable to the needs of those people who have ears to hear. As the author of Hebrews states, "For the word of God is living and active and sharper than any two-edged sword . . . and able to judge the thoughts and intentions of the heart" (Heb. 4:12). Efforts to translate the Scriptures into the vernacular of additional people groups and energies spent in making God's Word relevant through well-crafted lessons are worthwhile and can reap eternal benefits.

4. Lay leaders are the foundation of long-term ministry efforts.

We have seen throughout the history of ministry that God is more than able to use lay leaders to reach the lost. God tells us in His Word that one of the primary emphases of the church should be the equipping of lay leaders for the work of the ministry (Eph. 4:11–16). As we help volunteers identify their giftedness, train them in the use of those gifts, and then provide them with the necessary resources, the work of the church is multiplied logarithmically.

Although we saw God working through the efforts of relatively few people in the early days of the Old Testament (i.e., the Patriarchs), He later branched out His efforts through the priestly tribe of Levi. Once the church was established, He distributed His Spirit's blessings upon everyone who chose to join His eternal family (1 Peter 4:10). Now every member is considered a priest, and each believer has been ordained into the gospel ministry. A Bible college education or a seminary degree is not a requirement for service in the kingdom.

Robert Raikes is an excellent example of what God can do through the efforts of a Christian businessman who simply desires to be used as a willing vessel. He took the resources at hand and used them in the work of the ministry. God had given him a vision, and with that vision came a responsibility. Raikes's ministry threatened the church because it required that ministry leaders make a paradigm shift and realize that different ways existed to reach the lost. Not until many years later did the church reluctantly accept the methods developed by Raikes and brought them into the church. As a result, the Sunday school ministry has become one of the church's biggest success stories, but it was clearly not designed or spearheaded by a professional ministry leader.

Likewise, many of the revivals that came about in the eighteenth and nineteenth centuries were begun by untrained volunteers. A few of them were unsuspecting college students whose only qualification for service was a willing heart. We have seen in history that sometimes that is the only requirement for accomplishing great things for God. Service can certainly be enhanced through advanced education and training (which is the ultimate purpose of seminary), but it can also be an obstacle. When students graduate with an attitude of arrogance and overconfidence in their own capabilities, they can sometimes become a detriment to ministry effectiveness. Perhaps that is why some of the greatest movements of God have been led by volunteers rather than by professional ministry leaders. We would do well to remember the Old Testament admonition, "'Not by might nor by power, but by My Spirit,' says the LORD of hosts" (Zech. 4:6).

5. Learn how to exegete culture.

Part of the reason many of the efforts put forward in the church today meet with such little spiritual success is that ministry leaders have not learned this lesson from history. Understanding culture has a great deal to do with making God's Word relevant and appealing to the lost. Cultural art forms of contemporary music, videos, movies, and art reveal the values and norms of society. Too many Christians have misapplied James 1:27: "Pure and undefiled religion in the sight of our God and Father is this: to visit orphans and widows in their distress, *and to keep oneself unstained by the world*" (emphasis added). Many ministry leaders pride themselves in being unstained by the world because they have removed themselves so far from the world. They have no unsaved friends, they do not associate with their neighbors, and they have nothing to do with the public school where their children attend. In their quest to remain unstained by the world, they have lost the ability to reach it in the name of Christ.

One of the principle criticisms that Jesus received from the religious leaders of His day related to this point. They were distressed because Jesus had so many nonreligious and unsaved acquaintances. Jesus went to social gatherings because He knew that they would be attended by unrighteous people. Jesus' response was simply, "It is not those who are healthy who need a physician, but those who are sick" (Matt. 9:12). Jesus understood that to reach the lost one must be among them, eat where they eat, and develop friendships with them.

The twenty-first century continues to demonstrate the characteristics of a postmodern society. Values are relative, and social morals are almost nonexistent. The Bible has been blocked from entering the classroom, and the Ten Commandments have been banned from our nation's courts. Those who espouse a value system based on natural law are ridiculed as naive. Biblical standards of conduct are cast aside for a lifestyle that is immoral and hedonistic. If ever the church should step into this moral gap and declare "Thus saith the Lord," it is now. But how do you declare the teachings of Christ if no one is listening?

The answer to the dilemma is clear: the church has to learn better methods of communication. It isn't that the lost aren't listening; indeed, their lives are full of information being directed at them through a host of technology, media, and creative art forms. The problem is that the church has not learned to speak their language. Ministry leaders in the twenty-first century must learn to speak the language of the postmodern generation. Until they do, the church's message will continue to fall on deaf ears.

   6. Critical thinking is a characteristic of spiritual maturity.

When the media portrays a minister in a television show or film, it generally presents him as an ignorant, bumbling, disengaged individual; or worse, as a womanizing fraud. Rarely do they portray the religious leader as an intelligent, rational, and critically thinking leader.

Ministry leaders of the twenty-first century must develop their critical thinking skills. The Enlightenment was a time when the church ignored the discoveries of science and preferred religious experience or tradition instead. This conduct resulted in a tremendous loss of credibility and respect. Rather than embracing these new discoveries and integrating them into our biblical worldview, the church rejected science and has never regained its respect. This attitude of anti-intellectualism still permeates many ministry leaders in the church today.

Christian university and seminary students are pursuing the intellectual development of the mind. As such, they are interacting with new insights from the social sciences regularly. These intellectual pursuits call us to challenge preconceived notions about our faith. This can either stimulate our thinking to determine whether the social sciences are accurate and credible or force us to negate their benefits. Critical thinking is the key to this process. A spiritually mature individual does not reject discoveries just because they come from unbelieving scientists or psychologists. We should take the time to examine their findings, find ways we can draw from them principles for ministry application, and, when appropriate, reject those claims that are contrary to the teachings of Scripture.

Nowhere is this need more critical than in the realm of science and the argument for the intelligent design of the universe. We saw remarkable progress in the intelligent design debate during the last decade of the twentieth century. This progress hasn't come because we have learned to argue or debate better; it has come because we gained the necessary scientific credentials and entered into the analysis of the data ourselves. We learned to analyze their arguments critically and to refute their claims. Christian scientists (an oxymoron to some people) have defended their faith in the laboratories, at meetings of professional scientific associations, in public debates with the critics, and by writing credible alternative science textbooks. We have carried the day based on sound reasoning, not verbal passion and misguided emotion. If only we had learned this lesson a few hundred years earlier and had developed the ability to think critically about science's discoveries, perhaps we would have been able to integrate these new scientific advances in light of biblical teaching rather than wholeheartedly rejecting them and becoming the recipient of academic scorn. There is a place for Christian scientists, chemists, astronomers, biologists, and physicists. Only as we enter these fields will we develop the credibility to critique them and offer a Christian alternative to their reasoning and arguments. The key to doing so is a mind trained in critical thinking skills. Spiritual maturity involves both the mind and the heart. Throughout the past few hundred years, we have tended to operate on the latter at the expense of the former. A blending of both is ideal.

7. Change is necessary.

Throughout history, the church has resisted change. For example, Hebrew Christians didn't want to accept people who came to the faith from a non-Jewish background. The leaders of the Catholic Church resisted all efforts to reform the multiple layers of bureaucracy that had developed over the years. Even the colonial church in America resisted accepting the new methods presented by Raikes for reaching the lost. Change is generally not well received.

Men and women prefer the safety and security of existing structures. Those in ministry leadership are no different. Human nature resists change because of the uncertainty it brings to our world. However, if we have seen one thing throughout the history of God's dealings with humanity, it is that God is rarely predictable. God seems to delight in doing things differently from the expected or the routine.

God did the unexpected when He chose an old couple living in Ur to become the starting point of an entire generation of God-fearing believers. He also went outside the paradigm when He sent Joseph to prison and forced him to wait many years before raising him to a position of power and authority. God certainly went beyond the bounds of normal operation when He chose to send His Son to be born into the world through an unmarried virgin. And who would have ever chosen that particular configuration of twelve men to lead the world in radical spiritual renewal? God is anything but predictable!

If we know this from observing history, then why are we so amazed when He brings change to the church today as well? As ministry leaders, we should welcome change as God's method of renewal. We must learn methods of leading change in the church. We should become the change agents and assist others who are resistant to its effect on their lives. Change is inevitable, and we should not view it as a threat to ministry effectiveness but rather as a necessary requirement.

Time does not allow a comprehensive assessment of all of the principles that can be applied to ministry, but certainly more of them exist than what we have identified here in this short list of seven. Perhaps you can identify a few more and develop them as your own observations from this book. Our desire has been to illustrate the means by which God has worked in the world, and we have sought ways of applying our observations to ministry effectiveness. We believe that the study of history and philosophy as applied to the context of the church will make the ministry leader more intentional and reflective in their leadership. To this end, we trust that this text has been a helpful guide in your ministry training and development.

INDEX